Keeper of
Concentration Camp

ALSO BY RICHARD DRINNON

Rebel in Paradise: A Biography of Emma Goldman (1961)

White Savage: The Case of John Dunn Hunter (1972)

Editor, *Memoirs of a Captivity* by John Dunn Hunter (1973)

Coeditor (with Anna Maria Drinnon), *Nowhere at Home: Letters from Exile of Emma Goldman and Alexander Berkman* (1975)

Coeditor (with Anna Maria Drinnon), *Living My Life* by Emma Goldman (1977)

Facing West: The Metaphysics of Indian-Hating and Empire-Building (1980)

Keeper of
Concentration Camps

Dillon S. Myer and American Racism

Richard Drinnon

UNIVERSITY OF CALIFORNIA PRESS
Berkeley · *Los Angeles* · *London*

University of California Press
Berkeley and Los Angeles, California

University of California Press, Ltd.
London, England

First Paperback Printing 1989

Library of Congress Cataloging-in-Publication Data

Drinnon, Richard.
  Keeper of concentration camps.

  Bibliography: p.
  Includes index.
  1. Myer, Dillon S. (Dillon Seymour), 1891–1982.
2. Japanese Americans—Evacuation and relocation,
1942–1945. 3. Indians of North America—Government
relations—1934–   . 4. Racism—United States—
History—20th century. 5. United States—Officials
and employees—Biography.   I. Title.
E748.M93D74 1987   305.8′00973   86-7058
ISBN 0-520-06601-4 (alk. paper)

Printed in the United States of America

2   3   4   5   6   7   8   9

To

Mitsuye Endo, James Matsumoto Omura,
Harry Yoshio Ueno, Kiyoshi Okamoto,
Hisato K., and all the other Japanese
Americans who said no,

and to Sarah and Avery Winnemucca,
Rufus Wallowing, Thomas Main, Severino
Martinez, and all the other Native Ameri-
cans who said no,

and to Emily Light, Wayne M. Collins,
Ernest Besig, Alida C. Bowler, Felix S.
Cohen, John Collier, and the few other
Anglo-Americans who crossed the color
line to say no *with them,*

this book is respectfully dedicated.

I would like to ask the Committee: Has the Gestapo come to America? Have we not risen in righteous anger at Hitler's mistreatment of the Jews? Then is it not incongruous that citizen Americans of Japanese descent should be similarly mistreated and persecuted?

James Matsumoto Omura speaking before the Select Committee Investigating National Defense Migration, February 23, 1942

Now you may wonder, Mr. Secretary, why our Montana tribes are so much concerned about these attorney regulations and I want to tell you in my $40 cowboy language. We Indians in Montana thought we were making real progress towards freedom until a couple of years ago. Then something happened. . . . And during the last couple of years that attitude of paternalism, treating us like prisoners in a concentration camp, has become the attitude of the Indian Bureau.

Thomas Main speaking at the Hearing before the Secretary of the Interior on Proposed Regulations to Govern Indian Tribal Attorney Contracts, January 3–4, 1952

Contents

PART III. NATIVE AMERICANS

Illustrations

Acknowledgments

Like happiness, my indebtedness to Anna Maria Drinnon can be mentioned once again but never measured. And proving that former editors can become lasting friends, John F. Thornton demonstrated undiminished faith in my work through his astonishingly determined efforts to put it in the hands of a likely publisher. Finally our mixedblood friend and scout Gerald Vizenor stepped in to guide us over the Donner Pass and into the able hands of Alain Hénon at the University of California Press.

A senior fellowship from the National Endowment for the Humanities (1980–81) made possible research in major repositories on both coasts and our visits to the sites of the concentration camps and to Indian reservations.

By the time I had worked my way through thousands of pages of files from the Federal Bureau of Investigation and was prepared to ask some of the right questions, Dillon S. Myer was too infirm to be interviewed. Through the courtesy of his widow, Jenness Wirt Myer, I received permission to quote his oral autobiography.

In the late fifties graduate students in my seminars at the University of California, Berkeley, made initial, but substantial, contributions to my understanding of the great internment. From start to finish, Arthur A. Hansen of the Japanese American Oral History Project, California State University at Fullerton, proved himself a true friend of this undertaking by answering queries, calling my attention to sources I might have overlooked, and guiding me to memorable interviews with James Matsumoto Omura and Harry Yoshio Ueno. For her timely assistance I am also grateful to Aiko Herzig-Yoshinaga of the Commission on the Wartime Relocation and Internment of Civilians.

For access to relevant files of their respective organizations, I thank Executive Directors Steven Unger of the Association on American Indian Affairs and Dorothy M. Ehrlich of the Northern California American Civil Liberties Union (NCACLU). On opposite sides of the continent, the younger Wayne M. Collins in Berkeley and Doctor Lewis A. Opler in Stamford, Connecticut, made their fathers' papers available and then garnished these gifts with the hospitality of their homes.

From the outset Vine Deloria, Jr., provided support and helped me see the national policy of "termination" as an ill-concealed weapon that has been used "against Indian people in a modern war of conquest." Simon J. Ortiz, the poet from Acoma Pueblo, kindly granted permission to reproduce sharp-edged imagery that captures the inner meaning of "relocation."

A list of all my debts to librarians would be interminable. But I must express my gratitude for the unfailing helpfulness of Director James D. Hart, Irene M. Moran, and other members of the staff of the Bancroft Library in Berkeley. In San Francisco Waverly B. Lowell of the California Historical Society also assisted my research in every possible way. And in Washington Sara Dunlap Jackson and Jerry N. Hess went out of their way to turn up relevant files in the National Archives.

Finally, I have two special debts.

With "a one-man office with a half-time secretary," as former Director Besig apologetically describes his wartime NCACLU, I think he did wonders—inadequately recognized in the dedication of this book—in bringing the plight of camp inmates to national attention. I am deeply grateful to Ernest Besig for that, for an enlightening interview, and for his painstaking responses to my written queries.

Rounded up and penned with her people, Michi Weglyn refused to forget that enormity and decades later broke the stone of Japanese American silence with the best book on the camps, *Years of Infamy* (1976). Through it and through a clear-running stream of letters, she has taken me inside her insightful experience, shared documents and directed me to others, and gently but persistently nudged me toward the final title of this work. For all that and for her daring to be who she is, Michi Nishiura Weglyn has my profound respect and appreciation.

Abbreviations

AAA	Agricultural Adjustment Administration
AAIA	The archives of the Association on American Indian Affairs in Princeton University Library. This collection contains important letters and memoranda of President Oliver La Farge, Executive Director Alexander Lesser, and, especially, General Counsel Felix S. Cohen.
ACLU	American Civil Liberties Union
Affidavit	Affidavit of Ernest Besig, WCP, 78/177, *Tadayasu Abo v. Tom Clark* (77 F. Suppl. 806 [1948]).
APs	Appointed Personnel [in WRA camps; also known as "Caucasians"]
Auto	"An Autobiography of Dillon S. Myer." Regional Oral History Office, Bancroft Library, University of California, Berkeley, 1970. Courtesy The Bancroft Library.
Auto 2	"Japanese-American Relocation Reviewed," vol. 1, "Decision and Exodus," interview with James Rowe and Dillon S. Myer; vol. 2, "The Internment," interview with Dillon S. Myer on November 6, 1969, "to more fully explicate the chapter on the WRA in his autobiography." Regional Oral History Office, Bancroft Library, University of California, Berkeley, 1974. Courtesy The Bancroft Library.

BIA	Bureau of Indian Affairs
CC	Roger Daniels, *Concentration Camps USA: Japanese Americans and World War II*. New York: Holt, Rinehart and Winston, 1971.
CCC	Civilian Conservation Corps
CHS	California Historical Society, San Francisco, file no. 3580, containing the correspondence and documents of the NCACLU.
"Crisis"	Frank Shotaro Miyamoto, "The Registration Crisis at Tule Lake," JERS, 67/14, R.20.36.
CWRIC	Commission on the Wartime Relocation and Internment of Civilians
FBI	The main WRA file of the Federal Bureau of Investigation is no. 62-69030, consisting of some 3,000 pages and containing materials from the Office of Naval Intelligence (ONI) and the Military Intelligence Service (MIS or G-2). In addition, there are 3,500 pages of FBI documents on the camps at Tule Lake (62-70564), Manzanar (100-140363), and Heart Mountain (100-164195); on Myer and the Pine Ridge Reservation (100-378472); and on his adversary Felix S. Cohen (46-16318; 70-17072; 121-6680). References include the relevant file numbers.
IIAA	Institute of Inter-American Affairs
JACL	Japanese American Citizens League
JACL	William Hosokawa, *JACL in Quest of Justice*. New York: William Morrow, 1982.
JCP	John Collier Papers, 1922–68, Yale University Library. Part 3 (1945–56), series 1, contains correspondence with Harold L. Ickes, Felix S. Cohen, James E. Curry, E. Reeseman Fryer, Avery Winnemucca, and other Myer critics. Series 2 contains no less valuable materials on the Bosone Resolution, the Paiutes of Pyramid Lake, the Attorney Contract Dispute, the Indian Bureau Police Powers Bill, and memoranda, notes, statements, and letters under the heading "Dillon S. Myer, Commissioner of Indian Affairs."

JERS	Japanese American Evacuation and Resettlement Study files in the Bancroft Library, University of California, Berkeley. Courtesy The Bancroft Library.
MIS	Military Intelligence Service
MKO	Marvin K. Opler papers in the possession of his son, Dr. Lewis A. Opler of Stamford, Connecticut.
NA	National Archives. Among the relevant groups are the following: RG 48, secretary of the interior; RG 75, Bureau of Indian Affairs; RG 107, secretary of war; and RG 210, War Relocation Authority.
NCACLU	American Civil Liberties Union of Northern California
NCAI	National Congress of American Indians
NCJAR	National Council for Japanese American Redress
NRC	Myer Desk Files, accession no. 67A721, Records of the Bureau of Indian Affairs (Record Group 75), National Records Center, Suitland, Maryland. Before he left the BIA in 1953, Myer and his aides must have gone through these files with considerable care. Nevertheless, they failed to remove a few "sensitive" items among all the official memoranda, policy statements, speeches, and routine correspondence.
ONI	Office of Naval Intelligence
SAC	Special Agent in Charge [FBI]
SCS	Soil Conservation Service
SSS	Selective Service System
UA	Dillon S. Myer, *Uprooted Americans: The Japanese Americans and the War Relocation Authority During World War II.* Tucson: University of Arizona Press, 1971.
WCP	Wayne M. Collins papers in the Bancroft Library, University of California, Berkeley. Courtesy The Bancroft Library.
WCP2	Wayne M. Collins papers in the possession of his son, Wayne M. Collins of Berkeley, California.

WRA   War Relocation Authority

YoI   Michi Weglyn, *Years of Infamy: The Untold Story of America's Concentration Camps.* New York: William Morrow, 1976.

Prologue

It is a big country.
—*Dillon S. Myer,*
Press Conference,
May 14, 1943

"Oh, the Jap Camp!" exclaimed the manager of Pfeiffer's Liquor Store in Granada, Colorado, when we asked for directions to what had been Camp Amache. In 1980 and 1981 Anna Maria Drinnon and I learned to expect this stale misidentification from local residents as we drove to all of the ten officially listed camp sites scattered across the country, from the Mississippi Delta to the Sierras. Even a member of the tribal council on the Gila River Indian Reservation at Sacaton, Arizona, suspiciously questioned us about why we were applying for permission to visit "the Jap Camp."

Well, why *were* we tramping through cactus and sand looking for the ghost towns that in the 1940s confined tens of thousands of American citizens? It was surely not because we hoped to find in place those happy faces that we had seen in the War Relocation Authority photographs: families in "apartment" cubicles showing off their scrap-lumber furniture, primary school children pledging allegiance, Boy Scouts of America marching on Memorial Day, drum majorettes prancing on Flag Day, couples jitterbugging at USO dances, Gold Star mothers receiving medals, and the mandatory shots of kids playing marbles and smiling right up into the camera.

The quick of real suffering behind these WRA promotional stills has long since disappeared, along with the inmates; so have the keepers in their business suits and the armed MPs in their lookout towers and the square miles of barracks lined up like tar-papered soldiers. Today jack rabbits and lizards run over the remnant foundations and Herefords graze around them; the sentry house still stands at Manzanar, California; a few structures remain at Poston, Arizona; camp chimneys still thrust into the sky above what are now rice fields at Jerome, Arkansas; and at several sites cemeteries contain those who never "relocated" again, though at Granada a grave was recently reopened so that the family could take the remains to Chicago. And at Gila River I photographed a strand of barbed wire, coiled and rusting away in the greasewood and sagebrush.

Near the camp sites are small towns with names that wryly memorialize their founders' extravagant expectations: *Independence*, California, near Manzanar; *Vocation*, Wyoming, near Heart Mountain, the camp with an Orwellian name of its own; and my favorite, *Eden*, Idaho, near Minidoka. In these and other nearby towns I slipped uneasily and unsystematically into the role of an oral historian by asking older residents for their past and present views on the camps. Virtually every one concurred with the assertions of the American Legion plaque at the Heart Mountain site that the inmates had been well treated and "loosely confined," and had enjoyed a "modern waterworks and sewer system and a modern hospital and dental clinic, staffed with people from the ranks of the evacuees. First rate schooling was provided for the children of the evacuees through the high school grades."

An exception was a high school teacher in Granada, a woman of Navaho ancestry married to a Chicano. She related that she had been there when the trains came in and had seen "the people crying and herded like cattle into army trucks and hauled up to the camp." With her empathy for these people stirred up by my queries, she came right out with the tabooed words: "We [Granadians] were the recipients of the concentration camp." But had no one in town protested at the time that American citizens were being locked up in what you yourself call a concentration camp? No, she could not recall anyone protesting: "There was a lot of prejudice here in the Arkansas Valley then. Stores in Lamar [the county seat] had signs: 'NO JAPS ALLOWED.'"

Typical of the other respondents was a woman in Independence who had been in charge of the Manzanar telephone switchboard while her husband ran the camp motor pool. Now a widow, she spoke proudly of her pioneer grandmother who had been one of the first white settlers in the Owens Valley. She also manifestly nursed some sour wartime memories, although she insisted that she would not be interviewed about matters "it is better to leave in the past." Nonetheless eager to set us straight, she emphatically added that the people in the camp had had an easy life and ate better than she and her husband: "We were rationed but they had everything at the camp and the coop store." But what about those sent to a penal colony after the shootings in December 1942? "They asked for it." One of her neighbors, the current superintendent of the Inyo County roads, echoed this opinion when I asked him why he thought citizens had been corralled in the camp: "We were at war with their race."

In different ways, all of those who answered our queries—and even some who did not—told us part of what we had come to find out. All made clear that for them at least the camps cannot be dismissed as ancient history. Forty years after they were in full swing, they still raise issues that live on in the minds and hearts of these local witnesses.

Of course, our primary purpose in coming was not to gather current opinions but to see for ourselves these "godforsaken" sites, as they have been called, and to inspect the scenes of the crime personally. Curiously enough, we found the graveyards had more to tell us than nearby townspeople.

At Heart Mountain we were taking notes on one of the memorials when a man in a pickup stopped and obligingly wondered if we needed any help. Unable to find the camp cemetery, we asked what had happened to it. Sure, he knew where that had been—as a matter of fact, it had been on land he had homesteaded in the 1950s, when the outlines of five graves were still visible, though someone had since told him there had originally been twenty-one. "Would you like to get in your car and follow me to see something interesting?" Near his house and barn was one of the old camp barracks, which his wife had made over into a craft shop. Inside he told us that years ago a man working on one of his irrigation ditches had turned up a fifty-five-gallon drum with the blade of a caterpillar tractor. When they pried the top off, they found the drum filled to the brim with tiny stones, each carefully inscribed. "Here are some—if you want, help yourselves to a handful." Thanks to the homesteader's generosity, we came away with a dozen or so of these exotic, marble-sized artifacts.

Once translated, the Japanese characters thereon all turn out to be fragments from the dialogues of the Buddha—Kannon (Buddhist goddess), seed, flower, youth, sky, equal(ity), goodness, dead/deceased, and the like. These fragments memorialized the dead and kept them company until they joined the spiritual world of their ancestors. But these are literal translations and this is a surface reading of their meaning.

In *Farewell to Manzanar* (1974), Jeanne Wakatsuki Houston remarked that the old rock gardens of her father and other inmates of his generation still spoke to her when she returned to the site in 1972: "Each stone was a mouth, speaking for a family, for some man who had beautified his doorstep" (p. 137). Our smaller versions speak to me of a time when such stones grew in their myths into massive rocks and into the 354 sacred mountains worshiped in ancient Japan. Quietly gathered from dry stream beds and uplands on what was part of the Shoshone Project of the Bureau of Reclamation, and then inscribed with infinite patience and surreptitiously buried, these stones speak of a time when the ancestors of both the Japanese Americans and the Shoshones and other Native Americans believed in such voices. Today they still broadcast good news: cultures die hard. On the other hand, from their mouths comes the ultimate indictment of those who rounded up and penned those buried nearby. The great internment was an attack not merely on the bodies of the inmates but on their cultural heritage, and hence on their spiritual existence as such. Or so the stones have emboldened me to venture in the pages that follow.

Since the inmates customarily cremated their dead, the very existence of these camp cemeteries was perplexing. Why were the graves there at all? If some of the deceased had no families, why had they not been buried in the neighboring community cemeteries? Later I chanced upon a letter dated October 25, 1945, from the Granada director to national WRA Director Dillon S. Myer urging that the camp cemetery be permanently dedicated to those interred there: eight infants, most of them stillborn, and three adults, two of whom "had no close friends or known relatives" (the third, no doubt, had been in that freshly reopened grave we saw). But up to that point no one outside had shown interest in the remains and "our failure previously to secure acceptance of bodies by other cemeteries is an indication of the same problem now" (James G. Lindley to Myer, JERS, 67/14, L1. 22A). So that was it. In death as in life these "places of despair," as my companion calls the camps, contained unwanted non-Caucasians.

"The Jap camps" did not collectively constitute "Our Worst Wartime Mistake," as Eugene V. Rostow charged and I shall dispute, but had deep roots in our traditional racism that made them as American as the Jamestown weed.

2

It is a big country. After the European invaders had overrun much of it, they attempted between 1824 and 1844 to make it literally a white man's country—save for the Afro-American chattels—by removing more than 100,000 Native Americans from the East and relocating them westward in what was to be, as long as the waters flow, Indian Territory. A century later those Trails of Tears constituted the prototypes for the removal of more than 100,000 Japanese immigrants and Japanese Americans from the West Coast and, in a reversal of direction, their relocation eastward in the intermountain states and beyond. Other more tangible threads tied the Japanese-hating 1940s to this Indian-hating past. Two of the officially listed Arizona camps were on Indian lands, that of the Pimas and Maricopas at Gila River and that of the Mohaves and Chemehuevis at Colorado River. Heart Mountain was on what had once been Indian land, but so were all the other camps. And WRA Director Myer hid away what was in effect his eleventh camp, a penal colony near Cañon Diablo on the fourteen-million-acre Navaho Reservation. Even had we wanted to, we could not have avoided interlacing our inspections of the camp sites with visits to the reservations.

Down in Cañon de Chelly near Chinle, Arizona, the Anasazi, as the Navahos call the "ancient ones," had perhaps a millennium ago chipped carvings into the cliffs that tell truly primordial tales. Birds, deer, antelope, mountain sheep, snakes, and other petroglyphs move rhythmically across the sheer rock walls, while a reclining, ithyphallic anthropomorph—one of the humpbacked Kokopelli—provides suitable accompaniment on his flute. In company with a Japanese historian from Kyoto and other tourists, we stood under gold-leaved cottonwood trees and marveled at this outdoor art gallery. Then or a little later our Navaho guide mentioned the bone-freezing January more than a century ago when Kit Carson's troops had swept through this great chasm, splattering its walls with the blood of his people and destroying their hogans and peach orchards, gathering up the survivors, and starting them on their Long Walk into an exile in the mesquite along the Pecos River three hundred miles away. It was as though I had been discovered by an Indian and guided from the floor of his sacred cañon to a still more direct anticipation of the WRA camps.

In *The Kit Carson Campaign* (1982), Clifford E. Trafzer helpfully filled in the details. The preceding summer Carson had approached the west end of the cañon and there "arrived at a large bottom containing not less than one hundred acres of as fine corn as I have ever seen," some of which he fed to his horses and mules but most of which he ordered trampled and burned. With the cañon finally "pacified" in January 1864, he pushed forward the roundup of the starving and freezing people and the walk into captivity, under military escort, that by spring was to put 8,474 of them in the forty-square-mile tract of semiarid land called the Bosque Redondo. One of the first of the reservations in their modern form, Bosque Redondo resembled the WRA camps in its prison atmosphere, the fact that no one could leave without permission, and the ceaseless indoctrination to "civilize"—in Myer's camps it was called "Americanize"—the inmates. Old photographs show the Navahos being used as forced labor to build the adobe structures at Fort Sumner. In the WRA camps the inmates received pittances for their work, and at Tule Lake in California, as we shall see, troublesome inmates were also forced to work under military guard. Like Myer later, General James H. Carleton undertook to destroy the cultural heritage of his Navaho charges so that "soon they will acquire new habits, new ideas, new modes of life." The Navahos were confined in their camp for four years until they were finally allowed to return to their sacred cañons and mountains—inmates in the WRA camps spent an average of nine hundred days behind barbed wire, or a roughly comparable eternity. Give or take a few particulars, the likenesses between Bosque Redondo and a WRA camp were close and instructive. Both embodied attitudes toward nonwhite inmates that had remained remarkably constant over the decades.

As head of the Bureau of Indian Affairs in the 1950s, Commissioner Myer launched the attack on tribal rights and identities known as "termination," sought to break up the reservations and lure peoples away from their homelands through a program of "relocation," and used boarding schools to speed up the process—he arranged, as he put it, to have "Navaho youngsters go to school in other areas in order to get them out of the reservation complex and milieu." In towns such as Gallup and Flagstaff we saw the empty faces of those he and his successors had gotten out of that milieu and who had then come home homeless, as depicted in the lines of Simon J. Ortiz, the Acoma Pueblo poet:

> West, California is too far,
> once I been to California, got lost
> in L. A., got laid in Fresno,
> got jailed in Oakland, got fired in Barstow,

and came home,
Gallup, Indian Capital of The World, shit. . . .

In his simply titled "Relocation," Ortiz has a lost Indian tell his story:

so i agreed to move
i see me walking in sleep
down streets down streets grey with cement
and glaring glass and oily wind
armed with a pint of wine
i cheated my children to buy
i am ashamed
i am tired
i am hungry
i speak words
i am lonely for hills
i am lonely for myself

Or as the late Clyde Warrior, a Ponca Indian of Oklahoma, wondered, "Is this an American way of hollowing out the insides of people?"

All along our zigzag expedition to the Pacific and back were threads that could be teased out into illuminating connections. On August 17, 1866, Indian Agent D. N. Cooley at the Tule River Farm drew this sketch in his annual report: "A cruel, cowardly vagabond, given to thieving, gambling, drunkenness, and all that is vicious, without one redeeming trait, is a true picture of the California Digger." It followed that his life was not worth much and that he had no rights the white man was bound to respect. Those self-evident truths led to "The Biggest Little War in American History," as a nineteenth-century chronicler grandiloquently called the Modoc War of 1872–73. Following the execution by hanging of the Modoc patriot Kintpuash, or Captain Jack, on October 3, 1873, his body was dug up, embalmed, and exhibited at carnivals before being shipped to the U.S. Army Medical Museum in Washington, D.C. For understanding the historical reach of the later terror at Tule Lake, it matters that the most infamous of the WRA camps was on what had been Modoc land.

Just up the road across the Oregon state line lies what once was Klamath land. When Peter Skene Ogden traveled through their country in the 1820s he found the Klamath Indians a "happy race" with few wants. When we passed through in the 1980s no one would have called the survivors happy. As a boy growing up in Oregon I had heard that the tribe still owned some fabulously rich timber and later learned that it consisted of a prime stand of 720,000 acres of ponderosa pine. But in the 1950s the Klamaths had been one of the first large tribes (2,133 enrolled members) to be victimized by the termination policy Myer had launched but which hit them in 1954 (Public Law 587) after he had stepped down as commissioner. Tempted by per capita payments of nearly $44,000 for their shares of the timber and other tribal assets, 78 percent of the members had taken their money in 1959 and vanished in red ghettos scattered from Klamath Falls, Portland, and Seattle to Los Angeles, Minneapolis, and Chicago.

Before they disappeared, many of the terminated individuals bought flashy cars or otherwise demonstrated limitless wants. White neighbors helped relieve them of their inheritance through excessive attorneys' fees, exorbitant interest rates, and outright fraud. Young red women suddenly found themselves besieged by white suitors and married and nearly as quickly stripped of their trust shares. Increasing numbers of young red men found themselves in the Oregon State Penitentiary in Salem. Two hundred and twenty Klamaths died of violence and alcoholism in the ten years following termination.

All we could do was try to imagine their unhappiness and drive on by with the scarcely comforting thought that the suffering wreaked by the scattering of their people and the loss of their homes and cultural identities could never be quantified. "Termination is genocide," a former Klamath tribal official has recently concluded:

> The white man has a talent for killing us. He's been doing it ever since he came into this country, and he's good at it—we just can't always see what the hell he's doing. But you can't see the scars of termination. They're inside of us.

Termination was an attack not merely on the persons and possessions of tribal peoples but on their cultural heritages, and hence on their spiritual existence as such.

And termination did not constitute "Our Worst Peacetime Mistake," as former Interior Secretary Harold L. Ickes suggested. No "mistake," it had deep roots in our traditional racism that made it as American as the Trails of Tears and the Navahos' Long Walk.

3

As head of the WRA (1942–46) and of the BIA (1950–53), Dillon S. Myer was director and commissioner of twin calamities. His career enables us to bring together vast bodies of evidence on the treatment of

Native Americans and of Japanese Americans—materials too often studied separately—and trace these to their common matrix. And since I shall be arguing that the common matrix was our traditional racism, readers have a right to know what I mean by the word. Terribly hard to define, as a number of writers have ruefully acknowledged, *racism* as I use the term in these pages consists in habitual practice by a people of treating, feeling, and viewing physically dissimilar peoples—identified as such by skin color and other shared hereditary characteristics—as less than persons.

"Six feet tall," read Myer's entry in *Current Biography*, "he has gray-green eyes and gray hair." In 1944 Ruth Gruber, then one of Interior Secretary Ickes's assistants, met him for the first time at the WRA head-quarters in the old Barr Building on Seventeenth Street and detected no warmth in his greeting: "A tall man with steel-rimmed glasses and steel-gray hair, he stared down at me as I entered. He looked like the engineers I had seen on construction projects in Alaska, hard-driving men who seemed closer to machines and mortar than to people." Gray-green eyes, steel-gray hair, frequently gray-suited, Myer was a study in dull shades. A lifelong bureaucrat, he had achieved a certain distinction in gray office buildings by having no distinguishing characteristics. In speech as in writing, his was the gray language of official memoranda. In appearance and outlook, he was the gray "normalcy" another Ohioan, Warren G. Harding, had wanted to get back to. Normality personified, Myer was emphatically not a monster and not even an interesting villain and therein lies a difficulty.

On November 8, 1950, former BIA Commissioner John Collier sent his old boss Ickes an update on "the yes-group" of opportunists with whom the new commissioner had surrounded himself and then almost audibly sighed over the problem they all presented: "But the fact that there is not one interesting villain among them all does present a real difficulty" (JCP). Unquestionably the grayness of Myer and company did hamper Collier and Ickes in their efforts to oppose what they considered his disastrous policies. No less certainly, it presents here the problem of detaching the man from the similarly colored background to which he cleaved and of then establishing his responsibility for his actions. It is a ticklish, but by no means unique, challenge.

With such notable exceptions as Adolf Hitler and Joseph Stalin, our age has lacked easily identifiable villains of stature commensurate with their crimes against humanity. No longer the transgressions of exceptionally cruel individuals, evil has been bureaucratized by the twentieth-century state and made the charge of relatively faceless administrators, small in character and comprehension. In the West, in the East, and in the Third World, natty figures in suits or uniforms have carried out monstrous suppressions, uprootings, and scatterings without entering the pages of history as striking despots—considered individually, their outstanding characteristic is their mediocrity. As for political leaders with recognizable faces and some stature, the problem of identification remains. Though Franklin Delano Roosevelt signed the executive order for the great internment, who thinks of the debonair Hudson River squire as the commander in chief of concentration camps? Next to FDR, Henry L. Stimson was the official most responsible for that calamity, but he has been permanently typecast as a distinguished elder statesman. Stimson's right-hand man, John J. McCloy, comes close to being the only identifiable villain on the scene, but the undersides of his role have only recently been exposed. Myer and his associates in the WRA and the BIA were more like the gray president who ordered the bombing of Hiroshima, heard the outcome, and declared elatedly: "This is the greatest thing in history."

Undeniably, Myer's career reached out laterally to become an expression of Western racism, nationalism, imperialism, and colonialism and in that global context added confirmation to Hannah Arendt's insight into "the banality of evil." Yet just as undeniably, as I have emphasized, Myer was as American as the Stars and Stripes, and this is of necessity a study of him in that narrower context. Born in the white Protestant heartland, he was a walking repository of the Puritan virtues and traditional hostility to the very idea of the survival of separate peoples with separate cultures. Always sure he did good, he did great wrongs. How did he come to be? How did he come to be a member of the "helping professions"? Why was he made the keeper of hundreds of thousands of souls? Who were his allies and his enemies? Who were his victims? Do such questions matter?

Obviously, I think they do and hope that readers will too before they put the book down. Two worst "mistakes," after all, have their own intrinsic interest. At all events, this is my report on the banality of evil, U.S. style.

Lewisburg, Pennsylvania

PART I

Origins

And of course I didn't know any Japanese. . . . The Bill of
Rights was our endpost to hook our fence to. [Laughter.] As
a farm boy, you see, I use the kind of similes that come from
a farm boy's life.

—Dillon S. Myer,
Interview, November 6, 1969

CHAPTER I

The WRA Story of Human Conservation

Neither I nor most of my staff were well informed regarding the problems we faced. We lacked information about the evacuees and their history. We were generally uninformed regarding the anti-Oriental movements on the West Coast, and the pressures, rumors and fears that had led to the evacuation.
—*Dillon S. Myer,* Uprooted Americans, *1971*

In early 1944 key officials in the Washington office of the War Relocation Authority discussed their agency with Dorothy Swaine Thomas of the University of California. Head of the "Japanese American Evacuation and Resettlement Study" (JERS) in Berkeley, Professor Thomas chatted knowledgeably with them about various matters, learned they proposed to close one of their two camps in Arkansas, and concluded that the morale of Director Dillon S. Myer, Solicitor Philip M. Glick, Morrill M. Tozier, chief of the Reports Division, and other members of the staff was very high indeed:

> There is, in the first place, enormous admiration for Myer. Tozier, in particular, has an extreme case of hero worship. "The boss was magnificent yesterday. He knew all the answers, etc. etc. etc." (Tozier writes Myer's speeches for him.) In the second place, WRA is a typical, New Deal, idealistic agency (I worked for FERA [Federal Emergency Relief Administration] for quite a period under Harry Hopkins and observed exactly the same phenomena). They carry the torch for the Japanese people, but always in abstract, idealistic terms without much understanding of the problems that are being faced in the projects, or of what the people themselves really want. . . . In the third place, the Washington group is held together by the attacks they are receiving from the outside, which makes crusaders of them, and by a terrible fear they will lose their agency.
>
> ["High Points in Conversation. . . ," January 20, 1944, JERS 67/14, suppl., cart. 2]

Thomas's few lines catch, for a moment, the WRA leaders in their natural habitat and correctly identify them. The men who ran America's
concentration camps were liberals of the genus New Deal.

2

From second and third levels of the administration, these officials had
little understanding of their charges and less of what had called their
agency into being. Milton S. Eisenhower has related in his memoirs, *The
President Is Calling* (*PIC*; 1974), that Franklin Delano Roosevelt sum-
moned him to the White House on March 10 or 11, 1942, and abruptly
enjoined him: "Milton, your war job, starting immediately, is to set up
a War Relocation Authority to move the Japanese-Americans off the
Pacific coast. I have signed an executive order which will give you full
authority to do what is essential. . . . And Milton . . . the greatest possible speed is imperative" (p. 95). Told that Budget Director Harold
Smith would fill him in on the details, the startled appointee barely had
a chance to ask and get permission to take along his staff from the
Agriculture Co-ordinating Office.

"Like most Americans at the time," Eisenhower explained, "I knew
very little about the problem of the Japanese-Americans on the West
Coast." The administration's fledgling expert on the "problem" even
had to be informed by the budget director that it broke down into *Issei*,
the immigrants from Japan; *Nisei*, their children who were born and
educated in this country; and *Kibei*, their children who were born here
but educated in Japan—among the last, he learned, "were people who
probably posed the threats to our security." It was all very confusing,
especially when Harold Smith added that Lieutenant General John L.
DeWitt of the Western Defense Command had pronounced it impossible to "tell the difference between a loyal and a disloyal Japanese-
American."

Eisenhower also knew very little about the events after Pearl Harbor
that led Roosevelt to sign Executive Order 9066 on February 19, 1942.
Earlier Admiral Ernest Stark, chief of Naval Operations, should have
put to rest fears of an invasion with his flat statement that a full-scale
Japanese attack on the West Coast was "impossible." And just the preceding week the army's general staff had recommended against mass
evacuation, holding in effect that there was no military necessity. General Mark W. Clark and the other staff officers had, however, been opposed and outmaneuvered by their civilian heads, Secretary of War

Henry L. Stimson and his assistant John J. McCloy, who acted in concert with Provost Marshal General Allen W. Gullion and his assistant Karl R. Bendetsen, along with General DeWitt, and drew support from West Coast congressmen, municipal and state officials, columnists, and assorted patriotic and economic interest groups. Eisenhower knew nothing of this infighting or of the conflict between the Departments of Justice and War, with Attorney General Francis Biddle's wavering efforts to forestall exclusion defeated by Stimson, who easily gained the upper hand with Roosevelt. And, finally, the appointee knew nothing of the cabinet meeting *after* Roosevelt's command decision when, according to Stimson's notes of February 27, 1942, "there was general confusion around the table arising from the fact that nobody had realized how big it was, nobody wanted to take care of the evacuees. . . . Biddle suggested that a single head should be chosen to handle the resettlement instead of the pulling and hauling of all the different agencies, and the President seemed to accept this."* That single head became Eisenhower and out of the ashes of these conflicts and confusions—all unknown to him—arose the agency that he ran for the first three months of its existence.

"I can hardly believe that at the time of the events I knew so little about them," Eisenhower wrote decades later while trying to put some of the pieces together by drawing on the historian Stetson Conn and others (*PIC*, p. 112). And if he knew so little at the time, Philip Glick and the other members of the "well-knit team" who followed him into the WRA knew even less, so to speak, and their unfathomable ignorance was shared by the amiable fifty-year-old bureaucrat he chose as his successor, his old friend and protégé Dillon S. Myer, who had risen through the ranks with his help to become assistant chief of the Soil Conservation Service and then acting administrator of the Agriculture Conservation and Adjustment Administration. Not under either director were the keepers in the WRA ever distinguished by knowledge of their charges or by understanding of what had placed these particular people behind their barbed-wire fences. Given their careers in agriculture, they would have been more at home in the Farm Security Administration and more qualified for resettling subsistence farmers on productive lands. Yet for the public servants who went from land conservation to people keeping, administration was administration.

---

*See "Notes and Bibliographic Essay" at the conclusion of the book for a running commentary on sources mentioned in the text and others used as a general background in each chapter.

3

Did the keepers never weigh the moral implications of their new duties? "I must confess that I spent little time pondering the moral implications of the President's decision. We were at war. Our nation had been viciously attacked without warning," Eisenhower explained in *The President Is Calling*. "President Roosevelt was the Commander-in-Chief and he had given me my war assignment" (pp. 97–98).

The assignment was in fact to run *concentration* camps, and these were hardly modern innovations. Perhaps the first on this continent was the bleak rock in Boston harbor named Deer Island on which the Bay Puritans dumped their "praying" Indians during the crisis of the 1670s. Here and elsewhere plenty of others followed. At the turn of this century the Spanish had built such concentration camps in Cuba, the British in South Africa, and the Americans in the Philippines. In *The Origins of Totalitarianism* (1958) Hannah Arendt aptly divided them and their successors "into three types corresponding to three basic Western conceptions of life after death": *Hades* corresponded to "those relatively mild forms, once popular even in nontotalitarian countries," such as the historical forerunners of the WRA camps just mentioned; *Purgatory* corresponded to the Soviet Union's slave labor camps; and *Hell* corresponded to the Nazi camps that were "systematically organized with a view to the greatest possible torment" (p. 445). Under this typology, the first WRA director had the comparatively moderate task of administering Hades in the sand and cactus of the American West.

Unsurprisingly, Eisenhower rejected such comparisons out of hand: "We called the relocation camps 'evacuation centers,'" he wrote in his memoirs. "Never did we think of them as concentration camps. Technically, the Japanese-Americans were not restricted to the camps, although in fact they could not return to the Pacific coast and movement without safeguards to any other location would probably have endangered their lives, at least in the beginning" (p. 122). Movement surely endangered their lives, from beginning to end. Technically, the inmates were free to walk to the barbed wire and be killed, as happened to James Hatsuaki Wakasa at Topaz, Utah, on April 11, 1943. At the time and still decades later, Eisenhower tried to shield himself and his readers from the simple truth that enclosures where people, most of them citizens, have been penned without being charged with crimes and without being sentenced by ordinary process of law, and then shot if they try to leave, are enclosures correctly called concentration camps. By insisting

Endangered Lives at Manzanar, April 2, 1942. The WRA legend made no reference to the soldier's battle readiness: "While [a] military policeman stands guard, this detachment watches arrival of other evacuees of Japanese ancestry at this War Relocation Center."
[The Bancroft Library]

they were merely "evacuation centers," Eisenhower hid their grim realities under the official lies the WRA called "definitions."

To his lasting credit, Eisenhower hated his job, did what he could to make the camps more bearable, and was permanently scarred by the experience: "I have brooded about this whole episode on and off for the past three decades, for it is illustrative of how an entire society can somehow plunge off course" (*PIC*, p. 125). At the time he found his duties "agonizing" and word soon reached Roosevelt that he was "sick of the job" (*YoI*, p. 114). A way out came in mid-June when he was asked to become the deputy of Elmer Davis in the Office of War Information. Before taking up his new post he went to a party at the home of Dillon and Jenness Wirt Myer and enjoyed himself playing their piano and talking to friends. After the other guests had gone, he spoke to Myer about taking over the WRA. The latter already knew something about the agency, for they had talked about its problems riding back and forth to work in the same car pool and three months before had collaborated to select the top WRA staff from among their colleagues in the Department of Agriculture.

Dillon Myer always mentioned Eisenhower's piano playing when he related how he became director. Afterward they discussed the proposition for a couple of hours, Myer has reported, and when "I asked Milton if he really thought I should take the job, he replied, 'Yes, if you can do the job and sleep at night.' He said that he had been unable to do so. I was sure that I could sleep, and so agreed to accept the position if he felt that I was the one to do it, although it was not something that I would have chosen for myself" (Auto, pp. 183–84). On June 17, 1942, Roosevelt appointed him director.

"I was requested to take on a special war-time job with a Presidential appointment," he added elsewhere, "and unless you have a very good reason you don't turn down a Presidential request during wartime" (Auto, p. 185). Eisenhower's weighing of moral implications was profound contrasted with his own: "I was sure that I could sleep." Actually, he had always been "a good sleeper," and over the next four years—until the official termination of the WRA on June 30, 1946—he prided himself that "with very few exceptions I went to bed at night and slept soundly until time to get up the next morning" (Auto, p. 185).

Myer slept soundly nights as ruler of a vast American archipelago. Originally he had his own independent civilian agency—it was moved into the Department of the Interior by executive order on February 16, 1944—that ran concentration camps scattered throughout the country from the Mississippi Delta across the Rockies and into the Sierras. Officially, the WRA had ten camps. The two in Arkansas, Jerome and Rohwer, were on lands the Farm Security Administration had purchased for poor southern farm families. Three camps were on federal reclamation lands: Tule Lake, California; Minidoka, Idaho; and Heart Mountain, Wyoming. Three camps were on lands obtained from various sources, federal, municipal, and private: Manzanar, California; Topaz, Utah; and Granada, or Amache, Colorado. Finally, the two Arizona camps, Gila River and Poston, were on Indian reservations. In all, the WRA had under its jurisdiction over a hundred million dollars worth of government property and within the camps confined altogether 119,803 men, women, and children, almost two-thirds of them (64.9 percent) American-born.

At peak confinements (January 1, 1943) the mean number of inmates per camp was 11,031, with less than 8,000 in the smallest (Granada) and over 18,000 in the largest (Poston). In each camp were about a square mile of flimsy barracks, usually tar-papered, mess halls, schools, hospitals, stores, police stations, and administration buildings. Military police patrolled the perimeters, served as sentries at the gates, and manned the guard towers, but were under orders to move into the centers only upon formal request from the WRA. Within the camps "appointed personnel" (APs) or "Caucasians" counted inmates called "evacuees," studied them, enticed some into the all-Nisei combat team and registered others for the draft, cleared many for "leave," and sorted the remainder into bins labeled "loyal" and "disloyal." In all, about 3,000 APs worked in the camps, in the chief field offices in San Francisco, Denver, and Little Rock, in smaller "relocation" offices in other cities, and in the Washington headquarters. From beginning to end the WRA received appropriations of over 190 million dollars, of which the keepers spent over 160 million.

It was a huge job, a difficult job, and a "Job Well Done," editorialized the civil libertarian Alan Barth in the *Washington Post* of March 28, 1946: "All the men associated in this undertaking, and in particular Mr. Myer, who fought valiantly and pertinaciously against prejudice for the rights of the unfortunates in his charge, can take pride in a difficult job exceedingly well done." By then about 57,000 "evacuees" had moved back to the West Coast, but about 50,000 had settled eastward in new homes, a planned dispersal Barth hoped would "have some benefits in better integration of the Japanese-Americans into American society." President Harry S. Truman awarded Myer the nation's Medal for Merit for his outstanding service, offered to make him the last appointed governor of Puerto Rico, a post he declined, and then did appoint him commissioner of Indian affairs, another people-keeping role we shall consider later on. And claiming to represent not only its own members "but also the vast majority of all persons of Japanese ancestry in the United States," the Japanese American Citizens League (JACL) held a banquet in his honor at the Roosevelt Hotel in New York on May 22, 1946, celebrated him as a "champion of human rights and common decency," and presented him with a testimonial scroll for his "courageous and inspired leadership" (*UA*, p. 342).

This inspired leadership had already been trumpeted everywhere by the WRA's many publications. While laying bare the keepers' roots in agriculture, Morrill M. Tozier caught the general tone of WRA propaganda in the title of his final report: *WRA: A Story of Human Conser-*

vation (1946). And having grown larger than life-size in a job Eisenhower could not stomach, Dillon Myer naturally did not spend the next decades brooding over his finest hour. Indeed, in his "inside story" on *Uprooted Americans* (1971) Myer came close to exulting: The camps had been innocent "way stations," places that "a large number of the evacuees looked upon . . . as havens of rest and security. This was especially true of the elderly Issei. . . . Of the 70,000 people left in centers in 1944, probably at least half had never had it so good" (pp. 291–92). And, looking back over the decades, he stressed the beneficent consequences: "in spite of mistakes the results have generally been good. It was important to prove to the world that World War II was not a racial war but rather a war to maintain our democratic way of life and to leave the way open for other countries to develop the democratic concept" (p. xiv).

With few notable exceptions, popular writers and historians have simply repeated and perpetuated the keepers' story of their own benevolence. It drew plausibility from the undeniable truth that the WRA did not treat the Issei and the Nisei with the harshness Congress, military and intelligence agencies, and perhaps a majority of American citizens thought fitting—this undeniable, but relative, "benevolence" has been so often detailed as to need no restatement here.

But there was another story, one of illegal imprisonment, of systematically breaking up a subculture by the "dispersal" of families and individuals away from the West Coast, of penal colonies for citizens called "troublemakers," of forced labor, of shootings, of arbitrary internment of aliens, of drafting young men for military service from behind barbed wire, and of the basic denial of common decency characteristic of total institutions, including spying and informing, humiliation and intimidation, and such physical abuse as beating and kicking. This was a story not of conservation but of human betrayal, and to understand it we must go back to the chief keeper's beginnings.

CHAPTER II

Farm Boy

[Being director of the WRA was] a tough job without precedents or guidelines. I learned many things for sure during
that four years including the confirmation that many of the
tenets which I had grown up with were still valid.

—*Dillon S. Myer, "Autobiography," 1970*

In *Historical Collections of Ohio* (1889, 1891), the renowned traveler
Henry Howe began his chronicle of Licking County with the pioneers
who streamed in shortly after General ("Mad") Anthony Wayne's victory at the Battle of Fallen Timbers in 1794. They came in from Maryland, like Dillon Myer's grandfather, from Virginia, Pennsylvania, New
Jersey, and New England, or directly from Wales and Germany.

Blazing the way was a Virginian named Ellis Hughes, who raised his
cabin "in some old Indian corn-fields, about five miles below [present-
day] Newark." Said to have been "bred in the hot-bed of Indian warfare," Hughes did not let the return of relative peace "mitigate his hatred
of the race." That he demonstrated unforgettably after two Indians supposedly stole his horses one night in April 1800. Accompanied by neighbors, Hughes trailed them all day and camped part of that night deep
in the woods. When the alleged thieves awoke in the gray of the next
morning, there stood the white men with their rifles leveled:

> Just at that moment one of the Indians discovered them, and instinctively
> clapping his hand on his breast, as if to ward off the fatal ball, exclaimed in
> tones of affright, "me bad Indian!—me no do so more!" The appeal was in
> vain, the smoke curled from the glistening barrels, the report rang in the
> morning air, and the poor Indians fell dead.
>
> [Howe, II, 317]

The smoke curling up in this woodland tableau signaled the imminence
of a day when the rolling hills and pleasant valleys of the county would
be cleared of both woods and Indians.

11

From 1828 to 1864 the Reverend Jacob Little ministered to his flock in Granville, a small town six miles west of Newark. In the early days, Pastor Little once remarked, "snakes, wolves and Indians abounded in this region" (Howe, II, 330). Like snakes and wolves, Indians did not abound long, and those who made them vanish earned the lasting gratitude of their neighbors. When the remorseless Ellis Hughes died in 1845, for instance, after living to "an advanced age, in the hope of a happy future," he was "buried with military honors and other demonstrations of respect" (Howe, II, 317). This respect for Indian-haters was so pandemic we may simply assume, in the absence of evidence to the contrary, that it was shared by Dillon Myer's grandfather, who by then had been in Licking County for over a decade.

Of German extraction and from Allegheny County, Maryland, Jacob H. Myer (1800–67) bought land in 1834 on the banks of what is now Buckeye Lake—his sheepskin deed, his grandson was to note proudly, had been signed by President Andrew Jackson. After the death of his wife Nancy in 1855, Jacob Myer married Mary Oldaker (1818–1912), a relatively young woman who had grown up in the Shenandoah Valley of Virginia. Six years before the aging Jacob died, Mary Oldaker gave birth to a boy they named John Hyson Myer (1861–1941). Their son stayed on the farm after his father's death and later married Harriet Estella Seymour (1864–1959), a woman of Scotch-Irish descent. John and Harriet Myer had four children. Their son Dillon Seymour, born on September 4, 1891, had an older brother and two younger sisters.

Born and raised on what he called "a typical corn belt farm of 135 acres in central Ohio," Dillon Myer became a typical boy in a typical home near a typical nineteenth-century country town. From his seventh birthday on he milked cows mornings and evenings and in between sawed and split wood and did other chores. When he was about fourteen years old he made some money raising potatoes and with that bought his first shotgun, a Remington: "I don't suppose I ever bought anything that I got more pleasure out of as a kid than I did that." Thereafter, "rabbit and quail hunting were fun times," as was fishing in the summer; winter evenings around the fire with apples and popcorn "were also fun." On Sundays he would sometimes sneak away to attend baseball games: "I had to sneak because my Dad did not favor Sunday baseball games." He also remembered with pleasure the County Quartet in which Uncle George "was a good tenor," the horseback riding, taffy pulls, box socials, playing "post office" at parties, and going to dances at Buckeye Lake Park with "our gang from Hebron" (Auto, pp. 1, 32, 81, 69, 58, 77).

Still, life was a serious business. In his oral history of those early years about all that Dillon Myer saw fit to include about his mother was her insistence on correct spelling and good posture. Spelling was "a very important matter in our family." And day after day as he passed by, Harriet Myer would slap him on the shoulder blades and drum into him that he had "to straighten up so I wouldn't be stooped" (Auto, pp. 9–10).

"Methodism was to the West all that Puritanism was to New England," Edward Eggleston explained in *The Circuit Rider* (1897). "Both of them are sublime when considered historically; neither of them were very agreeable to live with, maybe." For many years secretary of the board of trustees of the Methodist Episcopal Church in nearby Hebron, John Hyson Myer was not very agreeable to live with, maybe. When his son Dillon was old enough, he had him pass the collection baskets during Sunday services. Everyday at home, "my dad sat at the head of the table and always gave the blessing" (Auto, p. 10). Such domestic worship was usual in their neighborhood, and church attendance was very nearly universal. Dillon Myer remembered only one family, the Robys, who did not go to church much, though "it wasn't that they were complete heathens in the sense that we thought of heathens" (Auto, p. 51).

Between 1850 and 1900 the Myers and other Americans purchased a hundred million copies of William Holmes McGuffey's school readers, and with them came a flood tide of piety and morality with strong undercurrents of New England Puritanism. When Dillon Myer was three years old, his father placed a copy in his hands and taught him how to read. In McGuffey's *Eclectic First Reader for Young Children* (1837), the toddler soon mastered sentences such as these from Lesson XVIII:

> All that live get life from God.
> He made the poor man, as well as the rich man.
> He made the dark man, as well as the fair man.
> He made the fool, as well as the wise man.

The precocious reader was soon walking a little over a mile to a one-room school where these contrasts of class and color joined a cluster of self-evident truths such as "God Blesses the Industrious." Industry, self-reliance, punctuality, neatness, honesty, acquisitiveness, and thriftiness were all divinely sanctioned according to the McGuffey readers. In grade school Dillon Myer had his character built upon these unchallenged tenets. (Classmates kidded him about being "the good little boy.") In high school he was a cheerleader.

Also on the debating team, "which was pretty good," Myer once went up the pike six miles to debate Kirkersville High. When he and the gang from Hebron came out afterward to catch the electric interurban, "we were egged by a bunch of hoodlums and most of us went home with eggs all over our overcoats" (Auto, p. 76).

Another "strange interlude" in his oral history hinted that he was not always a good boy. When he was a teenager the Hebron Methodist Church sponsored two "so-called fresh air kids" from Columbus to a summer outing on the Myer farm. Named Willie and Harry Graham, they kept Dillon and his brother Ernest Myer enthralled for a few days by their stories of life in the metropolis. Tiring of these, the farm boys decided to entertain their guests by boosting them up on the bare backs of a pair of carriage horses. Old Queen and Gyp were then whacked across the "back" ends and started "down the field as hard as they could run. It happened that the boys did survive. I think at least one of them fell off." The Grahams also survived being led into bumblebee nests, but were again made painfully aware of their lack of rural lore. Decades later Dillon Myer's sly pleasure at the discomfiture of these city slickers still endured in the moral he drew for an interviewer: "These experiences and others taught a couple of city boys that all the excitement did not lie in the cities" (Auto, pp. 73–74).

Nearby Hebron was not a city. "In the dusty tramp of civilization westward," as Ed Howe put it in *The Story of a Country Town* (1883; p. 1), Hebron had heroically, but vainly, tried to keep pace. It lay some twenty miles east of Columbus, nine miles southwest of Newark, and a little over a mile north of the Myer farm. It was strategically situated at the one place in the state where the pike, or National Road, crossed the Ohio and Erie Canal. After the canal was completed through Hebron in 1828 and the pike in 1834, the town seemed destined for booming good times. Alas, the census of 1840 showed a population of only 473 souls and that of 1880 of 489. Hebronites still ponder over the mystery of why their town never grew. One explanation in the form of a rumor—the mystery awaits its historian—has it that Hebron lost out to Newark by one vote in the race to be named county seat. At all events, lacking a courthouse square, Hebron hung onto its portion of the pike and called that Main Street, with frame buildings strung along it that included a blacksmith shop, general store, feed mill, lumber yard, volunteer fire station, school, and four churches—one Methodist, two Baptist, and one Disciples.

Like townspeople all across the heartland, the inhabitants had made "success" synonymous with "progress" and measured that by rapid population growth and spiraling real estate values. By their own standards Hebron's failure was so dismal it made the air on their Main Street hard to breathe. By the end of the century the town had become a museum piece, a case of arrested development, a cramped, prudish, shallow, conventional, rigidly pious world. It dozed in the twilight of the agrarian era and could only daydream that the advance of mechanization might kiss it awake. Ironically, the advance of the automobile put it to sleep for good as a bedroom of Newark and Columbus.

Dillon Myer's recollections of the coming of the new technology were untroubled by insight or second thoughts. He was eight years old when he saw his first car, a "one-lunger" (Auto, p. 8). In about 1900 Rural Free Delivery (RFD) reached out to the family farm. In 1901 the electric interurban began service through Hebron. In about 1903 the Myers got free fuel for allowing the natural gas company right of way across their land—over in a flash was the drudgery of sawing and splitting wood, for all they had to do then was light a match, turn on the gas, and "boom! away it went. I'll tell you that was a real thrill" (Auto, p. 18). And in 1913, the year before he graduated from college, his father purchased their first automobile. Myer's celebration of these happenings reads like a chamber of commerce retrospect: all the technological innovations were "important in widening the scope of communications and contact with the world outside of the traditional rural neighborhoods" (Auto, p. 80).

Applied science was the catalyst of these "big events," as Myer called them. Added to Puritan virtues and middle-class values such as those broadcast by the McGuffey readers, it sped up the formation of a new class of "professionals," technicians who were charged with nothing less than the perfection of industrial America. At the highest level their vocation was *national efficiency*, a goal Theodore Roosevelt defined in 1908 as "the patriotic duty of insuring the safety and continuance of the Nation." On every level they worked to supplant the sprawling disorder of the past with up-to-date centralized planning based on rationalized administrative methods and new scientific knowledge. Even in the countryside specialists coming out of the land grant colleges and experiment stations were effectively combating the farmers' traditional scorn for "book farming." Not fully in step with this new order of things, John Hyson Myer urged his son to become a Methodist minister. In an act of disobedience less grave than either of them might have imagined, the young man enrolled instead in the College of Agriculture at Ohio State University.

2

Of Dillon Myer's undergraduate years (1910–14) in Columbus not much can be said, for not much happened. His grades were average and his life in general "somewhat uneventful." He did join "an agricultural fraternity," Alpha Zeta, made some "wonderful friends," liked the parties, and benefited from "a great deal of contact with agricultural leaders." On balance, he felt he had profited from being a fraternity member. In fact, "the greatest thing that happened to me was that I was given an opportunity to become an Alpha Zeta" (Auto, pp. 84–85).

In 1914 the graduate became an instructor in agronomy at the University of Kentucky. He had "two wonderful bosses" and taught cereal crops for "two wonderful years in the lush and beautiful blue grass country" (Auto, p. 86). Then on March 1, 1916, he became the first agricultural demonstration agent for Vanderburgh County at Evansville, Indiana. Therewith he had successfully completed the leap from the family farm to the vast governmental complex called "agriculture."

In his new job Dillon Myer became a key mover in the transformation of farming into agriculture. The rural representative of the corporate state and the consolidating economy, the county agent had first appeared in 1904 as a technician dispatched from Washington to demonstrate to Southerners how to fight the boll weevil in their cotton crops. These and other specialists soon gained the support of railroad directors, farm implement manufacturers, bankers, and other business executives who believed agriculture was out of step with the rest of the economy, who remembered vividly and uneasily the impassioned mass movement of the Populists in the 1890s, and who thus had both economic and political motives for promoting more businesslike attitudes among agriculturalists. In the first few years the county agent was employed by the Department of Agriculture, by state agricultural societies, by county appropriation boards and farm bureaus, by private firms and groups, or by some combination of these organizations. With the passage of the Smith-Lever Co-operative Extension Act on May 8, 1914, Congress established a national system that made the agent a joint appointee of the U.S. government, the state agricultural college, the county government, and in some measure of the conservative, ostensibly private, farm bureaus. These bureaus evolved from county to state organizations and in 1920 took national form as the American Farm Bureau Federation.

Myer had joined a far-flung adult extension service that reached from Washington down to the county level, where it was charged, under the Smith-Lever Act, with "diffusing among the people of the United States useful and practical information on subjects relating to agriculture and home economics." Instead of becoming a Methodist minister, he had swerved only slightly from parental urgings in becoming an "agricultural missionary" who preached the gospel of efficiency. Recently ordained an expert in one of the proliferating "helping professions" and dressed in newly pressed trousers, white shirt, bow tie, and cap, the young man liked instructing work-worn farmers on crop pests, livestock production and marketing, new machines, new techniques of tillage, new fertilizers, new strains of seeds. As for the young folks he habitually called youngsters, he took pride in being the first to introduce 4-H clubs to Vanderburgh County: "It was fun watching these youngsters come along and develop" (Auto, p. 131). Toward all age groups his paternalism was unmistakable. To Myer and county agents generally, as the historian Grant McConnell has observed in *The Decline of Agrarian Democracy* (1953), "the farmer was a figure to be lifted out of the mire of his own ignorance and backwardness" (p. 26).

Early in World War I, Myer managed to get himself promoted to "assistant county agent leader" at Purdue University, a position that gained him deferred draft status. For reasons that will become quite clear when we consider his relentless harrying of draft resisters and draft evaders behind WRA barbed wire during World War II, his reminiscence of this "embarrassing" exemption is very nearly diverting: "During the first ten months of 1918 I found myself in quite an embarrassing situation, because I was not in uniform." He himself felt "a bit of a slacker," but luckily nobody made that charge to his face (Auto, pp. 146, 147).

In the 1920s "the most wonderful girl" came to Ohio State University "as a specialist in the field of Interior Decorating, and as a Clothing

Specialist in the Extension Service." Jenness Wirt was a "county home demonstration agent," in fine, with an overlapping "field"—his was farm management and hers was home management, or "home beautification," as it was sometimes called. The extension agents married in 1924, when Myer was thirty-three; afterward "three very wonderful daughters" blessed their union (Auto, p. 159).

In 1925 Myer interrupted his extension work to enroll in the Teachers College of Columbia University. While earning a master's degree in education he also took several courses at Columbia College. These made no discernible impact and their instructors mattered so little he apparently soon forgot their names. No Franz Boas or any other teacher ever set his imagination ablaze. In the mountain of government documents and letters issued over his name in the 1940s and 1950s there was no trace of the literary and scientific allusions one might have expected of a man whose reading ranged beyond newspapers and the technical publications of the Government Printing Office.

In 1933 Myer became a state supervisor of the Agricultural Adjustment Administration (AAA). To bring supply down and prices up, the AAA sought to curtail production and destroy the existing "surplus." Myer thus implemented the "Killing Little Pigs" program in Ohio, a program that throughout the country slaughtered six million pigs and impregnated sows. Such enforced scarcity struck many farmers as organized madness, especially during a year when over fourteen million persons were unemployed and at least a third of the nation was undernourished. But Myer had no misgivings at the time or afterward. Brushing aside the criticisms of "unbelieving farmers," he went ahead with the killing secure in his conviction that the experts knew best. Even in retrospect he maintained that it had been merely the first step toward a comprehensive "corn-hog program" (Auto, p. 161).

On April 12, 1934, Myer finally joined the headquarters staff of the Department of Agriculture. Milton Eisenhower went "to bat" to get him an "appropriate pay grade" (Auto, p. 167). It began at $6,500, a salary on which he and his family could live pretty well in Washington "at that time." The time was of course the Great Depression, and in those days that amount was pretty nearly a princely stipend.

The time was also that of the huge cloud of Great Plains soil that blew all the way back to the national seat as a dusty reminder of the need to do something about conservation. Set up in 1933 in the Department of the Interior, the Soil Erosion Service was moved over to the Department of Agriculture in 1935 and renamed the Soil Conservation

Service (SCS). On September 15, 1935, Myer moved from the AAA to the new SCS; in 1938 he became its assistant chief.

By then agriculture was subject to a network of compulsory market-ing quotas, tax penalties, and payments that mocked the old ideal of the farmer as prototypal free entrepreneur. Semiautonomous agencies in the Department of Agriculture administered their own programs of parity, extension, credit, forestry, electrification, and conservation. Each had its own turf, sought to extend that, and meanwhile fought off trespass-ers. In 1938 Milton Eisenhower, then head of the Office of Land-Use Coordination, negotiated the famous Mount Weather Agreement, which was supposed to achieve a measure of coordination and pacify the warring agencies and land grant colleges. It did not, and the suc-cessful onslaught against the Farm Security Administration would soon demonstrate that dramatically. The new SCS, a relatively weak agency, was also an inviting target since it organized farmers at the grass roots in soil conservation districts not under the direct control of the Ameri-can Farm Bureau Federation and its client agency, Dillon Myer's old outfit, the Extension Service.

In this shadow dance of the administrators, Myer became a formi-dable performer. As a county agent he had worked comfortably for years with the large-scale commercial producers who ran the Farm Bu-reau Federation and through it dominated the system of which he was a part. But now that the agency of which he was assistant chief had come under their attack, he led the bitter fight against what he described as the attempted "take over" of the SCS by the Extension Service. Lost forever in the shadows are the letters and telegrams he must have sum-moned forth, his informal telephone calls and visits with individual con-gressmen, his councils of war with other agency leaders, and his strategy sessions with men like Eisenhower. Whatever the precise details of this obscure campaign, his final triumphant moment became radiantly visi-ble when he laid the whole matter before Secretary of Agriculture Henry A. Wallace and gained his support: "This was a major victory for the SCS and for me personally" (Auto, p. 178).

For Myer politics was always administration. Before he left the De-partment of Agriculture he had learned the ins and outs of the congres-sional committee system and had developed relationships with individ-ual lawmakers that would come in handy later on. Within the beleaguered SCS he had made allies who would follow him elsewhere as a virtual band of disciples. And he believed he had established an earned reputation as a bureaucratic infighter, as a man who was handed, he noted proudly, "the tough problems which nobody else wanted to handle." It was "kind of dirty work," he admitted, and it was to be handed to him more than once (Auto, pp. 181, 182).

3

The "good little boy" from a typical corn-belt farm had become a typical Washington bureaucrat. To be sure, a career in agriculture imposed special claims: "Anyone who has spent much time about the department," Grant McConnell has observed, "is aware of the degree to which the protective coloration of rustic ways is cultivated in the offices of the vast buildings on the Mall. Failure to achieve this coloration is itself ground for suspicion" (*Decline*, p. 72). No one could suspect affable Dillon Myer on that ground. An aura of rusticity always covered his trim business suit like a topcoat. It hung lightly from his shoulders as he preached the fundamental value of self-reliance and simultaneously subjected farmers to controls that made them substantially dependent on government handouts. It protected his faith that America was the land of equal opportunity while he implemented programs designed to benefit the already prosperous minority of large-unit producers. And it kept him snug in his urban setting as he cultivated rural figures of speech. The Bill of Rights, he told an interviewer in 1969, had been the WRA "endpost to hook our fence to. . . . [Laughter.] As a farm boy, you see, I use the kind of similes that come from a farm boy's life" (Auto 2, II, 4).

In *The Farm* (1933), native son Louis Bromfield lamented the speedy transition of Ohio from wilderness paradise through an interlude of Jeffersonian democracy to the current urban carcinoma and commercialized agriculture. Earlier, in *Winesburg, Ohio* (1919) and then elsewhere, Sherwood Anderson, another and greater native son, pursued his lifelong quest for, in his words, "some lost, some hidden and half-forgotten loveliness." Not gifted with the imaginative awareness of these Ohioans, Myer planted his rustic stock phrases in shifting surfaces and remained serenely unaware of any paradise lost or of any half-forgotten dream of loveliness. The "good sleeper" who slept soundly as director of the WRA seemingly never dreamed—at least his reminiscences lack any hint of visions, fantasies, or dreams, even bad dreams.

"It surpasses understanding," said the former county agent Russell Lord, "how completely insensitive most Land Grant College graduates were to the widespread spectacle of grinding rural poverty and degradation of rural labor" (McConnell, *Decline*, p. 165). Myer was a prime case in point. Never for a moment did he entertain the radical proposition that grave injustices existed; never, to my knowledge, did he even betray historical interest in the Populists, who had built a mass movement on that proposition in the years when he was growing up. He later lacked interest also in urban reformers such as Mayors Tom Johnson and Samuel ("Golden Rule") Jones, who sought to give the citizens of Cleveland and Toledo a fair shake. For him politics was administration, and that was a matter for objective experts like himself.

A report from Myer of a dream or two would have suggested an inner self sending up signals from beneath his layers of repression. Even desultory historical study of agrarian protest movements might have given him some inkling of his current *political* role in agriculture. And respectful attention to what was after all his "field" might have given him some appreciation of what was happening to it. But the land itself had disappeared under his production statistics—so many acres with yields per acre of so many bushels of corn or soybeans that would in turn feed so many head of hogs or steers. But in this he was like Anglo-Americans generally—as Alexis de Tocqueville had remarked, they were "insensible to the wonders of inanimate Nature, and they may be said not to perceive the mighty forests which surround them till they fall beneath the hatchet."

Nature's children, who like the wolves had pretty much vanished from Licking County during the years Myer was growing up, became his responsibility when he ran the Bureau of Indian Affairs for Harry S. Truman. An authority by virtue of that service, he later helped an interviewer understand "The Indian Problem." It stemmed from the fact that "many Indians are still primitive," he said, still like their hunting and fishing forefathers who had "lived the life of the nomad, because they moved from place to place and many of the tribes lived in part by poaching on the richer tribes and stealing their produce" (Auto, p. 286). Where that produce came from was something of a mystery, for most Indians had never been farmers:

> The only Indians who did extensive farming were the Pueblo and Hopi Indians in the New Mexico–Arizona area, who had received their grants of land from the Spanish conquistadors many, many years ago and who were able to carry on undisturbed for a great many years in their farming operations. . . . Outside of these, however, the forest Indians of the East and North

and the Plains Indians of the Midwest and the fishing Indians of the Northwest did practically no farming and any farming that was done by these
Indian groups was done by squaws, who simply raised patches of squash to
dry, corn which could be used as meal, and used as part of their pemican
which was made from buffalo meat, berries and many other things which
they packed together into a kind of combination of meat, grain and fruit that
they could slice down all winter long.

[Auto, p. 285]

This explanation measured precisely Myer's stature as an expert on
farming and on Indians. To hold up a yardstick beside his prejudices,
consider just three of the sources he might have drawn on for antidotes.

1. In *The Beginnings of Agriculture in America* (1923), agronomist
Lyman Carrier formulated virtually in Myer's words "the most common
belief" that "Indians were not agriculturalists, but lived mainly by hunting and fishing" and marveled at its longevity, "despite the fact that the
evidence without any likelihood for refutation proves the contrary." Nor
did most Indians live Myer's "life of the nomad":

The great majority of the Indians lived in fixed habitations, tilled the soil,
and subsisted fully as much if not more on their agricultural products, than
they did on those of the chase. The more the matter is studied from an un-
prejudiced point of view the more remarkable appear their achievements in
farming. No people anywhere in the world ever made greater strides in plant
breeding than did the American Indians. . . . A comparison crop by crop
taking into consideration acreage and value of these products with all the
other crops now grown in the United States shows quite clearly that our
agriculture is at least one-third native American.

[p. 41]

Had Myer consulted this still useful source, he would have at least
known the origins of many of the crops he worked with. It was at his
fingertips—Carrier was a colleague in the Bureau of Plant Industry of
the Department of Agriculture.

2. In *Archaeological History of Ohio: The Mound Builders and
Later Indians* (1902), Gerard Fowke piled up quotations to show that
assertions of Indian "improvidence, lack of energy, and dependence
upon spontaneous growth of natural productions for subsistence, are
utterly without foundation." From his convenient list, let us select two
extracts from Lucien Carr's "Mounds of the Mississippi Valley Historically Considered":

The testimony is so uniform that of the main fact—the cultivation of corn in
greater or less quantities by all the tribes living east of the Mississippi and

south of the St. Lawrence and Great Lakes—there can not be a shadow of doubt. . . . Instead of cultivating it in small patches as a summer luxury, it can be shown on undoubted authority that everywhere, within the limits named, the Indian looked upon it as a staple article of food, both in summer and winter; that he cultivated it in large fields. . . . [Of the Maumee country in 1794, General Anthony Wayne said] "nor have I ever before beheld such immense fields of corn in any part of America, from Canada to Florida."

[pp. 478, 480]

A major publication of the Ohio State Archaeological and Historical Society, Fowke's volume was accessible to Myer in Columbus and elsewhere.

3.   In *Historical Collections of Ohio* (1889, 1891), Henry Howe added substantially to this accumulation of evidence. After the punitive 1780 expedition of General George Rogers Clark, for instance, "it was estimated that at the two [Shawnee] Indian towns, Chillicothe and Piqua, more than five hundred acres of corn were destroyed, as well as every species of eatable vegetables" (I, 389). Chillicothe was only about sixty miles from what became the Myer farm. And after Fallen Timbers in 1794, the battle that cleared the way for white settlement of Ohio, General ("Mad") Anthony Wayne reported that "we remained three days and nights on the banks of the Maumee, in front of the field of battle, during which time all the houses and corn-fields were consumed and destroyed for a considerable distance, both above and below Fort Miami." Wayne's army laid waste what he described as "immense fields of corn" for about fifty miles on both sides of the Maumee (II, 394). All this destruction took place about a hundred and fifty miles from what became the Myer farm. And Myer grew up surrounded by Howe's volumes—of the first edition alone, the proud compiler claimed that "a third of a million of my books have gone out among the people and done good" (I, 16). Had one done good to Myer, he would have known that the Indian-hater who blazed the way to Licking County had first settled "in some old Indian corn-fields, about five miles below Newark." That placed those old Indian cornfields about five miles above the Myer farm. Every time the agricultural expert walked through a new white cornfield in his "corn-hog program," he might properly have paid thanks to the Native American farmers who had domesticated and developed the precious plant in the first place.

Actually, those first farmers had been in residence since time immemorial. Of the ten thousand effigy, burial, and temple mounds in the

Ohio Valley, a goodly number were in Licking County; with all the others, they have been traced back to the Adena people (c. 500 B.C. to A.D. 100) and to the magnificently creative Hopewell people (c. 100 B.C. to A.D. 300). At Newark, ten miles northeast of the Myer farm, were impressive Indian earthworks that originally covered an area of over two square miles. When young Dillon Myer went to the Licking County Fair there, he walked over an enclosure made up by the Great Circle Earthworks, an area of twenty-six acres enclosed by earthen walls eight to fourteen feet in height. In the yard of the Fairmount Presbyterian Church six miles down the pike from his home, he could climb a conical mound about thirty feet in height and on a clear day see the tall buildings in Columbus on the western horizon. Other mounds were nearer still. David Morrow, a retired RFD mailman, estimates that he used to see fifteen to twenty within a five-mile radius of Hebron, and it may even be that Dillon's brother Ernest Myer built his home on a mound just across the lane from their father's house. And each mound heightened the irony of the expert's wonderful incomprehension, for it was the work of the ancestors of certain modern tribespeople: the Adena and Hopewell peoples were ancient farm folk who lived in permanent villages and grew corn in the rich bottomlands. Myer grew up blind to what his feet were stumbling over.

Faced with the obvious absurdity of making tumuli of such number and magnitude the work of nomadic hunters/gatherers, financier and ethnologist Albert Gallatin, General William Henry Harrison, Ephraim George Squier, the Ohio newspaper editor, and other antiquaries and scholars invented a vanished race of "Mound Builders." They came into their fabulous existence for a few decades to meet an embarrassingly pressing need: living Indians were said to be wandering hordes of savages; the mysterious folk who built the mounds had to have been farming peoples. In *Pre-historic Races of the United States of America* (1873), for instance, John Wells Foster, a former president of the American Association for the Advancement of Science, adopted the lost-race theory for reasons he put bluntly. The Indian could never have been the Mound Builder:

> His character, since first known to the white man has been signalized by treachery and cruelty. He repels all efforts to raise him from his degraded position: and whilst he has not the moral nature to adopt the virtues of civilization, his brutal instincts lead him to welcome its vices. He was never known voluntarily to engage in an enterprise requiring methodical labor; he

dwells in temporary and movable habitations; he follows the game in their migrations; he imposes the drudgery of life upon his squaw.

[p. 300]

By the early 1900s archaeologists had deflated such notions of a separate prehistoric race, as Gerard Fowke's subtitle *The Mound Builders and Later Indians* suggested. Myer may well have been as unaware of the great nineteenth-century controversy over the origins of the builders as he was uninterested in the mounds themselves. But his "primitive" Indians were those of Foster and the rest of the fabulists. His contempt for "squaws" tending their "patches" came straight out of this Indian-hating past and indeed out of his grandfather's first days in Licking County when Indians were seen as encumbrances on the land—recall the Reverend Jacob Little's linkage group, "snakes, wolves and Indians."

Wonderfully unreflective about his own roots, Myer was such a typical product of his time and place as to seem the mythic heartland American in thin disguise. If this well-intentioned man tends to appear a monster of incomprehension, that is only because he was so normal in his contempt for the land and its original indwellers. After all, his delusion that Indians were nomadic hunters was "the most common belief" into the 1920s and after. No evidence can be found anywhere that he ever made a painful search for meaning outside these common beliefs. That meaning he found in ready-made rights and wrongs. Improving on Ralph Waldo Emerson's injunction to "hitch your wagon to a star," he hitched his wagon to technology and organization charts. He had and has significance not as an individual but as a carrier of Progressive white values, as a walking repository "of the tenets which I had grown up with."

As for the Japanese immigrants and the Japanese Americans, Myer took over the WRA knowing even less about them, so to speak, than he knew about the Native Americans. That may have been fortunate, he suggested to an interviewer in 1969:

And of course I didn't know any Japanese. The only Japanese that I ever remembered knowing before I took this job were two boys that were in my class in the College of Agriculture at Ohio State University in 1910–14. And I didn't remember ever meeting any others in the interim period. . . . In a way that was good because I came in, fortunately, with an open mind.

[Auto 2, II, 3–4]

PART II

Japanese Americans

After all these people were Japanese. The emotions against
the Japanese were great.

—Dillon S. Myer,
Interview, November 6, 1969

CHAPTER III

Director

I sincerely believe, gentlemen, that if we don't handle this
problem in a way to get these people absorbed as best we can
while the war is going on, we may have something akin to
Indian reservations after the war. . . . We will have a racial
issue which I don't think we need to have, and I am frankly
hoping that quite a number of those people will get established in positions in different parts of the country other than
on the Pacific coast, where they can be accepted as part of the
population, where they can gradually be absorbed as American citizens, and thus dispose of a racial problem that has
been a pretty tough one for the coast people and for the
United States.

> —*Dillon S. Myer,*
> *Testimony before the U.S. Senate Military*
> *Affairs Subcommittee, January 20, 1943*

Even when they tried, white officials failed to keep more than half buried their conviction that not only the Japanese immigrants (Issei) but
also the American-born (Nisei) were ineradicably alien. It cropped up
time and time again in their perplexity over what to call the latter. On
February 3, 1942, for instance, Assistant Secretary of War John J.
McCloy talked on the telephone with General John L. DeWitt of the
Western Defense Command about the complicated problem of evacu-
ating "the native born Japanese," and then had to explain whom he
meant: "That is[,] the American citizens." After finding "American citizens of the Japanese race" almost as cumbersome, McCloy actually
tried out "Japanese Americans" and proposed a licensing system
whereby everyone would be evacuated and "you permit to come back
into that area all non-suspected citizens." Whatever their other desig-
nations, Japanese Americans were not called "non-suspected citizens."
Let us eavesdrop:

MCCLOY: You may, by that [licensing] process, eliminate all of the Japs, but
             you might conceivably permit some to come back whom you are
             quite certain are free from any suspicion, as well as the fact that
             you might let some Italians come back. Now that has sound legal
             basis for it.

DEWITT: Particularly about the Germans and the Italians because you don't
             have to worry about them as a group. You have to worry about
             them purely as certain individuals. Out here, Mr. Secretary, a Jap
             is a Jap to these people now.

MCCLOY: Yes, I can understand that. [NA, RG 107]

In his *Final Report: Japanese Evacuation from the West Coast* (1943),
DeWitt called all the impounded people "Japanese," as indicated by his
subtitle. He, Colonel Karl R. Bendetsen, and their fellow officers infor-
mally used the epithet "Japs," a great leveler of distinctions between
citizens and aliens.

At the Federal Bureau of Investigation officials also referred to "the
Japs" in intra-agency memoranda. When that pejorative term seemed ill
advised, they almost invariably addressed themselves to "the Japanese"
and let the fractured meanings fend for themselves. On February 24,
1943, for instance, Director J. Edgar Hoover wrote a special agent in
Cleveland alerting him to the fact that "the Japanese granted leave from
the War Relocation Centers will include both citizens and aliens." That
seemed to place the Japanese Americans in a curious category, and, sure
enough, on March 4, 1943, Hoover wrote Edward J. Ennis, director of
the Alien Enemy Control Unit in the Department of Justice, about "the
handling of Japanese aliens and nonaliens" (FBI 62-69030). Hoover and
his staff saw the second-generation citizens as "Japanese nonaliens."

In the War Relocation Authority, Myer and his staff were not always
more circumspect. A few months after he took over, the WRA negotiated a memorandum of understanding with the Department of the Interior "covering the relocation of ten thousand Japanese on the Gila
River Indian Reservation in Arizona." In a fateful first encounter, Acting
Interior Solicitor Felix S. Cohen objected to Myer's term "Japanese" and
suggested to Commissioner John Collier of the Bureau of Indian Affairs
that they insist it be stricken, since "the agreement between the War
Relocation Authority and this Department does not restrict the use of
the Gila River Relocation Project to Japanese evacuees only." Collier
agreed: "The use of the term 'Japanese' to apply to native-born Americans of Japanese descent is at least as objectionable to those concerned
as would be the application of the terms 'Britishers' or 'Germans' to

native-born citizens of British or German descent" (letter and memoranda, July 18, August 12, and August 20, 1942, NA, RG 75).

After this galling mishap in his own field of expertise, Myer usually called his charges "these people," "evacuees," "relocatees," "persons of Japanese ancestry," and, less often, "Japanese Americans." Yet at a project directors' conference at Little Rock, Arkansas, on February 1–3, 1943, Myer welcomed "induction of Japanese into the United States Army"—a weird prospect throughout World War II—and concluded emotionally: "I deeply believe that our program must succeed in order we won't feel we lost part of the battle. We must not let the Japanese [which? where?] feel we are making a racial question out of it" (JERS, 67/14, E2.11B). In a speech at Eagle Rock, California, on June 19, 1945, after heading up the WRA for three years, he fell back into a reference to "American-born Japanese," a misnomer that mirrored Hoover's "Japanese nonaliens."

And decades later (in 1969) Myer recalled wartime passions against his charges for an interviewer: "After all these people were Japanese. The emotions against the Japanese were great" (Auto 2, II, 3). From beginning to end, despite the reproof of Felix Cohen and John Collier, the director literally did not know how to identify those behind his barbed wire. When his guard was down "these people" were simply "the Japanese."

2

Underlying all the confusion over nomenclature was the half-buried conviction General DeWitt blurted out in his testimony before the House Naval Affairs Subcommittee: "A Jap's a Jap. . . . There is no way to determine their loyalty. . . . It makes no difference whether he is an American; theoretically he is still a Japanese and you can't change him" (*San Francisco Chronicle*, April 14, 1943). Subsequently excoriated for such overtly racist assertions, the general was merely voicing what the other architects of exclusion kept camouflaged under less blatant language: no matter how long the Issei had been in the country and no matter how Westernized the Nisei had become, both generations were and would always be "the Japanese." Orientals.

Inscrutable Orientals. Governor Culbert L. Olson and Attorney General Earl Warren of California agreed with DeWitt that it was impossible to tell which ones could be trusted. Said Olson to a group of Japanese American editors in February 1942: "You know, when I look out at a group of Americans of German or Italian descent, I can tell whether they're loyal or not. I can tell how they think and even perhaps what they are thinking. But it is impossible for me to do this with the inscrutable Orientals, and particularly the Japanese." Said Warren to the House Select (Tolan) Committee Investigating National Defense Migration that same month: "We believe that when we are dealing with the Caucasian race, we have methods that will test the loyalty of them. . . . But when we deal with the Japanese, we are in an entirely different field and we cannot form any opinion that we believe to be sound." Federal Judge William Denman stated this inability more succinctly in his concurring opinion in *Korematsu* v. *United States* (140 F. [2d] 289, 300 [C.C.A. 9th, 1943]): "They all look alike." Why? Earlier, in the draft of an article cheerily titled "Goodbye Mr. Moto" (April 7, 1942), the liberal Carey McWilliams, then head of the California State Division of Immigration and Housing, had picturesquely suggested why in a phrase that was to have wide currency: the Nisei were "Americans with Japanese faces."

Decades of agitation against the "yellow peril" by the Native Sons and Daughters of the Golden West, the California Joint Immigration Committee, the American Legion, and other champions of white supremacy, including the Hearst and the McClatchy newspapers, chambers of commerce, and agricultural, labor, and business organizations, had indeed created a "pretty tough" racial problem for "the coast people," as Myer put it (though he did not have the Issei and Nisei in mind). That problem was scarcely limited to the Pacific slope, but notwithstanding overwhelming evidence of current prejudice against the Japanese Americans and their parents in the intermountain West and eastward, Myer let on that race-baiters on the coast were the only truly infectious carriers and treated the virus as though it could be placed under quarantine there. By this stratagem he helped implement standing administration policy to make the whole matter appear "regional," a West Coast aberration, as documents turned up by Michi Weglyn demonstrate. According to a State Department memorandum of April 6, 1942, "McCloy advised that every effort is being made to handle this problem as a 'regional' one, and is anxious to have as little publicity or instructions emanate from this end as possible" (*YoI*, pp. 298–99). That anxiety also appeared in a call from McCloy in Washington to Bendetsen in San Francisco on July 10, 1943: "I want to give you another strong warning," he admonished the colonel. "I certainly don't want to have the Chief's [i.e., FDR's] name in any way tied up with this whole business out there" (*YoI*, p. 299). But a whole battalion of Bendetsens could not have effectively distanced Franklin Delano Roosevelt.

Aside from his Executive Order 9066, which had started the whole business, FDR was tied up with it through Bendetsen, the ambitious young lawyer in uniform whom McCloy had sent out to San Francisco to serve as his liaison officer with DeWitt. McCloy promoted him from major to full colonel before he turned thirty-five and placed him at the head of the Wartime Civil Control Administration (WCCA), the agency that conducted the roundup of Japanese Americans, ran the sixteen assembly centers, and oversaw transfer of the impounded people to the WRA camps. Bendetsen worked out the licensing formula for mass exclusion, a move he advocated as "undoubtedly the safest course to follow, that is to say as you cannot tell which ones are loyal and which ones are not" (*YoI*, p. 95). First the protégé of Provost Marshal Allen W. Gullion and then McCloy's man in San Francisco, Bendetsen became the principal military apologist for exclusion and detention. His grateful superiors awarded him the army's Distinguished Service Medal in late 1942 and a decade later pulled him up into the equivalent of McCloy's old position by making him assistant secretary of the army (1950–52).

In Washington FDR was also tied in directly through John Jay McCloy himself. The principal assistant—he later liked to remember that he was "The" assistant—of his hero Henry Lewis Stimson, McCloy was a Philadelphian by birth, a Republican, and a product of the Ivy League (Amherst, Harvard Law) and Wall Street. He belonged to what C. Wright Mills called "the inner core of the power elite"—a corporation lawyer who moved easily from investment banking to the political arena and back, as he demonstrated after the war, when he was president of the World Bank (1947–49); U.S. military governor and high commissioner for Germany (1949–52), a position that ironically placed him in control of those convicted of war crimes in the Nuremberg proceedings and enabled him to set free *all* the convicted industrialists, even the notorious human rights violater Alfried Krupp, whose sentence was reduced to time served and whose personal fortune was restored intact; chairman of the board of Chase National (1953) and, after a merger, of Chase Manhattan (1955–60), the third largest bank in the United States; chairman of the Ford Foundation (1953–65); and, among his public services, a member of the Warren Commission (1963–64), on which he was the strongest proponent of the notion that a single bullet

had struck President Kennedy and Governor Connally. But back in 1942
he was already adept at insinuating himself into the centers of power
and dedicated to protecting superiors who embodied, at least temporarily, the image of national greatness and virtue. Placed in charge of
West Coast matters by his chief, and thus the key link between the
White House and Bendetsen and DeWitt, McCloy could readily understand and support their views of how to handle "the Japs" since he
shared those views and differed only in stating them more discreetly.

Roosevelt was tied in to "this whole business out there" still more
directly through the Republican elder statesman he had brought in as
his secretary of war. A member of the Eastern establishment and an
architect of U.S. Asian policy, Stimson also shouldered the white man's
burden and dealt firmly with subject peoples wherever he found them,
whether in Nicaragua, where he served as Calvin Coolidge's special executive agent, or in the Philippines, where he served as governor-general
in 1928 and 1929. The Filipinos were racially unfit to govern themselves, he declared, and though "capable of hopeful progress while under our supervision," they had, as Malays, "that racial tendency towards
backsliding." After he became Herbert Hoover's secretary of state, the
two men had a memorable conversation one day in February 1932.
Stimson asked the president if

> he really believed that the United States was not enough of a gov-
> ernmental power and did not have enough of a constitutional
> freedom to evolve [a] relationship to another country like the
> Philippines similar to the relationship of England to the British
> Commonwealth of Nations.

HOOVER: Well, that's the white man's burden.
STIMSON: Yes, that's what it comes down to and I believe in assuming it. I
           believe it would be better for the world and better for us.

Early in 1942 Roosevelt had placed in Stimson's hands the responsibility he in turn delegated to McCloy. A number of Stimson's diary en-
tries then make it clear that he shared the attitudes of his subordinates—
both on the West Coast and in Washington—toward "the younger generation of Japanese," by which he meant the American citizens of Japanese descent. An entry on February 3 shows that he, too, had to struggle with the vexed problem of what to call them: "If we base our
evacuation upon the ground of removing enemy aliens, it will not get
rid of the Nichis who are the second generation naturalized Japanese,
and, as I said, are the more dangerous ones." Later he drew a line

through his phonetic *Nichis* and substituted *Nisei,* but he let stand *naturalized Japanese*, which they were not. This early he still worried about the constitutional issue of discriminating "among our citizens on the ground of racial origin." By February 10, however, after a conference with McCloy, he recorded that "the second generation Japanese can only be evacuated either as part of a total evacuation, giving access to the areas only by permits, or by frankly trying to put them out on the ground that their racial characteristics are such that we cannot understand or trust even the citizen Japanese [*sic*]. This latter is the fact but I am afraid that it will make a tremendous hole in our constitutional system to apply it." The next day he took up "the west coast matter" with Roosevelt "and fortunately found he was very vigorous about it and told me to go ahead on the line that I had myself thought the best." And on February 18, the day before FDR signed Executive Order 9066, Stimson wrote that he had no illusions "as to the magnitude of the task that lies before us and the wails which will go up in relation to some of the actions which will be taken under it."

The task was staggering. It was nothing less than confinement of the "yellow peril," the concentration in camps of those Japanese hordes already within our borders. In the very diary entry that posited the Japanese Americans as beyond understanding, Stimson went on to invoke the prophecies of Homer Lea, "a little humpback man who wrote a book on the Japanese peril entitled *The Valor of Ignorance* [1909]." Lea's turn-of-the-century racism lived on in Stimson and other members of the administration. From FDR—we shall return in another context to why the president was so "vigorous about it"—down through the national to the state level, officials saw those of Japanese birth or ancestry not as persons, but as mysteries to be solved, inscrutable Orientals, perils to be guarded against, abstractions, symbols, all subsumed under the epithet "Japs." White officials could not tell them apart, in short, good from bad, loyal from disloyal, because whites had been conditioned not to look at them, *see* their individuality, but to look through them to their racial essence. And this was what U.S. authorities fenced in: "The Enemy That Never Was," as Ken Adachi aptly titled his study (1976) of the still more horrendous exclusion of Japanese Canadians from British Columbia.

The confinement of these Oriental shadows in desert camps presented the great opportunity, at long last, to fathom their inscrutability. After a tour of the camps John J. McCloy wrote the civil libertarian

Alexander Meiklejohn on September 30, 1942, that he was "doubtful about the wisdom of widespread release of the Japanese at the present time." His letter merits quoting at length:

> We would be missing a very big opportunity if we failed to study the Japanese in these Camps at some length before they are dispersed. We have not done a very good job thus far in solving the Japanese problem in this country. I believe we have a great opportunity to give the thing intelligent thought now and to reach solid conclusions for the future. These people, gathered as they now are in these communities, afford a means of sampling their opinion and studying their customs and habits in a way we have never before had possible. We could find out what they are thinking about and we might very well influence their thinking in the right direction before they are again distributed into communities.
>
> I am aware that such a suggestion may provoke a charge that we have no right to treat these people as "guinea pigs", but I would rather treat them as guinea pigs and learn something useful than merely to treat them, or have them treated, as they have been in the past with such unsuccessful results.
>
> For the sake of the Japanese themselves, I would therefore wish that Dillon Myer would take some very long thoughts before committing himself to a principle of immediate and extensive release.
>
> [JERS, 67/14, E1.020]

As indicated by the epigraph to this chapter, the letter, or a copy, found its way into WRA files as forceful advocacy of the kind of social engineering Myer championed in his testimony before the Senate Military Affairs Subcommittee. The director obviously had taken some very long thoughts. Not only was the assistant secretary of war "always sympathetic and helpful" to the WRA, as Myer acknowledged in *Uprooted Americans*; McCloy was also directive.

3

Compared with movers and shakers such as Stimson and McCloy, Myer was a mere implementer, the chief keeper and head distributor of the concentration and dispersion phases of administration policy. Myer had so little contact with the White House that almost a year after his "presidential appointment" Roosevelt wrote Eisenhower under the misapprehension that the latter was still director. Budget Director "Harold Smith served as the President's go-between on both Milton's appointment and mine," Myer told an interviewer in 1969. "I used to go over to see him. I'd walk in, and he'd grin and he'd say, 'You know I'm not your boss, don't you?' And I'd say, 'Yes, I know you're not my boss, [but] you will

The Director and Eleanor Roosevelt at Gila River, April 23, 1943. According to the WRA legend, "they were greeted by crowds of enthusiastic evacuees." [The Bancroft Library]

listen, won't you?' [Laughter]. . . . I wanted him to *listen* about my problem and get any reactions, because I was reporting only to God. . . . You know I wasn't seeing Roosevelt" (Auto 2, I, 23). Through Eleanor Roosevelt he contrived to be invited to a White House luncheon on May 23, 1943, but that was the one and only time he conferred directly with the president (*UA*, p. 95). On all other occasions Budget Director Smith, McCloy, and, after the WRA moved into the Department of the Interior (February 1944), Undersecretary Abe Fortas were the go-betweens.

By the late spring of 1942, when Myer took over the WRA, exclusion of Issei and Nisei from the Pacific rim had already been decided upon and was pretty much an accomplished fact. But what, precisely, was his stand on the administration policy that had created his job in the first place? "As director of the WRA," he affirmed in 1971, "I believed, and still believe, that a selective evacuation of people of Japanese descent from the West Coast military area *may have been* justified and feasible in early 1943 [*sic*], but I do not believe that a mass evacuation was ever justified" (*UA*, p. 285; emphasis added). In *WRA: A Story of Human Conservation*, published in 1946 under his direction, the sentence he was misquoting had read—and not in the subjunctive mood—that selective evacuation "*was* justified and administratively feasible in the spring of 1942" (p. 182; emphasis added).

The truth of the matter is that as director Myer had in fact believed that mass exclusion was justified. On July 7, 1943, he presented a prepared statement on "Constitutional Principles Involved in the Relocation Program" to the House (Costello) Un-American Activities Subcommittee (JERS, 67/14, T1.02). His paragraph on exclusion was explicit:

> We believe, in the first place, that the evacuation was within the constitutional power of the National Government. The concentration of the Japanese-Americans along the West Coast, the danger of invasion of that Coast by Japan, the possibility that an unknown and unrecognizable minority of them might have greater allegiance to Japan than to the United States, the fact that the Japanese-Americans were not wholly assimilated in the general life of communities on the West Coast, and the danger of civil disturbance due to fear and misunderstanding—all these facts, and related facts, created a situation which the National Government could, we believe, deal with by extraordinary measures in the interest of military security. The need for speed created the unfortunate necessity for evacuating the whole group instead of attempting to determine who were dangerous among them, so that only those might be evacuated. That same need made it impossible to hold adequate investigations or to grant hearings to the evacuees before evacuation.

Myer's pseudojustifications for this "unfortunate necessity" matched General DeWitt's in every particular. They were pseudo for familiar reasons that bear repeating: no military estimate after December 1941 even raised the possibility of an invasion of the Pacific states; the FBI had already conducted a "selective evacuation" of Japanese nationals deemed dangerous; and not a single Japanese American had been convicted of espionage or sabotage. Moreover, eight months elapsed between Pearl Harbor and the completion of exclusion—time enough and more for investigations and hearings, had there been reason for them.

4

"The evacuation and establishment of relocation centers were actions without precedent in American history," Myer asserted, in another demonstration of his ignorance of the American past (*UA*, p. 4). Descendants of Cherokee, Creek, Chickasaw, Choctaw, Seminole, Shawnee, Delaware, Seneca, and other tribes forcibly "removed" across the Mississippi from 1813 to 1855 could have told him of precedent uprootings and earlier Trails of Tears. The parallel was not lost on Edward H. Spicer and other anthropologists among the WRA community analysts, though in *Impounded People* (1946, 1969) they claimed that the forced migration of 1942 was bigger and better than its forerunners: a marvel of human engineering, "a magnificent tour de force, as different and superior in technique and administrative management from the transfer of Indians as the oxcart differs from the latest bomber" (p. 43).

Still, the brave new world of the 1940s was tied to the past at Colorado River and Gila River, the two camps on Indian reservations in Arizona. In other camps old hands at dealing with dislocated peoples flocked into the WRA from the Bureau of Indian Affairs until they almost came to equal the number of appointees from the Soil Conservation Service and other agriculture agencies. On the lower levels especially they brought with them attitudes straight out of the Indian-hating past. A young penal officer named Francis S. Frederick, who first worked for the WRA at Gila River, later passed on his assessment of the Gila police chief to a member of Dorothy Swaine Thomas's JERS team:

> Every trade has its tricks and every workman leaves his own particular ear marks. In my racket one gets to recognize techniques. Take [Fred J.] Graves. Indian Service for ten years and like all of those guys feels that there are only two kinds of Indians—gooduns and baduns—and feels that Japs are Indians. You tell one to jump off a bridge and if he does without question, he is a goodun—but if he as much as questions the order he is a badun.
> [to Robert Spencer, August 20, 1943, JERS, 67/14, S1.10]

In *The Governing of Men* (1945), the psychiatrist Alexander H. Leighton classified such WRA staff members as the "stereotype-minded"—those for whom the impounded people "were Japanese first and people secondarily" (p. 84).

The staff members who reversed the order Leighton called "people-minded." Those for whom their charges were people first included Poston project director Wade Head, the former superintendent of the Papago Indian Reservation and one of the more creative young officials in the BIA. Falling somewhere between these ideal types was E. Reeseman ("Si") Fryer, the former superintendent of the Navaho Indian Reservation. Following his appointment as WRA regional director in San Francisco, Fryer succeeded so well in the scramble for power that he bothered the contingent from agriculture. To neutralize leadership that threatened to outdistance his own, Myer centralized authority in his Washington headquarters and eliminated the regional offices as line offices (December 1, 1942). Early in 1943 Fryer left to administer food to North Africans, but he was destined to meet Myer one day on another administrative battlefield. His job in San Francisco went to the garrulous Robert B. Cozzens, a crony of Eisenhower's and Myer's from the SCS.

By a sly irony of history, BIA Commissioner John Collier had himself aspired to direct the WRA. At his request, Vice President Henry A. Wallace put Collier's name in the running at a cabinet meeting and Secretary of the Interior Harold L. Ickes seconded the nomination. What the WRA would have been like under Collier makes for fascinating speculation. The commissioner was a charismatic contradiction, a bureau official who treated tribal cultures with respect. He worked to promote their revival, extend religious freedom, foster political self-determination, and "curb the administrative absolutism" of the Indian Service. With his personal record under sustained attack in Congress and his program virtually stalemated, he proposed to turn his considerable energies toward helping the most recently uprooted people. FDR had other plans, as we have seen, but had he given Collier the job, the former commissioner would have been a landmark link between past and present experience in dealing with subject peoples. As it was, under Myer the WRA was a Johnny-come-lately to the business of people keeping, a sort of upstart Bureau of Japanese Affairs.

Still, the link with the past was visible at Poston. In his memoir *From Every Zenith* (1963) Collier recounted his high hopes for what he bluntly called a concentration camp:

> Milton Eisenhower had been appointed by President Roosevelt to administer Poston and the other concentration camps. Eisenhower sent for me, to urge that the Indian Service take the whole responsibility for operating the Poston camp. I agreed to do so, on the express condition that we be allowed to discharge the trust in the spirit of the Indian New Deal and the Indian Re-

organization Act [1934]. Eisenhower agreed, heartily. The agreement, as later events proved, ought to have been a written one. It was left verbal, and Eisenhower's successor, Dillon Myer, considered the agreement not binding on himself at all.

[pp. 301–2]

In accordance with Eisenhower's plan to keep both Issei and Nisei—with relatively few exceptions—in camps for the duration of the war, Collier fixed on their cultural heritage as the only way to make their lives endurable until they could all be sent back together to their homes on the West Coast.

In the meantime, Collier hoped the large irrigation project already on the reservation and the farming experience of the inmates would enable them to bring 25,000 acres of land under cultivation. From the navy he borrowed Alexander Leighton, who had some previous experience studying Navahos and Eskimos, put him at the head of what was called the Bureau of Sociological Research, and appointed the anthropologist Edward H. Spicer as his assistant. From such ambitious beginnings came schemes for "practically a complete self-government," in Collier's words; for adult education, including Great Books study; and for consumer cooperatives, recreation councils, and community credit organizations. Even at Poston the inmates might demonstrate to the whole country "the efficiency and splendor of the cooperative way of living." In addresses at the three units or subcamps, "I pleaded that life could be lived even here; and that even though the imprisonment should last for years, a deep democracy could be achieved, and a shared happiness" (p. 302).

Such was the essential background of what Myer called "The Poston Incident" (*UA*, pp. 61–62). On November 17, 1942, Myer visited the camp "and made a speech announcing the WRA policy of all-out relocation outside of the centers and the abandonment of plans to establish further industry at the centers." Only later did he learn that Collier had been there just the preceding week (November 11) stressing the importance of community stability "and had painted pretty pictures about how they would probably be there for forty years or more and they would develop land and they would be able to have a fine brand new community, etc. etc. . . . [My speech] was entirely opposite from what John had said and he never quite forgave me" (Auto, p. 255). Or Myer him. The director was not one to allow for honest differences of opinion, to assume responsibility for Eisenhower's commitments in the name of the WRA, or to be too scrupulous in representing the views of Collier, who had not in fact told the Poston inmates they would "probably be there for forty years." Leighton was at the camp, heard Collier speak, and recorded in *The Governing of Men* that he had "said that the community must face the reality of their situation and the war and must build for a period of between five and ten years" (p. 103). As it turned out, Collier was not too wide of the mark: the WRA did not close Poston for over three years (on December 1, 1945).

In the early days the inmates had diverted little streams from the irrigation ditches for vegetable and flower plots that became, according to Collier, "gardens of the ancient Japanese beauty." When Myer saw them he was less impressed, Collier learned, and had said, "as quoted by our headquarters men: 'This is the worst thing I have come on in all my inspections of the camps.' The intangibles of happiness which were flowering, and the cooperative institutions which were their vehicles, were, it became apparent, equally distasteful to Dillon Myer" (*From Every Zenith*, p. 302). As reported to Collier, this was probably very nearly a verbatim quotation. The director differed fundamentally with the commissioner on gardens, the need for community stability, the value of subcultures, the lot. After eighteen frustrating months, Collier, Wade Head, D'Arcy McNickle, and others in the Indian Service formally pulled their agency out of Poston, convinced that they had been totally blocked by the WRA.

Yet a concentration camp was a concentration camp. For all of John Collier's fine visions, his conflict with Myer must be placed in its proper context. While Poston was still under BIA supervision, Leighton was repeatedly asked by Japanese American inmates "if they would be 'kept' all the rest of their lives on 'reservations like Indians'" (*The Governing of Men*, p. 104). Though the questioners may well have resented this comparison with "a lower race of people," as Leighton observed, the parallels were foreboding for the inmates and disturbing for their 1,200 Native American neighbors. The Mohaves and Chemehuevis on the Colorado River Reservation resented the camp, saw both inmates and keepers as intruders, and disliked Collier for bringing these outsiders onto their land. In good colonialist fashion, BIA and WRA keepers at Colorado River subjected old-timers and newcomers alike to programs of forced compliance.

And while Collier and Myer debated questions of policy for their wards, the army was methodically stapling up barbed wire around the three subcamps.

5

The barbed wire around Poston and the other camps mocked the possibility of "community." Inmates climbed over or crawled under the wires at the risk of being shot by a bored or trigger-happy sentry. Even being near these boundaries of their lives could prove fatal. With the sun still above the horizon on Sunday evening, April 11, 1943, a former chef from San Francisco walked toward a fence at Topaz (Central Utah). After careful investigation, the Topaz reports officer recorded that "at 7:30 P.M. James Hatsuaki Wakasa, age 63, a Japanese national, was fatally shot by a Military Police sentry near the west fence, but inside the center about three hundred yards north of the southwest corner sentry tower No. 8." Accompanying photographs showed that the body of the elderly bachelor fell "from 40 to 65 inches inside the fence." In California stopping a construction truck at the main gate of the Tule Lake camp for permission to pass likewise proved fatal to Soichi James Okamoto on May 24, 1944. The officious sentry on duty, Private Bernard Goe, put an end to their angry exchange of words by shooting the young Nisei at close range—witnesses maintained he shot without provocation. Four Issei and Nisei in all were slain by military police in or at the camps, and others were wounded, events that made Myer's euphemisms "temporary havens" and "wayside stations" grotesqueries. That such killings were relatively infrequent made them no less exemplary. The possibility was always no farther away than the nearest armed sentry.

Decades later (on November 1, 1980) in Granada, Colorado, a retired farmer and former inmate of the nearby Camp Amache, who was manifestly still riled by his recollections, said to this interviewer: "There were soldiers with machine guns at the camps. If we were being protected, why weren't the machine guns pointed outside? They were pointed into the camps."

It does not follow that those inside lived from day to day in terror. Camp memoirs and other evidence indicate that—apart from crises such as the general strike at Poston in November 1942, the so-called riot at Manzanar the following month, and continuing turmoil at Tule Lake from the fall of 1943 until the camp closed—most of the inmates found their circumstances bearable for the average of nine hundred days they spent behind barbed wire, though extremely unpleasant in their lack of privacy, soul-deadening in their boredom, uncomfortable inside flimsy barracks subject to temperatures that soared and plummeted, and harsh outside in the sand and cactus, dust and snow storms. Elderly Issei farmers, orchardists, fishermen, and their wives no doubt found some solace in their respite from constant toil. No doubt many children welcomed being out from under rigorous parental discipline and felt as though they had indeed been sent away to camp. Nisei in their teens and twenties exploited the opportunity to loosen the tight constraints of the immigrant generation. Even if all these "positive" aspects of camp life are figured in, they still would not support Myer's claim that "of the 70,000 people still left in the centers in 1944, probably at least half had never had it so good" (*UA*, p. 292). Of someone else's good there is no measure. The most that can be said is that incarceration had unintended consequences and by-products, not all of which were negative.

In the WRA's *Community Government* (1946), Solon T. Kimball cited a directive to the project directors on December 15, 1942, wherein Myer "pointed out that the existing policy on community government represented a liberal interpretation of the executive order [No. 9102, March 18, 1942, Fed. Reg. 2165] and that WRA was under no obligation to allow or to encourage self-government in the centers" (p. 41). Unlike Collier, Myer encouraged nothing of the sort, as Kimball, the social anthropologist who oversaw these "communities," conceded: "Community government became in actuality an adjunct of administration" (p. 5). From beginning to end Myer ran the WRA on the same set of principles he had found serviceable in agriculture. Knowing nothing about their charges, really, he and his staff still thought through their problems and presented them with decisions. To the Poston inmates, for instance, he said that nothing "above decent minimum subsistence" would be allowed and that was that. Also not negotiable were their "wages," set at $12 and $16 per month, with a few professionals receiving a high of $19. Inmates had infinitely less chance to change such policies than the farmers who had protested Myer's administration of the AAA "Killing Little Pigs" program. The experts knew best.

White experts. Under Myer the WRA never permitted inmates to rise to the level of the decision makers. They were the objects administered. Again the language of the keepers is revealing. What should they call themselves and their charges? *Whites* versus *Japanese*? At first this binomial opposition was pressed into use but shortly it gave way to *Caucasians* or *appointed personnel* (APs) versus *colonists*, *residents*, or, more frequently, *evacuees*. Myer and his staff tried to make "Japs" a tabooed word, but APs used it among themselves and on occasion even a project director let it slip out. Probably a majority of the lower-level personnel were "stereotype-minded," as Leighton called them, and continued to think of their charges as "Japs" even if they did not call them such to their faces.

Myer's camps institutionalized the racism intrinsic to the exclusion he justified. Inmates slept in segregated quarters, worked in the fields in segregated gangs, ate in segregated mess halls, and relaxed in segregated facilities. Project directors formally discouraged "fraternization." For administrative purposes even Afro-American APs were classified as "Caucasians" at Tule Lake, as Daisuke Kitagawa, an Episcopalian priest, wryly noted in his memoir of the internment years, *Issei and Nisei* (1967; p. 75). At Tule camp life made an indelible impression on older children in particular, Kitagawa observed:

> The center was a place where Caucasian people governed and Japanese people were governed. Everything they saw, day in and day out, indicated that racial difference was identical with caste distinction. They were all Americans, but those with white skins were, by virtue of their skin color, superior to those with colored skin.
>
> [p. 94]

At Manzanar a young inmate wrote about the resentment against

> "obvious preferred treatment" of "whites." Typical comment: "You can't eat in the Caucasian mess hall"; they call this democracy where everyone is supposed to be equal; look at our housing . . . and the Project Director ordered his quarters completely re-made. . . . A perennial discussion topic among virtually all groupings . . . is the "color line."
>
> [*Impounded People*, p. 88]

At Heart Mountain, Wyoming, Kiyoshi Okamoto, a soil chemist and perhaps the first Nisei to teach in a mainland public high school, blasted the color line in a paper, "Questions, Fears and Doubts" (February 1, 1943). Inmates found it impossible, he wrote,

> to minimize the feeling of degradation, inferiority and resentment in the knowledge that only Caucasians are placed over them. This is an invitation to Racial discrimination and bigotry by means of actual practice . . . [through the] ruling of ten thousand Souls by a handful who are backed by bullets and bayonets of a Company of soldiers. It is like India. And Africa.
>
> [Sproul Papers, Bancroft Library, CU-5]

Okamoto had keen insight into colonial parallels but, as we shall see, ran a grave risk in speaking his mind so directly—Myer and his project directors had no greater tolerance for such outspoken inmates than their counterparts in India and Africa had for sassy natives.

The Director at Heart Mountain, n.d. One of Myer's favorite photographs, it shows him posing in front of a painting of the mountain, barracks, and chimney of the camp hospital.
[The Bancroft Library]

Everybody knew that Orientals made splendid servants. On June 30, 1942, Elmer Shirrell, then project director at Tule Lake, wrote Regional Director E. R. Fryer a letter marked "confidential": "What would be the Regional Office thought on the employment of enlistees [inmates] in the private homes of personnel living on the Project? Several of them have asked for help in looking after children, cooking and other household tasks which are beyond the scope of usual maintenance of personnel quarters by the War Relocation Authority" (JERS, 67/14, R1.40). In an affidavit dated December 6, 1946, Director Ernest Besig of the American Civil Liberties Union of Northern California deposed that when he had visited Tule Lake the preceding January

> I discovered that a slave labor racket was being carried on and had been continuously carried on since the inception of that Center. It then was and all during said period of time had been the practice of the Caucasian personnel to hire, for their own private purposes, internees who were hired in the capacities of nursemaids, cooks, domestics and cleaning women at concentration camp bargain prices of $30 a month for a forty-hour week. Of this sum, the internees hired received $19 and a $3.75 clothing allowance and the balance of the $30 was deposited in the treasury of the Recreation Club in the administration section of the Center which was operated only for the benefit of the Caucasian personnel. A Personnel Mess Hall served cheap meals only because such concentration camp labor was paid slave wages. Indeed, the waitresses received only $16 a month for a forty-hour week. The Recreation Club had a barber shop where men's hair cuts could be secured for 40¢ at a time when the price in San Francisco was 85¢ for like service performed by free men. . . . The beauty parlors operated by internees for the benefit of the Caucasian personnel charged 75¢ for shampoos and $4.50 for permanents but the operators received only $16 per month for a 40-hour week.
>
> [WCP, 78/177, *Tadayasu Abo* v. *Tom Clark*
> (77 F. Suppl. 806 [1948])]

Like fatherly Prospero in *The Tempest* (1611), Myer and his project directors pretended that they had no selfish interests of their own and simply acted toward their wards out of their own upswelling benevolence. But also like William Shakespeare's prefiguration of all the paternal colonizers to come, they in reality indulged hidden psychological cravings for power and attention by keeping those wards in a state of childish dependence.

A case in point was the project director criticized by the young Manzanar inmate for ordering "his quarters completely re-made." Federal Food Administrator for California during World War I, a former comptroller of the University of California, an executive in the Sun Maid Raisin Growers organization before it went bankrupt, and a mining promoter, Ralph P. Merritt was "a big man," according to his project reports officer—"big in his thinking, big in his ideas." In some extraordinary notes titled "The Caucasians Make the Rules" (n.d.—February 1945?), Solon T. Kimball recorded highlights of an interview with Merritt at Manzanar. The project director told him that the

only relationship that Japanese understand is that of father and child. He has
become the father of Manzanar. The people are his children. Sometimes he
is stupid in their eyes because he doesn't understand [Japanese]. He talks to
them about the need for speaking only English, learning American ways,
having their children speak English, having no Japanese entertainment, yet
they still persist and it is a worry to him. . . . Also mentioned . . . [inmate
X], said he was in bad because when the new servant policy came out . . .
[inmate X] quit work. Merritt said if you will continue to work, then I will
be willing to help you out when the time comes, but if you do not, then you
can expect no assistance from me. . . . At block meeting he was introduced
as the father of Manzanar. . . . Merritt made reference to it and to his children, and how he was trying to help his children to see the right way.

[JERS, 67/14, 05.00]

Myer's administrative style was not as flamboyant as Merritt's, but
it was no less paternalistic. Since he was based in Washington, we can
catch glimpses of this style in the camps only during his inspection tours.
On the evening of March 7, 1945, for instance, he had a long conference
with Richard Shigeaki Nishimoto, the block managers' supervisor of
Unit 1 at Poston. Myer rightly suspected Nishimoto of being a key member of Dorothy Swaine Thomas's JERS team, wanted to find out what
he knew, and did his best to charm the camp-wise Issei. Born in Tokyo
in 1904, Nishimoto had come to the United States to attend Lowell
High School in San Francisco, graduated from Stanford University in
1929, and before the roundup lived in Gardena, California. Wary and
unwilling as yet to reveal his JERS connection—after the war he coauthored *The Spoilage* with Thomas—he was nonetheless flattered that
Myer should be so cordial and treat him "as a scientist and not as an
evacuee," as an anthropologist who was present afterward put it. Nishimoto reported to Thomas on March 9, 1945:

He wanted to know how he was received by the evacuees here. I said, "You're
old enough to take a compliment without getting conceited. So I'll tell you."
I said the reactions could be summarized in one sentence. I placed the finger
nails of my right hand to my teeth and made a love lorn look. I said in an
adoring tone, "Gee, what a man!" He smiled genuinely. He liked it. (I wasn't
kidding him here.) . . . He said he was a close friend of Milt Eisenhower. . . .
He said he enjoy[ed] playing politics with members of the Congress. He
spends every Saturday afternoon on "the Hill."

[JERS, 67/14, W1.25B]

Nishimoto was not charmed by the sequel, as his correspondence
with Professor Thomas revealed. The following June he learned that
Myer had written Poston Project Director Duncan Mills

that I was working for the Evacuation and Resettlement Study . . . and requested that I be converted into a terminal [or indefinite] leave status. . . . This makes me damn mad. . . . Mills questioned me on this this morning, but I did not admit anything. He says the instruction is from Myer and he cannot ignore it. . . . Myer seems to be going all the way in getting after us.

In another letter to Thomas he quoted what he had said to Edward H. Spicer about her recent disagreement with Myer: "One thing you must remember: Myer would not have agreed with her conclusion, because Myer does not listen to anything contrary to his own beliefs." Thomas responded by deploring his "eviction" from Poston: "I had no idea that Mr. Myer was such a vindictive person and I am naturally worried about other steps he might take," and later added:

> Re Myer, the only time I ever had more than fifteen minutes with him was the day I took him to the Mark Hopkins for drinks. At that time I tried to give him the "benefit" of my observations, but instead had to listen to what a great man and what a martyr he was.
>
> [Nishimoto/Thomas letters, June 14, 18, 25, 28, 1945,
> JERS, 67/14, W1.25B]

Obviously the correspondents had learned some painful truths about Myer's administrative style. If he had his way, Thomas's JERS team would not be allowed to interfere with "his" inmates. As he said to an interviewer about the camps in 1969: "I'm the kind of guy who likes to run my *own* show" (Auto 2, I, 13). As for Nishimoto, he realized to his chagrin that he had been taken in at their first meeting—the director had been treating him all along as an "evacuee."

CHAPTER IV

Scatterer

It would be good for the United States generally and I think
it would be good from the standpoint of the Japanese-Americans themselves, to be scattered over a much wider area and
not to be bunched up in groups as they were along the
Coast. . . . [WRA relocation helps solve] a serious racial
problem by having them scattered throughout the United
States instead of bunched up in three or four states.

—*Dillon S. Myer,*
Press Conference, May 14, 1943

At the Poston Center Fair in January 1945 an inmate displayed a hand-
some model of a swimming pool in a green patch of grass, but that was
about all that was left of John Collier's dream of making the camp an
"ideal community." In the intervening three years the dream never quite
died, it had just been denied daily there and in the other camps by the
barbed wire, the arbitrary paternalism of the WRA, and the never-end-
ing sorting and skimming of inmates that left behind mostly the young
(under seventeen) and the old (over fifty). But what had happened to
Myer's announced policy of "all-out relocation"? In practice it had
turned out to be neither all nor out, not for *all* inmates and not *out*, or
only conditionally out, for the others, somewhat in the way that sailors
were "out" of the navy when they were ashore on leave.

In the fall of 1942 "indefinite leaves" became the keystone of the
makeshift arch that held the rest of Myer's program in place. Under
Eisenhower the WRA had already granted farm workers "seasonal
leaves" and Nisei students "college leaves" to pursue their studies in the
Midwest and East under the sponsorship of the National Japanese
American Student Relocation Council, a private group of educators and
church people organized by Clarence Pickett of the American Friends
Service Committee. But Myer wanted to go much further once he became convinced that "life in a relocation center is an unnatural and un-
American sort of life" (*UA*, p. 158). Mindful of John J. McCloy's clout
and his concern over the "wisdom of widespread release," Myer first

went to him, found him "sympathetic" to proposals that did not in fact mean turning the inmates loose, and received his assurances "that the Army probably would have no objections to the development of a program of private employment." Next he placed his plan before Francis Biddle and J. Edgar Hoover at the Department of Justice (Myer to Biddle, September 24, 1942, FBI 62-69030). With their qualified approval in hand, he issued the WRA leave regulations on September 26, 1942 (7 Fed. Reg. 7656–57).

These regulations in fact provided for the loyalty investigations and hearings that supposedly could not have taken place on the West Coast because of lack of time and because those rounded up all looked alike. Earlier Myer and his staff had requested the FBI to conduct such investigations for them so that the WRA "will not be launching upon the country subversive tendencies" (R. P. Kramer, memo for D. M. Ladd, June 23, 1942, FBI 62-69030). Given the numbers involved and, as Hoover sensibly noted in a memorandum for Biddle on July 7, 1942, given "the fact there is no allegation that the individuals are subversive in character," he turned the WRA down and the attorney general concurred. The FBI did agree to check its files for derogatory data on individuals. The WRA then asked the bureau to locate any citizen who traveled beyond the extent of his WRA permission, but at a meeting with FBI officials, "Mr. Myer was not in a position to state definitely that such a citizen of Japanese descent would be violating any Federal statute or regulation other than the specific permission which had been given him for travel. He said that he would like very much to have the FBI locate such individuals and that he would have this question discussed" (D. M. Ladd, memorandum for Hoover, August 6, 1942, FBI 62-69030). In other words, Myer very much wanted the FBI to locate errant leave-takers, even though no federal law had given him authority to tell citizens where to go. It is a pity that no test case ever challenged his assumption of power to recall former inmates to the camps.

After the FBI refused to conduct investigations by the tens of thousands in the camps, Myer had his staff put together the leave regulations as his do-it-yourself loyalty kit. Periodically the WRA revised the regulations—particularly after the imposition of a mass loyalty oath in early 1943—but left their essentials unaltered. On January 18, 1943, Myer summarized these for Hoover (FBI 62-69030). Any Issei or Nisei was theoretically eligible for three kinds of leave: short-term, work-group, or indefinite. To receive the last an inmate had to apply first for leave clearance and then for the leave itself by filling out Form WRA-126, a questionnaire, and Form WRA-26, an individual record sheet. The project director and his staff then investigated the inmate's record for "the period spent at the relocation center." Myer's letter to Hoover made clear that racism was built into the application process itself:

> The applicant is requested to submit references, preferably Caucasian persons, such as school teachers, ministers, neighbors, and former employers. . . . A recommendation is made by the Project Director as to the disposition of the application . . . and the entire file on the case is sent in to the Washington office. When the file arrives in Washington, two copies of the Form WRA-26 are sent at once to the Federal Bureau of Investigation.

Along with the Office of Naval Intelligence (ONI) and the Military Intelligence Service (MIS), the FBI checked its files for derogatory data on the applicant and reported its findings to the WRA. Myer then made the final decision on the application and so notified project directors. Inmates who objected to his negative rulings could refer their cases to a board of appeals.

But that was merely the first step in getting out of the holding pens. If the inmate had been "cleared" and had submitted an application for the leave, he or she might leave the camp, provided

> employment is secured outside or other means of support have been arranged for, provided that the Director of the War Relocation Authority is satisfied as to the adequacy of the employment or other means of support and provided that the relocation of the evacuee in the intended place of residence will not be accompanied, insofar as can be determined, by an unusual and substantially negative reaction in the community which would prevent the evacuee from making a satisfactory adjustment in his new surroundings. The Director of the War Relocation Authority is able to keep in touch with job opportunities that are offered and with community sentiment through the relocation staff of the War Relocation Authority in the field. . . . One of the requirements for indefinite leave is that the evacuee must agree to keep the War Relocation Authority informed of any change of address after the first destination. We hope through the means of change-of-address cards to be able to have at all times a reasonably accurate and comprehensive check on the location of evacuees who have left the relocation centers for residence outside.
>
> [Myer to Hoover, January 18, 1943, FBI 62-69030]

Special conditions might be attached to a leave in any particular case, and all leaves were revocable at any time.

For a moment or two imagine yourself an inmate who has filed for leave clearance on Form WRA-126, executed in duplicate, accompanied by Form WRA-26, executed in sextuplicate. Today your turn for a leave-clearance interview comes up, breaking the monotony of camp life. Among the questions you answer under oath are these:

Before questioning you any further, we would like to ask if you have any objection to signing a Pledge of Allegiance to the United States.

Will you assist in the general resettlement program by staying away from large groups of Japanese?

Will you try to develop such American habits which will cause you to be accepted readily into American social groups?

Are you willing to give information to the proper authorities regarding any subversive activity . . . both in the relocation centers and in the communities in which you are resettling?

Would you consider an informer of this nature an "Inu"? (Stool-pigeon)

Will you conform to the customs and dress of your new home?

Have you been associated with any radical groups, clubs, or gangs which have been accused of anti-social conduct within the center?

Can you furnish any proof that you have always been loyal to the United States? [NA, RG 107]

After you have said yes, you will pledge allegiance, will stay away from concentrations of "Japanese," and will become an informer, you wait and hope another inmate has not already performed a like service for the administration by saying something real or imaginary about you, hope you are not in bad for other reasons with the project director and his staff, and hope the FBI does not know of your existence. It will after your application.

You have been "cleared" and have a job in Chicago, a favorite city of "resettlers." With a grant of $25 and a one-way coach ticket you speed to your WRA-approved destination. Once there you report your arrival within twenty-four hours to Director Myer, as you have pledged, and confirm your address. Meanwhile the FBI has two copies of the Form WRA-26 you filled out in sextuplicate and has already sent the information thereon out to the nearest SAC (Special Agent in Charge), in your case the SAC of the Chicago field office.

In Chicago your first residence is a hostel, Issei-organized and WRA-approved, at 537 North Wells Street, in a run-down neighborhood just north of the Loop District. Though you may not know it as you mind your own business, refrain from fraternizing with the other nineteen residents, who have also promised to be informers, and only have a relative or close camp friend visit on Sundays, you still are under close observation. As Chicago SAC S. J. Drayton advised Hoover on September 27, 1943, his "confidential informants" had turned up "no evidence that this place has been used as a center for subversive activity among the Japanese. . . . However, it is a potential meeting place for subversive activity and will be closely observed and the Bureau advised accordingly" (FBI 62-69030).

As for your job, let us pretend that you are one of the former inmates Professor Thomas has installed in the JERS branch office at the University of Chicago. After work you oblige a friend who expresses great interest in the Thomas project by loaning him documents under the express condition that they be kept in strict confidence so as not to betray JERS sources. Perhaps by now you should suspect, given your own response under oath to the leave-clearance questions, that your supposed friend is a "confidential informant." At all events, so he is, and he promptly photostats copies of the documents for SAC Drayton, who in turn transmits them to Washington (to Hoover, July 31, 1943, FBI 62-69030). After careful scrutiny of the copies, Hoover concludes that "the study being made of evacuated Japanese is largely a sociological study" but asks Drayton to "maintain contact . . . [with your blacked out "friend" in an] effort to secure additional data which might be compiled by the committee interested in this study" (August 19, 1943, FBI 62-69030). Your supposed friend will be back for more confidential data.

Though a citizen who has been "cleared," you have been told where to live, with whom to associate, how to dress and act, and what to do for a livelihood. You have been and will continue to be spied upon. In fine, your indefinite leave has most of the earmarks of a parole, no?

All of this continuing surveillance of citizens was with the connivance of the WRA director who had conceded that they were "loyal" by approving their leaves. After a few months in office Myer had undertaken (through a subordinate on August 28, 1942) to keep the FBI "advised of the locations of these Japanese at all times" (J. C. Strickland, memorandum for D. M. Ladd, FBI 62-69030). The following spring he wrote Hoover reaffirming that the Washington office of the FBI would be notified of the name and destination of each inmate who left a camp, but hoped that their two investigative agencies could handle the matter with professional delicacy:

> I prefer that the Project Directors not send these notices direct to your field offices because of the undesirability of emphasizing at the centers the fact that citizen evacuees who are granted leave will be subject to special surveillance by an intelligence agency after they leave the center.
> [April 5, 1943, FBI 62-69030]

In the camps Myer understandably preferred not to rub in the fact that one of the fringe benefits for "citizen evacuees" on the outside was special surveillance. Inside or outside, to paraphrase General DeWitt's dictum "A Jap's a Jap" (quoted in chapter 3), "an evacuee's an evacuee."

2

Wheresoever they resettled, "evacuees" were "Japanese": "Will you assist in the general resettlement program by staying away from large groups of Japanese?" read the WRA leave-clearance question. A slight reformulation lays bare its racist roots: "Will you stay away from large groups of yourselves?" As individuals they were suspect, and as large groups they were a peril, a yellow peril.

Some victims apologized for these stigmas the keepers burned more deeply into their identities. On May 22, 1942, the chapter secretary of the Japanese American Citizens League at Florin, California, expressed this internalized shame in a letter to President Roosevelt: "We, who are Americans to the core, but in appearance betray our oriental ancestry, feel ashamed that the people of our own race are greatly responsible for the present conflict" (JERS, 67/14, T6.10). "And I am black," said the poet William Blake's Little Black Boy, "but O! my soul is white." "And I am oriental in appearance," said the chapter secretary in unconscious paraphrase of Blake, "but O! my core is American!" It had become national JACL policy to stand "For Better Americans in a Greater America" and to eliminate "those mannerisms and thoughts which mark us apart, aside from our physical characteristics." Impossible to eliminate, those betraying physical characteristics could at least be strewn among white characteristics from the Sierras to the Atlantic: "If we're going to be American we have got to get away from ourselves," said a like-minded Nisei in an interview at Poston. "There can't be any such thing as a Japanese-American . . . and we're not saps enough to think there could" (*Washington Star*, November 4, 1942).

For these fugitives from themselves, Myer's resettlement program provided a one-way ticket to *relative* anonymity—let us not forget the "special surveillance"—in Salt Lake City, Denver, Chicago, and points eastward. Yet the JACL did not speak for most Nisei, despite the organization's windy claims that it did, and some surely rejected the submissiveness and self-denigration it encouraged. "Now they're trying to push us to the east," said an older Nisei to Manzanar Community Analyst Morris E. Opler. WRA policy was "always 'further inland, further inland.' I say, 'To hell with it!' Either they let me go to the coast and prove my loyalty there or they can do what they want with me" (July 26, 1943, NA, RG 210).

In the epigraph to chapter 3 we observed that Myer did indeed "frankly" hope to do precisely what the Manzanar Nisei charged, namely push his "citizen evacuees" east. Not with equal frankness did he face the implications of "the racial problem that has been a pretty tough one for the coast people" or the fact that his resettlement program institutionalized their attitudes and assumptions: All "bunched up" before the roundup, both Issei and Nisei had been an undesirable presence on the Pacific slope. Myer sympathized with his beset fellow whites, who were also not incidentally voters, and moved to relieve them of their problem, pretty much as Andrew Jackson had taken pity on the white Georgians a century earlier and removed the Cherokee Indians from their midst. But in the 1940s there was no Great American Desert for a collective dump, and in any event this push had to be from the West eastward. Myer and his modern crew of removers thus had to reverse the historic pattern by scattering their unwanted charges back across the continent.

In the hearings of the Senate Military Affairs Subcommittee on *War Relocation Centers*, Senator Edward C. Johnson of Colorado extracted from Director Myer some of the assumptions underlying his resettlement program:

SENATOR JOHNSON: Is it your underlying idea that the Jap, no matter how long he is here, will finally merge with our citizenship the same as any white man?

MR. MYER: My underlying idea is that since these people are going to continue to be American citizens, they will have to merge into our economy and be accepted as part of it, otherwise we are always going to have a racial problem.

SENATOR JOHNSON: Of course, you know that no Pacific States allow intermarriage. They are always going to be brown men. Do you think they will finally merge and just be accepted in every way like a white man?

MR. MYER: Well, I can't predict that. I can say this, that there are a good many hundreds of the youngsters of college age and many who have gone to college in the past who have been accepted in the professions and otherwise.

Now, I think that you will find, other than color, that after about four or five generations these people will be living under the same standards as any other American citizens. They won't know anything else. I don't know what the ancestry of all the people around this room is. I know what my own is. We have been

> a melting pot of the nations here and we have ac-
> cepted these people. [January 20, 1943, 78th Cong.,
> 1st sess., pp. 55–56]

Myer's response to Johnson's pointed question was not a model of clarity.

Despite his gesture toward mixed ancestry, he certainly never would have considered being as daring as William Byrd of Westover, who had advocated just such intermarriage across the color line in 1728 and had argued that the Englishman should have stomached Indian darkness of skin for the good of the colonies: "Nor would the shade of skin have been any reproach at this day," he had added reassuringly, "for if a Moor might be washed white in three generations, surely an Indian might have been blanched in two." But Myer foresaw no such washing white of the color of his charges even after four or five generations. His "melting pot" was not, in fact, biological but political and economic, a matter of citizenship and absorption in the wartime manpower pool. What he proposed to melt or boil away was the cultural heritage of his redistributed "evacuees": "They won't know anything else." They would know nothing else but mainstream Anglo-American culture because his removal program set Issei against Nisei, sliced into kin and generational groupings, and scattered the severed members like leaves blown by prevailing westerlies.

By the centennial year 1876 forced migrations of tribal peoples had become so convulsively common—the Delaware tribe, for instance, had been broken up and removed six times—that a Sioux named Red Dog offered a suggestion to treaty commissioners: "I think you had better put the Indian on wheels. Then you can run them about whenever you wish." After the turn of the century Woodrow Wilson's secretary of state, William Jennings Bryan, proposed to free the West Coast of its "problem" by putting the "Japanese" on train wheels and dispersing them throughout the country. The proposal was premature, but Roger Daniels has calculated that had the Japanese Americans enumerated in the census of 1940 been so dispatched, about forty of them would have rolled into each U.S. county. Ignorant of all these pioneering precedents in the field of racist race relations, Myer still followed their patterns faithfully when he undertook to implement what Bryan had only proposed. To Governor Herbert B. Maw, who had expressed anger over the "filtering of Japanese into Utah," Myer explained reassuringly: "One of our primary objectives is to secure a rapid and widespread dispersal of the evacuees, thereby permitting them to regain their full rights as citizens or aliens as soon as possible without over-populating any particular areas" (March 23, 1943, JERS, 67/14, E2.04).

3

In the camps Myer's project directors and their staffs subjected "cleared" inmates to endless exhortations, "Go East, young man," and to endless warnings against even the thought of recreating "Little Tokyos" after the war. From the regional offices WRA public relations men fueled this propaganda with handouts to the press that portrayed tens of thousands gladly boarding the bandwagon. "NISEI MAY FORSAKE PACIFIC COAST—50,000 PLAN TO REMAIN EAST OF SIERRAS" read the banner headline in the *San Francisco Chronicle* of February 27, 1944: "A 'pioneering' movement which leads them toward the 'New America' they have found east of the Sierra Nevada mountains already is underway. Its steady growth indicates that one of the mountainous post-war social problems faced by California, Washington and Oregon rapidly is becoming a molehill." These sensible Nisei realized that the Japanese empire and its descendants "are the natural enemies of the United States in the current war," knew they would be subject "to some degree of racial persecution wherever they go," but believed it would be less in their "New America." So for these reverse pioneers, Eastward Ho!

To keep from "over-populating any particular areas" Myer established forty-two WRA field offices—eight of them were area offices located in major cities—scattered like the "evacuees" they processed from Spokane to Little Rock to Boston (*UA*, pp. 135–36). These offices were supported by almost as many volunteer local resettlement committees, made up of church people, civic leaders, and social workers. Together the field offices and the local committees helped the resettlers pioneer new jobs in new places, a process made all the easier by wartime labor shortages. Relocation officers also acted as public relations men for the program in their areas. In Chicago, for instance, Elmer Shirrell, who had become Midwest WRA director, dealt with complaints by white citizens that resettlers were forming cultural and social clubs and loitering on corners of North Clark Street "in undesirable sections," according to the *Chicago American*, July 8, 1943: "Shirrell said one-sixth of all the Japs released from internment camps have come to Chicago. But, he added, the WRA 'spreads them thin' over the country."

Myer said he wanted this kind of spread to help out "the coast people," meaning whites there, to avoid "having something akin to Indian reservations after the war," and to help his charges "merge into our economy"—as the legal analyst Nanette Dembitz once observed, "the theme of benefaction" ran throughout WRA utterances. But mostly Myer wanted the spread because it was administration policy to have it. After all, he did not announce his leave regulations until he had conferred at length with John J. McCloy. The announced policy coincided at every critical point with the strong opinions McCloy had expressed in his letter to Alexander Meiklejohn on September 30, 1942 (JERS, 67/14, E.1.020). Myer did not muff what McCloy called the very big opportunity of studying "the Japanese in these Camps at some length before they are dispersed." Through WRA leave-clearance procedures he had studied "their customs and habits" to "find out what they are thinking about" and had done his best to "influence their thinking in the right direction before they are again distributed into communities." Moreover, McCloy's terms *distributed* and *dispersed* implied Myer's unremitting efforts to "spread them thin" over the country.

On June 2, 1944, on Myer's recommendation, Secretary of the Interior Ickes wrote to the president urging revocation of the exclusion orders (*UA*, pp. 178–79). Roosevelt's response in a memorandum of June 12, 1944, made it absolutely clear that Myer's leave regulations merely implemented the dispersion phase of administration policy:

> The more I think of this problem of suddenly ending the orders excluding Japanese Americans from the west coast the more I think it would be a mistake to do anything drastic or sudden. As I said at Cabinet, I think the whole problem, for the sake of internal quiet, should be handled gradually, i.e., I am thinking of two methods: (a) Seeing, with great discretion, how many Japanese families would be acceptable to public opinion in definite localities on the west coast. (b) Seeking to extend greatly the distribution of other families in many parts of the United States. . . . In talking to people from the Middle West, the East and the South, I am sure that there would be no bitterness if they were distributed—one or two families to each county as a start. Dissemination and distribution constitute a great method of avoiding public outcry. Why not proceed along the above line—for a while at least?
> [PPF File 4849, Franklin D. Roosevelt Library, Hyde Park, N.Y.]

Only with his reelection in November did Roosevelt agree to release the majority of inmates and give them permission to return to the West Coast if they could not be induced to "forsake" the region. In effect FDR had held tens of thousands of impounded citizens hostage to his reelection and his insouciant willingness to prolong their suffering has rightly drawn the fire of writers.* Yet for the president "dissemination and distribution" were not only short-term means to avoid a politically embarrassing outcry; they were also long-term solutions of the "Japanese problem."

How otherwise are we to understand orders to step up the scattering that came down to Myer *after* the election? On December 19, 1944, for instance, Undersecretary Abe Fortas sent a strongly worded memorandum to Myer: "I want again to call your attention to the necessity for a vigorous program to persuade evacuees in the centers to relocate outside of the West Coast, and to encourage evacuees who have been relocated to refrain from returning to the West Coast" (NA, RG 48). On the same day Secretary Ickes addressed a memorandum to the entire WRA staff: "Before you is the task of carrying out the desire of the President to continue and intensify the effort to relocate as many of these people as possible in areas other than the West Coast area, as well as the tasks of continuing orderly administration of the centers and of regulating the return of those persons who choose to go back to the West Coast" (NA, RG 48). Roosevelt, Ickes, McCloy, Fortas, and Myer at their respective levels were all believers in the preposterous notion that the way to solve a "pretty tough" racial problem was to accommodate the racists.

The great social-engineering experiment of rounding up, penning, and strewing was less than half successful from the keepers' point of view. Despite all the relocation machinery, propaganda, and badgering to move east, about 57,000 former inmates crossed back over the mountains; only about 50,000 resettled east of the Sierras. Yet the enormity of the scattering that did take place had racist and totalitarian implications of a piece with the antecedent exclusion and incarceration. Through Myer's executive agency the Roosevelt administration told citizens where they might live, what to do there for a living, how to dress, how to behave, how to talk, and with whom to associate. Then on December 18, 1944, the day after the War Department announced revocation of the exclusion orders, the Supreme Court ruled in the Mitsuye Endo case that Myer's WRA had had no legal authority to detain a "concededly loyal" U.S. citizen and no legal authority to impose conditions on the release of such a person (*Ex parte Endo*, 323 U.S. 283). But this came as no surprise to the director, for he had good reason to

---

*Most recently in the report of the Commission on Wartime Relocation and Internment of Civilians, *Personal Justice Denied* (Washington, D.C.: Government Printing Office, 1982), pp. 228–36.

believe that he had been trampling on the rights and invading the privacy of "citizen evacuees." On June 8, 1944, over six months before the Endo decision was handed down, Myer revealed his supposition that he was acting outside the law in a memorandum for Undersecretary Fortas: "I have little confidence that the courts will sustain even the leave clearance regulations of the War Relocation Authority and the related segregation program" (*UA*, pp. 181–82).

Was the director repentant or at least apologetic about the years of detention and conditional release? Not a bit of it. The noble end justified the illegal means. Primary among the "excellent results" of the WRA program he bragged about later was the scattering of "these people": "This dispersion of the population led to an understanding and an acceptance on the part of the great American public that would never have been possible otherwise" (*UA*, p. 286).

CHAPTER V

Segregator

Never, of course, was there any policy of confinement for the
duration. . . . Punitive measures were not resorted to by the
WRA administration, since these were not prison camps.
—*Dillon S. Myer,*
Uprooted Americans, *1971*

In his lengthy outline of WRA policy for the FBI, Director Myer assured
Director Hoover that "those among the evacuees who do not meet the
conditions stated in the Leave Regulations should not be allowed their
freedom until the War is over. It is not intended that this element will
have access to indefinite leave" (January 18, 1943, FBI 62-69030). Of
"this element," Myer estimated for his project directors that "we will
have something like 2,000 of the total who could be put away for the
duration" (minutes of Little Rock Meeting, February 1–3, 1943, JERS,
67/14, E2.11B). As for "punitive measures," Myer also informed them
that "at the present time, WRA is in the uncomfortable position of having 16 people stuck out in a CCC [Civilian Conservation Corps] camp
in the desert [at Moab, Utah] with I think about 15 soldiers to guard
them, with no particular plan in mind as to how they are to be kept
peacefully, with their families not with them and with no provision for
having their families with them, with no work program laid out for
them other than service of the camp. In its physical layout it is probably
something worse than an internment camp or detention camp." And in
an earlier burst of candor he had gone the whole way, referring to Moab
as "nothing more than a concentration camp" (minutes of Denver Meeting, January 28–30, 1943, JERS, 67/14, E2.11B).

Such candor was permissible only within the inner circle of key staff
members and project directors. Solicitor Philip M. Glick was, of course,
privy to the agency's secrets and could write Myer about the "special

kind of jail or penal colony" they had established at Moab on December 10, 1942, and then moved into an old boarding school on the Navaho Indian Reservation at Leupp, Arizona, on April 27, 1943 (JERS, 67/14, E6.00). Among those they considered too junior to have a need to know was Francis S. Frederick, the young penologist who served as acting chief of internal security at Moab and then Leupp. When he took up his duties, Frederick recalled, "I attempted to ascertain whether I should make a regular count of the inmates and other routine steps taken in penal institutions . . . [and then] was given to understand in no uncertain terms that we were absolutely not running a penal colony." Later he reported this admonition to Lieutenant Colonel Frank E. Meek of the Ninth Service Command in Salt Lake City, "whereupon he blew his top. He quoted a letter to him from Dillon Myer stating in the most definite terminology that Leupp was indeed a penal institution. The moral to this story is that they are a damn two-faced hypocritical outfit who lie glibly whenever it suits their purpose" (Frederick to Robert Spencer, December 9, 1943, JERS, 67/14, S1.10). The moral Frederick drew was true enough, if a bit harshly put—as a professional jailer he was understandably angered by the disorienting experience of running a penal colony that was officially not a penal colony. Yet even Frederick, who was an unusually perceptive subordinate, never quite understood why lies were so necessary to the top WRA administrators.

The truth was that Myer and his staff could not admit to outsiders, to the victims, and indeed to their own normal everyday selves that within Republican America they were in fact running ten *concentration camps* (and one penal colony)—the term became so taboo Myer even identified Dachau in the index of *Uprooted Americans* as a "German Internment Camp." So the head keepers doggedly clung to their euphemisms and hid the reality of what they were doing under what the WRA called "definitions."

"Keep These Definitions in Mind" enjoined the WRA under Milton Eisenhower. Among them was "*Relocation Center*—A pioneer community, with basic housing and protective services provided by the Federal Government, for occupancy by evacuees for the duration of the war," a definition that by itself gave the lie to Myer's bald assertion: "Never, of course, was there any policy of confinement for the duration." From beginning to end inmates were "evacuees," even in the penal colony, and concentration camps were "relocation centers," Myer's "wayside stations," "temporary homes," those "havens of rest and security." Building on the foundation lie that "military necessity" had dictated exclusion, the WRA leaders hid from outsiders, from the victims themselves, and from their own normal, everyday selves the truth that they were holding citizens in indeterminate detention—for "the duration"—and presumed to punish those who protested. "Definitions" were official lies integral to the whole WRA program. They formed the shield against reality that enabled the American keepers to run concentration camps without seeming to do so.

Ironically, congressional, press, and military critics helped pin Myer's shield in place. From the first some legislators demanded a tougher policy. "I am for catching every Japanese in America, Alaska, and Hawaii now and putting him in concentration camps and shipping them back to Asia as soon as possible," declared Representative John E. Rankin of Mississippi. "Do not forget that once a Japanese always a Japanese. . . . Damn them! Let us get rid of them now!" (*Cong. Rec.*, March 20, 1942, pp. A-691–92). "As I have said before in this House," reiterated Representative Alfred Elliott of California, "the only good Jap is a dead Jap" (*Cong. Rec.*, October 11, 1943, p. 8286). In 1943 the 78th Congress considered turning the camps over to the army and authorized investigations of the WRA by the Senate Military Affairs Subcommittee chaired by Albert B. ("Happy") Chandler of Kentucky and by the House Un-American Activities Subcommittee chaired by John M. Costello of California. Representative Clair Engle of California and other witnesses appeared before the subcommittees to demand army takeover and to charge that the WRA was "coddling" the inmates (*Washington Post*, November 25, 1943).

Similar allegations had already appeared in the Hearst, the McClatchy, and numerous other newspapers. "AMERICA'S JAP 'GUESTS' REFUSE TO WORK BUT NIPS ENSLAVE YANKEES," read the *Denver Post* headline of April 24, 1943. "HOSTILE GROUP IS PAMPERED AT WYOMING CAMP."

The army did not want to take on operation of the camps, but voiced its own dissatisfaction with WRA "soft-on-Japs" policies. After the revolt at Manzanar, General John L. DeWitt advised the FBI that he had "heretofore made five separate recommendations, all suggesting that the known bad Japs be separated from the good to stop this trouble" (N. J. L. Pieper to Hoover, December 11, 1942, FBI 100-140363). During Senator Chandler's speedy "investigation" of Manzanar, Mrs. Happy Chandler vehemently expressed the opinion that all the Issei and Nisei "should be put on shipboard and dumped in the ocean when Tokyo was bombed" and Major Smith of the Judge Advocate's Staff, another member of their party, "freely admitted" to accompanying FBI agents "that he was not at all in sympathy with what he termed 'the social workers' who were administrating the Center. . . . While visiting the Japanese orphanage [the so-called Children's Village], Major Smith openly remarked that he felt it would be an excellent idea to segregate the male and female Japanese, in order to prevent the birth of any more Japanese in the United States" (R. B. Hood to Hoover, March 5, 8, 1943, FBI 100-140363).

The strident racism of their military and civilian critics made the WRA "social workers" appear veritable models of liberal goodwill. It added a protective layer to their carapace of lies by enabling Myer to wage, seemingly, "The Continuing Battle of the Racists," as he called a chapter of *Uprooted Americans*, and to pose as the fearless champion of his vilified wards.

The small minority of victims who trumpeted unquestioning acceptance of their chief jailer in this dubious role made his beneficence all the more believable.

2

In June 1943 agents of Costello's House Un-American Activities Subcommittee raided the Washington office of the Japanese American Citizens League. "SEIZED FILES REVEAL NIPPONESE AT SECRET FEDERAL PARLEYS," blared one headline, "EVEN SHAPED U.S. POLICIES" (*Los Angeles Examiner*, June 17, 1943). Many confidential letters to and from Mike Masaoka, JACL national secretary, provided the most sensational revelations. "I spent over 15 hours" with Myer this week, he bragged in one, "and got a lot of answers." In a report to JACL headquarters in Salt Lake City he gave the director high marks for his handling of troublemakers: "I have been impressed by the way he has nursed things along, and his attitude toward the agitators has been admirable." Still more important to the subcommittee was a memorandum in which he proudly claimed that Myer had "said that he and his staff deal with me on the same basis of confidence and mutual trust as they do among themselves. . . . He is afraid that certain guys in Congress would jump down their collective throats if they could only imagine a part of the part which we play in forming WRA policy." Jump they did—it was, said a spokesman for the subcommittee, "one of the most astounding cases on record of collusion between a pressure group and Government officials."

But when the subcommittee grilled the collaborators, their testimony yielded only an anticlimax. With paternal indulgence, Myer pictured "Mike" as a well-intentioned young man who had "allowed his imagination to run wild, occasionally, on how much influence he had on WRA policy." Masaoka agreeably acknowledged that he liked "to pat himself on the back" and that he had exaggerated the formative influence of the JACL. As an FBI agent present at the hearings summarized their testimony for his superiors, "Mr. Myer said that . . . [Masaoka's] statements were overly expansive and were the results of wishful thinking. . . . He did admit having conferred with Masaoka and other members of the Japanese-American Citizens League on numerous occasions." And frequently in the questioning of the younger man, "Masaoka was compelled to admit that he had made these statements for the purpose of impressing the Japanese-American Citizens League with his own importance and the excellence of his contacts" (memoranda of D. M. Ladd, July 3, 7, 9, 1943, FBI 62-69030). The agent's conclusion was acute: "Masaoka impressed Agent Ranstad as being exceptionally intelligent, shrewd, wily, quick-witted, persuasive, and not altogether scrupulous."

Had the JACL leader not existed, Myer would have had to invent him—or someone like him. Born in 1915, Mike Masaru Masaoka had grown up in Salt Lake City, become a Mormon, and graduated from the University of Utah. Before President Saburo Kido made him the JACL's first full-time staff employee in 1941, he had known few other Nisei and knew hardly more than Myer about Japanese culture and the history of his people in the United States. But the JACL had been organized in 1930 to promote assimilation of the Nisei and to reject the Japanese traditions and ties of the Issei, ends that made Kido pick Masaoka as just the man to lead young Japanese Americans out of Little Tokyos into mainstream America. Ambitious, energetic, and as arbitrary toward subordinates as John J. McCloy—whom he discussed in highly flattering terms in the seized letters—Masaoka identified with the white jailers and vividly illustrated the pattern Albert Memmi identified in *The Colonizer and the Colonized* (1965), the attempt of the colonized "to assume the identity of the colonizer" (pp. 135–36).

Shortly after Pearl Harbor Masaoka and his JACL brethren attempted to become one with the colonizer. From the Seattle chapter came a statement drafted by James Y. Sakamoto pledging that its members would continue informing on their parents "to uncover all subversive activity in our midst, and if need be we are ready to stand as protective custodians over our parent generation to guard against danger to the United States arising from their midst" (statement enclosed in a letter from William Hosokawa to Cordell Hull, January 23, 1942, NA, RG 107). From San Francisco came Masaoka's still more notorious plan for dealing with the old folks. In a final effort to keep citizens out of the mass internment, he proposed the army establish a "suicide battalion" (*YoI*, p. 38). After turning their parents over to U.S. authorities as hostages, Nisei volunteers in the unit would throw themselves into combat against the Japanese in a demonstration by blood of their undying loyalty. Observing that America did not believe in the concept of hostages, the army rejected his offer and thereby at least for the time being spared parents the ordeal of demonstrating how they felt about being held as living guarantees of their sons' patriotism.

At that climactic moment Masaoka, Kido, Sakamoto, Bill Hosokawa, and the other JACL schemers were manifestly not overly solicitous about Issei feelings or properly scornful of allegations that these "enemy aliens" posed a subversive threat. Indeed, in a sense, to them their parent generation *was* the enemy. Like the chapter secretary I quoted earlier (in chapter 4), they were "Americans to the core" although their appearance "betrayed" their oriental ancestry. With wry logic their goal of total assimilation had led them to total self-rejection. Their rejection of the Issei "took on the complexion of self-hate," observed Daisuke Kitagawa in *Issei and Nisei* (1967). "In his parents the Nisei found that element in himself which made it difficult for him to be accepted by American society" (p. 29).

Kitagawa's insight was forcibly confirmed by the eighteen-page list of JACL recommendations Masaoka handed Milton Eisenhower on April 6, 1942 (NA, RG 210). Now that the Nisei could not be exempted from the great roundup, he swung around to embrace the line that the camps represented the cause of democracy—that is, "the humane and democratic resettlement of us unfortunate people who have been called upon to leave our homes and businesses in order that the military defenses of our country may be strengthened." He invited the WRA to take the JACL under its wing in a kind of junior partnership: "By having Japanese Americans laud the work of the War Relocation Authority, we may be able to create a favorable public sentiment which will permit your office to do that which you desire in the relocation of our group." In return the WRA should treat the citizen sons and daughters with greater consideration than the "enemy aliens" who were their parents: "We recommend that only citizens who have attained their majority be

The Great White Father at Topaz, October 21–23, 1943. Presumably extended by inmates, the welcome beside the unabashed Myer illustrated the self-hate Daisuke Kitagawa observed among the Nisei.
[National Archives]

permitted to vote and hold offices of any sort, elective or appointive." Anticipating John J. McCloy's proposal to treat "evacuees" as guinea pigs, Masaoka recommended that the WRA and the JACL work together to turn the camps into indoctrination centers for the creation of "Better Americans in a Greater America." To insure inculcation of the right kind of "Americanism," he recommended maximum permissible "intercourse with 'white' Americans":

> We do not relish the thought of "Little Tokyos" springing up in these resettlement projects, for by so doing we are only perpetuating the very things which we hope to eliminate: those mannerisms and thoughts which mark us apart, aside from our physical characteristics. We hope for a one hundred per cent American community.

Although the "physical characteristics" of his "Better Americans" could not be whitened in the near future, their speech could be—he recommended language classes in which "special stress should be laid on the enunciation and pronunciation of words so that awkward and 'Oriental' sounds will be eliminated."

The next day Masaoka rushed to head off "self-styled martyrs" from challenging this indoctrination program on the legal level. Dated April 7, 1942, his Bulletin 142 warned JACL members: "*National Headquarters is unalterably opposed to test cases to determine the constitutionality of military regulations at this time*" (JERS 67/14, T6.10; Masaoka's italics).

Masaoka had prefaced his recommendations with an obsequious tribute to Eisenhower for his "sympathetic understanding and vision." On behalf of "the 20,000 members of the Japanese American Citizens League," he expressed his heartfelt gratitude "that our Federal Government has appointed a man of your calibre to direct the humane and democratic resettlement of us unfortunate people." When Eisenhower left for the Office of War Information, Masaoka understandably regretted losing his inspired leadership. Still, after a few wary days of feeling out and stroking his successor, he discerned in Dillon Myer a man of comparable caliber, fully deserving of the later JACL testimonial scroll for his "courageous and inspired leadership" (*UA*, p. 342). And Myer soon came around, according to Bill Hosokawa's JACL-inspired *JACL in Quest of Justice* (1982; henceforth *JACL*): Both men "realized they were thinking along the same lines and would have no problem working together" (p. 190).

So began the "collusion" charged by the Costello subcommittee. In reality the relationship of WRA and JACL officials embodied the traditional symbiosis of jailers and trustees. Through the head jailer and his staff, head trustee Masaoka sought and got favors for his members and helped them share the modicum of power WRA regulations allowed compliant inmates. With Masaoka in his vest pocket, as it were, Myer could point out that Japanese Americans accepted his proposition that the camps were democratic makeshifts, "temporary homes." With Myer behind him, as it were, Masaoka could count on official sanction of the complementary lie that the JACL represented the inmates—or as he put it later in the foreword to Myer's *Uprooted Americans*, the JACL represented "not only its members but also the vast majority of all persons of Japanese ancestry in the United States."

Led on by assurances that the JACL was their only bulwark against exclusion, numerous Nisei had joined the league following Pearl Harbor, but this influx still left the membership at considerably less than

half of the 20,000 claimed by the inventive Masaoka in April 1942.*
They did not stay long, a fact confirmed four years later by Saburo Kido's sad recital at the JACL's first postwar convention:

> It is the irony of fate that I was president when the organization with 66
> chapters and close to 20,000 members dwindled down to only ten active
> chapters and about 1,700 members. I went through the years when it no
> longer was a matter of pride to belong to the JACL, but rather a thing to be
> shunned. Only those brave in heart and determined in purpose . . . remained
> with JACL. [Hosokawa, *JACL*, p. 275]

Even before mass exclusion the JACL had become a thing to be both
shunned and despised by its victims.

At least as early as August 1941, JACL informers had assisted intelligence agencies in identifying supposedly dangerous Issei and thus in
fingering rival leaders for future internment in Department of Justice
camps, acts that did not endear the organization to the internees and
their families. Later JACL leaders even fingered their own members, or
so Los Angeles journalist Togo Tanaka concluded after having been
picked up by the FBI and held incommunicado for eleven days: "For
years afterward I figured that a couple of my fellow Nisei, prominent in
the national JACL and overzealous in their American patriotism, who
took great pride in their close association with Navy Intelligence officers, had bird-dogged a number of us whose pre–Pearl Harbor itinerary
looked suspicious or confusing" (Hosokawa, *JACL*, p. 137). In the
camps the JACL-recommended exclusion of Issei from elective office
(implemented by the WRA on June 5, 1942, and not rescinded until
April 19, 1943) provoked angry controversy over "child councils" (i.e.,
councils run by Nisei in their early twenties) and "administration
stooges" and provided the essential background for the general strike at
Poston I (November 18–24, 1942) and for the revolt at Manzanar (December 6, 1942).

"Opposition to JACL leadership was undoubtedly the underlying
factor in the Manzanar incident," observed Togo Tanaka of the events
that began with the beating of JACLer Fred Tayama and culminated in
military police shooting into a crowd of unarmed inmates, killing two

---

*In a review of Bill Hosokawa's *JACL in Quest of Justice*, James Omura has indicted
the JACL's numbers game and the invented "20,000" figure: "Its own inhouse historian
confesses it ballooned its membership to 'impress' the government (Togo Tanaka: Unpublished History of the JACL, Bancroft Library). The actual figure was nearer to seventy-
five hundred with the influx of sixteen additional chapters after Pearl Harbor" (*Amerasia
Journal* 11 [1984]: 97–102).

and wounding eight or more. In the sequel the WRA pulled out Harry Yoshio Ueno, Joseph Yoshisuke Kurihara, and fourteen other "troublemakers" for Myer's penal colony at Moab and concurrently whisked Tanaka and other JACL "leaders" out of the camp for their own safety. By then JACL claims to leadership at Manzanar and elsewhere had been contemptuously cast off and the popularity of the organization was roughly measured by widespread inmate approval of the numerous beatings some of them administered to its officials, including those of Tayama, Saburo Kido at Poston, and Tom Yatabe at Jerome.

Had Masaoka been with inmates behind barbed wire, he surely would have felt their wrath, but he never did any hard time in a camp. After comprehensively investigating conditions in all the camps, FBI Inspector Myron E. Gurnea reported that the JACL was "one of the greatest causes for disorder" and found some indications that the views of its members were "as political as patriotic. It is the consensus of opinion among the Japanese that the Japanese-American Citizens League, in collaboration with the United States Government, 'sold them out' and did not put up a fight to block relocation. . . . [Inmates refer to the national secretary as] 'Moses Masaoka,' stating that he 'led them out of California'" (transmitted by Hoover to Myer, March 22, 1943, FBI 62-69030).

A contretemps at the Wyoming camp amusingly underlined the hollowness of Masaoka's claims to speak for the impounded people. Originally he had planned to marry Etsu Mineta at Heart Mountain, where she had been interned with her parents and brothers, according to Bill Hosokawa, "but reports of rising feelings against Masaoka made it prudent to shift the site to Salt Lake City" (*JACL*, p. 213). In a letter that wound up in FBI files—probably courtesy of Masaoka—Hosokawa, then editor of the *Heart Mountain Sentinel*, had explained "the situation" in greater detail on January 16, 1943:

> The project director, GUY ROBERTSON, is scared to death of the consequences of your visit. He admits that in all probability nothing would happen, but at the same time he is afraid of the possibility that your arrival might be the cause of a riot on the order of Poston and Manzanar. He seems to be under the impression that the JACL was the spark that touched off the riots in those two centers. I have talked to him at length, but . . . his fears persist. . . . I have it from second hand sources that ROBERTSON has written to MYER asking him about the matter. It would appear that you should also contact MYER immediately to present your side of the story.
>
> [FBI 100-140363]

Myer must have agreed that it was prudent to keep this latter-day Moses out of the hands of the people he led into bondage, for Masaoka and his fiancée entered into the conjugal state in Utah.

Thoroughly repudiated by inmates in the camps, Masaoka could still depend on WRA support in Washington. Never in a position to have "dictated" the agency's policies, as Congressman Costello was to charge, he could still be confident that his recommendations would be heard and carefully considered. After all, with Eisenhower's and then Myer's paternal sanction, he and his tiny league had become the only officially recognized voice of all the Nikkei (that is, all Americans of Japanese ancestry). As the Chinese American writer Frank Chin recently observed with a sharp eye, "The JACL had no power over Japanese America before camp. No power of its own. The JACL became the Nikkei leadership at the government's pleasure, not by any form of popular Japanese American approval. The rift between the JACL and the Japanese Americans was created by the government when they imposed JACL leadership and Mike Masaoka on the Nikkei."

All the essentials of Myer's symbiotic relationship with Masaoka came out in their exchange of "CONFIDENTIAL" letters after the upheavals at Poston and Manzanar. Writing "Dear Mike" on December 24, 1942, Myer asked for his views on segregation of "disloyal evacuees" and invited him to finger individuals and name specific incidents: "Several of us here know generally your feelings on the whole problem and value the judgments you have given us from time to time" (JERS, 67/14, T6.10).

Belatedly replying to "Dear Mr. Myer" on January 14, 1943, Masaoka apologized for his tardiness and explained that he had been ill but mainly had waited "to obtain the thinking and collaboration of certain of our key people in the centers in order to give you a composite impression of our views" (NA, RG 210). Angered by "the fact that practically every person who has been 'beaten up' in the centers is a member of our Japanese American Citizens League" and by the lenient "overlooking" attitude of project administrators that had, in his judgment, contributed to such assaults, he and his key people believed in immediate and summary action "whereby, without warning or hearing, known agitators and troublemakers are moved out of the relocation centers and placed in special camps of their own." As for serving as informers, "most of our chapter leaders have signified their willingness to name those whom they consider inimical to center welfare if their own names are not revealed. The names which they might submit could be checked with others who are reliable and who are not members of the JACL in order to insure against possible prejudices simply because of organizational differences."

Myer and Masaoka were indeed "thinking along the same lines." Both believed in making the camps into indoctrination centers for "Americanism," in excluding Issei from positions of trust, in subjecting Nisei to Selective Service, in scattering both generations across the country, and in pulling out and holding for the duration all "agitators and troublemakers." With first-name condescension, Myer asked "Mike" for his views on segregation and then confirmed the latter's status as a para-administrator by tabulating his replies side by side with those of project directors (replies to Myer's "Segregation Letter," December 24, 1942, JERS, 67/14, E6.00). With becoming deference, Masaoka gave "Mr. Myer" the benefit of his opinions and later could boast of the part the JACL played "in forming WRA policy" only because he had out-colonized the colonizer.

3

For his impossible task Myer needed all the help he could get from Masaoka and his key JACL informers, from his own internal security officers and their "dogs," or *Inu*, as the victims called the finks in their midst, from the FBI and other intelligence agencies, from volunteer sleuths, and, for that matter, from professional diviners. His task was no less than to ferret out from among all the impounded people the putative "unknown and unrecognizable minority" that had made exclusion from the West Coast an "unfortunate necessity" in the first place, as he testified before the Costello subcommittee—namely, those who "might have greater allegiance to Japan than to the United States" (July 7, 1943, JERS, 67/14, T1.02). Ultimately inscrutable, these specters were not only unknown and unrecognizable, he might have added, they were also unconvictable in any court of law.

Under the Constitution the crime of treason is defined in very narrow and explicit terms. Existing federal law—including the Espionage Act of 1917 and the Smith Alien Registration Act of 1940—made indictable offenses of espionage, sabotage, and seditious conspiracy, but no statute made "disloyalty" a crime. In their heart of hearts persons of German or Italian descent could legally champion the regimes of Hitler or Mussolini. Even those who actively propagandized for their favorite dictator could not be convicted of sedition or, in the case of members of the

German-American Bund, of conspiracy to obstruct the draft (*Keegan* v. *United States*, 65 Sup. Ct. 1203 [1945]). Myer could not have gone through the court system to secure the conviction of a single one of his charges for having "greater allegiance to Japan than to the United States." Their cultural heritage and current political opinions were quite literally none of his business. They nevertheless became his unremitting concern and his agency's reason for being. Under his direction the WRA became a huge detention and investigative machine that incessantly processed and reprocessed inmates to determine their "loyalty." Somehow he and the other experts from the Soil Conservation Service had to make themselves expert in recognizing the rotten apples in their barrels. And all their "sorting," to borrow a homey word from Myer's chapter on "Sorting . . . and Segregation" (*UA*, pp. 67–80), grew naturally into their mass segregation program.

"On May 31, 1943," Myer noted long afterward, "we had called all project directors to Washington, D.C. . . . After a thorough discussion the directors were unanimous in their recommendation that we proceed with a mass segregation program. Because I did not feel that I could ignore their unanimous judgment, I capitulated, although reluctantly" (*UA*, p. 76). The claim that he had yielded reluctantly to pressures from Stimson, McCloy, DeWitt, congressional subcommittees, racist groups, Masaoka and the JACL, and finally his own directors was marred by the fact that a few weeks earlier, at his first national press conference, he had come out unequivocally for mass segregation (May 14, 1943, JERS, 67/14, E2.04). And it was destroyed by the fact that at his very first "policy conference" with his directors almost a year earlier (San Francisco, August 13–20, 1942), he had accepted segregation in principle and merely questioned how and where it could be implemented:

> I was urged to accede to a policy of segregation. "Remove the troublemakers," I was urged. "How can we pick them out?" I replied. And nobody could tell me how it could be done. But, after much discussion, I did tell them I was ready to move on those people who had clearly decided to throw in their lot with Japan, that is, the repatriates and expatriates. I told them we would move with this segregation policy if we could find a place to put these groups to be segregated. The trouble, of course, was that we couldn't find the space. . . . It is interesting to know that we actually had a definite first policy as early as August, 1942—we just could find no means of carrying it out.
>
> [Morton Grodzins, "Myer Interview,"
> September 29, 1943, JERS, 67/14, E2.10]

Before Myer and his staff made space and came up with means of sorts in 1943, "segregation" had several meanings. In the most inclusive, it meant pulling the Nikkei out of the population on the West Coast and penning them up in the WRA camps. Less inclusively, it meant imprisonment for the duration of all those who could not thread their way through the labyrinth of trick interview questions and loyalty investigations to the exit marked "indefinite leaves." Still less inclusively, it meant the initial roundup after Pearl Harbor of some two thousand Issei suspects and their indeterminate detention in Crystal City, Texas; Santa Fe, New Mexico; Bismarck, North Dakota; and other distant Department of Justice internment camps.

When little or no evidence could be found against many of the interned men, they were "paroled" back to the WRA camps, where they remained, along with all other Issei males, especially subject to arbitrary removal and detention. Shortly after the upheavals at Poston and Manzanar, Solicitor Philip M. Glick confidentially reported to Myer that Edward J. Ennis and Thomas Cooley of the Alien Enemy Control Unit in the Department of Justice had agreed to take "alien evacuees whom we may wish to segregate. . . . We indicated to them the kind of data we shall normally have available as our justification for asking that a particular alien evacuee be removed to a detention center. Mr. Ennis and Mr. Cooley felt that the kind of data we summarized would be adequate for their purposes" (December 30, 1942, JERS, 67/14, E2.05). The kind of data the WRA normally had available would even fall short of the bare minimum Attorney General Biddle had hitherto expected before he would issue a "Presidential Warrant" for the removal of an alien to an internment camp. As Ennis explained his deal with the WRA to J. Edgar Hoover on March 8, 1943:

> A special limited arrangement has been agreed to at the request of the War Relocation Authority. WRA inquired whether Japanese aliens who by their conduct in the camps proved to be a disturbing element could be taken off their hands and interned. In the interests of promoting the success of a difficult task in administering the war relocation camps involving the detention of citizens and aliens together, it was agreed that a limited number of troublesome Japanese aliens would be taken and interned even though their conduct did not establish subversive activity under the standards heretofore applied.
>
> [FBI 62-69030]

Thanks to this friendly, informal arrangement with Ennis's Alien Enemy Control Unit, Myer's WRA had an open hunting season on Issei "troublemakers."

At one stroke the keepers had solved their alien "problem." Myer quickly passed on the good news to project directors that when they

"Democracy at Work" at *Heart Mountain,* January 11, 1943. The WRA legend explained that "night school classes in advanced English are very popular. For the first time, many of the old people are now able to take advantage of the opportunity to read and write the language of their chosen country."
[The Bancroft Library]

had Issei "who are anti-administration, who are causing real trouble in the Centers," they could simply turn these troublesome Japanese nationals over to the Department of Justice (minutes of Denver Meeting, January 28–30, 1943, JERS, 67/14, E2.11B). Inmates without rights anyone had to respect, they had convicted themselves, or rather had obligingly made themselves "known and recognizable" as being pro-Axis, by being anti-administration. Did not his concentration camps represent the cause of democracy?

Of course, that curious calculus also applied to the Nisei, among whom, he also informed his directors in Denver, were "some problem boys whom I should like to segregate." Alas, these citizens posed "the toughest problem that we have today, as I see it, in relation to the whole segregation program. This involves the question of people who are not probably going back [*sic!*] to Japan—not aliens but people presumed to have rights as citizens. What will we do," he asked, if Nisei and Kibei (i.e., Nisei who had received some education in Japan) were anti-administration: "What will we do with them?" In a word, their presumptive rights as citizens were a vexing hindrance.

Back in Washington a few days later Myer demonstrated why Masaoka thought "his attitude toward the agitators has been admirable." At a staff meeting his mood was plainly punitive: Now that they could put the "tough aliens" where they belonged, he yearned to perform a like operation on the "hardboiled boys" among the Nisei—"I wish we could put them in the same place but we can't" (minutes, February 5, 1943, JERS, 67/14, E2.11B). Their quandary had its taproot in those presumptive rights: "Our main problem is that we are going to have a very difficult time to get the courts to act normally in putting people in prison and holding them, and when they don't hold them, they come back to us and become more or less martyrs, so we have a very difficult problem." As in his disposition of the Issei "problem," that of the Nisei would have been eased or expunged had he only been able to count on the courts to act "normally" by putting people in ordinary prisons and holding them there indefinitely for their noncrimes.

To be sure, the WRA had already done precisely that on its own to the inmates stuck in Moab, the penal colony Myer had characterized at Denver as "nothing more than a concentration camp and I hope we can work out something better." Something more sweeping, if not much better, came out of the loyalty oath they were about to administer to "all Japanese [sic] people in the centers."

In the meantime, the army had apparently undergone a change of heart about the concept of hostages, for it came up with plans reminiscent of Mike Masaoka's original proposal for a battalion of volunteers who would throw themselves into battle while their Issei parents remained behind government barbed wire. On January 28, 1943, Secretary Stimson announced plans to recruit 4,500 Nisei from Hawaii and from the mainland camps for an infantry unit later known as the 442nd Regimental Combat Team (*YoI*, pp. 134–36; *CC*, p. 112). Ten army recruiting teams of four men each readied themselves to go out from Washington to the camps to register all draft-age Nisei males and to administer a questionnaire to determine their loyalty. Though he had been urging that these young wards be subjected to Selective Service in the same way as other draft-age males, Myer welcomed the segregated unit as a "first step" and jumped at the chance to use their upcoming registration as an occasion to administer a mass loyalty oath: "In the hopes of expediting our leave-clearance operation, WRA proposed that the registration and questionnaires be presented to all persons, both male and female, over 17 [actually 17 or older] years of age. The forms used were labeled 'Application for Leave Clearance,' which proved to be disturbing to many Issei and others who did not want to leave the centers" (*UA*, p. 72). Not incidentally, the obverse of expediting leave clearance was expediting the sorting and continued segregation of those who flunked their loyalty tests.

The critical moment had arrived for finding out what the impounded people were "thinking about," as McCloy had urged, and for smoking out the "unknown and unrecognizable minority," as Myer had hitherto futilely sought to do. First distributed on February 10, 1943, the imperfect instrument—"adapted from ones in use in the Intelligence Unit of the Navy," Myer informed his staff in Denver—was a four-page questionnaire that inquired in great detail into the inmate's history, interests, and opinions in the manner of the interview questions I quoted in chapter 4. But this document also contained questions 27 and 28:

> No. 27.   Are you willing to serve in the armed forces of the United States on combat duty wherever ordered?
>
> No. 28.   Will you swear unqualified allegiance to the United States of America and faithfully defend the United States from any or all attack by foreign or domestic forces, and forswear any form of allegiance or obedience to the Japanese emperor, to any other foreign government, power or organization? [Selective Service Form 304A]

Intended for Nisei men, question 27 was modified on another form for Nisei women and for all the Issei: "If the opportunity presents itself and you are found qualified, would you be willing to volunteer for the Army Nurse Corps or the WAAC [Women's Auxiliary Army Corps]?"—a prospect that must have seemed odd to elderly farmers and fishermen. As it stood, question 28 merely asked the Issei to become stateless persons by renouncing the only citizenship they had and by affirming their unswerving fealty to a government that had made their race the legal basis for denying them U.S. citizenship. In the wake of bitter outcry, question 28 was reformulated for the Issei: "Will you swear to abide by the laws of the United States and to take no action which would in any way interfere with the war effort of the United States?" But by then, Myer recorded, "much confusion had already been produced" (*UA*, p. 72).

Much furor and pain is more precise. Even under the modified form, were Issei who had no place to go asking to be turned out of the camps by applying for "leave clearance"? Were Nisei who answered question 27 in the affirmative in effect volunteering for the "Jap Crow" outfit? In response to question 28, why should they forswear a nonexistent allegiance to the Japanese emperor? Might not a "yes" trap them into admitting such allegiance? And a "no" trap them into admitting disloyalty to the United States? Anyway, why were they alone among citizens required to take a loyalty oath? And especially why when they were in detention without formal charges? Why answer at all and become a "No-No boy" or a "Yes-Yes JACLer"? Should parents urge their Nisei children to become one or the other? Should sons and daughters respect Issei urgings? If they volunteered for the combat team or expressed their willingness to serve in the WAAC, who would look after the old folks? Did they have to choose between family and country? What did that say about the country that had forced such a choice upon them? "People walked the roads, tears streaming down their troubled faces, silent and suffering," remembered one inmate. "The little apartments were not big enough for the tremendous battle that [was being] waged in practically every room" (*YoI*, p. 141).

In his 1976 presidential address to members of the American Anthropological Association, Walter Goldschmidt remarked that "the incarceration of the Japanese, citizens as well as aliens, was a case of rape." Incarceration laid the cruel scene, but the mass loyalty oath consummated the act.

At the time anthropologist Morris E. Opler, then a WRA community analyst, and eight of his colleagues at Manzanar petitioned "that the answers to the so-called loyalty question, question 28, be thrown in the waste basket where they belong." The petitioners proposed to Myer and top WRA officials "that the same standard of measurement of loyalty and worthiness be applied to the Nisei that are applied to other young Americans of their age class, namely their record of obedience to law and the evidence of past behavior, character, activity, associations and affiliations." *Loyalty*, they contended, was a matter of activity and record and if nothing in the latter proved culpable, then it "must be assumed." They provided a valuable summary of reasons why in this instance it was emphatically unfair to assume the contrary:

> The matter of questionnaires and the persistent inquiries about "loyalty" was becoming galling to the Nisei. At the beginning of the war their "loyalty" was questioned. They pointed to their good record and to the lack of sabotage—but to no avail. They met and pledged their loyalty in statements, resolutions, and letters to government officials. They volunteered for the armed services, they bought bonds, they became blood donors, they did everything and more than other American citizens were doing to demonstrate their loyalty. They were told that the evacuation and their attitude toward it would be considered a test of their loyalty. After evacuation they were expected to take an oath of loyalty before becoming members of the WRA Work Corps. Those who had been inducted into the armed forces and

later dismissed had taken the soldier's oath. Even all this fanfare about "loyalty" was paralleled by a chain of events which clearly indicated that their protestations of loyalty were viewed with suspicion, that they were not trusted and that their citizenship rights were being disregarded. Now, from behind barbed wire, after all that had gone before, they were being asked for another affirmation of loyalty.

[Opler et al., "The Loyalty Controversy," n.d.
(February 1943?), JERS, 67/14, 05.00]

Wrung from victims of repeated assaults on their integrity, their monosyllabic responses to the "loyalty" question, cogently asserted Opler and his associates, amounted to "no more than an evidence of witchcraft."

An unfunny administrative farce that might have been properly billed as "Trial by Questionnaire," the oath split camp populations into "Yes-Yeses" and "No-Noes," the "loyals" and the "disloyals." Of the nearly 78,000 "eligible" inmates, about 75,000 finally took the oath, with all but a handful of the "nonregistrants" concentrated at Tule Lake. About 7,600 of those who filled out the questionnaire entered negative or qualified answers to question 28 (*UA*, p. 73). Only 1,181 volunteered for the combat team for which the administrators had set a quota of 3,000 (*YoI*, pp. 143–44). Results varied from camp to camp depending on past events, on how skillfully project directors and their staffs cajoled and threatened those who opposed the oath, on the resisters' level of organization and tactical decisions, and on like factors. At Heart Mountain, for instance, Nisei resisters made the project director doubt he could administer the oath until they beat "a strategic retreat," shifting their opposition first to the combat team and then (1944) to the draft (*CC*, p. 121). Even at Granada, or Amache, another "happy camp," Solon T. Kimball pointed out that "there was a point at which 100 citizens were answering 'No' to the loyalty question and only 30 had volunteered" (*Community Government* [1946], pp. 37–39). Resistance was highest at Tule Lake (42 percent, February–March 1943), high at Jerome and Manzanar (both 26 percent), substantial at Topaz (15 percent) and Gila River (13 percent), and then shaded down from Minidoka (9 percent) to Granada (2 percent). But these figures tend to strip the farce of its pathos and meaning—blasted marriages, still more estranged parents and children, deadly enmities, a subculture sliced into warring majorities and minorities, with only victims of the oath on both sides. After all, the "Yes-Yeses" bought their compliance at the high price of swallowing and internalizing their further mortification.

Among the various reasons Myer later assigned to negative responses

Typical Block at Tule Lake, 1943. According to an FBI agent, "this photograph is a close-up showing the end portion of a typical Japanese block in the colony itself. Rows of apartments extend on both the left and the right sides of the picture. The smaller buildings located in the center to the rear of the basketball court comprise laundry rooms, toilet facilities, and utility rooms. Each block is similarly constructed. . . . It is to be noted in the report that there was considerable discussion between the Japanese and the Administration on the subject of porches for the apartments."
[FBI 62-70564]

to the oath were family loyalties, avoidance of the draft, freedom from pressures to "relocate," and then his lay reading of the psychological factor: "Some of the segregants were defiant individuals who said 'no' to the loyalty question mainly because they had developed persecution complexes" (*UA*, p. 76). Such self-revealing, retrospective etiology aside, he proceeded at the time as though their negative answers were sure signs of "disloyalty" or "potential disloyalty." The mass segregation program he formally decided upon in the spring and carried out in the fall of 1943 had always been implicit in the mass oath. Abortive data collected from the latter became the basis for the former. As he wrote Stimson on June 8, 1943: "Now, on the basis of information developed during registration, I feel that for the first time the War Relocation Authority has a reasonably adequate background of information on which to proceed with the process of screening out disloyal or potentially disloyal individuals" (*UA*, p. 170).

On the eve of the massive reshuffling, Myer proudly heralded it a truly novel experiment in social engineering:

> According to Dillon S. Myer, director of WRA, the people who will live in the Tule Lake center will include: those who have asked to be repatriated or expatriated; a group which has refused to pledge loyalty to the United States; and those who had pledged loyalty to the United States but whose behavior in relocation centers or before evacuation has indicated that they are not truly loyal. . . . It is believed to be the first time that any group in the country has been sorted and segregated on the basis of National loyalty.
>
> [Press Release, September 14, 1943, NA, RG 210]

From their perplexity as beginners the keepers had graduated to cockiness as veterans about their ability to weed out the formerly unknown and unrecognizable "disloyals." All of their sorting and weeding and grading sent trainloads of inmates back and forth in September and October 1943, with eventually about 12,000 "disloyals" moved into Tule Lake and with about the same number of "loyals" moved out to the other camps. Left behind were about 6,000 "Old Tuleans" who for one reason or another stayed on in what was officially designated the "Segregation Center." Including their families, over 18,000 "disloyals" and "loyals" fought for space meant for 15,000 at most. It was a time bomb with a short fuse—army takeover and martial law were only weeks away.

CHAPTER VI

"Troublemakers"

So our position on the matter is simply this: One, that we are removing the agitators.

Q: To where?

A: Aliens to internment camps through agreement with the Justice Department; citizens to Leupp. That is in Arizona and is about 27 miles out from Winslow. It is a big country. It is an old Indian school we have just taken over recently. It is an isolation center that we are using for those people who are, I might say, mostly pro-Japanese but who are American citizens, who are not eligible for internment camps and who are trouble-makers and agitators and are causing difficulty. They are not pro-Axis, generally speaking.

—*Dillon S. Myer,*
Press Conference, May 14, 1943

To make the acquaintance of "aggravated and incorrigible troublemakers" Myer and his men put away for the duration, we must leave their side in Washington, go out into the field, and go back to the beginning of the oath crisis. So as not to be distracted by side excursions to a number of camps, let us go directly to Tule Lake, the eye of the storm.

Troublemaker #1. Nisei; Buddhist; grammar-school education; married with no children—Masao I.* stated in his own behalf:

On, or about, February 15, 1943 Block #42 was ordered to register on Special Selective Service forms and on February 18 I had my wife obtain forms for repatriation to Japan in preference to registering. . . . We were told to apply for repatriation to Japan or register on the Selective Service forms. . . .

My reasons for refusing to register for Selective Service are: On October 16, 1940 at . . . Sacramento, California I registered for Selective Service and

*For obvious reasons I refrain from inflicting further injury on inmates who wound up in the WRA penal colony. From their first or second names and the initials of their surnames only, qualified students can find these individual case histories—unless otherwise noted—among the others in JERS, 67/14, S1.20A.

was classified as 3A because of my farm which I was operating with my wife. Later I moved to Gridley, California to do similar farming, truck gardening. Then evacuation came along and I was put in camp despite my American citizenship and never got a full and equal right as a citizen of America.

On February 19, the majority of Block #42 took same action bringing repatriation form witnessed of signing. I chose to do it on my own accord. . . .

On February 21st at 4:45 P.M. Block #42 was surrounded by Army guard with machine guns and bayoneted rifles and we were arrested without warrant and taken to Alturas County Jail and Klamath Falls Jail. There were about 27 arrested.

Now, since Masao I. had never been out of California, how could he possibly have been repatriated or "sent back" to Japan? Once again giving themselves away by their language (cf. Myer on p. 76), the keepers had to mean *expatriation* forms for Nisei like Masao I. and *repatriation* forms for Issei, who could indeed be sent back to their country of birth.

Myer's deputy director had in fact asserted that registration was compulsory "except in the case of those who have requested repatriation" (Elmer M. Rowalt to Project Directors, January 30, 1943, NA, RG 210). In the nine days following the start of registration on February 10, 1943, 2,656 inmates lined up outside administration offices to apply for "repatriation." These lines angered "Caucasians" and provoked Project Attorney Anthony O'Brien to voice a murderous impulse: "When I came back and saw these people lined up for repatriation, I wished for a machine gun for five minutes" (quoted by Frank Shotaro Miyamoto, "The Registration Crisis at Tule Lake" [hereafter "Crisis"], JERS, 67/ 14, R20.36). In Washington Myer's staff tardily rushed to close their barn door. As Tule Project Director Harvey Coverley explained to FBI agents:

According to Mr. COVERLEY there had been some confusion regarding repatriation. His original instructions from Washington had stated that if a citizen had signed papers for repatriation such citizen would not be required to register. Then on February 18, 1943, he was instructed that all citizens had to register regardless of repatriation and that a registration card was a prerequisite for a citizen who wished to repatriate. A public announcement of this was made on February 18 and 19, 1943. Following orders from the WRA in Washington, D.C., repatriation applications were not accepted after 12 noon on February 19, 1943. Those who were waiting in line to file application for repatriation were so notified and public announcements were made immediately.

[March 10, 1943, FBI 62-70564]

At that point Masao I. and thirty-four other inmates of Block 42 presented Coverley with their petition: "We the undersigned do not wish to sign to the Selective Service. But to repatriate we will sign anytime. So until then there won't be any business" (N. J. L. Pieper to Hoover, February 20, 1943, FBI 62-70564).

Troublemaker #2. Kibei; Buddhist; graduate of a Seattle high school, with three additional years in a Tokyo Buddhist seminary; single—Kentaro T. had previously managed a Seattle hotel. In the camp he had been helping out with registration by interpreting and filling out forms when he was shocked by the "Commando style method" with which the Block 42 petitioners were captured and hustled away in trucks:

> An army of soldiers surrounded block 42 and at bayonet points, plus light machine guns, captured thirty-five boys of that block. I have heard about this occurrence from an eye witness. Tears swelled my eyes as I heard his description of the heart rending scene. Where little brothers and sisters clung tenaciously to their departing brothers, tearfully hysterical in their demand . . . to accompany them. Old men stood by helplessly, their eyes wet, dimmed, their lips hard pressed by angry teeth. Mothers pathetically waved farewells to boys who they never expected to see again, their choked voices bade the boys "to take care of themselves—goodbye." Some men raised their voices above the tumult of the crowd and shouted lusty "Banzais" to impart to the departing boys that they would not be forgotten. . . . After all their hardships, the populace of Tule Lake was stirred with indignation at the army's unnecessary method of apprehending the boys of block 42. Needless to say, I was aggravated too. I decided not to register. If they were treating those boys like prisoners for refusing to register—then I would join them too. With deep conviction in the righteousness of my cause and with firm reliance on the protection of divine providence, I acted against registration. . . . My brother had volunteered and enlisted in the American army almost a year before Pearl Harbor. For my brother's sake and because America is my birthplace, I harbor no ill will towards this country. I am classified as a Kibei, and labelled a pro-Axis. It is strange indeed to be gazed upon with suspicion when I am not in a position to do harm. I have never published propaganda, nor organized a "Bund" or spoken against the government of the United States while living in Seattle those many years. My father, mother and sister are now residing in Japan; that is the basic reason why I will not fire a gun against Japan. Of a certainty I will gladly work for America on the production front but I will not bear arms against my father's country. I will not bear arms against America either.
> [Kentaro T., "The Factual Causes and Reasons Why I Refused to Register," JERS, 67/14, R30.25]

Soon identified or misidentified by Project Attorney O'Brien as one of the key leaders of the Kibei, Kentaro T. was also hauled away to a smaller prison.

How military police came to be in the camp helping with arrests was a tale with its own tortuous antecedents. Originally Director Coverley had responded to rising resistance by urgently requesting the FBI field office in San Francisco to send agents to remove the resisters. But SAC N. J. L. Pieper had then advised him "that this office had no authority to summarily arrest or incarcerate any individuals or groups of individuals to assist in the camp's registration program" (Pieper to Hoover, February 17, 1943, FBI 62-70564). Thus rebuffed, the director worked out his own plan for summary arrests and incarceration. Assisted by the army recruiting team led by Major S. L. A. Marshall, Coverley "decided to select various blocks known to be centers of agitation and force the registration in those blocks," according to the project attorney's detailed report to Washington (O'Brien to Glick, March 17, 1943, JERS, 67/14, R6.20). "Block 42 was selected as the first guinea pig." But when thirty-five of these first guinea pigs had the gall to hand him their petition, Coverley "again, and again, telephoned the FBI in San Francisco for help" but to no avail. Thereupon he appealed to Washington for permission to "borrow" some soldiers, and Dillon Myer quickly obliged, as Coverley's teletype message made clear: "Acting on your telephonic assurance I requested Military Police Commander yesterday for eight soldiers to assist in making arrests then necessary. Commanding Officer consented but on contacting Ninth Service Command was instructed no soldiers might enter Center unless control of entire project placed in military hands." And that, after all, was one of the stipulations in the WRA's written agreement with the army. But the WRA headquarters staff prevailed upon the War Department to make an exception in this dire emergency, and on February 21 Coverley finally received military assistance for his show of force. Without Myer's direct approval and intercession in his project director's behalf, those soldiers with rifles and machine guns would never have been in position around Block 42 to move Kentaro T. and his fellow inmates to anger, disgust, and heightened resistance.

Troublemaker #3. Kibei (that is, if a year in a Japanese grammar school made a Kibei of a Nisei); Buddhist; high-school education; single—like Masao I. (#1), who had married his sister, Saburo M. was a farmer who listed similar reasons for refusing to register and for joining the petitioners. Saburo M.'s case history fleshed out his brother-in-law's account of what happened to the young men caught up in these first twenty-seven arrests:

On the 21st of February, we were surrounded by a force of army guards and thrown into an army truck at the point of bayonets and machine guns without any warrants. We were taken to the county jail[s] at Klamath Falls [Oregon] and Alturas [California]. I was taken with a group to Alturas County jail. At Alturas I was questioned by F.B.I. agents and also by the Tule Lake project attorney. The object of the questioning appeared to be discovering a person responsible for our conduct. But, I said to them that, so far as I was concerned I acted on my own accord. . . . They asked me if I knew the penalty for not registering. . . . I told them I knew the penalty was 20 yrs and 10,000 dollars fine but that I have already registered for the draft and have been classified 4C. With neither explanation nor trial we were detained in jail for 8 days. Then we were transferred to Tule Lake Army Prisoners' Camp. We were compelled to work without compensation and were told that those who didn't work wouldn't be fed. The army guards followed us closely each step we took until the WRA took over several days later. All the incoming and outgoing letters were being strictly censored. Several of my letters were intercepted and sent back to the sender. One of my friends was stricken by a disease but it was many days after when he was finally given medical attention.

One of those "problem boys" Myer yearned to put away, Saburo M. was a victim of the WRA's do-it-yourself lawless enforcement of the law. Along with the other prisoners from Tule Lake, he had been arrested without a warrant, manhandled, given no opportunity to seek legal counsel, held incommunicado over a week in the Modoc County Jail in Alturas, grilled during this time by FBI agents and by Attorney O'Brien, and never taken before a U.S. judge or commissioner for a hearing, commitment, or taking of bail for trial, as provided by federal law (18 U.S.C., Sec. 595).

On the other hand, Saburo M. and his comrades could not allege that they had not been warned. On February 17 Coverley had published a notice on "Registration Penalty" in the *Tulean Dispatch*:

Mr. Dillon S. Myer, Director, War Relocation Authority, has instructed me to call to the attention of all residents of this Project the fact that Title 50 of the United States Code, Section 33, provides that "whoever shall willfully obstruct the recruiting or enlistment service of the United States shall be punished by a fine of not more than $10,000 or imprisonment for not more than 20 years. Section 34 of the same Title, provides the same punishment for a conspiracy to violate Section 33. . . . Under such circumstances, we have no alternative but to see that the law is enforced." Mr. Myer has called this matter to my attention, because he has reason to believe that in this Relocation Center, there have been infringements of these laws.

And even their families had been warned by "Director Coverley's Message to Parents" in the *Tulean Dispatch* of February 25:

> Mothers and Fathers: If you have a son of military age who is required to register . . . DO NOT advise your son not to register or in any way to fail to comply with the Selective Service regulations. If you do and if your son should follow your advice, he may be subject to a long prison term for which YOU will be responsible.

Myer followed through on these warnings by teletyping authorization for a sedition investigation of the Block 42 petitioners and by delegating Project Attorney O'Brien to make a case against them.

Once they heard of Myer's authorization, FBI agents forcefully instructed Coverley and O'Brien that any such sedition investigation was their responsibility and theirs alone (Pieper to Hoover, February 24, 1943, FBI 62-70564). The agents also made clear to the sheriffs in Klamath Falls and in Alturas that the Japanese Americans in their jails were there as prisoners of the WRA and not of the FBI.

In San Francisco, meanwhile, Ernest Besig, the energetic director of the Northern California branch of the American Civil Liberties Union (NCACLU), had repeatedly and futilely written to Myer, Glick, and Coverley asking for "the official facts about this matter" (see, for example, Besig to Myer, March 9, 1943, CHS 3580). Frustrated also by his inability to communicate with the jailed resisters, he wired the sheriffs in Alturas and Klamath Falls on March 12 setting forth his understanding that they had been holding certain men from Tule Lake "for the federal authorities and that they have been detained for some weeks without the filing of formal charges, presentation before a committing officer and the privilege of counsel. May we request that you kindly inform such evacuees to contact . . . [the NCACLU] and that we will be glad to advise them" (CHS 3580). Enclosing a copy of this telegram from Besig—his invitation almost certainly never reached the jailed men—Klamath County Sheriff Lloyd L. Lowe anxiously reminded Coverley on March 16 that he had twenty-one "Jap prisoners . . . which I have never received a letter of commitment for. I have asked several of the officers to see that I receive this commitment, but as yet I have heard nothing. Please write one up and send it immediately as I must have something for my records" (NA, RG 210). Merely by raising the threat of due process, Besig had come within a hairsbreadth of blowing "the official facts" out of their hiding places. That would happen when the NCACLU director appeared in person at Tule Lake, as we shall see, but only after troublesome inmates had been victimized for another year and more.

At the time WRA Principal Attorney Edgar Bernhardt, who had been sent up from San Francisco to help out during the crisis, "was very much concerned" about the unbooked inmates in the Klamath jail and wanted the men removed forthwith. To the Tule director he explained "the risks involved in keeping a man jailed (as, for example, an A.C.L.U. habeas corpus case, suits for false arrest against Coverley himself and others)" (Bernhardt to Glick, March 17, 1943, JERS, 67/14, R6.20). Coverley reluctantly agreed, pulled the remaining resisters out of jail, and stuck them in what Myer and his aides playfully called "Shangri-La," a smaller prison located across the lake on the site of an old CCC camp about thirteen miles northwest of the main camp. In this hidden paradise, under the keepers' exclusive control, the presumptive rights of their citizen wards posed less of a threat.

Troublemaker #4. Kibei; Methodist; graduate of a commercial school in Japan and a technical high school in California; married with one child—Yoshio Y. had been the manager of a food store in San Francisco before his internment. In his "legal history" Yoshio Y. explained that he had not refused to register "but merely failed to register until he understood clearly what it was all about." Nonetheless, he was pulled out of bed in the early morning hours of February 28, hauled off to jail, questioned by FBI agents and by O'Brien, and after a week transferred to the so-called isolation center at the former CCC camp. From there on March 13 he wrote his wife a vitriolic denunciation of his tormentors:

> The wizard of the WRA Enterprises is Coverley himself and one of the general staff is the false arrests expert extraordinary O'Brien. . . . As the climax of white savage dance I was made the WRA made bachelor separating [me from] my family without any definite evidences or witnesses to prove. It is just [a] horrible inhuman act. . . . WRA Board of Directors are living the double life, one is pretending to help the Japanese people and [the] other is put[ting] Japanese into jail pitfalls and hardships and slave laborers. . . . Undeclared juice of WRA football team is racial prejudice. Poor law abiding Japanese are used as footballs. . . . Please remember that I was picked up and put into jail pitfall by tricks in the early morning when I was sleeping at 2:15 A.M. . . . Someday WRA will pay for the crime, committed injustice way. Please take good care of yourself.
>
> ["Crisis," JERS, 67/14, R20.36]

In this and other letters that reached his wife in censored form, Yoshio Y. inveighed against WRA "Gestapo methods" and declared his intention to enlist the aid of ACLU lawyers. With reason he believed this exercise in free speech "infuriated the officials at Tule Lake. . . . He states that he regarded the whole procedure of arrest and incarceration as unconstitutional and un-American and felt that as a citizen of this country he was within his rights to protest against such treatment" (JERS, 67/14, S1.20A).

Perhaps Yoshio Y.'s most threatening charge was that he and the others had been made into "slave laborers." Even after the war that was an explosive accusation, as Dorothy Swaine Thomas discovered when she attempted to learn whether it had any validity and how "the CCC isolation camp" had been established. A spokesman for the Western Defense Command informed her that their files revealed, "principally in telephone conversations with Washington," that the WRA had requested an officer and fifty men to guard the camp, but General DeWitt had objected to opening such subcamps within the exclusion zone and recommended instead that "these people" be sent to Moab, Utah:

> After the discussion with the Assistant Secretary of War's [McCloy's] office, they were able to obtain a promise from Mr. Myer that he would not open this camp except under an extreme emergency and then only for a limited period not to exceed two weeks. Mr. Myer apologized for not having made the request of General DeWitt, and stated he would move them to Moab just as fast as he could and further, that they were then negotiating for the Leuppe [sic] Camp in Arizona. . . . [As for the explosive accusation,] I would like to suggest, unless you have some documentation of your belief that the military guard utilized forced labor, that it is a rather dangerous allegation.
> [Victor W. Nielson to Thomas, August 7, 1946, JERS, 67/14, suppl. cart.2]

What extraordinary intelligence had come oozing out of DeWitt's files! It revealed chief jailer Myer in top form, pleading for the old CCC camp as a temporary penal colony for American citizens, promising to send these citizens to another penal colony just as fast as he could, and simultaneously negotiating for yet another, larger penal colony for the selfsame citizens, whose only crime was being who they were. Not surprisingly defensive about the army's role in all this, the spokesman demanded documentation that the military guard utilized forced labor.

It existed.

Once flushed from official cover, the documents supported the resisters' other major allegations against the keepers, as we have seen, and so why should they fail to substantiate what was perhaps their most shocking charge? Saburo M. (#3) stated, you will recall, that when he and the other Block 42 petitioners were put in the "Tule Lake Army Prisoners' Camp," they "were compelled to work without compensation and were told that those who didn't work wouldn't be fed. The army guards followed us closely each step we took until the WRA took over several days later." Yoshio Y. (#4) came in after the WRA had taken over, but things had not changed much, according to his "legal history": he was forced to surrender his pocket knife, received a number that was stamped on the front and back of his dark blue coveralls, worked digging ditches, and heard that he was a war prisoner who would have to work without pay. Yoshio Y. "told one of the supervisors that he didn't think he was a war prisoner and that he didn't come [t]here to work from jail. He states that the supervisor became angry, recorded his name in a note book and told [him] . . . he was going to report this to the office. Following this, all the boys (some 110 of them) were told that those who did not work would not eat."

And that was precisely the regime of forced labor that WRA Attorney Edgar Bernhardt found upon his arrival from San Francisco. It "bothered me very much," this officer of the court reported to the WRA solicitor in Washington, so he checked with Coverley at once:

> I told him that I felt that there was no legal basis for forced labor at the camp any more than elsewhere and that I was therefore suggesting that he inform Mr. Powell (in charge of the CCC camp) to assign work only to those who wanted to work. I pointed out that it would probably be only a matter of time until someone refused to work; then we would have the issue raised directly. We would find ourselves on the wrong side of that issue—and would have to back down. Coverley said that he thought I was right; that as a matter of fact he had heard that day that there were rumors of a strike. . . . At any rate we agreed that forced labor should end at once. Nevertheless, when I went to the camp the following morning I found all the men working and that there had been some trouble with one or two of them; that they had nevertheless been required to go out into the fields with a group. On my return to the project I reported to Coverley on my day's activities, and also spoke to him again about forced labor. He said that he would see to it that it was stopped. However, with the press of other work and the constant tension at the center, the situation remained unchanged for several days.
>
> [Bernhardt to Glick, March 17, 1943,
> JERS, 67/14, R6.20]

Some 110 Tule inmates had been made into "slave laborers," as Yoshio Y. charged, and Myer's headquarters staff had knowledge of that grim truth.

Troublemaker #5. Kibei; graduate of a Japanese middle school and a California college; single—Masao K. had been running a fruit ranch

before he was corralled at Tule Lake. Arrested on March 5 with ten
other young Kibei, he then told an AP why he refused to register:

> Firstly, I told him, it is an insult to ask us our loyalty in view of the fact
> that we had such a clean record and that we were placed in the camp without
> due process of law. Secondly, I have already registered for the selective service
> . . . and have been classified as 1B in 1940, [and] hence I can not see any
> reason for re-registration. Thirdly, I cannot trust what the administration
> and the army officers told us as to its compulsionness, because [the] admin-
> istration's order was changed many times in succession since the beginning
> of registration. Fourthly, I, therefore, don't believe it could be a War Depart-
> ment order.
>
> I also told him that I have more sympathy for Japan, when I was com-
> pelled to answer my loyalty.
>
> He . . . urged me to register with the threat of 20 years imprisonment and
> 10,000 dollar fine. But I showed my determination not to register under any
> condition at least for the time being until everything is cleared [up]. Conse-
> quently together with other boys I was sent to the isolation camp in the army
> truck.
>
> [JERS, 67/14, S1.20A]

You can fool some of the people some of the time—Masao K. rightly
knew that he could not trust his keepers. Moreover, he had shrewdly
and intuitively understood that they were lying to him about one of their
most closely guarded secrets. Registration was not a War Department
order, and neither was failure to register or reregister a violation of Selective Service regulations.

A month before registration commenced on February 10, McCloy
and Myer had met with leaders of the Selective Service System and then
thought they had reached an agreement that participation would be required. Later while Myer was out of the capital for field conferences,
another group in the War Department reconsidered the matter, decided
participation should be voluntary, and so advised the SSS officials. Thus
when FBI agents challenged Coverley's authority and checked with
Washington, they discovered the Tule director had no right under the
Selective Service Act to jail inmates or terrorize them—and their parents—with threats of twenty-year prison terms and/or fines of 10,000
dollars. The frantic Coverley wired Myer, who became no less frantic
when he made inquiries and learned they were in "a real mess." As he
both wired and wrote the Tule director on February 26, nonregistrants
were merely guilty of violating a regulation of the WRA—which infrac-
tion carried a maximum penalty of ninety days in jail—"but their mere

refusal to complete the questionnaires did not make them guilty of violating the Selective Service Act" (JERS, 67/14, E2.04).

That same day, February 26, Myer called FBI headquarters and had a long talk about the "little trouble" at Tule Lake, about the "little mixup" over Selective Service, and about his big need for help in filing charges against the some sixty inmates already arrested, "if the FBI thinks they can under the Espionage Act." According to Assistant Director D. M. Ladd's notes on their conversation:

> There are some aliens that he thinks are being picked up this weekend and he has asked that they be processed, if possible, under Presidential Warrant on their [i.e., the WRA's] documentation; that he is hoping there are some people in this group in jail that Federal charges can be filed against under the Espionage Act or some other way and then they will take action on the rest of it; that he would like for it to be made clear, if it is not clear to our men, that they have a very tough problem there and have to act; that they do have certain authority which they have not been able to clarify with our men which our men do not know about, which is more or less WRA law under their Executive Orders that are being worked out there, which is the only basis they have for operating and cracking that thing if they do not have Federal charges against them. . . . So he wired Coverley and told him to see if FBI could expedite their investigations and be able to file charges against any who might have charges filed under the normal Federal laws.
>
> [memorandum for E. A. Tamm, February 26, 1943,
> FBI 62-70564]

"WRA law" was to normal law what WRA truth was to normal truth— shortly afterward officials in the Department of Justice reviewed the evidence against the Tule resisters and concluded that it did not warrant "the prosecution of any of the subjects under the Sedition Act" (Wendell Berge to Hoover, April 1, 1943, FBI 62-70564). Director Hoover's sour, handwritten comment on Ladd's memorandum was apt: "This looks like another storm brewing. Be certain that our field offices are cautioned re handling of WRA matters. This outfit is bad & is inclined to pass buck to FBI or jam FBI. Do for WRA *only* what we are required to do under the law since there apparently appears resentment on their part."

Friday, *February 26, 1943*, was the date, then, that Myer was "greatly surprised and disappointed" to learn that registration was not compulsory: "It is now definite that the problem is ours" (Myer to Coverley, February 27, 1943, JERS, 67/14, E2.04). From his end Myer used all the power of his office to keep this definite truth from distracted inmates who sought counsel from the American Friends Service Committee and other outside organizations. On March 3, for example, Myer wired Coverley:

> FURTHER CONVERSATION WITH [CLARENCE] PICKETT AND FOLLOWING WIRE BEING SENT TO CHAIRMAN NISEI GROUP IMMEDIATELY SIGNED BY BOTH PICKETT AND CAREY [MCWILLIAMS] COLON QUOTE RE WIRE TO AMERICAN FRIENDS SERVICE COMMITTEE REGARDING REGISTRATION UPON FURTHER INQUIRY FIND THAT REGULATIONS ARE APPLICABLE TO AMERICAN CITIZENS OF JAPANESE ANCESTRY IN RELOCATION CENTERS WE THEREFORE STRONGLY ADVISE YOU TO REGISTER UNQUOTE
> [JERS, 67/14, R1.40]

Sent five days after the WRA knew definitely that Selective Service regulations were not applicable to their charges, this wire from AFSC Director Clarence Pickett and Carey McWilliams, elicited only after "further conversation," was deliberately misleading. Either Myer had made the two men privy to his official lie or he had simply conned them into perpetuating it.

At Tule Coverley clung to his end of the limb by never telling his charges the truth. On the contrary, he informed them in the *Tulean Dispatch* of March 2 that as a special concession to citizens who had not yet registered, they could continue to do so until March 10: "Those who have not registered by that date will be considered as having violated the orders of the War Department and War Relocation Authority and subject to such penalties as may be imposed." To this lie about "orders of the War Department," the project director added evasiveness about exactly what penalties would be imposed on Issei who refused to register, especially once he learned that their registration too was not compulsory even under WRA regulations. "Frankly," he complained to Myer, "I do not know how we are going to get out of this predicament without so great a loss of face that we would have no further control over the project" (March 6, 1943, JERS, 67/14, E2.04). Apparently not only Orientals dreaded losing face. Still, Coverley's and Myer's apprehensions about the risks of telling the truth were grounded in the reality of their predicament. Frank Shotaro Miyamoto, who was then in the camp as a member of the JERS team, put the probable consequences succinctly: "Had the evacuees learned that the maximum penalty for refusal to register was 90 days, the administration and those who cooperated in the registration would have become ridiculous in the eyes of the oppositionists" ("Crisis," JERS, 67/14, R20.36). Among those oppositionists, Masao K. had had the good sense to realize on his

Mount Abalone to the East of Tule Lake, n.d. This photograph of a painting by an unknown inmate shows the mountain, guard towers, and lighted fence topped by the customary barbed wire.
[Doctor Lewis A. Opler]

own that his keepers were lying to him before and after his arrest on March 5.

Not the combined forces of Myer, Coverley, their staffs, army recruiters, and army guards were ever sufficient to break the back of the resistance and "crack that thing." For all their attempts to terrorize an already victimized people through threats of long prison terms, show of armed might, false arrests and illegal jailings, censorship, forced labor, and lies, when the crisis subsided in late March, some 3,000 inmates still refused to register. Among them were 666 citizens. All told, the administration arrested and removed from the camp 140 inmates and returned most of them after their hearings; sent 6 aliens to Department of Justice internment camps; and shipped off 15 citizens—among them our 5 "ringleaders"—to the penal colony at Moab.

At the end of March the "trials" of the five (and of ten others) revealed the nature of WRA justice. All five were charged with the first of two counts and some were also charged with the second: (1) refusing to obey the project director's orders to register; (2) conspiring with others to impede registration, an act that was, among other things, "against the peace and dignity of the War Relocation Authority, an agency of the United States Government." Of the five, only Yoshio Y. (#4) pleaded not guilty to the first count, and "trial" on that single count against him was set forward until April 16 at 2:00 P.M. All the others pleaded guilty to refusing to register and received sentences ranging from sixty to the maximum of ninety days ("Crisis," JERS, 67/14, R20.36).

But for the flavor and character of the proceedings, let us follow Masao K. (#5) into the "Caucasian recreation hall" where they took place:

> That was the first time I saw the court in the center, but it must have been the regular W.R.A. project court. The U.S. flag was displayed in the front; judge, attorney and a few others were seated in front; and there were audience seats for public witnesses. When I was seated in front of the judge, Mr. [Paul] Fleming announced that he was acting in the capacity of a judge for Mr. Coverley and that Mr. O'Brien was acting as a defense attorney for W.R.A. . . .
>
> I was charged on one count . . . refusal to comply with the W.R.A. order to register. (Note the fact that nothing was mention[ed] about the War Department order!) I pleaded guilty of course. No lawyer or consultant was allowed for me to defend [myself], contrary to my expectation. It can hardly be said a hearing under the democratic form of government. Nevertheless it was true in this particular case.
>
> The judge communicated the sentence of two months in isolation camp or any place that the W.R.A. may designate, provided that the sentence be computed from the date of arrest.
>
> [JERS, 67/14, S1.20A]

That Wednesday, March 31, the "court" recessed at about 8:30 P.M.

By 9:00 P.M. the fifteen defendants—including Yoshio Y. (#4), who still had not had his "trial"—had been pushed into an enclosed truck and the rear doors had been padlocked from the outside. Dressed in their ordinary clothing with no overcoats or heavy jackets with them, the men assumed that they were being hauled back to their bunks in the smaller prison at the old CCC camp. But let us join Masao K. (#5) again and ride along:

> Until 1:30 o'clock in the next morning the truck sped with only one stop through very cold icy air. It was so cold that we shivered almost to death, because we were not told of such an unexpected journey and thus [were] unprepared. Even when we reached the small train depot at Doyle, California, we were not allowed to get off the truck to take a warm place in the depot's waiting room, despite our repeated request, while those Caucasian guards took themselves a warm place inside the building. We were told not to make any noise and to converse only in English, so that there would not be any trouble with the nearby residents. Not even a second could we sleep;

we had to keep on moving in order to keep ourselves warm. To such condition[s] we were exposed for more than five hours!! Was that the instruction given to those guards by Mr. Coverley? Whoever it may be, the person who is responsible for such inhumane treatment should have no excuse whatever morally and legally. . . .

At long last when we boarded . . . the Union Pacific train our destination was disclosed to be Moab Isolation camp in Utah.

[JERS, 67/14, S1.20A]

Therewith Masao K. and his mates joined the other inmates Myer had "stuck out in a CCC camp in the desert."

Only later did Masao K. learn from an item in the *Tulean Dispatch* of April 3, 1943, that Coverley had generously dismissed all outstanding charges against him and the fourteen other Tuleans, commuted their sentences to time served, and then had acted on orders of his superior:

Mr. Coverley had submitted records on these men to Director Dillon S. Myer in Washington for his action, following trials on Wednesday [March 31]. However, before Mr. Coverley had time to act on Mr. Fleming's recommendations, Director Myer determined that these men were so dangerous to the security of the Project that he ordered them removed to the permanent Isolation Center at Moab, Utah. They left the Project immediately after the last trial, at 8:15 P.M. Wednesday evening.

[JERS, 67/14, S1.20A]

Properly scornful of this clumsy cover story, Masao K. wrote Coverley demanding to know just how he could have presented records of the hearings to Myer in Washington and have received the latter's answer "between 8:30 o'clock P.M. and 8:50 o'clock P.M. on March 31, 1943"? Five months later he still had received no reply from the Tule director.

Again this canny victim drew the right conclusion: "Tracing the steps that were taken to handle us, I can say that there is not a speck of doubt that the whole scheme was carefully planned beforehand." All that was missing from what Masao K. had imaginatively inferred was the reason he and the others had been rushed off in the night and that was another nasty little secret he could have known nothing about: Myer was merely fulfilling, belatedly, his pledge to General DeWitt that I quoted a few paragraphs back, namely, that he would move "these people" to Moab "just as fast as he could."

2

Like the lie about "orders of the War Department," nasty little secrets have always been the earmarks of reformatories, Indian boarding

schools, jails, penitentiaries, and other enclosures containing binary societies of captors and captives. Just as in those other total institutions
of twenty-four-hour surveillance and control, in WRA concentration
camps knowledge of certain truths was the prerogative of the captors
and forbidden information for the captives. The power to hold their
bodies carried two correlatives: the power to punish and the power to
withhold knowledge of decisions that shaped their lives. Like the keepers in, say, the Federal Bureau of Prisons, Myer and his staff merged
legislative, executive, and judicial functions by arresting, judging, and
punishing inmates who allegedly disobeyed their orders and regulations.
Still less threatened by judicial restraints than these professional counterparts, Myer and his men could administer punishments not legiti-
mated by statutes, as we have seen, and not sanctioned by the general
social norm of treating each individual as an end in himself. Finally, like
these counterparts with their "holes" or closed cells, the WRA keepers
had to establish punishment pens that were out of sight. Secrecy also
became their prime solvent for moving waste through their human
sewers.

The physical remoteness of Tule Lake and Myer's other camps
screened off unwelcome scrutiny by the outside world. Unless granted
prior approval for a visit, any concerned citizen who collected his gas
coupons and drove all the way to a camp was confronted at the boundaries by barbed wire that kept inmates in and him out. So far distance
alone had discouraged most outsiders.

Inside, the keepers still had to find means to conceal punishment
from the rest of the inmates. Believing that they had to move fast, Myer
and Coverley had made use of the old CCC camp near Tule Lake. Yet
even apart from General DeWitt's opposition, this subcamp could only
serve as a makeshift. It was too open and too close to the main camp
to keep messages from being smuggled back and forth, and even censored letters carried their own revelations. It was also relatively too accessible to the meddlesome NCACLU in San Francisco. What if Ernest
Besig decided to face the ordeal of the trip and showed up one day
demanding to speak to the sequestered men? No, the safest bet was a
complete separation of "aggravated and incorrigible troublemakers"
from their families and potential counsel by dumping them far away in
the Indian country of the Southwest. First near Moab, Utah, a small
town nestled at the foot of cliffs and the towering La Sal Mountains,
and then at Leupp (pronounced "loop"), Arizona, the subagency

perched on the Little Colorado River at the edge of the Painted Desert, these camp outcasts would sink out of sight and out of mind in the old red sandstone buildings that had once confined some five hundred Navaho children. But Myer failed to reckon with his unusual subordinate I have already had occasion to quote.

According to his "Personal Narrative Report" (JERS, 67/14, S1.00), Francis S. Frederick had come out from New York City in the late summer of 1942 to work in the Federal Prison on Alcatraz Island, turned the job down upon arrival in San Francisco, and instead joined the WRA as an assistant chief of internal security in the camp at Gila River, Arizona. After several months in that position he had run afoul of his immediate superior, W. E. Williamson, and of the Gila River director, Leroy H. Bennett. As Regional Director E. Reeseman Fryer explained the case in a confidential letter to Myer, Frederick "is a good officer. However, he and Williamson form a combination that won't 'jell.' In my judgment Fredericks [sic] is a better officer than Williamson. . . . [and] should be transferred to another project. Future action . . . is indicated on Williamson" (February 10, 1943, JERS, 67/14, E2.04). Accordingly, Frederick was transferred and put in charge of internal security at Moab and later (April 27, 1943) at Leupp.

These biographical details matter, for at Gila River Frederick and his wife Jane had become friendly with Robert Spencer, a graduate student in anthropology who was working for Dorothy Swaine Thomas. About the same age and holding about the same irreverent view of WRA officials, the two men stayed in touch after they were both posted elsewhere. Frequently Frederick sent Spencer voluminous letters that amounted to a running account of developments inside the penal colony. Properly appreciative, Spencer acknowledged one batch of data with collective JERS thanks: "Like all the other materials I have been getting from you, we regard this as very valuable" (July 20, 1943; all their letters quoted below are in JERS, 67/14, S1.10). Frederick playfully identified his own role by signing off another long report as a worn-out informer: "Gettin' tired, so to hell with you and your guinea pigs—what am I saying? Am I not one of your choicest rodents?" (July 22, 1943). Myer and his staff might have said one of JERS's "choicest rats," had they known what he was doing—but let us say rather that he was a choice "mole" strategically placed behind the walls of their nastiest secret. In effect he was serving the Thomas team as an undercover agent, a wry turn of events given the earlier unsuccessful attempts of WRA officials to gain access to her confidential findings. Nothing more conclusively identified Myer's enclosures as concentration camps than the secrecy that spawned such spies and counterspies.

In his "Personal Narrative" Frederick recorded that he had gone to work for the WRA with "the ardent enthusiasm of a pioneer." Less loftily and more ironically, he had gone to work hoping his government job would keep him out of military service. No stranger himself to the arrogance of power, he liked working in the penal colony and even in 1946 still associated his "fondest memories of the agency . . . with the Isolation Center." On one occasion at Moab, he bragged,

> I enjoyed the unique position of passing a law [against "unlawful assembly"!]—by the powers vested in me as Acting Project Director—directing the arrest of twenty-one evacuees, presiding as judge in their individual trials, sentencing eight leaders to three months in jail [the Grand County Jail at Moab] and placing the others on probation. Besides being in charge of the jail, I was probation and parole officer. It has been said that the law mentioned in the foregoing was a deliberate design to goad the leaders into doing something for which they could be arrested. While I do not choose to enter into a discussion on this point at this time, I do recall having rescinded the same law within six hours after it was passed. Where else but WRA could one gain such extraordinary experience?

In America, where else indeed? Obviously Frederick had a sense of humor in an outfit not noted for that precious attribute.*

For all his mixed motives and capacity for cruelty, Frederick proved to be an invaluable channel of information. In his breezily effective style, he presented the Thomas team with shrewd portraits of WRA leaders. Raymond R. Best, another official from the Soil Conservation Service and the first director of the penal colony, he characterized as a "strong admirer of Myer and [Robert B.] Cozzens. The enthusiastic back-slapping Rotarian type—prone to jump at conclusions—susceptible to flattery but not a fool—soft hearted and takes the underdog's side. . . . He is a politician—former Republican county chairman—likes a drink oc-

---

*Not surprisingly, Frederick's charges did not find him very funny. In a recent interview (August 18, 1985), Harry Yoshio Ueno related that they used to call him "See Me" after his habit of fending them off by saying "See me later" when they came to him with grievances. In an unpublished reminiscence "I Was a Captive of the U.S. Government," Ueno has recounted how Frederick had him and four other inmates locked in a coffinlike box on the back of a flat-bed truck for the transfer from Moab to the new penal colony in Arizona. Wedged together in a five-by-six-foot space with only one small hole in back for air, the five men nearly suffocated and "the 11 hour long drive never seemed to end. In 36 years of my life this was the first time I had ever experienced such a painful, agonizing and helpless feeling. . . . I wouldn't transport any animal in this manner even if I knew they were going to be slaughtered."

casionally—very fine wife and family—former Marine and has a boy in the army." His successor, Paul G. Robertson, who took over at Leupp after Best left to become director at Tule Lake, was "the finest guy I have met yet in WRA. Honest, sincere, law trained, capable, and *likes* Japanese." By contrast Dillon S. Myer struck him as "one of the smoothest, suavest racketeers I have ever run across, and I know quite a few personally, and was probably selected because of his disarming speech and manners. He is fundamentally a politician which, in his case, makes him a racketeer for my money in his exploitation of this minority group for his own benefit and the benefit of others of his ilk such as Bennett, Cozzens, Best, etc." (Frederick to Spencer, August 20, December 9, 1943, JERS, 67/14, S1.10).

From his vantage point in the penal colony, Frederick came up with an insight of fundamental importance. Shortly after his arrival he wrote that "this business is nothing but the evacuation all over again. The camps had to clean house in a hurry and dumped them all [i.e., the refuse] here without any definite plans or ideas as to what to do with them. What some of these guys (W.R.A.) call dangerous is certainly questionable!" (Frederick to Spencer, April 20, 1943, JERS, 67/14, S1.10). Another letter revealed his keen awareness of the constitutional implications, as "many of them do have legally sound reasons for suit against the government and that is a problem not to be sneezed at. One might say what good will it do them but brother it becomes in reality a test of our constitution—an acid test" (Frederick to Spencer, December 9, 1943, JERS, 67/14, S1.10). Later the receipt of a letter from Myer strengthened his conviction that if the legality "of holding the Japs in camps" came to a head, he would be called as a key witness. As he wrote his wife:

> The best cases would naturally emanate from Leupp and Moab and there is a possibility that Robertson and Best notified the brass hats [i.e., Myer et al.] that I could probably be an important witness. Robertson was the one who really appreciated the position I was in and the possibilities the information I had could do for either side of the litigation. They little suspected or realized that Leupp was, in reality, the hub or the exchange for the whole intricate network of the entire system. I believe that they have now come to realize it. Discuss this with Spence and get his ideas. [Quoted in Jane Frederick to Robert Spencer, January 9, 1945, JERS, 67/14, S1.10]

Moab and then Leupp moved the other ten concentration camps over rough spots by serving precisely the same function for refractory citizens as the internment camps had for refractory aliens. And from the keepers' point of view, it had the great virtue of being pretty much their own secret. "Do you notice how it is never referred to in any publicity?" Frederick asked Spencer. "For example, reference is always made to the ten centers—Leupp makes eleven. I expected the Dies Committee to come here when they were making their investigations and so did the Japs. And were they ever prepared to tell them the works! But they never did come. I doubt if they know there is such a place which, if true, is fortunate for the WRA because they could really learn plenty here" (Frederick to Spencer, August 30, 1943, JERS, 67/14, S1.10).

Perhaps only Franz Kafka could have done justice to the daily nightmare within this American *Strafkolonie*, but Frederick caught reflections of its capricious tyranny in his inmate profiles. One "pure case of mistaken identity" was still seeking his release six months after the fact had been admitted. "Got another guy from Gila that called a Caucasian nurse an old maid. Such blasphemy!" Still another had come to Leupp as a "suspected troublemaker," but, "other than the possibility of his being a 'fat person with a beard,' which is hardly a crime unto itself, there is no evidence of just what he is suspected of having done."

From Manzanar came the father of four children, separated from them and his wife by an informer's accusations, but denied an opportunity to confront his accuser and submit evidence in his own behalf. Despite this, and despite the likelihood that he was yet another case of mistaken identity, the man "steadfastly believed in the democracy of these United States and is still a loyal American citizen. Such treatment would most certainly be a test of anyone's loyalty." With understandable exasperation, Frederick rhetorically asked Spencer "how in hell can you Americanize the Japs when Gestapo methods are used in sending them to Leupp—no warrants, no trials, no sentence, separated from their families, etc." (Frederick to Spencer, August 30, 1943, JERS, 67/14, S1.10).

On paper the WRA punitive system had a trace of due process. A docket was supposed to have accompanied each of the incoming prisoners, of whom there were sixty-seven in August 1943. The Leupp chief of internal security was assigned to study these, watch the men at work and at leisure, and then from their dockets and his analyses compile their case histories. These he submitted to the project director, who usually concurred in his findings and passed them on to Washington. There the Leupp Review Board, composed originally of Deputy Director Elmer M. Rowalt, Community Management Chief John H. Provinse, and Solicitor Philip M. Glick, reexamined these records and in turn submitted their recommendations to Myer for his final approval or disapproval. But in practice the system produced the absurdities we have just sampled, prisoners without dockets, without correct identification, without rhyme or reason beyond the keepers' arbitrariness.

With a professional jailer's disdain for such hit or miss confinements and with signs of sympathy for some of the men in his lockup, Frederick packed into his case histories more than enough dynamite to blow the lid off the whole mess. As he energetically documented, the cases fell into groups, six of which were in Leupp for reasons shared by their members (JERS, 67/14, S1.20A):

1. *The Manzanar Sixteen*—arrived January 11, 1943, to become the colony's first prisoners; allegedly connected with the events that included the beating of Fred Tayama and the subsequent revolt. Manzanar Director Ralph P. Merritt had assured them, in a letter dated January 8, 1943, that he had "been informed by Director Myer that each of you will be given a fair and speedy hearing." Eight months later that speedy justice was still beyond reach.

2. *The Gila Thirteen*—arrived February 18, 1943; charged with being members of the Gila Young People's Association. Given a charter by camp officials after a review of its constitution and bylaws, the organization was allowed to continue its activities even after the thirteen were transferred to Leupp. With such continuing official sanction, Frederick asked, "how can it be a crime to belong to it?" Understandably Gila Director Leroy H. Bennett developed the habit of referring to him, as he gleefully learned, as "that Goddamned Frederick."

3. *The Manzanar Ten*—arrived February 24, 1943; not charged with anything, but transferred as "suspected troublemakers" after having been fingered by individuals Frederick called "highly questionable informers." Later on we shall follow the case of Hisato K., one of these suspects.

4. *The Tule Fifteen*—arrived April 2, 1943; charged with refusing to register. This group included the five "ringleaders" we followed to the penal colony. Though they languished in Leupp months later, as Frederick observed, "yet there were still several thousand who refused to register and were not apprehended." Yoshio Y. (#4) still had not had his "trial" and nevertheless still served his indefinite sentence alongside all the others who had not been convicted of anything.

5. *The Tule Five*—arrived May 6, 1943; not charged with anything, but transferred after they had served sentences in the Modoc County Jail for attempted assault and battery. Apart from this first offense, Frederick could find no evidence whatsoever that they were "aggravated and incorrigible troublemakers."

6. *The Topaz Eleven*—arrived about July 1943; not charged with anything, but transferred after they had been interviewed by FBI agents. As Frederick explained to Spencer on July 22, 1943, Leupp Director "Best took it

upon himself about a week ago to interview some of the parents of these boys at Topaz and came back convinced that they were bullied by the FBI. . . . It does appear that the whole thing was much of a farce and the kids have taken a stand and feel that they have to stick to it. . . . One of the questions that was asked them was—if an authorized agent of the Jap gov't. ordered you to commit sabotage against this country, would you do it? Do you worship or feel that Hirohito is a divine person? This was another one."

7. *Miscellaneous*—this odd lot included individuals who arrived at various times. Among them was the Gila man who called "a Caucasian nurse an old maid" and another who "drew some pictures that did not meet with their approval. No leader, no organizer, merely an individual act. They gave him a hearing (some joke, these hearings) and sentenced him to Tule Lake via Leupp." From Heart Mountain came the head chef and the warehouse-chief at the camp hospital, charged with insubordination and leading a walk-out. Said the pro-American, but bewildered, former chef: "I just can't understand why I was arrested for insubordination. If I were guilty of this, why didn't they fire me from my job? I never knew that I could be arrested for walking out on my job."

And so these were the tens and fifteens and scores the WRA interned in the old Indian school behind the customary props—barbed wire, guard towers, and, in this instance, 150 military police to watch over less than half that number of unarmed outcasts.

Now, from half a continent away did National Director Myer know of the suffering in his penal colony? Of the enforced solitude, lack of meaningful work, separation from families, denial of heterosexual intercourse, and other deprivations made all the worse by the psychic strain of serving indefinite sentences, of doing time without end? As head of the WRA, of course, he was ultimately responsible for policy and the acts of his men, but that aside—did he have personal knowledge of the daily degradation and mortification at Moab and Leupp? Yes, he did, and had that personal knowledge from the beginning.

On February 12, 1943, Moab Director Best had informed Myer by letter of an outburst among the Manzanar Sixteen. After each had received a letter from the national director that morning, "a window was broken, a fire was started, one cook[']s bed was turned over and he had been pushed around so I decided that I must act and act fast before some actual bloodshed got started in earnest. . . . Not getting any definite decision in their case, is what keeps them constantly irritated and hard to handle." Best had already isolated four men in a separate barracks under constant guard, for "these men must not be allowed to come in contact with the balance of this group or some one will get killed." Myer had thus been informed directly of the lacerating pressures under which these men were doing their hard time, "waiting for a hearing that never came," as Best put it (NA, RG 210).

In the other ten camps hearings were explicitly ruled out a few days later by Myer in his confidential administrative instruction (unnumbered) on "Removal from Relocation Centers of Aggravated and Incorrigible Troublemakers": "In no case should the investigation be permitted to become a formal hearing" (February 16, 1943, FBI 62-69030). Long months later, prodded by the well-founded worries of Solicitor Glick over their legal position and alarmed over the abandon with which camp directors dumped their problems in Leupp, Myer rescinded the unnumbered instruction and replaced it with Administrative Instruction No. 95, which called for a hearing before an inmate was transferred. In a covering letter to his staff in the field, he explained their new policy:

> Previously some of us had conceived the isolation procedure as being primarily one to facilitate the maintenance of law and order within the relocation centers, necessary because of the unique conditions within the centers. It was not conceived as a punishment for the transferee. As we watch the isolation procedure in operation and see more clearly the implications of isolation, however, it is becoming increasingly evident that transfer to the isolation center is a punishment. This being the case, it is hardly appropriate to provide a punishment without giving the transferee a hearing and an opportunity to present his side of the case, if he has one.
> [June 5, 1943, JERS, 67/14, S1.10]

Already labeled a "transferee," the inmate was about to go even if he had "his side of the case." As Frederick acidly commented, "some joke, these hearings." Moreover, in emergencies camp directors could telephone Myer for permission to effect immediate transfers without hearings, an escape hatch that had "promiscuous use" (Frederick to Paul G. Robertson, August 21, 1943, JERS, 67/14, S1.10).

But what about those prisoners currently in Leupp who had been punished for months without ever having had their hearings? Among them were Hisato K. and the other members of the Manzanar Ten. On June 18, 1943, Myer wrote Leupp Director Best that he had approved the Board of Review's conclusion that the ten should stay in the colony. Their removal from Manzanar had been recommended by unnamed persons in that camp: *"The factual basis for these recommendations is not known and cannot be readily ascertained.* Under the circumstances, however, I believe that their removal is proper" (NA, RG 210; emphasis added). Another case in point was Yoshio Y. of the Tule Fifteen. On

June 22, 1943, Myer wrote Coverley that the Board of Review had advised him that the men he named—a list that included Masao I. (#1), Kentaro T. (#2), Saburo M. (#3), Yoshio Y. (#4), and Masao K. (#5)—had defective dockets:

> *The present dockets do not present adequate evidence to make it clear that the evacuees were appropriately transferred to Leupp, inasmuch as the dockets do not establish that these evacuees were "aggravated trouble makers."*
> . . . I have noted, however, that these men are all now living at Leupp, and that you have stated that you feel that their presence at Tule Lake would be detrimental to the internal security of the Project. I believe, therefore, that it is best for these men to remain at Leupp until we can determine whether they should *remain indefinitely at Leupp*, be transferred to another relocation center, or be transferred to the segregation center on its establishment.
> [NA, RG 210; emphasis added]

In fine, Myer knew that some inmates had been sent to Leupp without hearings; knew that being there was a punishment; and knew that the WRA had *no* evidence to justify their imprisonment there in the first place. Under these circumstances, however, he believed it "best for these men" to remain in the punishment pen for the time being and perhaps indefinitely.

Whirling up out of the desert air, Frederick's findings cut short this indefinite idyl. Matters no proper "Caucasian" would put on paper had been highlighted in the files he presented to Paul G. Robertson upon his arrival. "In reviewing the dockets of these evacuees," the new Leupp director wrote Myer a few days later, "I was very much amazed at the lack of evidence I had believed necessary to warrant a transfer to this center. . . . I expect to be in Washington around the latter part of August and would like to discuss these cases with you personally" (August 11, 1943, NA, RG 210). Robertson's letter arrived in the WRA headquarters just after Acting Solicitor Lewis A. Sigler had finished dictating an anxious memorandum for Solicitor Glick: "We have had reports from several sources indicating that the Project Director at Leupp does not know why some of the men were sent there, that the men themselves don't know why they were sent there, and that requests for information go unanswered. . . . I should like to see a reexamination made of the advisability of continuing the Leupp Center. I think it is an un-American institution, corresponds to and is premised on Gestapo methods" (August 14, 1943, NA, RG 210). At the end of the month Frederick informed Spencer that "Robertson is now in Washington and has taken an armful of my case histories which he says are so hot that there may be kick-backs but that he is going to show them to them anyway." Ten days later he reported that the Leupp director had returned from seeing Myer and his aides: "He went armed with my case histories which aroused them unfavorably toward me but still produced the desired results" (August 30, September 9, 1943, JERS, 67/14, S1.10).

The brash young officer could lay claim to having changed history—a little bit. Frederick had put the "WRA on the spot legally," as he confided to Spencer, and thereby made a crucial contribution to the closing of Leupp. Without his case histories, the out-of-sight prisoners might have languished indefinitely in the old Indian school as jailer Myer patiently refrained from tempering injustice with mercy.

Moving swiftly for bureaucrats, John H. Provinse and Philip M. Glick formally recommended "the liquidation of Leupp" and then added a prudent counsel: "The Leupp Center is not to be explained as a mistake, despite the fact that it was unfortunate that such a center had to be established" (Leupp Review Committee to Myer, October 12, 1943, NA, RG 210). Their counsel was superfluous. Certainly no less than his subordinates, Myer had made standard operating procedure of the old army motto "Cover your ass."

Leupp was to have been shut down without fanfare on November 5, 1943, but the pull-out was delayed for a month by what WRA officials called "The Tule Lake Incident" (*UA*, pp. 316–21). The skeleton of that, with the bones more or less rearranged, appeared in Myer's chronology:

> October 15—A truck accident, which killed one evacuee, led to a farm strike at Tule Lake.
>
> November 1—A mass demonstration was staged at Tule Lake for the benefit of the National Director, who was there on a visit.
>
> November 4—An outbreak of violence occurred at Tule Lake between WRA internal security staff and a group of dissident young evacuees. Troops were called in, and the center was transferred to military control. [*UA*, p. xxviii]

Not surprisingly in the light of the short-fused time bomb mentioned earlier, there had been an explosion, and part of the fallout was martial law in the "Segregation Center." Not until December 2—eight months to the day since we followed Masao K. (#5) and the rest of the Tule Fifteen into the penal colony—was the WRA ready to pull out the remaining fifty-two prisoners and put them aboard a train in Winslow, Arizona.

3

The trouble with skeletal chronologies, spent metaphors, and prisoner tallies is that they leave individual inmates faceless, hidden under masks of supposedly objective data. Let us introduce ourselves, therefore, to yet another of the "problem boys," as Myer called vexatious citizens, and tag along with him from one jail to another. Maybe with a few of the particulars from his case history and a bit of luck we can put a face on deprivation and mortification.

Selected troublemaker.   Kibei; no declared religion; seven years in a Japanese grammar school and almost three in Los Angeles high schools; single—Hisato K. had worked in his mother's restaurant before the uprooting. In the early morning hours of February 19, 1943, he and the rest of the Manzanar Ten had been picked up as "suspected trouble-makers" and taken to the jail in nearby Independence, California. After three days in that lockup they were carted off to Moab, where they arrived on February 24. Only nineteen years old and "unusually healthy and full of spirit," as Frederick noted on August 9 in Hisato K.'s case history, he had had trouble adjusting to life in the penal colony:

> It doesn't require much imagination to picture a boy of this type being apprehended . . . held in jail for a few days, and then whisked off to a new and strange environment without being told what he was supposed to have done or without being given a trial or opportunity to defend himself. Upon arriving at Moab, he saw a small area enclosed in barbed wire with armed guards patrolling the fences. Not knowing why he was sent here, nor how long he would be required to stay, together with the reaction that must have been his when he saw the lay-out of the camp, all had its effect. . . . There is no doubt in the mind of the writer that he was just plain angry at the W.R.A. and everyone connected with it.
>
> [JERS, 67/14, S1.20A]

In view of his only having been arrested on suspicion, of his tender age, and of his having seemingly "learned much since he has been in Moab and Leupp," Frederick recommended his release to Tule Lake: "Further exposure to life in the Isolation Center might destroy any hope for rehabilitation in this case." But in Myer's judgment, as we have seen, it was "proper" for this suspect to stay in Leupp. Further exposed for four long months, Hisato K. gained a "release" of sorts when armed guards put him on the train in Winslow on December 2.

"The trip to Tule Lake was a very interesting one," Leupp Director

Leupp Penal Colony, 1943. "Suspected troublemaker" Hisato K. stands at the far left of a cluster of inmates that includes Harry Yoshio Ueno (right front), through whose courtesy this photograph is reprinted.

Robertson wrote Frederick, who by then was a staff sergeant in the military police:

> I sincerely regret that you were not able to accompany us and remain to assist in the rehabilitation. . . . Our train was five hours late into Stockton so we missed connections and were scheduled to leave Stockton at 7:30 A.M. The train was so over loaded when it arrived that they refused to hook our cars on so we remained there until 7:45 that evening. The fellows were so anxious to have some Chinese food that . . . [with two assistants] I went down in town and ordered $65.00 worth of food. They were so grateful. I also permitted them to detrain at Stockton, under guard, for about two hours and stretch their legs. . . . Oh yes, just after you left I received a telegram from Washington saying that our request for deferment for you came too late for them to take any action.
>
> [December 27, 1943, JERS, 67/14, S1.10]

At Tule Lake ten of the fifty-two "boys" went into the military stockade for an indefinite stay, among them Hisato K. and four companions "because they were the Manzanar dead end group who might be easily led in case of further trouble." One of the ten told Robertson that he and the other "boys in the stockade felt like I had betrayed them and they had lost confidence. I assured him that the Army was responsible for them being there and that I had recommended release of the entire group but he would not believe me." Hisato K. was in for more rehabilitation.

"Apparently things are in very bad shape at Tule," Robertson reported in masterful understatement. The army had built up its forces to about 1,200 men, with eight tanks and tear gas; 300 guards were in the camp itself, with 4 armed soldiers stationed at every block; 5 or 6 radio cars patrolled the intervening roads and the periphery (John P. Frank to Undersecretary Abe Fortas, March 9, 1944, NA, RG 48). After the army moved in following the so-called riot of November 4, suspected "troublemakers" had been picked up at all hours of the day and night—209 in November and 107 in December—and placed in what the WRA euphemistically called "Area B" or the "Surveillance Area." Barracks-to-barracks searches for "contraband" occurred almost daily. Curfew was from 7:00 P.M. to 6:00 A.M. The administration buildings and hospital in the "Caucasian" area had been blocked off from the nonwhite inmates by manproof fences. Hisato K. and the other men from Leupp could not have been cheered by those fences spiked with barbed wire, the *four* gates they had to pass through, the guard towers, the powerful searchlights at night, the unceasing roar of jeeps and squad cars, all of which spread terror and made the very air breathe "mistrust and suspicion," as we shall hear from one sober witness who visited the camp a short while later.

Now, "Area B"—with the rest of the camp designated "Area A"—was in harsh reality the stockade, the tight inner prison that became Hisato K.'s new home. According to the WRA's official "History of Area B," the rules mandated that residence of any individual therein "shall be for an indefinite period." It "was situated at approximately the same location northwest of the hospital for the entire period of its existence, November 5, 1943, to August 24, 1944. [The WRA took over the stockade on May 24, though the army continued to man the watchtowers.] It grew in size from one Army tent to five barracks, a mess-hall and a bathhouse. The final site covered about two-thirds of an acre. It was enclosed by a high wire fence" (September 12, 1944, JERS, 67/14, R12.15). Under twenty-four-hour surveillance from the watchtowers by soldiers armed with submachine guns, the high fence was topped by the usual barbed wire and brightly lighted at night. All mail going into and coming out of the stockade was subject to strict censorship. No visitors were permitted except by permission of the Tule director. When Hisato K. joined the stockade prisoners, about forty were jammed into each of the five barracks in space built to house twenty at most. None of the barracks had laundry facilities. The army—and later the WRA—conducted regular "roll calls," or prisoner counts, and disciplined supereminent "troublemakers" by placing them in the tents that had been left standing. Called the "bull pen," the flimsy tents were, of course, unheated and scant protection for bunks placed directly on the ground. Inside inmates shivered on these bunks with no extra clothing and with only one or two blankets to cover what one of them, Tokio Yamane, identified as "a life and death struggle for survival" (CWRIC, *Personal Justice Denied* [1982], p. 247).

In all likelihood the cold was biting that New Year's Eve, by which date Hisato K. had been in the stockade for twenty-five days. In the afternoon the army commander inspected the mess hall, found it not to his liking, and ordered two inmates placed in the "tent stockade on bread and water until conditions were remedied," according to an FBI report. "He then inquired if there were any others present who desired to join . . . [prisoners X and Y]. The Japanese talked briefly among themselves and then all stepped forward out of line and presented themselves for removal to the tents" (N. J. L. Pieper to J. C. Strickland, January 25, 1944, FBI 62-70564). Angered by their forwardness and his predicament, since he "could not take care of all of them in the tents,"

Lieutenant Colonel Verne Austin confiscated the cigarettes, nuts, fruit, candy, and the like in their personal possession and ordered them all placed on bread and water for twenty-four hours. Thus began a hunger strike, precipitated by Austin's bread-and-water order, but stemming from the prisoners' root grievance that they were doing indefinite time with no assurance of ever being released.

This holiday tableau yields a glimpse of Hisato K. behind the man-proof fence. He had to have stepped forward to raise the colonel's ire, since all the "Japanese" did. He had to have signed the prisoners' petition, since all the 199 men in the stockade did. It read as follows:

As of Supper
December 31, 1943

> We the undersigned have voluntarily vowed to undergo hunger strike until such time as everyone here in the stockade is released back to the Colony simultaneously and unconditionally. [FBI 62-70564]

Hisato K. thus began the New Year with a hunger strike that ended at suppertime on January 6, 1944, when the prisoners collectively decided "there was little use in continuing" in the face of official intransigence. The WRA "History of Area B" insinuated that spokesmen for the prisoners had been "cheating by eating fruit, candy and vitamin pills" but then added this laconic observation: "During the hunger strike the Army held a medical inspection daily of the men. Some were growing weak at the end of the week's demonstration" (September 12, 1944, JERS, 67/14, R12.15).

A month or so later *Life* magazine sent Carl Mydans to Tule Lake for a pictorial report on the "Segregation Center." Having just returned after spending sixteen months himself in Japanese internment camps, Mydans was keenly interested in the stockade and introduced his report with a photograph of smiling Lieutenant Colonel Verne Austin and another of five "pressure boys" who were "among the 155 trouble makers imprisoned in the stockade." Thanks to the cooperation of the WRA and the army—not everyone could hope to have his picture in *Life!*— the photographer was permitted to enter their secret place and in one barracks, as chance would have it, encountered Hisato K. strumming a guitar and singing *Home on the Range*. Mydans's note of surprise set off the scene perfectly:

> He sang it like an American. There was no Japanese accent. He looked at me the same way I guess I looked at a Japanese official when he came to check on me at Camp Santo Tomás in Manila. At the back of my mind was

"What It Feels Like to Be a Prisoner," March 20, 1944.
[Carl Mydans, *Life* Magazine, © 1944 Time Inc.]

the thought, "Come on, get it over and get out. Leave me alone." This boy felt the same way. He was just waiting, killing time.

[*Life*, March 20, 1944, p. 31]

His memorable snapshot of "this young Japanese 'pressure boy'" was fittingly captioned "What It Feels Like to Be a Prisoner." By then Hisato K. was a natural for the part—for over a year he had been Myer's prisoner in jails, penal colonies, and the stockade, all the while uncharged, unheard, untried, and unconvicted.

A couple of months later Field Secretary Thomas R. Bodine of the National Japanese American Student Relocation Council came to Tule Lake and found the air filled with "mistrust and suspicion." In a long, sympathetic report back to his office in Philadelphia, he called the stockade "a tragic place" that confined many who did not belong there. Especially moving was the sight of

> mothers and children pressing against the barbed wire of the camp [i.e., "Area A"]—peering across . . . [the] parking lot to the stockade where the husbands and fathers lean on the barbed wire there. Waving—trying to shout across. The children jumping up and down and waving their arms to show that they're o.k. and in good health. And then the soldiers stopping them, on the ground that they are signaling secret and subversive messages. And, then, the children and mothers standing still just looking. And the husbands and fathers just looking back across the 100 feet [or 100 yards, actually].

Now that Bodine was at Tule he planned to reread Mydans's praiseworthy *Life* article:

> Particularly neat was the photo of the men in the Stockade. It just shows in their faces how gentle and innocuous most of them are. The photo of the boy strumming the guitar haunts me. There are so *many* here who look at me like that as I wander around.

[April 4, 1944, JERS, 67/14, R1.40]

The sensitive field secretary was right. The photograph of Hisato K. was haunting. It put a face on endemic deprivation and mortification.

In the meantime, if Myer and Tule Director Best did not find Hisato K.'s photograph haunting—and they did not—they did find highly disturbing the relative openness of their secret place. They did not fancy the sight of distraught families pressing up against the barbed wire and worried that individuals might, however remote the possibility, wave messages across the parking lot. Having soldiers and later internal security officers drive away mothers and children was a nuisance and having them shoot over their heads to frighten them away, as on occasion

"Five Japs . . . among 155 Trouble Makers Imprisoned in the Stockade," March 20, 1944. "Here they are answering roll call" or, less euphemistically, undergoing prisoner count.

[Carl Mydans, *Life* Magazine, © 1944 Time Inc.]

they did, was worse—should the shootings touch off another "incident," who knew what might happen?

Like an insomniac welcoming the return of a bad dream, Myer went ahead with plans to move all his prisoners back to Leupp. This time it would be for "the super-disloyal," as an Interior Department official put it (John P. Frank to Undersecretary Abe Fortas, March 9, 1944, NA, RG 48). On April 11, 1944, Myer informed John J. McCloy of the arrangements then underway: "WRA has planned to administer the Leupp Center as a sub-center of Tule Lake and initially to transfer there approximately 175 segregants now held in the stockade at Tule Lake. It is contemplated that the number necessary to maintain at the Leupp

Center will vary, depending upon the conduct of the segregees at both centers" (NA, RG 210). From Washington two weeks later Secretary Harold L. Ickes formally announced the reopening of Leupp (*San Francisco Chronicle*, April 27, 1944) but then three months later announced that the WRA had cancelled these plans (*Newell Star*, July 20, 1944). What had happened? In unsettling language, the WRA's official history of the stockade offered this explanation: as the months passed "the prospect of liquidating the entire population of the isolation area grew strong enough to cause the abandonment of these plans." More probably the case histories of that "Goddamned Frederick," as their former internal security chief was unaffectionately called, had made Leupp still too hot for reuse as a punishment pen.

Whatever the obscurities surrounding this turnabout, the record makes this much clear. Myer sought to reopen a penal colony his own assistant solicitor had stigmatized as "premised on Gestapo methods." When that failed, he did the next best thing. In early July WRA officials had workers place large pieces of beaverboard on the manproof fence to put an end to the touching scenes of prisoners and their loved ones waving to each other across the parking lot. If the "pressure boys" could not be put out of mind in the Tule stockade, they could at least be put out of sight.

Yet the very next month, August 1944, Myer was forced to open the gates and let every last one of his prisoners walk through the manproof fence into the relative freedom of the main camp. Why? And tied to that was the gnawing prior question: How had Myer gotten away with it so long? How had he managed to hold innocent citizens in durance vile for so many months without legal challenges to his authority to do so? To find an answer to this root question, we must temporarily leave Tule, return to the East, and go back to the beginning of the chief jailer's extraordinary alliance with leading civil libertarians.

CHAPTER VII

Jailer

We are fighting for the principle of individual rights.
　　　　　—*Dillon S. Myer,*
　　　　　　"Address . . . ," June 19, 1945

In the fall of 1943 Morton Grodzins of the JERS staff had interviewed Myer in Washington and found the chief captor in an expansive mood. Yes, he had worried from the beginning about "due process" in the penal colony. Neither he nor any other WRA official had known what Moab was going to be, "a jail, a rehabilitation camp, or what. We still don't know about Leupp." It was still a place for "troublemakers" against whom, "speaking very frankly, we don't have enough evidence to take into civil courts." No, he had never liked "the Leupp idea" and hoped "to be able to get rid of it someday":

> Now don't [put] me on the spot about the legality of Leupp. I have said from the first that it's illegal and I still think so. I'm not at all proud of Leupp even though it has been effective. At first, we weren't even giving hearings to those that were sent there. Now, of course, we are. But that doesn't improve things very much at all. At least, though, I did one thing before I gave the O.K. sign for Moab. That is, I got Roger Baldwin and Alexander Meiklejohn into this office and told them what we were going to do. I told them that it was a purely emergency matter and I told them frankly why it was necessary. I also told them to hold off any action—or at least, if I didn't do it that directly, I indicated that we needed their sympathetic understanding in the whole process. We have always been very cordial in our relations with the Civil Liberties group, and both men showed a fine understanding.
> 　　　　　[Grodzins, "Myer Interview," September 29, 1943,
> 　　　　　　　　　　　　　　　　　JERS, 67/14, E2.10]

Myer's mellow confidences set another scene worthy of a *Life* photographer.

In addition to the smiling, but earnest, Myer, "speaking very frankly," the fanciful photograph I have in mind would portray two improbable confidants: Roger Baldwin, the erstwhile protégé of Emma Goldman, and himself an avowed "philosophical" anarchist, had founded the American Civil Liberties Union in 1920. According to his self-description, he was "the only man who ever made a professional career out of defending the Bill of Rights." Alexander Meiklejohn, after the war an untiring advocate of the First Amendment as an absolute guarantee of free speech and press, was the legendary former president of Amherst College (1912–23), presumably fired because of his devotion to academic freedom. The legend below the snapshot of this bizarre scene would explain that these two celebrated libertarians were extending to the head jailer their fine understanding and sympathetic sanction of his admittedly illegal penal colony. Placed alongside "What It Feels Like to Be a Prisoner," it might have been no less fittingly captioned "A Jailer's Dream."

From all appearances the organization that Baldwin once characterized as "the watchdog for the underdog" had declined by World War II into a toothless and barkless old age. An instance of the national ACLU's cringing posture emerged in a letter from three of its officers to Lieutenant General John L. DeWitt of the Western Defense Command. Sent over the signatures of John Haynes Holmes, the liberal clergyman who was chairman of the board of directors, General Counsel Arthur Garfield Hays, and Director Baldwin, the writers assured the general that, although they were opposed to "wholesale" evacuation, "we cannot refrain from expressing to you our congratulations on so difficult a job accomplished with a minimum of hardship, considering its unprecedented character. Never before were American military authorities confronted with an evacuation of this magnitude; and it is testimony to a high order of administrative organization that it was accomplished with so comparatively few complaints of injustice and mismanagement" (November 3, 1942, CHS 3580). Baldwin enclosed the letter with a covering note to Ernest Besig in San Francisco: "If you think this is not entirely improper, will you forward this and advise us?" Besig obliged, but curtly advised Baldwin that he had "better keep your letter of thanks for a form letter. In the years to come there may be many humane American army officers engaged in establishing ghettos" (November 7, 1942, CHS 3580). And a little later Besig apologized to Norman Thomas, the democratic socialist who was also on the ACLU board of directors, for having let the letter to General DeWitt get by him: "It's quite true that

Ernest Besig in San Francisco, 1945.
 [E. Besig]

the evacuation was carried out very smoothly, but we often come across officials who are not vicious in violating civil liberties, and this is the first time we've congratulated them upon not being vicious" (November 17, 1942, CHS 3580). This exchange over the dismal letter to DeWitt revealed differences in outlooks and temperaments that contributed to the protracted conflict between Baldwin and Besig, and between their respective ACLU offices in New York and San Francisco.

In the early months following Pearl Harbor nary a warning yelp came from the New York office as events audibly and visibly moved toward what the ACLU would denounce one day in 1943, long and safely after the fact, as "the worst single wholesale violation of civil rights of American citizens in our history." Not until March 2, 1942, eleven days *after* Roosevelt signed Executive Order 9066, did Baldwin speak out for the union, perfunctorily criticizing the order, but accepting its legitimacy: it was, he said, "undoubtedly legal in principle, but may readily result in illegal action" ([Northern California] *American Civil Liberties Union-News*—hereafter *ACLU-News*—March 9, 1942). Two weeks later he appealed to Roosevelt directly in a letter that urged modification of the order so that citizens and aliens alike could have individual hearings and thereby "minimize injustice" (Press Release, March 16, 1942, CHS).

Although at first the New York office had invited a legal test of exclusion, it changed that policy after four months of acrimonious debate, with the board of directors split into two definite factions, one led by Norman Thomas and the other by Whitney North Seymour, a Wall Street lawyer who gave the war effort precedence over civil liberties. By a two-to-one joint vote (51 to 26) the board and the national committee accepted Seymour's assertion that Roosevelt's order was constitutional. To implement this decision Baldwin drafted a statement, called the Seymour resolution, and ultimately accepted by the warring factions, that committed the ACLU not to participate, "except where fundamentals of due process are denied—in cases where, after investigation, there are grounds for belief that the defendant is cooperating with . . . the enemy." In the *Christian Century* a month later the discouraged Thomas bewailed this spectacle of individuals boasting of their liberalism while taking the lead "in justifying the presidential assumption of dictatorial power" (59 [July 29, 1942]: 929).

In San Francisco Ernest Besig also had to contend with those Thomas called "totalitarian liberals." When polled, a slight plurality of NCA-CLU members (120 to 117) and of its executive committee (9 to 8) were of the opinion that the union should not challenge the exclusion (*ACLU-News*, April 1942; Besig to Baldwin, March 21, 1942, CHS 3580). At a meeting of the committee on April 12, 1942, for instance, Alexander Meiklejohn voted against a motion to test General DeWitt's curfew orders and even voted against another to test his contraband regulations (data on this and other meetings are in the minutes, CHS 3580). At this meeting Meiklejohn was granted a leave of absence—we shall encounter him again in Washington—and afterward Besig managed to swing the committee around, so that on June 4, 1942, he could be instructed to provide legal defense for Fred Toyosaburo Korematsu, "citizen of Japanese extraction, arrested for remaining illegally within a Military Zone." In response to notification of the Seymour resolution by the New York office, the committee adopted the following motion on July 2, 1942: "a) that the new national policy be followed in any future cases; b) that in view of the reliance of the local branch on existing policy when it intervened in the Korematsu case, we cannot in good conscience withdraw from that case at this late date."

Baldwin and his board tried requests, instructions, and threats, but never budged Besig and his committee from their commitment to Korematsu. Baldwin began by requesting them politely to withdraw from the case. Besig replied in a letter to Clifford Forster, a staff attorney in the New York office and the national director's right-hand man: "We don't intend to trim our sails to suit the Board's vacillating policy. Surely the Corporation's members could not have intended us to be faithless to our client" (July 8, 1942, CHS 3580).

Acting Chairman Walter Frank shot back a telegram from New York: "OVERWHELMING VOTE OF NATIONAL COMMITTEE ON THE WEST COAST ORDER IS A MANDATE LAYING DOWN POLICY WHICH MUST BE FOLLOWED UNDER BY LAWS BY ALL AFFILIATED COMMITTEES" (July 10, 1942, CHS 3580). As the controversy boiled over into the autumn, Frank went over Besig's head to the Right Reverend Edward L. Parsons, the Episcopalian bishop who was chairman of the NCACLU executive committee, urging him to "conform" to national policy in handling Korematsu's appeal:

> Your attorneys could file a brief amicus which would not raise the issue of the underlying presidential power and would raise only the points authorized under our national policy. Personal counsel can, of course, raise whatever points he may desire. . . . We ask you now that in the handling of the case on appeal both in the briefs and in publicity the position of the Union be made clear, as distinguished from contentions which may be made on behalf

of the defendant by his own counsel. *It should be emphasized that the Union does not attack the underlying presidential power.*
[November 9, 1942, CHS 3580; emphasis added]

Replying for the bishop, Besig restrainedly pointed out that Korematsu had no money for legal fees, no counsel other than Wayne M. Collins, who had taken on the case for the NCACLU, and no place to turn after having been assured "before he accepted our help that in the event he was convicted, we would undertake an appeal, if necessary, because we regarded his as a test case. Our policy at the time conformed to your own" (November 11, 1942, CHS 3580).

And so the contention continued on into the next year and the next—but we already have before us ample evidence to lay to rest the misleading claims of Baldwin's successors on this score. On November 2, 1981, for instance, Edward J. Ennis appeared before the Commission on Wartime Relocation and Internment of Civilians as spokesman for the union and testified that, "as soon as it was known that an evacuation program was being considered, the ACLU, both the national organization with its headquarters in New York, and its West Coast affiliates, immediately, vigorously and continuously opposed the evacuation as unnecessary and unconstitutional."* On the contrary, after initial inertness the national organization continuously and with relative vigor did precisely the opposite.

In reality, with the passage of the Seymour resolution the national ACLU's policy on constitutional test cases became precisely that of the Japanese American Citizens League: *"unalterably opposed"* (see p. 69). It was a sameness that was not happenstance. Files seized by the Costello HUAC subcommittee showed Mike Masaoka bragging about conferring "at great length" with, among others, Roger Baldwin (*Los Angeles Times*, June 20, 1943). The FBI summary of Masaoka's testimony before the subcommittee noted that he had been questioned about "a conference he had attended at which there were present Roger Nash Baldwin of the American Civil Liberties Union, Mr. Dillon Myer, another person associated with Mr. Baldwin [almost certainly Alexander Meiklejohn], and some person from the Department of Justice" (memorandum of D. M. Ladd, July 3, 1943, FBI 62-69030). Headed in the

---

*See CWRIC, Testimony, Edward J. Ennis, Washington, D.C., November 2, 1981. As if to demonstrate personally the identity of aims and the intimacy of personnel of the national ACLU and the JACL, the former Justice Department officer became an attorney for both organizations after the war: "Ennis, in 1952, became a special Washington counsel for the JACL's Anti-Discrimination Committee and the Washington JACL office" (*YoI*, pp. 323–24).

same direction, Baldwin and Masaoka conferred and then coordinated their policies and efforts. Indeed, Baldwin was one of the half-dozen members of Masaoka's "informal, unofficial advisory committee," as Bill Hosokawa characterized it in *Nisei* (p. 382), a group that included Clarence Pickett of the American Friends Service Committee and Norman Thomas of the Post War World Council. Obviously, Masaoka listened more attentively to Baldwin than to Thomas. And since both Baldwin and Masaoka sought to harmonize their policies with Dillon Myer's, the consequence was the formation of a national ACLU-JACL-WRA line.

On leave from the San Francisco committee, Alexander Meiklejohn joined forces with Baldwin to become the key link between the New York board and Myer's headquarters. Slim, bright-eyed, and energetic, the self-proclaimed Kantian idealist sent reports back to the NCACLU that amounted to a sort of "Dr. Meiklejohn Goes to Washington." In the summer of 1942 he wrote Besig that he had been talking about him with WRA Solicitor Philip M. Glick:

> Perhaps you saw in the National Board minutes that they have arranged with me to act for them in Washington on questions about the Japanese relocation. I've been trying to get a grip on the problem and have seen a lot of people. Tomorrow night I take dinner with Jack McCloy, Asst. Sec. of War, who seems to be near the bottom of things. He's one of my favorite Amherst boys [*cum laude*, 1916] whom I used to lick at tennis . . . and so I'm likely to get the low-down. . . . Between you and me, I didn't like Glick, and I know that a lot of other people don't like him either. . . . I hope to see Roger [Baldwin] on Thursday to talk over the whole matter. . . . Glick told me he leaves today. . . . He may ask you and Bishop Parsons to sit in [on] some of those [WRA] meetings [in San Francisco]. . . . He is very eager to avoid "litigation," and hopes we won't initiate or back it.
>
> [August 4, 1942, CHS 3580]

The next night and other nights the apprentice lobbyist broke bread with his good old Amherst boy: "Last night I had dinner with Jack McCloy, Assistant Secretary of War, who is one of my best student friends from old Amherst days. But I guess I told you that" (to Besig, September 10, 1942, CHS 3580). Indeed he had told him that, but three weeks later understandably did not bother to tell him about the letter in which McCloy had nearly demanded that camp inmates be treated as "guinea pigs" from which the government could learn something useful (McCloy to Meiklejohn, September 30, 1942, JERS, 67/14, E1. 020).

By then Meiklejohn thought he had an insider's grip on the problem, had grown accustomed to the underside of the low-down, and had even come to believe that Solicitor Glick was not such a bad fellow after all. On September 22, 1942, he wrote Besig that he and Baldwin had conferred with Myer and Glick, and that a few days later the solicitor had shown him the new leave regulations: "Glick is better than he seemed. He was trying to construe authority to do what apparently they had to do to satisfy the army and the authority wasn't there. So he was straining" (CHS 3580). As for the leave regulations, "there are 'conditions' about leaving the camps, but they are, I think, essentially reasonable limits arising out of the Evacuation situation." And that was the WRA-JACL line in a nutshell. In double-quick time Meiklejohn had internalized it so completely that Myer and Glick had no further need to worry that the national ACLU would initiate litigation over their nonexistent authority for the "conditions" that kept the majority of inmates in the camps for the duration.

Of course the old-boy network extended beyond Meiklejohn and McCloy and helped the keepers chain the watchdogs to their definitions of reality. Still more to the point was the fact that the national ACLU looked upon Roosevelt as "so much our man there's no use mentioning him. Everyone in the White House was our friend in those days," Baldwin later declared to his biographer Peggy Lamson. Yes, that was the ACLU's golden era: "The office was stacked with our friends and supporters. Frank Roosevelt was very much aware of civil rights and civil liberties and the kind of staff he picked was too. People like Harold Ickes, Frances Perkins and Harry Hopkins. And all sorts of others; the attorney general, the head of the Indian Service . . . name them, they were our friends." With one of their own in the White House, Baldwin and Meiklejohn naturally supported his administration and gave their sympathetic understanding to McCloy, Attorney General Biddle and his assistant James Rowe, Edward J. Ennis of the Alien Enemy Control Unit, and, as we have seen, to Myer and Glick. In vain did Ernest Besig warn Baldwin and Meiklejohn against getting too attached to the government through their friends (interview, April 7, 1981).

Far from being critics of friends who ran concentration camps, members of the ACLU Board followed the example of Masaoka and the JACL in becoming propagandists for the WRA. On October 8, 1942, John Haynes Holmes, Arthur Garfield Hays, and Baldwin—the trio who could not restrain their admiration for General DeWitt's handling of the exclusion—complimented Dillon Myer on his statesmanship. His policy of breaking up the subculture and scattering its members across the country, they wrote, was "far preferable to their segregation in virtual ghettos on the Pacific Coast, and will go a long way toward the process of Americanization. We congratulate the War Relocation Authority on its far-sighted statesmanship in making provisions conforming to a sound national policy" (CHS 3580).

At the height of the loyalty oath crisis, Harry Mayeda of the Tule Lake Community Council wired Besig for advice on whether registration was mandatory. Having no way to know that it was not, Besig immediately wired back:

> IT IS OUR CONSIDERED OPINION THAT CITIZENS OF JAPANESE ANCESTRY IN CENTERS ARE SUBJECT TO SELECTIVE SERVICE REGULATIONS, AND, AS A PRACTICAL MATTER, WE URGE COMPLIANCE WITH RECENT REGISTRATION ORDERS. WE THINK THE GOVERNMENT'S INTENTIONS WERE GOOD BUT THE METHOD REPETITIOUS AND OTHERWISE POORLY PLANNED AND EXECUTED.
>
> [March 4, 1943, CHS 3580]

When a copy of this telegram came into his hands, Tule Director Harvey Coverley immediately forwarded it to Myer in Washington on March 5, 1943, exactly seven days after his boss had learned that registration was not compulsory and two days after his boss had helped Clarence Pickett of the American Friends Service Committee send similar misadvice to the Tuleans (see p. 94). Knowing what he did, Myer still had the effrontery to complain to Baldwin about Besig's criticisms. Thereupon Baldwin passed on Myer's objections to Besig and added his own recommendation that bordered on an instruction: "THINK YOU OVERLOOKED LARGER ISSUE . . . AND TRUST YOU WILL RECONSIDER" (March 8, 1943, CHS 3580). Besig did not. But again we confront a forced choice. Either Myer had made Baldwin privy to his official lie or he had conned him into perpetuating it. And either way, wittingly or unwittingly, Baldwin had rushed into the field to assist his friend.

With evenhanded justice Myer acknowledged such assistance in his account of those years:

> Roger Baldwin, executive officer of the American Civil Liberties Union, was helpful at all times and was a great source of comfort and support in times of trouble. Al Wirin of the Los Angeles ACLU was continuously busy in behalf of fairness and justice, and he and his legal staff made a great contribution. The late Alexander Meiklejohn, who served with the ACLU during the war, was in the forefront of the fighters for liberty and justice.
>
> [UA, p. xix]

No doubt this warm puff for Abraham Lincoln Wirin had something to do with his cordial relations with Myer and other WRA officials, the fact that he was the law partner of JACL President Saburo Kido, and the related fact that he acted as counsel for both the JACL and the New York ACLU "in so many of the Japanese American cases," as Baldwin once approvingly noted (to Besig, October 17, 1945, CHS 3580). Conspicuously absent from Myer's list of fighters for liberty and justice were Ernest Besig and Wayne M. Collins. To find out why, we need now to go back out into the field and pick up the thread of things where we left off.

2

In the summer of 1944 Tule Lake had become Hades with the WRA lid still on. Prisoners still did their hard time in the stockade, with release days entirely subject to the whim and caprice of their keepers. Children and mothers still cried and waved across the parking lot—until camp officials put a stop to that on July 2. That same night Yaozo Hitomi, the proadministration manager of the cooperative store, had his throat cut with a knife, a crime that sent out widening ripples of fear, as the murderer remained unidentified and loose in the camp. Teams of two or three overbearing WRA "Caucasian" policemen added to the terror by ransacking barracks in search of evidence, by mistreating suspects, by simultaneously conducting the forcible searches and seizures the army had initiated the past November, and by still holding over the heads of all adult males the threat of being thrown into the stockade.

Under the "disloyalty" label affixed to these "segregees," Community Analyst Marvin K. Opler found, not that elusive phenomenon, but more familiar emotions such as frustration, insecurity, humiliation, fear, indignation, and rising pride in their collective past. An anthropologist, Opler detected "culture revivalism" in this upsurge of commitment to their Japanese heritage and perceptively likened it to the Ghost Dance religion that swept through the Plains Indian tribes in the late 1800s (to D. S. Thomas, March 1, 1947, JERS, 67/14, suppl. cart. 1).

But this cultural revitalization movement "of a pent-up, hopeless people" also had an underside in the shape of ultranationalistic groups that formed to force all the Issei to apply for repatriation and then to take their children "back" to a homeland many of them had never seen. These zealots shaved their heads in imitation of the *bozu* haircuts of Japanese soldiers, wore sweatshirts emblazoned with the Rising Sun, pressed indoctrination programs on the Japanese-language schools, and staged early morning bugle blowing, drilling, and martial exercises.

They sent out gangs of thugs to hunt down the *Inu*, or alleged informers, assaulted or menaced "administration stooges," intimidated others
who opposed their strong-arm tactics, and generally spread fear, terror,
and despair throughout the camp. Most Tuleans were thus doubly op-
pressed, first by the keepers from without and then by these physical and
psychological terrorists from within. By the summer of 1944 their wails
finally carried all the way to San Francisco.

Among those who sent pleas for help was Kiyoshi Okamoto, the
Heart Mountain inmate who ran grave personal risk, I have ventured,
in publicly denouncing the WRA color line (p. 45). In late 1943 Okamoto had had the audacity to form his own one-man "Fair Play Committee," based, he later said, on "the principles and ideals of the Constitution and the Bill of Rights" (interview with Besig, July 10, 1944,
CHS 3580). These radical principles had intrigued upright Heart
Mountaineers such as Frank Seichi Emi, Isamu Horino, Paul Takeo Na-
kadate, Minoru Tamesa, Ben Wakaye, and Ken Yanagi. When Japanese
Americans became subject to Selective Service in January 1944, Okamoto had turned over the title of his organization to these younger men
and, over the age limit himself, henceforth took no active role in their
resistance save that of adviser when asked. Nevertheless, Myer and his
aides had continued to see Okamoto at the core of the Heart Mountain
opposition to the draft, proceeded to build up a case entitled "Fair Play
Committee; Kiyoshi Okamoto, et al., Sedition," held "hearings looking
toward transfer to Tule Lake," and in due course ordered him shipped
there. Now a "segregee," after trying "for a whole year" to get help from
the outside and after having been harshly rebuffed by Roger Baldwin,
Okamoto had at last got through to someone who would listen. Ernest
Besig replied to his letter promptly, but informed him that Regional
Director Robert B. Cozzens had denied his request to visit the camp: at
first Cozzens had said there would be no difficulty, but "after conferring
with Mr. Best and Mr. Myer . . . he informed me that the request was
being turned down because of a 'tense situation that persists at Tule
Lake'" (to Okamoto, June 8, 1944, JERS, 67/14, R12.10).

Nobody could deny the camp was tense, but the still more conspicuous truth was that Myer and company did not want Besig poking into
nasty little secrets that had grown larger. For weeks Besig requested and
Tule Director Best denied, whereupon over fifty inmates petitioned the
WRA for an opportunity to counsel with a representative of the ACLU
(affidavit of Ernest Besig, WCP, 78/177, *Tadayasu Abo* v. *Tom Clark*
[77 F. Suppl. 806 (1948)]—hereafter Affidavit). Reluctantly, ungra-

ciously, Best yielded and granted the NCACLU director permission to descend into the purgatory operated by the WRA on the drained lakebed from which its name derived. With his secretary Alice Adams, Besig drove the nearly five hundred miles from the Bay Area and passed through the gates on July 10, 1944.

Straightaway they became astonished witnesses to the sufferings of the inmates and their families:

> As soon as I arrived, accompanied by Mrs. Adams, I was besieged by scores of evacuees who wanted to register complaints with me. Mrs. Yukiko M . . . was the first woman I interviewed. She complained amid her tears that her husband had been placed in the Stockade for eight months and that she and her three children had not been permitted to visit him; that she had requested and been denied permission to do so by the Internal Security staff, and that she had been turned away when she sought to appeal the matter to Mr. R. R. Best, the camp director. . . . After hearing the complaint, I immediately prepared a written request to [or for] Mrs. M . . . to visit her husband, which she signed, and I presented it to Mr. Best. Mr. Best declared he had no objection to having Mrs. M . . . visit her husband but said she had never sought permission to do so. Mrs. M . . . was permitted to see her husband that afternoon.
>
> I had no sooner settled the M . . . case, however, when another woman came to complain tearfully that her husband had also been incarcerated in the Stockade for eight months, and that she had likewise never been permitted to visit him. I again prepared a written request and presented it to Mr. Best. This time, however, he merely stated he would consider the request but would give no assurances that the woman would ever be allowed to visit her husband.
>
> [Affidavit]

Other crying women lodged similar complaints and were likewise given no hope of ever seeing their husbands. Some had given birth to children their imprisoned fathers had never seen—perhaps their babies were among the messages mothers tried to wave across the parking lot. One young woman had not been allowed to see her sweetheart since his arrest on November 13, 1943, the day before they were to have married.

Almost swept off their feet by this outpouring of pain, the visitors again confronted the camp director:

> Mr. Best acknowledged the truth of these charges, but declined to do any more than consider individual applications with no promise that it would be favorable. I suggested that it was customary in all of our penal institutions to establish visiting regulations for relatives, and I urged that this should be done for the Stockade, but Mr. Best declined to do so.
>
> Until these women came to me with their complaints, I had no knowledge

that there was a Stockade at Tule Lake, nor that around 400 persons [396, according to the WRA] had been detained there for periods varying from one month to nine months without any charges being filed against them. Since the relatives of the prisoners not only sought visiting privileges but also my assistance in procuring the release of their men, I arranged with some difficulty to interview seven or eight of those whose relatives had specifically requested me to counsel with them.

[Affidavit]

Harassing difficulties placed in their way by their host did not make him seem the jovial "back-slapping Rotarian type" described by Francis S. Frederick (to Robert Spencer, August 20, 1943, JERS, 67/14, S1.10). A former marine, and another soil conservationist who had graduated into people keeping, Raymond R. Best was completely Myer's man before and after he took over as Tule director on August 1, 1943. Normally clothed in the dignity of his office, his prejudiced view of inmates thrust up through his testimony before an investigating subcommittee of the California state legislature on November 8, 1943, shortly after the so-called riot:

Q: What was the reason for not allowing the policemen to carry firearms?
A: I have heard it discussed several times and decided that one policeman with a gun was worse than one without a gun. One internal security man with even a small group of Japs wouldn't be too good. [JERS, 67/14, R11.50]

An old hand in dealing with "troublemakers" at Moab and Leupp, Best believed he knew how to handle his "Japs" at Tule without any help from the NCACLU.

When Best could no longer refuse outright, he granted Besig permission to interview men in the stockade, but only on the condition, as he bragged to FBI agents,

that an Internal Security Officer would have to be present during the interview to protect [sic] Besig and to prevent any escapes. Besig then objected to having a "cop on my lap," and finally became so obnoxious and caused so much interference that he was requested to leave. Before this took place, however, Besig was able to conduct interviews with the persons in the stockade while an Internal Security Officer sat in the next room with the door ajar. In each instance, Besig told the Japanese that he should retain his American citizenship and should [cancel] any request for expatriation.* Besig ex-

---

*Obligingly proposed by Attorney General Biddle, a special wartime statute, the so-called "denaturalization bill," had been passed by Congress and signed by President Roosevelt just a few days earlier (July 1, 1944) as Public Law 405. For the first time a U.S. citizen could therewith renounce his/her citizenship on U.S. soil in time of war.

plained that if the Japanese would keep his citizenship they could continue to cause the WRA a lot of trouble and as a citizen of the United States would have to be allowed free access to the courts. Besig told the persons whom he interviewed that the WRA was in a "spot" and was anxious to get rid of the stockade as it realized it was illegal. He also promised that he would take all the necessary steps to see that the WRA was put in its place.

[D. M. Ladd to Hoover, October 4, 1944,
FBI 62-70564]

This and other FBI documents fully substantiate Besig's charge that Best permitted him no privacy for his interviews, but compelled him to conduct them under the supervision of WRA police who eavesdropped and recorded what they heard (Affidavit). Along with their other deprivations, then, WRA prisoners had been denied the constitutional guaranty of due process of law that provided, among other protections, for the assistance of untrammeled counsel and the benefits of privileged communications with him or her.

Fully aware that their fundamental rights had been violated, stockade prisoners soon began another hunger strike. "Denial of due process of law to all of us," was among the reasons one striker listed for undertaking this protest of last resort: "In connection with the interview which we had with Mr. Ernest Besig of the American Civil Liberties Union, all right of privacy was denied to us" (Tom S.Y., "Diary since the Hunger Strike," JERS, 67/14, R26.30—save for a five-day intermission when the men were hospitalized, this second hunger strike lasted from July 19 to August 13, 1944).

Before Besig's abrupt departure after only two days of interviews, he was summoned to the Tule director's office "and informed by him that my presence at the camp was interfering with the investigation of the July 2nd Hitomi murder (which was wholly untrue), and even though I had not interviewed all of the people who had appointments with me,

---

Charges that this was discriminatory class legislation designed to secure renunciations of citizenship by native-born Americans of Japanese ancestry, especially the Kibei, were corroborated by Tule officials. In his interviews with men in the stockade, Besig discovered that Best and his staff "had pressed such renunciations upon them while they were imprisoned in the Stockade. Indeed, in my conversations with . . . W.R.A. officials, each of them stated quite frankly that they had gotten rid of some alien Japanese by sending them to the Santa Fe, New Mexico, internment camp, and that they expected to solve their Stockade problem by getting the imprisoned men to renounce their citizenship and then send them on to Santa Fe for internment" (Affidavit). In the overheard interviews Besig was thus warning prisoners not to fall into the administration's trap by voluntarily becoming "native-American aliens," a status that would subject them to the same arbitrary procedures established by Edward J. Ennis's deal with the WRA for getting rid of troublesome Issei.

I would be compelled to leave at once" (Affidavit). He was issuing this order to leave after having conferred with Dillon S. Myer on the telephone, Best informed the startled NCACLU director, and for good measure complacently assured him that "Roger Baldwin had agreed that if in the minds of the WRA we were interfering with the investigation . . . it was agreeable that we should be invited to leave because we were there without his approval. Of course, we might have stated that we were there with the approval and indeed at the instruction of the Northern California Committee of the American Civil Liberties Union" (Besig to Gloria Waldron, July 13, 1944, CHS 3580). Yet forthwith Besig and his secretary were ejected, with two armed internal security officers escorting them out past the gates. Only with great difficulty did they make it back to San Francisco, for some ill-wisher had dumped two sacks of salt, bags and all, in their gas tank. Since Besig's ancient automobile had been parked in the guarded "Caucasian" compound, this parting gift bore an unmistakable message from their hosts: NO DUE PROCESS WANTED HERE.

Immediately Besig gave the story to Bay Area newspapers and the WRA dismissed it "with a brusque statement" (*San Francisco Chronicle*, July 15, 1944). Regional Director Robert B. Cozzens denied that the NCACLU director had been ordered out of the camp and denied that the stockade inmates had been "imprisoned." But lies could no longer conceal the WRA's overgrown secret, which had become nastier than even a cynic might have imagined.

"TYRANNY REIGNS AT TULE LAKE" trumpeted Besig's headline in the *American Civil Liberties Union-News* (August 1944). He revealed the whole story of his ejection from the camp, the imprisonment of citizens for months without charges, and the rest, including shocking allegations "of brutality and third-degree methods that have been leveled against Caucasian Internal Security police. There is evidence that on the night of November 4, 1943 [after the so-called riot], the police dragged certain Japanese into the administration building and beat them with baseball bats. It is general knowledge among the Caucasian personnel, that the people who came to work in the administration building the next morning of Nov. 5 found a broken baseball bat and had to clean up a mess of blood and black hair." Besig also quoted at length the letter he had sent on July 14 to Interior Secretary Ickes. In meticulous detail he disclosed to Myer's superior the denial of due process to Tuleans and concluded with what had to be construed in Washington as a threat: "We appreciate, of course, that Tule Lake presents many difficult ad-

ministrative problems. At the same time, I venture to say that the present
policy of keeping the lid on can result only in further difficulties. I sincerely trust that some investigation will be made into what appear to
me as intolerable conditions and practices."

National Director Myer responded with a letter dated July 29, 1944:

> I have received the copy of your letter of July 14 to Secretary Ickes and
> want to notify you that you will be allowed to visit Tule Lake in the future
> only if you are requested in writing by evacuee residents to visit them or
> represent them and *if your proposed visit has been approved by the National
> Director of your organization.*
>
> The War Relocation Authority has always maintained an open door pol-
> icy in regard to visits at relocation centers, providing those who may wish to
> make visits have reasonable grounds for their requests. Because of the pecu-
> liar problems at the Tule Lake Center, however, we have found it necessary
> to limit permission to visit this center.
>
> [CHS 3580; emphasis added]

An aggrieved host, Myer sternly reprimanded Besig for his bad manners—his "complete lack of understanding of the numerous administrative problems involved" and his utter failure to "trust responsible persons connected with this Authority."

Unfortunately, Secretary Ickes did not personally look into Myer's
alleged "open door policy," but instead routinely accepted the construction his subordinate placed on Besig's revelations: "Neither the Director
of the War Relocation Authority nor I have any disposition whatever to
deny any resident of Tule Lake his right to counsel and advice with
respect to his legal rights," affirmed the usually forthright cabinet officer
in a letter that had obviously been drafted by Myer's staff. Over his
signature Ickes confirmed that Besig would not be allowed in Tule Lake
without the approval of the national director of the ACLU and ear-
marked a carbon copy of this confirmation for Roger Baldwin (Ickes to
Besig, August 3, 1944, CHS 3580).

Fortunately, Besig did not rely exclusively on appeals to intransigent
authority to blow the WRA lid off Tule Lake. In the meantime, he had
placed the prisoners' cases in the strong hands of Wayne M. Collins, his
close associate in many a civil liberties battle. While Collins confronted
regional WRA officials, Besig secured approval from his executive committee for NCACLU intervention in the proposed habeas corpus proceedings, "but to withhold action for a couple of weeks or so to allow
Roger Baldwin an opportunity to come to California to see the situation himself. The Director was instructed to wire Roger Baldwin to this

effect" (minutes, August 3, 1944, CHS 3580). Besig promptly invited Baldwin to come out to see for himself: "IT SEEMS TO US THE WRA IS RUNNING A PRIVATE PRISON AND THE CASE PRESENTS AN EMERGENCY."

Unlike the men on hunger strike in the stockade, Baldwin was on vacation and could take a more relaxed view of their imprisonment: "THANK YOU AND [BISHOP] PARSONS FOR INVITATION BUT BELIEVE MATTERS [MAY] BE WELL SETTLED WITHOUT VISIT," he tardily wired back on August 6 (this and the following communications were incorporated in minutes, September 7, 1944, CHS 3580). Speaking for Baldwin and the national board, Clifford Forster instructed Besig the following day: "TAKE NO ACTION NOW IN STOCKADE CASES PENDING CHECK WITH MYER OF ALLEGATIONS IN CURRENT PAPER"—namely, Besig's *J'accuse* in the August *American Civil Liberties Union-News*. And on August 22 Forster repeated that the board members wanted the NCACLU to withhold action until after their next meeting: "Roger will be back at that time and he will write you about the Board's action." But while Baldwin vacationed and his New York office stalled and obstructed, Myer was forced that very day, August 22, to agree to open up the gates of the stockade.

Like Besig, Wayne M. Collins had no illusions about the natural benevolence of governments and no friends among the WRA people keepers. A wiry, tense Irish-American, he made the courtroom his arena for battle after battle to make the Bill of Rights apply to everybody—communists, Nazis, nonwhites, everybody—and apply in wartime as well as in peacetime. Filled with outrage over the exclusion of "a wonderful people," and then further enraged by the official lies showered upon them, he became Korematsu's attorney of record, a leading counsel in the other cases, and virtually the single-handed savior of thousands of harassed and embittered Nisei who fell into the Roosevelt administration's trap when they renounced their citizenship. With immense tenacity and energy, he was to fight the Department of Justice for the next two decades and more, from Attorney General Tom Clark to his son, Attorney General Ramsey Clark, in behalf of victims called "renunciants."

Collins had a boundless contempt for those he saw conniving with monumental injustice—namely, men and organizations such as Mike Masaoka and the national JACL and Roger Baldwin and the national ACLU. As he wrote to Abraham Lincoln Wirin, Saburo Kido's law partner and Baldwin's favorite ACLU counsel on the West Coast:

Wayne M. Collins, n.d.
[Margaret Collins Weeks]

The JACL is as much to blame for the evacuation and imprisonment of these citizens and aliens as anyone because it did not raise any protest at the outset but willingly aided and abetted the evacuation. It is, therefore, in my opinion a cowardly group, bent upon satisfying the aspirations of its leaders the while it cheerfully betrayed the interests of the evacuees. It pretended to be a spokesman for all the deported people but it never represented anyone except its leaders. It has had about as much courage as the national office of the ACLU on the issues. If the JACL or the ACLU in their [amicus curiae] briefs adopt positions inconsistent with mine in the Korematsu and Endo cases [,] I shall ask the court for time to answer them in both.

[September 22, 1944, CHS 3580]

While the NCACLU director fruitlessly tried to persuade Baldwin to approve intervention in the stockade cases, Collins pressed ahead with them as the prisoners' private counsel. He responded to Regional Director Cozzens's abrupt dismissal of Besig's charges with a denunciation of WRA misdeeds and threatened habeas corpus proceedings that would expose them to the world. Fearful of that eventuality, Cozzens pleaded for time to get Solicitor Glick out from Washington and Director Best down from Tule Lake for an emergency conference. But the WRA officials continued to stall, as Collins later consulted his records and reconstructed what followed for Michi Weglyn:

> On August 19, 1944 I telephoned to the WRA office and spoke to Cozzens and delivered an ultimatum to the WRA. He stated he would see Glick and Best immediately and arrange for a conference date. At 3:06 P.M. I telephoned to Mr. Cozzens who stated that Glick and Best wished to confer with me on Tuesday [August 22]. . . . I stated that I would not brook any delay following the conference date (Tuesday) but would file suits and also go to the Tule Lake Center. He stated that "no one can see anyone in the Center unless he has a written request from inmates." I informed him I had written authority to represent the persons confined in the Stockade and that no one would dare prevent me from seeing my clients. . . .
> On Tuesday following Aug. 19, 1944, the conference was held at the WRA Office in the Sheldon Building; Best, Glick, Cozzens and I being present. I delivered another ultimatum. Then we went to another room in that office where Mr. Dillon Myer was found. He was suffering from some lameness and was tired. I was introduced to him. I delivered another ultimatum. They agreed to liberate all the persons confined in the Stockade. Mr. Best telephoned to the Center in my presence and ordered all the persons there confined released immediately. I informed Mr. Best that I intended to visit Tule and see the Stockade. He stated I would be welcomed.
>
> [*YoI*, pp. 215–16]

Actually, the last seven men in the stockade were not released until 9:00 A.M. on Thursday, August 24 (Besig to Gloria Waldron, August 25, 1944, CHS 3580). But when Collins arrived the next day "there was no vestige of the Stockade then discernible. Even the fence that surrounded it was gone." It was as though it had never existed.

Myer was understandably tired. Nothing had worked. Besig and Collins had not shown a trace of the "fine understanding" he had come to expect from Baldwin and Meiklejohn. He had tried to head off Besig at the pass by making the latter's visits to Tule Lake depend on approval he could not get from Baldwin, but as the prisoners' private attorney Collins could not be stopped by this condition, and no one—not Baldwin, Myer himself, Glick, Cozzens, Best, or anyone else—could block his threatened habeas corpus proceedings.

So, finally, Myer had to let every last one of his "troublemakers" walk out of the stockade and even suffer the manproof fence to come down. Still, he neither yielded gracefully nor limped off the field without leaving behind yet another little WRA untruth: "The isolation area, commonly called the 'stockade,'" had been emptied, according to the official explanation in the camp newspaper, because "conditions in the center at the present time are such that isolation of individuals is no longer considered necessary" (*Newell Star*, August 31, 1944).

3

"You can be sure that Mr. Best and the top officials in the WRA loathe me for my interference in the Tule Lake administrative problems," Besig assured Gloria Waldron, who had formerly worked in the camp. "Personally, if I had been the victim of their false imprisonment, I would sue them for damages. . . . We are still going after the WRA on the question of the beatings" (August 25, 1944, CHS 3580).

Again Myer tried to fend off the NCACLU director by enlisting the sympathetic understanding of Roger Baldwin. "Mr. Besig's article [in the August *ACLU-News*] also charges brutality on the part of the War Relocation Authority police force, particularly during the November incident," explained Myer's aide Malcolm E. Pitts. "Here again, he made no effort, to my knowledge, to substantiate the charges so made by the evacuees with whom he talked. The War Relocation Authority made a thorough investigation of these charges some time ago and uncovered absolutely no evidence to substantiate them" (to Baldwin, August 17, 1944, JERS, 67/14, R12.12). But Myer and Pitts had made the hopeful mistake of assuming that Besig's evidence had been gained only from the stockade men, but among his other sources, Gloria Waldron had informed him that "there have been many cases of beating up, particularly on the night of the famous 'riot.' . . . My own office [in the administration building] was used as a third-degree chamber last November and there was plenty of blood spilled. In that case, both the army and WRA Internal Security men participated" (July 19, 1944, CHS 3580).

After requesting the New York ACLU to secure a copy of the WRA's report on its "thorough investigation," the NCACLU executive committee finally recorded receipt of a letter from Roger Baldwin saying he would try to get one. He did not rush. Four months later the executive committee recorded receipt of a letter from Baldwin's office counsel Clifford Forster stating that the WRA "considers its report on the alleged beatings . . . as 'confidential.' The director was authorized to protest to Mr. Myer against the secret handling of a public matter" (minutes, October 5, 1944, February 1, 1945, CHS 3580). Besig forthwith protested to Myer, reciting this background, the many months of waiting for the report, and the difficulty his committee had "in understanding why a report of this kind should be confidential, when your Mr. Pitts had originally taken the position that there was absolutely no foundation to the charges contained in the story we ran in the August 1944 issue of the 'News.'" Again Myer's Mr. Pitts shouldered the responsibility of fending off these allegations: the army had been in charge on the night of November 4, 1943, he wrote Besig, and besides the WRA had no report but "statements by various persons of the events of that time." Furthermore, "we have discussed this matter with your national office and Mr. Baldwin has indicated his satisfaction with our judgment that the rumors referred to in your letter are untrue" (February 5, 16, 1945, CHS 3580).

"Untrue" rumors or rumors of truth? Driven underground by WRA lies, the truth had burrowed beyond Besig's reach into mountains of classified documents. On November 8, 1943, B. J. Glasgow, the Military Intelligence Service (MIS) agent stationed in nearby Medford, Oregon, had submitted a detailed report to his superiors on recent events at Tule Lake (declassified June 25, 1981; a copy is in FBI 62-70564). Inmates picked up in the "Caucasian" area on the night of November 4 had been taken to the administration building for questioning but proved uncooperative:

> Difficulty was encountered in obtaining information from these Japanese held in custody. Some variation from the normal procedure of questioning was necessitated by the circumstances. Mr. Schmidt, head of the Internal Security WRA, choked Bob H . . . , scared him and twisted his arm. In this manner he obtained the name of Tom Kobiyashi* as being one of the leaders.

---

*As I write this the Commission on Wartime Relocation and Internment of Civilians has just issued its report *Personal Justice Denied* (Washington, D.C.: Government Printing Office, December 1982), in which an excerpt from a deposition by Tokio Yamane appears (pp. 210–11). Yamane refers to Kobayashi by surname, making him like the Reverend Shizuo Kai and George Kuratomi, also mentioned by Yamane, and other inmates

This Japanese was also in custody and so he, in turn, was interrogated. Mr. Payne and Mr. Lewis, both officers of the Internal Security WRA, hit him in the face with their fists until he succumbed, then they proceeded to kick him until he revived. This procedure continued until Kubiyashi [*sic*] was induced to reveal further information (unknown to this Agent). The interrogation lasted until approximately 0400, 5 November 1943. All Japanese held in custody were questioned in approximately the same manner. . . . All Japanese persons apprehended were placed in the hospital after the interrogation.

Upon receipt of a photostatic copy of MIS Agent Glasgow's report, FBI Director Hoover reproduced it for the attorney general on December 15 and considered it sufficiently important to remind Biddle of it a week later, calling his particular attention to the passage just quoted and noting that "a copy of this memorandum is being forwarded to Mr. Henry A. Schweinhaut and to Mr. Tom C. Clark, Assistant Attorney General" (December 22, 1943, FBI 62-70564)—thus this graphic, ir-refragable evidence of duress, beatings, and terror at Tule Lake had been formally transmitted to the cabinet level of the Roosevelt admin-istration and to the upper echelons of the Department of Justice, facts that will receive our attention elsewhere. Hoover also sent an urgent telegram to FBI Inspector Myron E. Gurnea in San Francisco pointing out that Glasgow's report "INDICATES THESE ALLEGATIONS [OF DU-RESS] FOUNDED IN FACT. IF NOT ALREADY INVESTIGATED, COMPLETE DETAILS INCLUDING VERSION OF WRA AND ARMY REPRESENTATIVES REGARDING TREATMENT OF JAPANESE PRISONERS ON NOVEMBER FOUR, FORTYTHREE SHOULD BE OBTAINED AND REPORTED" (Decem-ber 21, 1943, FBI 62-70564). Inspector Gurnea complied with a thor-ough investigation and a series of reports (all in FBI 62-70564; hereafter Gurnea, FBI 62-70564) that further validated the allegations of torture and incidentally rendered still more improbable the claim that the vic-tims had just come hot from the historic "riot."

According to Myer's skeletal chronology of "The Tule Lake Inci-dent," on October 15, 1943, a truck accident killed one inmate and

---

such as Kiyoshi Okamoto, Joseph Kurihara, and Harry Yoshio Ueno, all of whom have been identified in print so often no point is served in trying to preserve their anonymity. Himself picked up and kicked and beaten "all night long," Yamane remembers vividly the interrogation of Kobayashi, who "was hit on the head with such force that blood gushed out and the baseball bat actually broke in two." Not quoted in the CWRIC report is a passage from the full deposition wherein Yamane relates what happened in the stockade afterward: "Mr. Kobayashi, who had been so severely beaten, was never given any medical aid even though he had suffered a brain concussion and his head wound was open and infected. He moaned and complained constantly, but no aid was ever given him. Once, at his request, I placed my finger on his wound and was shocked to see pus ooze out of his wound."

triggered a farm strike. Thereupon Myer and Best arranged for "loyal" workers to be brought in from other camps to harvest the crops. On November 1 this was one of the grievances Tuleans presented to Myer personally when they "staged" a mass demonstration, as he put it, "for the benefit of the National Director" (*UA*, p. xxviii). On that occasion he warned the protesters, reported MIS Agent Glasgow, "that if the WRA could not get along with the Japanese, they would have to come under the control of someone else," and Best had chimed in: "Should there be any further such outdoor gatherings of the Japanese at the Center, he would not hesitate to call in the Army." On November 4 some young men from the camp clashed with WRA police by the warehouse over the clandestine, nighttime loading of trucks with food for the strikebreakers. As Best had warned and had prearranged with Lieutenant Colonel Verne Austin, 753rd Military Police Battalion, he then (9:50 P.M.) called the army in. "We brought the Army into the Tule Lake center," Myer testified before the Senate Military Affairs Subcommittee on November 24, because "we had an incident which required force of arms *which we had arranged for previously*, and we utilized them when they were needed" (*War Relocation Centers*, 78th Cong., 1st sess., p. 223; emphasis added).

The only evidence that the WRA in truth "required force of arms" to quell what was at most a scuffle or skirmish between inmates and internal security officers came from witnesses whose testimony would have been insufficient in calmer times to convict the men in question of having walked on the grass. With significant variations, these WRA sources attested that a crowd of inmates had rushed from the site of the skirmish to surround Best's home, which was situated in the "Caucasian" area near the warehouse and in front of the motor pool, and had then and there menaced his safety. For MIS Agent Glasgow, Best estimated their number as 200, but for FBI agents he later scaled that figure down, advising them "that looking out the window he could see 30 or 40 Japanese with clubs circling around his house, yelling and hollering."* To Glasgow, Best mentioned no specific shouts, or at least the MIS agent inexplicably failed to report any, but to the FBI, Best later claimed "that he heard a shout, 'Get BEST.'" These two fateful words became the shaky pegs from which hung WRA assertions that a riot

---

*The number of "rioters" was elastic: "The 200 Kibei around Mr. Best's home were not the only Japanese in the area," reported Glasgow. "Various reports indicated that the number of Japanese in the administrative area varied from twenty-five (25) to two thousand five hundred (2,500)."

was under way. As gleaned from FBI Inspector Gurnea's reports, Assistant Director Clarence E. Zimmer, Best's old friend and fellow graduate from the Soil Conservation Service, first claimed "that he heard a shout, 'Get BEST,'" but later changed his claim to having heard *some* "of the Japanese shout: 'Let's get BEST.'" On February 11, 1944, former WRA officer Payne claimed he heard the more polite "Get Mr. BEST," but on December 2, 1943, in an earlier interview, he had claimed that he heard "We want BEST." And Chief Schmidt claimed he heard both "Get BEST" and the less ambiguous and more incriminating "Take BEST," but his veracity will be considered in a moment.

No inmate asserted he heard any of these variations. But for the sake of analysis, say that some men had shouted "Get BEST." What was more natural and innocent than for American citizens to bring their grievances to the director of their concentration camp and for them to want him to come to the scene of an altercation? Especially since, according to some inmates, he had pledged not to smuggle any more scarce foodstuffs out of the camp at night? To be sure, Assistant Director Zimmer told FBI agents that it was his "personal opinion" that inmates intended to seize Best and take him "as a hostage into the colony. He said he had nothing specific on which to base this belief except the chain of circumstances surrounding the incident." But that very chain of circumstances made his unsupported belief absurd. With a military police battalion ready and eager to come in, and with overwhelming reinforcements only a phone call away, the angry young Kibei in the administrative area would have been foolish to dream of kidnaping Best and hiding him away among the old folks and women and children in the inner camp. In my view, the summary of inmate opinion that the Reverend Shizuo Kai of the negotiation committee presented to FBI agents said all that needed to be said for those who had ears to hear: "Whereas, Mr. RAYMOND R. BEST, the Project Director, gave as his excuse for calling in the military that a group of Center residents threatened to kidnap the Caucasian personnel, which statement is a plain *false[hood]*. As a result many unnecessary arrests have [been] conducted."

Likely conclusions flow from this reading of the evidence: provoked by the effrontery of Tuleans in assembling for redress of their grievances or in "staging" a mass demonstration for his benefit, as Myer would have it, he and Best had *previously* arranged for the force of arms they called in three days later on the flimsiest of pretexts. To cover their exposed flanks, Myer, Best, Zimmer, Schmidt, and their underlings blew up a minor altercation into a raging "riot." But their underlying urge to punish was unmistakable—to their minds, troublemaking "hardboiled boys" deserved to be chastised, and so they were, in the stockade months that followed, by the searches and seizures and all the other abuses.

Widely regarded by other "Caucasians" as a "Jap lover" because she treated inmates with respect and sympathy, the Tule schoolteacher Emily Light wrote a paper on her experiences during the evening of November 4, and FBI agents incorporated excerpts from it in one of their reports:

> During the evening there were many expressions on the part of the staff members (who were all workers just as I was), which revealed one of two things— either how they actually felt toward the evacuees (and some of their attitudes were quite vicious), *or* how hysterical they could get in such circumstances. The concern for the most part seemed to be for our safety from "those Japs" who were at last getting "exactly what they deserved."
>
> [Gurnea, FBI 62-70564]

This racist spite extended to Colonel Austin's men and sparked the only riot that occurred, an authentic riot of WRA employees and military policemen that lasted for approximately ten days following the army takeover.* But the first was the worst night of terror, as a sampling from Inspector Gurnea's reports suggests.

WRA National Director of Internal Security Willard E. ("Huck") Schmidt was a big man, according to an FBI agent, "a six foot, two hundred and forty pound individual who makes a very tough and formidable appearance. He spent eighteen years with the Berkeley, California, Police Department, and, according to Agent [name blacked out] is not the type of individual that the Japanese would be eager to impede." He was a big "windbag," according to Francis S. Frederick, who worked for a spell with Schmidt at Leupp (to Robert Spencer, October 31, 1943, JERS, 67/14, S1.10). Questioned by FBI agents about "third degree methods" on the night of November 4, Schmidt categorically "denied that any force was used." But the Tule "Community Activities supervisor" advised agents that he had been in the middle wing of the administration building, where the "questioning" took place from

---

*In "Plaintiffs' Brief," Wayne M. Collins put the problem of loaded labels with characteristic vigor: "Troop violence is not called a riot—it always is justified as a necessary military measure taken to suppress violence. Institutionalized W.R.A. employees kept the rumor factory busy and spineless gossipers among them added fiction to fancy and substituted both for fact. A riot that never occurred was magnified by exaggeration of lies into a rebellion" (WCP, 78/177, *Abo* v. *Clark* [77 F. Suppl. 806 (1948)]).

midnight until about 2:00 A.M., that Schmidt came along and told him
to leave and then took an inmate (whose name has been blacked out in
the report) into a supply room that had no windows and only one door
that was closed behind them, and that

> Before going into the room, SCHMIDT apparently asked [X] a question and
> when he received what he considered an unsatisfactory answer, he twisted
> [X's] arm behind his back and as he increased the pressure kept repeating,
> "Don't give me that s——," "Don't give me that s——." [The activities su-
> pervisor] said he did not leave as requested by SCHMIDT, but stood in the
> hallway where he could hear [X] crying out in great pain. . . . On the follow-
> ing day [he] saw [X] walking from the hospital to the stockade and at that
> time [X] had his arm in a sling.

Camp Doctor John T. Mason "also recalled that he saw WILLARD
SCHMIDT take one Japanese into the supply room where SCHMIDT
twisted the arm of the Japanese and pushed him up against the wall
while he was asking him various questions. . . . [Also] he heard screams
and outcries from other individuals who were being questioned." These
were among the additional facts Glasgow's report had pried loose.
Whether Schmidt was categorically denying the use of force or claiming
that inmates had shouted, "Take BEST," his word was worthless.*

On February 11, 1944, an FBI agent secured a signed statement from
Clifford Leroy Payne, the "Get Mr. BEST" witness. By then an acting
deputy sheriff in Vancouver, Washington, the former Tule security officer looked back on November 4 with pride and exultation:

> None of the three Japs were unconscious but all three were groggy from the
> blows they received, especially the one [questioner Q] had hit with the base-
> ball bat. We picked the three of them up and got them on their feet and took
> them into the Administration Building . . . [where] we ordered the Japanese
> to lie down on the floor. They refused to do so whereupon I knocked my Jap
> down with my fist. He stayed down but was not unconscious. [Q] hit his Jap
> over the head again with the baseball bat. . . . [During the interrogation of
> another inmate] I had been itching to take a sock at the Jap so I shoved [Q2]
> aside and hit [Y] a hard right blow to the jaw with my fist. [Y] went down
> and out. I reached down and shook him hard in an effort to revive him. I
> even grabbed him by the hair and shook his head. After about three minutes

---

*Inmates were not fond of Schmidt, according to a confidential letter from Tule An-
alyst Marvin K. Opler to his superior in Washington: "People are certain . . . that Internal
Security Chief Schmidt beat up stockaders, uses grilling methods, and is in danger in the
center if he ever gets out of the police car without his gun . . . Besig is said also to have
heard the stories about Schmidt's handling of stockaders back in November. My guess is
that Besig believes these stories, has documented them, and is far from through with Tule
Lake" (to Edward H. Spicer, July 15, 1944, MKO).

he came to. In an effort to get him up I tried to get a grip under his arms
and accidentally got his shirt and tore it off his back. . . . [At one point] I
did hear screams which seemed to emanate from one of the back rooms.

[Gurnea, FBI 62-70564]

After such a full night's work Payne joined Willard Schmidt and three
other interrogators and before dawn's early light they all walked over
"to the mess hall for a cup of coffee."

Tule surgeon John T. Mason was less enthusiastic about the long
night, stating to agents it was not "the type of affair he would like to
watch, and that he certainly would not have stayed . . . had he not been
requested to do so [by an army officer in the reasonable expectation
that a doctor might be needed]. He stated that he remained at the
Administration Building until all of the Japanese had been questioned
and removed, and that as he recalled he arrived at his apartment about
5 A.M. on November 5, 1943." In addition to his recollection of
Schmidt's questioning techniques, Mason recalled another interrogator
(I1) hitting a

Japanese with a piece of baseball bat which he had in his hand. The blow
knocked the Japanese down, but not out. [I2] also proceeded to beat the
Japanese with his fists, and during the whole time they were accusing this
Japanese of calling various Caucasians "Sons of bitches." After each blow at
the Japanese [I1 or I2?] would again ask the Japanese "who is a son of a
bitch now[?]" . . . Finally someone mentioned to [I3] that it was "open season" for Japanese, and asked him if he would like to try his hand. [I3] replied
"It's like shooting ducks."

[Gurnea, FBI 62-70564]

With such fretful images on his conscience, Mason retired to his apartment to try to sleep.

The doctor had not done much for those who most needed his professional services. Former Tule Legal Aid Counsel Tetsujiro Nakamura,
who became Collins's associate in the renunciation cases, deposed that
of the eighteen inmates "severely beaten with baseball bats," some required "hospitalization for several months and the mentality of one was
impaired permanently as the result of the beating he had received" (Affidavit, WCP, 78/177, *Abo v. Clark* [77 F. Suppl. 806 (1948)]).

With reason, then, Myer and Best loathed and feared Besig and Collins. Not only had they been forced to close down their private prison,
commonly called the stockade, but the lawyers' allegations of beatings
threatened to expose the cornerstone lie upon which they had erected
that institution. Myer and Best therefore pretended to have made "a

Terror at Tule Lake, 1945. Understandably, no WRA "Caucasian" cared to commemorate the events of November 4, 1943, by taking snapshots of the beatings. But later, after Colonel Austin's MPs had been replaced by border patrolmen of the Immigration and Naturalization Service, an inmate with a contraband camera secretly snapped scenes from other nights and days of terror. From the files of Wayne M. Collins, the five photographs on this and the following pages are reprinted by courtesy of his son.

thorough investigation" that turned up "absolutely no evidence" of beatings. To cap that, they had Roger Baldwin express "his satisfaction with our judgment that the rumors referred to . . . are untrue." And by the dubious virtue of official secrecy and the classifier's stamp, they succeeded in the cover-up.

Yet decades later it is still pretty to think that one of our professional optimists may have been right: "Truth, crushed to earth, shall rise again." Thanks to the Freedom of Information Act, maybe, now and then, but later rather than sooner.

4

In 1945 the "exciting adventure" drew to a close. "The program of the War Relocation Authority has been an exciting adventure in the democratic method," declared Dillon S. Myer:

We had a mass evacuation, dictated by military necessity [*sic*], which over-rode the peacetime rights of one minority in our population. But in our grad-ual, slow, sometimes painful process of individual readjustment, we have furnished a guarantee that the American way is to repair and make restitu-tion; that even in a war, we do not forget the rights of individuals; and that while fighting on battlefronts around the world, we will not allow ourselves to forget the problems of democracy near at hand.

["Japanese American Relocation: Final Chapter,"
Common Ground 6 (Autumn 1945): 61–66]

Tule Lake was near at hand, and to the end Ernest Besig and Wayne M. Collins would not allow Myer to forget that individuals had rights even in that "problem of democracy."

On March 16, 1945, Myer's agency issued new regulations sharply curtailing the residual rights of individuals at Tule Lake. When Besig asked Raymond R. Best if limitations had been placed on their right of assemblage, he was told to take his troubles elsewhere: "It has been my understanding that your inquiries should be addressed to Mr. Dillon Myer. . . . I have therefore forwarded your letter to him for reply" (March 19, 1945, CHS 3580). On March 27, Myer curtly acknowl-edged that "certain regulations were put into effect at Tule Lake re-cently. I presume that is what you have reference to and am enclosing a copy for your information" (CHS 3580). By the end of the month fifteen men had received sentences of 90 to 110 days in the reestablished stock-ade for "pro-Japanese activities." As Besig observed to Lillie Rouda-bush, one of the teachers whose "belligerent" pacifism worried WRA officials, "no explanation was given by Mr. Myer why existing federal law is insufficient to cope with the situation. . . . But these regulations go far beyond any restraints authorized by Congress in war or in peace" (April 18, 1945, CHS 3580). Fortunately, Besig's executive committee had already authorized him "to oppose by whatever means possible, the regulations recently established at Tule Lake limiting the right of free speech, press and assemblage" (minutes, April 5, 1945, CHS 3580). The lines had thus formed for yet another set-to, with Myer and Best, sec-onded by Roger Baldwin, on the one side, and Besig and Collins, sec-onded by what was left of the Constitution, on the other.

On or about June 3, 1945, five young inmates, ranging in age from fifteen to seventeen, were charged with violating the new regulations by blowing bugles and wearing certain clothing, tried by Best, denied the right to bail, counsel, trial by jury, and the rest, and sentenced to the stockade for terms ranging from 120 to 370 days. On July 6 Besig sent

Terror at Tule Lake, 1945.
[II]

a strong protest to Interior Secretary Ickes, waited three weeks for a
satisfactory reply, and only then prepared to ask his executive committee
for authorization to institute habeas corpus proceedings. By telegram
on July 26 Baldwin urged him to hold off on the writs until the Interior
Department had a chance to act and followed that up the next day with
a letter in which he remonstrated that Besig was "rushing the federal
officials a little unreasonably." Thereupon he instructed Besig on the
facts of life in such institutions:

> I have no doubt that summary action was taken. But in a community like
> that, discipline must be enforced by measures similar to those in a prison.
> Almost all internment camps for aliens or otherwise are so run, and the
> ordinary protections of defense do not apply.
>
> [July 27, 1945, CHS 3580]

Now, this curious defense of WRA lawlessness from the illustrious
watchdog for the underdog raises a question that is both irrepressible
and, under the circumstances, necessarily rhetorical: would Baldwin

have been quite so nonchalant about the victims had they been five white teenagers from, say, his hometown in Massachusetts?*

As it happened, on the very day Baldwin sent his extraordinary justification of official absolutism to San Francisco, he was interviewed in his New York office by an FBI agent who overheard his no less extraordinary telephone conversation with someone. These eavesdroppings were then transmitted via urgent teletype from New York SAC Conroy to Director Hoover:

> BALDWIN CONVERSED WITH AN UNKNOWN INDIVIDUAL TO THE EFFECT THAT THE A.C.L.U. HAS A QUOTE HOT HEADED UNQUOTE ATTORNEY AT SAN FRANCISCO WHO WANTS TO TAKE THE MATTER INTO FEDERAL COURT BUT THAT HE BALDWIN DID NOT WANT TO DO SO AND FELT THAT AIRING THE MATTER OF SOME DISLOYAL JAPANESE AT TULE LAKE WOULD BE HARMFUL TO PUBLIC OPINION REGARDING ALL JAPANESE AMERICANS. BALDWIN'S CONVERSATION INDICATED THAT THE SAN FRANCISCO ATTORNEY WAS HOT HEADED ABOUT SOME DISCIPLINARY MEASURES THAT HAD BEEN TAKEN BY THE AUTHORITIES AT TULE LAKE AND BALDWIN SAID THE PERSONS, APPARENTLY THE JAPANESE, HAD NOT BEEN GIVEN FAIR HEARINGS, THAT THE CAMP DIRECTOR WAS JUDGE, JURY AND EXECUTIONER BUT HE FELT THAT THE MATTER SHOULD BE HANDLED ADMINISTRATIVELY RATHER THAN AIRED IN COURT.
>
> [July 27, 1945, FBI 62-69030]

Working closely with Interior Undersecretary Abe Fortas and with Director Myer, as his letters made clear, Baldwin did his frantic best to keep his administrative friends from having to go to court: "BOARD EARNESTLY REQUESTS YOU GIVE GOVERNMENT MORE TIME," he wired Besig and a week later his staff counsel Clifford Forster directed Besig not to proceed with the writs "UNTIL BOARD HAS ACTED ON MONDAY" (August 1, 8, 1945, CHS 3580).

But this time around earnest requests and impatient directives from New York had little impact in San Francisco. On August 10 Besig informed Clifford Forster that the writs had been filed that morning: "My

---

*Regrettably, Baldwin's death on August 26, 1981, kept me from putting the question to him personally. When I put it to Besig, he commented first on the passage just quoted: "The excerpts from Roger Baldwin's letter of July 27, 1945 are particularly shameful and almost unbelievable. I ask myself now, 'Why was a person with such beliefs about individual rights heading the American Civil Liberties Union?' Obviously, he was a part of our problem on the West Coast." As for the irrepressible question, it still seems to Besig nearly four decades later "that a civil liberties organization should have been more sensitive to the racial issue. Certainly, as I viewed the facts, the ACLU national office were defenders and justifiers of racism. Baldwin later admitted they were wrong and we were right but he never explained to me why he had made such a grievous error" (to Drinnon, May 18, 1981).

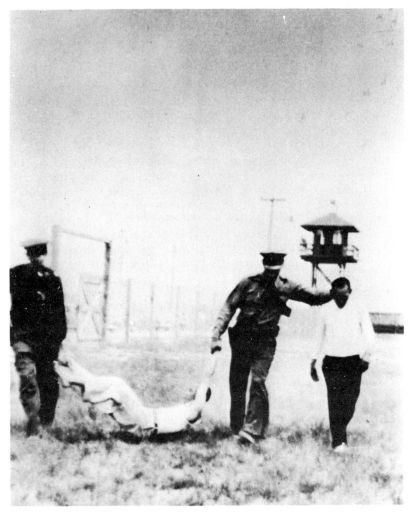

Terror at Tule Lake, 1945.
  [III]

committee authorized filing of the suits if we were unable to reach an
agreement with the Department of the Interior. Failing to reach an am-
icable settlement with Abe Fortas, the suits were filed" (CHS 3580). The
suits named Ickes, Myer, Cozzens, and Best as respondents and affirmed
that in each of the five cases the petitioner had been unlawfully imprisoned by the respondents and that none of these officials had "any authority to hold or imprison petitioner, and the holding, imprisonment

Terror at Tule Lake, 1945.
[IV]

and restraint of petitioner are illegal and in violation of the Constitution of the United States and the statutes of the United States." U.S. District Judge A. F. St. Sure ordered Ickes, Myer et al. to show cause why the writs should not be granted on August 20, which order was continued to August 27 and then to September 10 (N. J. L. Pieper to Hoover, August 29, 1945, FBI 62-70564). In New York, Baldwin's board of directors voted "to take no action" on the ostensible ground that they "had

Terror at Tule Lake, 1945.
[V]

not been furnished copies of the petitions" (NCACLU minutes, September 6, 1945, CHS 3580).

Risen renewed from the ashes of Myer's defeat the preceding summer, the stockade was back in business and seemingly destined to last as long as the WRA. Enter Wayne M. Collins to act out a scene redolent of déjà vu, which he later sketched for Michi Weglyn:

Arriving at the Tule Lake Center [on August 28, 1945, just over a year since the first memorable confrontation,] I discussed this new Stockade problem with Mr. Raymond Best, the Project Director, Mr. Lou Noyes, the Project Attorney, and other members of the WRA staff, upbraided them for having reopened the Stockade and for having incarcerated citizens therein without preferring charges against them. . . . Because they came to doubt whether their actions could be justified in court and because of their fear that if the outcome of habeas corpus proceedings was unfavorable to the WRA the facts would be publicized . . . they consented to release all the persons who were held in the Stockade and to close the Stockade permanently. The imprisoned persons were released immediately and they were brought from the Stockade into the room so that I could verify the fact of their release.

[*YoI*, p. 216]

By then the five teenagers had been unlawfully imprisoned in the stockade for about three months.

"You are of course familiar with the fact that we do not take every case put up to us," Baldwin reminded Besig a few weeks after the adolescents had been liberated. As for their "disciplinary" cases, "the real reason for our disinclination to raise the issue in the courts was solely a matter of public relations." Appalled, Besig shot back that this was the first time, so far as he knew,

that the flexible question of "public relations" has proved a bar to the board's entry into a case. On such grounds, the Union could always wriggle out of cases involving unpopular minorities such as Communists and thereby reduce our defense of civil liberties to a mockery. May I quote from your letter in our sheet? It seems to me that our membership ought to be apprised of this shift in our policy.

[September 25, 28, 1945, CHS 3580]

And he had already made plain for Baldwin that the NCACLU would not be reduced to subservience: "I suppose you can always kick us out of the Union" (September 21, 1945, CHS 3580).

From Washington came Alexander Meiklejohn's chatty letter about a conference on citizenship renunciation that he and Baldwin had just had with Assistant Attorney General "Herb Wechsler, who is [Edward J.] Ennis's boss. There was good hard plain talking, and the difficulties of the situation seemed to get clearer." Who had done the hard talking seemed clearer with Meiklejohn's admission that he and Baldwin had been persuaded that the legal position of the renunciants "seems hopeless," with their only hope lying in administrative remedies, the sympathetic treatment of each case by their kindly keepers. But before he and

Baldwin placed too much reliance on "administrative relief," Besig warned Meiklejohn in reply, they should have something concrete from their friends in the administration:

> I am not opposed to Roger's conferences in Washington, although I am inclined to think that he may be taken in by his friends. I say to the national office that its job is to establish national policy promptly and with clarity, but giving us a voice in the formulation of that policy, and that our job is the application of that policy. That is the old argument.
>
> [September 14, 25, 1945, CHS 3580]

And that old argument spilled over into the next year, with Besig and his executive committee charging Baldwin and his board of directors with "playing the government's game" by blinking the critical issue of *official* duress in the citizenship renunciations: "We submit that it is not the function of the Union to shield its friends in the War Relocation Authority and the Justice Department from legitimate charges at the expense of the renunciants. By doing so we open ourselves to charges of partisanship and failure to keep faith with our membership" (Besig to board of directors, March 11, 1946, CHS 3580).

For captors who sat down to play the government's game in the comfort of their offices, it was "an exciting adventure" that beat soil conservation any day. The principal players were in the triple alliance Myer had crafted: his WRA, Masaoka's JACL, and Baldwin's New York ACLU, with all three organizations working in concert with their friends in the War Department, the Department of Justice, the Department of the Interior, and elsewhere within the Roosevelt administration. The sacrificial pawns were the mysterious beings in Myer's "unknown and unrecognizable minority." Once self-identified or at least made more scrutable by their anti-administration attitudes and activities—real or merely imputed—dissident inmates became Issei internees or Nisei penal colony/stockade prisoners and renunciants. These "hopeless" cases, as Meiklejohn called them, were the human stakes, casualties of the triple alliance and its friends, victims of simultaneous betrayal from within and from without the camps. But the grand success of this game plan depended upon a gentlemanly observance of rules that kept Nisei inmates severed from their presumptive rights as citizens—or, alternatively, as Myer had ominously put it, upon getting "the courts to act normally in putting people in prison and holding them" (WRA staff minutes, February 5, 1943, JERS, 67/14, E2.11B).

From the players' point of view, then, the real trouble with Besig and

Collins was that they were "hot headed" spoilsports. They broke the rules and fouled up the game by threatening legal action and by actually aiding and abetting inmates in "airing" their grievances in court. But without their dedication to the proposition that the Bill of Rights belonged to nonwhites too, tyranny at Tule Lake would still have reigned unchallenged. "The measure of a man is not by pigmentation. The value of a citizen does not lie in his color," declared Collins: "When the definitive history of these times is written, that which the government has done to these citizens will be described in one word and that word is 'Shameful'" ("Plaintiffs' Brief," WCP, 78/177, *Abo* v. *Clark* [77 F. Suppl. 806 (1948)]).

Undeterred by official disapproval, Collins went ahead with his cases in behalf of thousands of renunciants and devoted the rest of his life to them and to others, most notably Iva Toguri D'Aquino, the Nisei misdubbed "Tokyo Rose." Besig, too, kept faith with civil liberties principles and NCACLU members. On February 7, 1946, his executive committee voted "to protest to Sec'y Ickes and Dillon Myer against the slave labor racket at Tule Lake" (minutes, CHS 3580). As we have seen in chapter 3, Besig did just that.

But the captors were already turning the last page of their "final chapter." In the Tule high school auditorium the last picture show had run through the projector, and on March 1, 1946, the editor of the *Newell Star* informed readers that they held the final issue of the camp newspaper in their hands. Myer's WRA was saying "thirty," the end, that is, of the "exciting adventure in the democratic method."

5

Some ten miles south of Newell are the lava beds where Kintpuash, the Modoc leader commonly called Captain Jack, and his band holed up and held off the U.S. Army for months until he was finally captured, and then hanged on October 3, 1873. Today a visitor sees a historical marker in Newell commemorating that other war, to the west sees Castle Rock, and to the east the flat-topped butte Tule inmates called Abalone Mountain and local residents less picturesquely still call Horse Mountain: "Nothing lives long," sang the dying Cheyenne White Antelope, "except the earth and the mountains."

The Newell Homestead Market, a grocery, is in what used to be the officers' quarters of Colonel Austin's military police battalion. Chicano families live in nearby shacks that were once the barracks of Tuleans. A

Castle Rock to the West of Tule Lake, April 30, 1981.
  [R. Drinnon]

visitor can even photograph Castle Rock through a section of the chain-link fence, topped by rusting barbed wire, that once made the captors feel more secure in their "Caucasian" area.

Of course, from May 1942 to March 1946 the town itself was strictly off-limits for Tule inmates. Former Community Analyst Marvin K.

Opler remembered that it had once taken him "six months to get permission to take our Japanese-American nursery-school kids across the road to the Center farm after one of them asked his teacher if a Japanese child was ever allowed to see real farm animals like the ones in the picture books." In contrast to this tight security was the relaxed informality enjoyed by former soldiers of the Third Reich in their prisoner-of-war camp less than fifteen miles away, an irony not lost on anthropologist Opler: German prisoners could ride their bicycles "into the town to buy in the stores. They picnicked in the hills in their bluejeans with 'P.O.W.' stenciled across the backs. One day I walked into their camp unchallenged and we stood around, speaking German, and they showed me photos of their families" ("Non-White Americans and Our 'Kid-Glove Concentration Camps,'" *Colleague* [SUNY, Buffalo] 6 [Fall 1969]: 4). Obviously for captors, to paraphrase Collins, the measure of a captive *was* by pigmentation.

A little to the north of the Homestead Market is California Registered Landmark No. 850-2, a plaque cemented in place by the State Department of Parks and Recreation on May 27, 1979:

> Tule Lake was one of ten American concentration camps established during World War II to incarcerate 110,000 persons of Japanese ancestry, of whom the majority were American citizens, behind barbed wire and guard towers without charge, trial or establishment of guilt. These camps are reminders of how racism, economic and political exploitation, and expediency can undermine the constitutional guarantees of United States citizens and aliens alike. May the injustices and humiliation suffered here never recur.

Almost a replica of the first Landmark No. 850, installed six years earlier in the facade of the sentry house at the entrance to Manzanar, the real fight over the wording on both plaques had occurred then. In this intense struggle the Manzanar Committee had run into surprisingly little opposition from the State Parks and Recreation Department to the term *concentration camps*, compromised on *economic exploitation* in lieu of *greed*, but had to fight right down to the wire to retain *racism*. Our political surrogates and their supporters still would like to keep us from seeing what the camps so plainly memorialized.

By March 1946 the soil conservation alumni—the back-slapping Raymond R. Best, the garrulous Robert B. Cozzens, the steadfast Clarence E. Zimmer, and the rest—had become veteran people keepers. All pulled up stakes and many pursued their careers as civil servants elsewhere. (Dillon Myer took a significant number of former WRA personnel with him into the Bureau of Indian Affairs, where we shall encounter them again.) For just one instance, Best went on to head the U.S. refugee camps in Germany, Austria, and Italy. When he died at eighty his obituarist noted this work with displaced persons, but started out with what he was best known for: "In 1943, after Raymond R. Best was involved in a night of terror at the Tulelake Relocation Center, his name went on front pages around the world. . . . His night of terror at the Japanese internment camp was an uprising among what was then said to be a hard core of camp troublemakers, out to 'get' him. A riot ensued, requiring tanks, armored cars, machine guns and fixed bayonets to secure the safety of the camp director and his family" (*Sacramento Bee*, September 1, 1976).

Screams from the back rooms of Best's administration building were the real stigmata of that night of terror: "It's like shooting ducks."

May the injustices and humiliation suffered here never recur.

Though some return on pilgrimages from time to time, the victims have gone, taking with them their hundreds and thousands of individual tragedies, Kiyoshi Okamoto's, the Reverend Shizuo Kai's, George Kuratomi's, Joseph Kurihara's, Harry Yoshio Ueno's, Tom Kobiyashi's, Tokio Yamane's, Masao I.'s, Kentaro T.'s, Saburo M.'s, Yoshio Y.'s, Masao K.'s, Hisato K.'s, and those of all the others. Their wounds scarred over, but never healed, as the recent outpouring of pain in their testimony before the commission of inquiry (CWRIC) established beyond question.

Since Myer's agency patriarchally excluded women from his "unknown and unrecognizable minority" as fit objects for punishment—he never made the penal colonies and stockade coeducational—my numbered and selected *troublemakers* have all been men. Women suffered no less, though differently and perhaps in some respects more, as they stood on the other side of the parking lot from the stockade or watched loved ones being dragged away, going into the army, or however their families were being torn apart.

Marvin K. Opler could never forget and often repeated the story of one mother:

> Few accounts have picked up this reviewer's possibly most poignant story of a segregated Nisei wife who went utterly schizophrenic and literally brained one infant of her own and was about to destroy a second. She smeared the brain cell material on inside barrack walls of her dwelling "space," announc-

ing that these were the unspoken thoughts of her deprived children. This violent projection and her total derangement disappeared within three months of her being remanded to a State Hospital for treatment and certainly tells, in bloody terms, the tortures felt by one hopeless "relocatee" transformed by government policy into a hopeless "segregee."

[*American Anthropologist* 75 (April 1973): 559]

For this woman, Opler might have added, Tule Lake had been an "extreme situation," whose psychological manifestations were comparable to schizophrenic phenomena observed by Bruno Bettelheim in the Nazi camps.

After Nisei volunteers went into what had originally been Mike Masaoka's proposed "suicide battalion" and after the 442nd Regimental Combat Team went into the thick of the fighting in Europe, Director Myer periodically sent body counts back to the camps that were to his mind honor rolls showing how many Japanese Americans had proved their patriotism with their lives. "MYER REPORTS 45 CENTER NISEI KILLED IN ITALY" read the headline of the *Newell Star* on September 21, 1944. The first name on the list was that of a technical sergeant, and my own most poignant story came in the form of a letter to Ernest Besig from the dead man's mother a year later (September 6, 1945, WCP, 78/177). With this little help, it speaks for itself and demands full quotation, minus surname but with errors and garbled sentence:

Dear Sir: RE: RENUNCIATION OF CITIZENSHIP OF
SOJI TOM, JACK YOSHIMI, YONE, YUKUYE,
AND BETTY ASAE A . . .

I am the mother of the four mentioned above. I am, also, the mother of George Zentaro A . . . , T/Sgt Company F, 442nd Division, who was killed in action in Italy, July 3, 1944.

George was inducted before our family was evacuated. it was ever the wish of my husband and of myself to keep our family intact while we waited for the was [*sic*] to end and bring our eldest son back to us again.

But on July 3, 1944 we received words of the death of son in action. I was grieved beyond comfort. My husband who was of advanced years, was stricken with a hopeless malady shortly after evacuation and confined to the hospital. He was too ill to be told the news. Words cannot express the agony, the anguish, the utter desolation of my heart.

My husband's condition became worse and on October 4th of the same year, he passed away not knowing that George had gone before him. Then I lost all perspective. I forgot how gladly George had gone to serve his country. I only knew that the rest of my children must be kept with me.

Another Inmate Gold Star Mother, April 21, 1945. Like Mrs. Tane A., a number of women behind barbed wire received word that their sons had been killed in action. This WRA promotional still shows a colonel from the Seventh Service Command in the camp at Granada, Colorado, as he presented the Distinguished Service Cross to the mother of a man killed near Sureveto, Italy.
[The Bancroft Library]

So when rumors spread through the colony that evacuees, other than aliens, would be ousted from the center, I was panic-stricken. I nagged the children to renounce their citizenship. They reasoned with me that it was not necessary to give up their birthright, that it would be possible to go to Japan even if they retained their citizenship. But I was frantic and urgent. It was their concern over my health, and over my sanity, and the love they had for me who had so lately lost two, which finally drove them, against their will and better judgment, to do my bidding.

Now, I have the children with me but they arelike so many strangers—they resent me—what I have made them do has alienated them. And thinking rationally, I have come to realize the enormity of the wrong I had done them to restore their citizenship, I will gladly do it. Will you, in your kindness, give me advice. Any light you may shed upon ttis [*sic*] problem will be gratefully accepted by a perturbed mother.

Very respectfully

[Sig.]

Mrs. Tane A . . .

Citizens had become anvils, said Wayne M. Collins, "upon which the government must hammer" ("Plaintiffs' Brief," WCP, 78/177, *Abo* v. *Clark* [77 F. Suppl. 806 (1948)]).

PART III

Native Americans

Many Indians Are Still Primitive.
> —*Dillon S. Myer,*
> *"Autobiography," 1970*

CHAPTER VIII

Commissioner

Now the Bill of Rights applies to Indians as it does to all of
us and I want to say at the very beginning that I believe in
the spirit as well as the letter of our Constitution. I intend to
administer the Bureau of Indian Affairs in accordance with
that belief. I have had some experience with the problems of
minorities in our country and I know that their finest hopes
and aspirations are as truly in the American tradition as
those of the rest of us.

> —Dillon S. Myer,
> "Statement . . . before the National Congress
> of American Indians," August 29, 1950

On March 28, 1946, a *Washington Post* editorial by Alan Barth assured
the country that Dillon S. Myer and his aides had handled valiantly "the
most distasteful of all war jobs" and could "take pride in a difficult job
exceedingly well done." On May 8, 1946, President Harry S. Truman
handed him the nation's Medal for Merit after Secretary Harold L. Ickes
had so recommended in words he lived to regret:

> By his scrupulous adherence to democratic concepts in his administration
> of the War Relocation Authority, Dillon Myer has established a precedent
> for equitable treatment of dislocated minorities. In doing so, he salvaged for
> American democracy a minority group that has proved itself well worth sav-
> ing, and at the same time he saved the United States from jeopardizing its
> standing as a democracy in the eyes of other nations. Finally, he succeeded
> in converting what was in 1941 the least known, most misunderstood and
> most locality-bound American minority into a well-known, widely distrib-
> uted one, whose Americanism has been recognized by fair-minded people
> throughout the Nation. . . .
> I know Dillon Myer and his work. For two years now the War Relocation
> Authority has operated within my Department, and I can vouch personally
> for his administrative competence, his clear vision, his indestructible integ-
> rity, and for the warmth of his human sympathies which more than any
> other quality in the man enabled him to keep alive in a bewildered and dis-

located people their faith in American democracy and their faith in themselves.

[NA, RG 48]

And on May 22, 1946, some 275 members and guests of the Japanese American Citizens League sat down to a banquet at the Roosevelt Hotel in New York City in honor of their head jailer and applauded the organization's "Citation Presented to Dillon S. Myer" for his "courageous and inspired leadership" (*UA*, p. 342).

The deskborne war hero had come a long way from the family farm. In his middle years, Myer had precociously become an elder statesman. Truman offered to appoint him governor of Puerto Rico. Myer knew nothing about the language and the rest of the cultural heritage of the islanders, or for that matter anything about their island, but then neither had he known anything about Americans of Japanese ancestry on the continent. "At that stage of the game," however, Myer wanted to stay in Washington and tackle slum clearance (Auto, p. 227). He knew nothing about that either, really, but during the war had visited his charges in Chicago and "the slummy parts" of other cities to which the WRA was scattering "relocatees" and had then been shocked by the conditions in which they were forced to live. Accordingly, he resolved to become commissioner of the Federal Public Housing Authority, an appointment he duly received in August 1946. After over a half century on the farm or in agriculture, he now launched a crusade to clean up the cities, with "basic principles wholly consistent with my previous experience in public administration." "We *will* move forward," he assured housing officials at a conference in Cleveland on October 12, 1946, "until the problem of decent housing for every American family is solved" (*Cong. Digest* 25: 278). Alas, Representative George H. Bender, an unkind critic from his home state, later held him partially responsible for the great forward movement that never occurred, asking "Is not this the same Dillon Myer who bungled the housing business?" (*Cong. Rec.*, April 25, 1951, p. 4374). Before he left the housing authority at the end of 1947, Myer himself came to realize that many of his subordinates "never quite understood the actions of a farm reared lad." As he reminisced later, had he sensed what would happen "in the public housing area during the period I was to take over the job I probably would have accepted the offer to become the last appointed Governor of Puerto Rico in spite of my antipathy to the social and protocol requirements of that office which led to my nonacceptance" (Auto, p. 239).

Greener pastures beckoned—in fact the whole Western Hemisphere lay at Myer's feet waiting to be cleaned up. Sponsored by John Drier, a former subordinate in the Soil Conservation Service and then an officer in the Department of State, Myer was named on January 1, 1948, to succeed Colonel Arthur R. Harris as president of the Institute of Inter-American Affairs (*Bulletin of the Pan American Union* 82 [1948]: 234). A precursor of Truman's Point Four program and of John Fitzgerald Kennedy's Alliance for Progress, the IIAA traced its ancestry all the way back to the Manifest Destiny propounded by Secretary of State James G. Blaine, who had established the Pan American Union in 1890 as "an ideal economic complement to the United States." In 1942 Assistant Secretary of State Nelson A. Rockefeller had updated Blaine's imperial vision by organizing the IIAA to run technical assistance programs of sanitary engineering, agriculture, and what was called education.

Myer now stepped into a position that put him in charge of extensive projects in eighteen Latin American countries. He knew nothing about any of these and nothing about their inhabitants and cultures, but to offset this lack of preparation, he visited cooperating republics on two field trips and took a beginning language course at the Foreign Service Institute, where after a year of diligent cramming he could at least "read the Spanish newspapers" (Auto, p. 246).

Through radio, movies, magazines, and other publications, Myer's IIAA showered Latin America with the appropriately translated imperatives of sanitary living, industry, self-reliance, acquisitiveness, and the like. For those misguided natives who shook off this indoctrination, he had no more patience than he had had for "hardboiled boys" in the camps. In Guatemala, he later observed bitterly, his agency was forced to cancel the *Servicio* or joint fund "where the Communists were moving in and wanted full control of all the educational activities" (Auto, p. 242). In fine, Myer's apparatus and projects heralded the network of repression and the sophisticated counterinsurgency campaigns of his successors.

In 1949 Myer ascended to global troubleshooting as head of a United Nations mission to the Middle East. He knew nothing about that part of the world and neither did H. Rex Lee, the former WRA relocation expert he took along on this junket into exotic terrain (Auto, pp. 247–50). After a quick reconnaissance, however, the proconsul and his aide had to return to Washington without solving the problem of the Palestinian refugees.

Anyway, Myer was shortly recalled from hemispheric and global social engineering to tend to homegrown natives in North America.

2

In 1947 the president had offered to make Myer head of the Indian Service. After Truman's surprising victory in 1948, he had called and repeated the offer, but Myer did not want to leave the Institute of Inter-American Affairs until he had pushed its charter through Congress. Finally, in 1950 Truman offered him the appointment for the third time, and Myer accepted after receiving assurances his new agency would have enlarged appropriations. In his unpublished autobiography Myer recalled that Truman (HT) kept his word and asked the budget director (BD) to give him more money:

BD: Why, Mr. President?
HT: I have a shitty ass job that I want him to do. [Auto, p. 244]

And in one of his memoranda for the secretary of the interior, Myer explained in greater detail how he had slid into his post as commissioner of the Bureau of Indian Affairs on May 8, 1950:

> I did not accept the job on the first two occasions because I knew something about the complexities of the problems involved and had some doubt as to whether I could do an adequate job with the tools at hand and when it was offered to me in the spring of 1950 I made it quite clear to the Secretary that I felt very strongly that the Bureau of Indian Affairs should get out of business as quickly as possible but that the job must be done with honor.
>   [for Douglas McKay, March 20, 1953, NRC]

Feeling "very strongly" that the BIA should get out of the Indian business, he had been given a free hand by Truman and the leverage of an increased budget. He had also secured "agreement on many points," he assured Secretary McKay, before taking over as commissioner.

Myer stepped into the command of a far-flung domestic empire that by comparison dwarfed his World War II dominions. Then he had kept only about 120,000 Japanese Americans (including their Issei parents) in the camps; now he became the keeper of about 450,000 Native Americans in several hundred tribes and bands, or of almost four times as many souls. During the war he had been chief jailer, with a staff of only some 3,000 WRA "Caucasians"; now he was commissioner, with a staff of about four times as many underlings that was entirely white at the top and predominantly white at the bottom. Of his some 12,000 BIA employees, nearly 4,500 were teachers and others who ran 93 boarding schools and 241 day schools, and another 3,000 were medical personnel who operated 62 hospitals in seventeen states and in Alaska.

Then he had had charge of only about 100 million dollars' worth of government property; now he took charge of many times that amount, especially if we include over 50 million acres of tribal and individual allotment land, with all the underlying riches of oil and gas, coal, uranium, and phosphate. And then he had made up "WRA law" as he went along; now he inherited out of the native-hating past and the more benign New Deal era the bureau's Indian Affairs Manual, the thirty-three volumes of which made a stack higher than his own six feet and included 389 treaties; 5,000 statutes; 2,000 federal court decisions; 500 attorney general opinions; over 2,200 BIA regulations; 95 tribal constitutions and 74 tribal charters; and a mass of Department of the Interior rulings. Myer knew nothing about this mountain of convoluted Indian law and nothing about his nearly half a million new charges, who had somehow survived under its weight.

Of course, the new commissioner could draw on the experience of seasoned BIA officials, some of whom cared about Native Americans. Instead he implemented his prior "agreement on many points" with Truman and Interior Secretary Oscar L. Chapman, which gave him a free hand in hiring and firing.

The first to go was Assistant Commissioner William Zimmerman, who had been working to implement the Indian Reorganization Act since it launched the Indian New Deal in 1934, and who was widely known and generally trusted in Indian country. To replace his intimate knowledge of personnel, policies, and unfulfilled commitments, Myer brought in Erwin J. ("Pop") Utz, who had been his chief of the WRA Operations Division and long before that one of his county agents in Ohio. Utz's major qualifications for this high position were a conditioned compliance to his chief's every wish and an inviolable ignorance of Indian affairs.

Perhaps an even more grievous loss for tribal peoples was BIA Chief Counsel Theodore H. Haas, the principal collaborator of Felix S. Cohen in writing the *Handbook of Federal Indian Law* (1941) and a champion over the years of Indian land rights, preference in employment, and tribal self-determination. As Cohen somberly observed in a letter to the chairman of the Omaha Tribal Council, "in losing Ted Haas, the Indian Bureau has lost its conscience, as in losing Bill Zimmerman it lost its memory. It is now free to disregard past promises and to repeat past mistakes without awareness of either" (to Amos Lamson, May 12, 1950, AAIA). Acting out this prediction, the new commissioner replaced Haas with Edwin E. Ferguson, who had succeeded Philip M.

Glick as WRA solicitor in 1944 and whose only experience with Indian affairs, as Cohen pointed out, "was an attempt to diminish rentals payable to an Indian tribe for reservation land taken for one of the concentration camps in which American citizens of Japanese ancestry were held during the war years under Dillon Myer's supervision." To second Ferguson's absolute inexperience in a very specialized branch of the law, Myer created the new position of "associate" chief counsel and filled it with Lewis A. Sigler, who had been his WRA assistant solicitor and whose sole claim on our memory is the daring with which he had secretly denounced the Leupp penal colony as "premised on Gestapo methods" (to Philip Glick, August 14, 1943, NA, RG 210).

Assistant Commissioner John H. Provinse, the applied anthropologist who had moved over to the BIA at the end of the war after serving as Myer's WRA chief of community management, kept his job not by virtue of his experience in the Indian Service but by virtue of his unblemished record of tractability. Apart from Provinse, Myer made a clean sweep of key staff positions both in Washington and in the field, as we shall see, and eventually drove out Assistant Commissioner Willard W. Beatty, the respected head of the Branch of Education, Joseph C. McCaskill, another assistant commissioner and head of the Indian Arts and Crafts Board, and a long list of others.

Thus did Myer surround himself with the same crew of career bureaucrats, many of whom had followed him from the SCS to the WRA and now to the BIA, and all of whom had a ready docility to orders from the top and a rigid hostility to any sign of resistance from the bottom. "Wily" reservation Indians, as the commissioner soon called restive natives, now replaced the camp "troublemakers" of unfond memory. To put a good face on the forthcoming benevolent repression, Myer demoted the head of the Information Service and in his stead brought in the ineffable Morrill M. Tozier, his former WRA publicity man, who was practiced at the art. And at the tip of this pyramid, just one niche below his own, Myer created the new position of "associate" commissioner and filled it with H. Rex Lee, his relocation expert, boon companion on the United Nations junket to the Middle East, and now undercommissioner, a man with a reputation in the Department of the Interior for having a low view of Indians.

Since his clash with Myer over policy for the WRA camp on the Colorado River Indian Reservation in 1942, John Collier had been repeatedly attacked in the press and in Congress for his "communistic" nurturing of tribal cultures and self-government and for his perverse insistence that the Indian Reorganization Act had laid down the radical principle that the U.S. government must keep its promises to tribes and not abrogate them without their consent. Representative of the growing number of congressmen who demanded that the Indian be "turned loose" or "freed" from all those solemn pledges was Senator Elbert Thomas of Oklahoma, who chaired a subcommittee that in 1943 called for "the liquidation of the Indian Bureau" and that charged Collier with wanting "to keep the Indian an Indian and make him satisfied with all the limitations of a primitive life" and with "tieing him to the land in perpetuity," an encumbrance white Westerners patently could do without. Forced to resign in 1945, Collier headed up the Institute of Ethnic Affairs and became a professor of anthropology at the City College of New York, from which vantage point he watched as Acting Commissioner William Zimmerman was pressured by Congress in 1948 to draw up a comprehensive program of BIA liquidation and as scores of bills designed to scrap Indian rights were introduced in both Houses.

In 1950 the "demolition enterprise" in the BIA alarmed Collier and moved him to caustic comment about Myer's "new broom." Still defending his friend, Roger Baldwin acknowledged "what you say about the new broom's clean sweep, but it might conceivably be for the better. I suppose only time will show, but Myer has demonstrated a very sensitive understanding of minority problems and the courage to resist pressures" (June 10, 1950, JCP). No, the new commissioner stood for "administration by formula," Collier replied, adding that Myer had once served

> as a model for a portrait of the men who come up through [the] state extension service to federal top jobs, believers in just one way to do things. The verbal portrait was shown him: he remarked, I have known thousands of them like that. He never suspected that the portrait was of himself. . . . Myer is a peculiarly crystallized mentality with a meagre frame of reference. Within this crystallization and meagreness he will always be faithful and forthright. But he cannot change himself; he doesn't even know what he himself is like. . . . But more: Myer has surrounded himself with an intimate culture of yes-men, not bad men but mere opportunists; they will insure that the miracle of the make-over of Myer will not even get started.
> [June 16, 1950, JCP]

Easily dismissed as the fulminations of a disappointed rival, Collier's predictions were soon proved prescient.

Myer's number two man in that intimate culture did have some talents Collier and other critics tended to overlook. When Richard Nishimoto encountered H. Rex Lee at Poston some years earlier, that shrewd inmate had not been impressed: "Lee is stupid and asinine," he had reported to Dorothy Swaine Thomas. "When I met him first (before my conversation with him), I described him as 'a traveling salesman of a wholesale hardware house.' I still hold the same opinion of him" (March 24, 1945, JERS, 67/14, W1.25B). Later Harold L. Ickes reported Lee's low view of Indians and characterized him as a man "who feels perfectly at home in a puppet show" (*New Republic* 125 [September 24, 1951]: 16). Lee was also, however, a political operator with experience his master prized, as Myer made clear in his autobiography. His associate commissioner, he noted proudly, "had been very close to Congressional committees during the four years or so [following the WRA] when he was in the [Interior] division of Territory and Insular Affairs" (Auto, p. 253). Although Myer himself enjoyed "playing politics with members of the Congress" (Nishimoto to Thomas, March 9, 1945, JERS, 67/14, W1.25B), he needed Lee as his fulltime lobbyist on the Hill and as his liaison with those committees.

With this key tool at hand, Myer's recycled apparatus first went into action in response to a congressional proposal known as the Bosone Joint Resolution. Described as "a red-haired freshman Congress-woman" from Utah, Reva Beck Bosone had been "only casually acquainted with the Indian problem" before she was put on the House Public Lands Committee. After a year of listening to Indians testify, she had an inspiration that solved the problem: They should be made "free, unrestricted Americans." With "education and health training," she believed, the red man "can hold his own with the white man." Myer and Lee took this emancipator in hand, after several conferences had revised her bill (House Joint Resolution—hereafter H.J. Res.—490), and "went to work for it as avidly as Mrs. Bosone," according to the *Washington Post* account of August 13, 1950. When the reporter asked Lee how it felt to be working for a bill that would eventually eliminate his agency, he replied: "Well, that's what we are in (the Indian ward) business for— to get ourselves out of it."

The forerunner of many bills to come that undertook "initiation of a procedure for the final termination of Federal supervision and control over the American Indian as such," H.J. Res. 490 passed the House and then went before the Senate Interior and Insular Affairs Committee. At the hearings on August 11, 1950, someone expressed concern for Indian welfare and survival, whereupon Representative Bosone exclaimed: "But, think of the American taxpayer! I'm worried about the taxpayer.

Do you know what it costs to keep up this Indian Bureau?" A bemused witness of this outburst, Collier found Associate Commissioner Lee's support of the bill still more revealing:

> Lee was asked if he had any idea how many treaties there were between the Federal Government and the Indians. Lee said that he did not have any idea. However, he did feel that many of the existing treaties could be adjusted in some way in order to terminate the Federal obligations. When consent of the Indians was brought into the discussion as an obstacle to "conversion" of treaty obligations, Lee said something like this: "Well, if they won't consent, some compromise will just have to be reached." Lee also said several times that the object was to sit down, get to work and get this thing wound up fast.
>
> ["Remembrances of the Hearing,"
> August 28, 1950, JCP]

The key word was *terminate*, and the main idea, Lee declared, was to get "the Indian problem" settled once and for all.

Of course no one, not Lee, not Myer, not Bosone, and not the committee members who favorably recommended her bill to the Senate, deigned to consult the tribes, let alone seek their consent. Still lacking that necessary "education and health training," Indians could not be expected to act responsibly for themselves. Belatedly learning that their keepers were once again settling their affairs once and for all, some tribes joined in the fight against the resolution. Collier attacked it through the Institute of Ethnic Affairs. In one of her columns Eleanor Roosevelt added her warning, "Bill Now on Hill May Strike at American Indians" (*Washington Daily News*, December 30, 1950). But the most telling opposition came from Harold L. Ickes, who frankly hoped that, if it came to his desk, Truman would veto the bill, for it was nothing less than an attempt "to breach contracts, to terminate present Federal protections and services, and undo all that the Indian Reorganization Act of 1934 . . . has made it possible for the Indians to accomplish for themselves." Still more in sorrow than in anger, Ickes added that "I have had faith in Indian Commissioner Dillon Myer, but it has been somewhat shaken by the fact that he has supported this legislation. I hesitate to believe that he understands what could be done under this legislation" (*Washington Post*, September 17, 1950). Scathing fire from such quarters killed the bill on the Senate floor, but friends of the tribes had merely won a skirmish, not a battle, and surely not the war.

Stung by his old boss's rebuke, Myer wrote recalling "the wonderful support you gave me during those troublous times. I shall always remember that had it not been for your sense of justice and fighting spirit, the War Relocation Authority would not have so readily achieved its humane and democratic goals during that period of adverse public temper. I honestly feel in this instance that you have not given me my day in court but have based your decision on presentation by the prosecution only" (September 22, 1950, JCP). "When a man wants his day in court, he asks for it," replied Ickes and in anticipation gave him the benefit of his opinions:

> Frankly, it seemed almost incredible to me that you should endorse this legislation and, whether you know it or not, there is a growing feeling of criticism of the action of the Bureau of Indian Affairs with reference to this bill. I even hear complaints that the Indians themselves have not been consulted. I have heard categorically that many Indians do not want their reservations disestablished. . . . Certainly, to turn the Indians generally footloose without any legal or moral obligation toward them, so far as the Government is concerned, would be a shameful thing to do.
>
> [October 4, 1950, JCP]

Perhaps spoiled by his long association with John Collier, Ickes still held "the idea" that it was the duty of any commissioner "to devote his first interest to the native Americans."

Myer had a different idea. By his embrace of the Bosone Resolution, he had already shown that his first impulse was to invite the fox into the chicken coop. With his pitchman Lee on the Hill, he was maneuvering the BIA into an alliance with its former enemies, the congressional network responsible for the many fierce assaults upon the Indian Reorganization Act. Shortly the alliance became unmistakable when Myer joined forces with the dean of the Senate Indian-haters, Democrat Patrick A. McCarran of Nevada, who had long coveted and long tried to bestow upon white squatters the water and some 2,000 acres of land belonging to the Pyramid Lake Paiutes. Said "old Pat," as white Nevadans called him, "an Indian ain't *got* no goddamn rights" (*New Yorker*, January 1, 1955, p. 38).

3

Back in January 1844 some local residents had walked into the pages of Anglo-American history by meeting up with and handing over to John C. Frémont and his men the delicacies of some cutthroat trout—big ones, Frémont remarked, "about as large as the Columbia River salmon." The gift-givers did not know who they were yet, according to that history, but called themselves the *Numa* or just the People, of whom there were about six hundred. Their tribal neighbors called them the Kuyuidökadö, or the Cui-Ui (kwee-we) Eaters, after the *Chamistes cujus*, a unique fish found in their lake alongside the big trout, as A. J. Liebling pointed out in his useful series in the *New Yorker* (January 1, 8, 15, 22, 1955). These fisherpeople of the desert and plateau country did not even know the name of their 120,000 acres of turquoise water—they called it Lake of the Cui-Ui—until its official discoverer thought of Cheops after seeing an islet off shore and called it Pyramid Lake. Although they did not know who they were or where they were, yet, they could claim to be permanent residents since they had been on the premises for some three thousand years. A Shoshonean dialect group of the Uto-Aztecan language family, as the anthropologists would later establish, they had stayed put beside their lake after their colinguals headed south to empire and to an earlier discovery by Cortez. The Numa knew a good place when they got to it.

But once the Paiutes of Pyramid Lake had been officially discovered, they were caught up in the convulsions of Anglo-American history. One of the ironies of their touch-and-go existence then became the way two women in different centuries contributed to their survival.

Born about the time Frémont discovered the Numa's lake, and first called by their name Thocmetony, or Shell Flower, Sarah Winnemucca was the daughter of the old headman Winnemucca, whose name meant "the giver" or "one who looks after the Numa" (in fact synonymous translations). Through her mother, Tuboitonie, she was the granddaughter of the man whites called Captain Truckee because of his agreeable habit of saying *truckee,* or "all right." The first whites she saw frightened her, but later she was sent off by her people to board with a white family in a mining camp, where she soon learned American English. Later she taught herself Spanish and two other Indian languages, returned to the Numa and became their interpreter and mediator with the dominant culture, and in 1880 journeyed across the continent to speak to the Great White Father in their behalf. An intelligent, determined, passionate patriot, Sarah Winnemucca earned the hatred and fear of men in the Indian Service. Prior to her Washington trip, for instance, Agent W. V. Rinehart collected and dispatched to BIA headquarters affidavits ostensibly showing

> that her influence with the Indians has always been to render them licentious, contumacious and profligate. That this woman has been several times married, but that by reason of her adulterous and drunken habits, neither squaw-

The Winnemucca Family, 1880. This photograph of Sarah, her father "the giver," her brothers Natchez and Captain Jim, and an unidentified boy was probably taken in Washington when the "Princess" fruitlessly asked the Great White Father for their rights.
[Nevada Historical Society]

men nor Indians would long live with her; that in addition to her character of Harlot and drunkard, she merits and possesses that of a notorious liar and malicious schemer.

The Paiute "princess" had to be doing something right.

Three years later she lectured on the plight of her people and of other Indians to audiences in six Eastern states, a tour made possible by the enthusiastic support of two remarkable Bostonians, Elizabeth Palmer Peabody and her sister Mary Mann, widow of the famed educator Horace Mann. With their encouragement she wrote *Life Among the Piutes: Their Wrongs and Claims* (1883). The book, said her editor, Mrs. Horace Mann, was "the first outbreak of the American Indian in human literature." More accurately the first by a Native American woman, this outbreak and the biography of its author by Gae Whitney Canfield, supplemented by A. J. Liebling's *New Yorker* series, allow us to piece together some of the early wrongs and claims of the Northern Paiutes.

In 1859, fifteen years after the nearly simultaneous appearances on the scene of the explorer Frémont and the infant Sarah, the appropriate authorities in Washington approved the recommendation of a special Indian agent that the land around Pyramid Lake and the delta of the Truckee River, some 300,000 acres of land in all, be set aside for the Winnemucca band. In May 1860, the month reservation notices were posted on the land, two girls from the band were kidnapped, raped, and thrown into a cellar by two white brothers who ran the saloon and provision station on the Carson River. Enraged kinsmen of the girls killed the perpetrators and thereby touched off what was called the Pyramid Lake War.* A hundred or so white irregulars undertook to teach these unruly natives a lesson, but were so outmaneuvered and outfought that only forty or so were left alive to straggle back to the mining camps. Even after the U.S. Army had been called out to quell the uprising, Paiute warriors still posed a problem. Thus both prudence and economy persuaded white authorities to hasten their plan to placate the lake people by giving them some of their land back in the form of a reservation. It was surveyed in 1865 and proclaimed by President Grant in 1874.

Yet forevermore white settlers buzzed around Paiute land and lit on choice morsels. Only a year after the reservation notices had been posted in 1860, Territorial Governor James W. Nye found five whites squatting on tracts along the Truckee at the southern end of the lake: "I here instructed the agent to warn them off, which he has done," he reported to Washington. "I understand they have promised to go as soon as they can secure the crops growing on their several ranches." Those crops took decades to secure, and in the experience of the Numa, such white promises became interchangeable with big white lies. Not chary of the rights of those they contemptuously called "diggers," the white invaders adopted a code formulated by the *Humboldt Register* on March 31, 1866: "Kill and lay waste everything pertaining to the tribes, whenever found—no trials, but at arms; no prisoners; no red tape."

One of Sarah Winnemucca's uncles was a victim of this code a year

---

*Other accounts trace the outbreak of hostilities to a quarrel over a Paiute's horse —see the interdisciplinary work, published since this was written, by Martha C. Knack and Omer C. Stewart, *As Long as the River Shall Run: An Ethnohistory of Pyramid Lake Indian Reservation* (Berkeley and Los Angeles: University of California Press, 1984), p. 71.

later. Called Truckee John, he had built a house at Pyramid Lake, fenced land, dug an irrigation ditch, and raised horses, hay, grain, and vegetables. According to the report of U.S. Army Lieutenant J. M. Lee, "his prosperity aroused the jealousy and hatred of a mean, worthless, and villainous white man named [Alexander] Fleming, who brutally murdered the Indian near his ranch on July 4, 1867. Afterwards, Indians were afraid to locate on it lest they meet the same fate, no cognizance having been taken of the dastardly murder by the civil or other authorities" (Liebling, *New Yorker*, January 15, 1955, p. 35).

The Humboldt code and the nonchalant noncognizance of dastardly murder were merely local expressions of the current national temper. Two illustrations will have to do:

1.   In the Indian commissioner's *Report for 1872*, Francis Amasa Walker bluntly stated that collective white disposition:

> There is no question of national dignity, be it remembered, involved in the treatment of savages by a civilized power. With wild men, as with wild beasts, the question whether in a given situation one shall fight, coax, or run, is a question merely of what is easiest and safest.

2.   From the field a year later an army officer reported his belief that young Paiute braves had been "greatly excited and elated at the delay in exterminating Jack's renegade Modocs"—I have already mentioned this small band of about 175, two-thirds of them women and children, who fled to the lava beds near Tule Lake and for months fought off nearly 1,000 soldiers. But before Sarah Winnemucca's people could make common cause with their tribal neighbors, had they decided to do so, Kintpuash, or Captain Jack, brought the so-called Modoc War to a close by surrendering on June 1, 1873. No one could deny that he had his day in front of a military tribunal before he was hanged that fall, but the truth was that his fate had never hung in the balance. From Washington on June 3, two days after the Modoc leader's surrender, General William Tecumseh Sherman had telegraphed orders to General J. C. Davis:

> I will submit to the War office for reference to the highest authority with a view to what disposition is to be made of prisoners according to law and Justice. Some should be tried by court martial and shot others to be delivered to the Civil authorities and the balance dispersed so that the name "Modoc" should cease.

The civil readiness to treat with Indians as with wild beasts and the military will to exterminate them right down to their names coalesced into a national policy that was merely the Humboldt code writ large.

Modoc Patriots in Chains, 1873. Kintpuash or Captain Jack (right) and Schonchin John shortly before they were hanged at Fort Klamath, Oregon.
[Smithsonian Institution, National Anthropological Archives, Neg. No. 3052]

In this atmosphere of official and free-lance Indian-hating, Sarah Winnemucca defended her people as best she could and set forth their wrongs and claims. At first hand she discovered they had few more white friends in the streets of Washington than they had in the deserts of Nevada, no matter how displaced, abused, and starving they were. As her brother Natchez once asked in exasperation, "Have the whites no hearts?" (Canfield, *Sarah Winnemucca*, p. 169). In her book she preserved some of their own pithy observations on what was happening to them, as when she quoted the protest of Egan, leader of the Malheur band in Oregon, to Indian Agent W. V. Rinehart: "Why do you want to play with us? We are men, not children" (*Life*, p. 125). And she quoted her father's summary of the Numa's plight in the centennial year 1876. Speaking to the commanding officer of Fort Harney, Oregon, the old gift-giver pointed out that they had a reservation at Pyramid Lake, but "for so many years not one of the agents ever gave me or my people an old rag. I am just from there. My people have nothing to live on there but what little fish they catch, and the best land is taken from them" (*Life*, pp. 121–22). Always, even when they had nothing else, the Numa had the white squatters. A year after Sarah Winnemucca's life story was published in 1883, an army lieutenant shooed off some, but they soon circled back and lit once again on aboriginal land.

Fifty years later Alida C. Bowler found these freebooters, or rather their successors, still in place. Appointed by John Collier in the 1930s to head up the Carson Agency in Stewart, Nevada, she was the first woman Indian superintendent ever. Soon she learned that there had been twelve families of squatters on the reservation as recently as 1924, the year Congress passed an act allowing them to buy what they had so long enjoyed for nothing. She also learned that seven families had taken advantage of Congress's generosity with Paiute land—the Numa had not been consulted—but five families made one payment and then defaulted. Formerly associated with Collier in the American Indian Defense Association, Alida Bowler was another determined woman who saw no reason why the people of Pyramid Lake should so long have been denied use of what was theirs. When she told them so, they laughed and dared her to do something about it, she later informed A. J. Liebling: "Being a woman, I imagine I felt under a greater obligation to show them." Show them she did by prodding Collier into taking up their cause. Through Collier and Ickes, the Departments of the Interior and of Justice finally moved to eject the unpaying and unpenitent squatters. And like Sarah Winnemucca, she showed the lake people by example how to stand up for their rights. "It was really she," one said to A. J. Liebling, "who started us to fight" (Liebling, *New Yorker*, January 22, 1955, pp. 62, 64).

Understandably upset by this untoward turn of events, the predaceous whites, their relatives, and the banks that held mortgages on their putative property all called on Senator Patrick A. McCarran to do something. In 1937 he obliged with S. 840, a bill that would have simply given "certain lands" to their white occupants. A good neighbor who had grown up only a few miles away, and like the squatters a true son of the West, with moral and intellectual roots reaching back and down to the Humboldt code, McCarran accommodated his friends and clients, and not out of crass political calculations alone. In the hearings on his bill before the Senate Committee on Indian Affairs, he took the principled position that fair play, justice, and equity were all on the side of the "honest, God-fearing citizens" who had made the land theirs by converting it from a "wilderness waste." By contrast he pictured the permanent residents at Pyramid Lake as not agriculturists at all, but fishermen, and "nomadic" ones at that: "They are a rambling tribe." Therefore, his bill took nothing whatsoever from them: "What they never had they never lost." As for Superintendent Bowler, he did not conceal how pained he was by her perversity: "The attitude of the lady who represents the department in the State of Nevada has been the most unfair that I have ever seen on the part of a Government official. The result has been to arouse class hatred between races"—a horrific upshot that made the lady agent, as A. J. Liebling aptly commented, "an amalgam of the evils of Marx *and* Hitler" (*New Yorker*, January 8, 1955, p. 51). Though his prototypal land-grab bill failed, McCarran soon had the satisfaction of having Alida C. Bowler transferred out of his bailiwick for being too "prejudiced."

Perhaps Ickes and Collier reluctantly acquiesced in Bowler's transfer on the assumption that it would satisfy the increasingly powerful senator. Whatever their motives for this grievous acquiescence, they unswervingly opposed his bill and refused to drop the eviction proceedings against his squatters. In 1942 and 1943 the U.S. Circuit Court of Appeals decided that the disputed acres, some 2,000 in all, indeed belonged to the Pyramid Lake Paiutes; in 1944 the U.S. Supreme Court refused to hear an appeal of that decision; and in 1948 the band reentered into possession of some of their land.

Undeterred, McCarran reintroduced his Pyramid Lake Bill in each new session of Congress, finally sweetening the pot with a proviso that the squatters pay a token amount for what had never been theirs. In his seventh attempt in 1949, he had the support of a new solon from Nevada, Senator George ("Molly") Malone, a Republican who owed the Democrat some political debts. Though this bill (S. 17) failed too, Malone had done his best to help and at one point enlivened the hearings before the Senate Interior and Insular Affairs Committee with a fantastic pledge and a dubious compliment. Malone said that he had known the Pyramid Lake Indians for a considerable time and that he himself intended "to introduce a bill that will make Indians people. . . . As a matter of fact, they are just as intelligent as we are" (Liebling, *New Yorker*, January 15, 1955, p. 49).

By mid century the people of Pyramid Lake had survived 13 years of their war with Senator McCarran, 106 years of Anglo-American history, and at least 3,500 years of their own. By then they had found another defender, this one a man whom we first met as the extremely able regional director Myer squeezed out of the WRA as a threatening rival (p. 40).

Also a former superintendent of the Navaho Reservation, E. Reeseman ("Si") Fryer had returned to the Indian Service after the war, and in 1949 he took over as superintendent at the Carson Agency, the post previously graced by the presence of Alida Bowler. Since her successor, Ralph Gelvin, had not done much, Fryer really took over where she left off, but of course had the advantage of the favorable court decisions since handed down. In the summer of 1950 he brought Collier, his old boss, up to date on his Nevada assignment:

> The fight for the repossessed land at Pyramid Lake still goes on though this is now the sixth year since the Supreme Court denied certeriori [*sic*]. The Indians only last year obtained physical possession of the land and began using it themselves. We are now urging a suit to quiet title to the ditches and to the headings that supply the irrigation water. The Government in its earlier suit to dispossess the squatters unfortunately neglected to include ditches and ditch rights.
>
> [August 24, 1950, JCP]

Under the guidance of their counsel and champion, McCarran's squatters had made the repossessed land waterless by cutting off the ditches. To quiet their dreamy title to trenches running through property that had never been theirs, Fryer secured the services of Judge E. P. Carville, an accomplished attorney and former U.S. senator and Nevada governor. Carville became the local associate of James E. Curry, the Paiute band's general counsel, who was based in Washington. While that litigation was pending, Fryer surveyed the possibility of making water more immediately available through a siphon from the Truckee River. With his encouragement the lake people put up fences to keep the trespassers from driving their stock in to destroy crops and organized patrols to mend the fences when the trespassers cut the wires. With Fryer standing by them, the people took hope they would get their water rights and might even free themselves at long last from the squatters.

Into this cause célèbre of the Indian country Commissioner Myer plunged in the fall of 1950. On August 29 McCarran had written him that the water of the Truckee River "has all been appropriated to beneficial use," meaning white use, and "that with everything in my being I shall oppose the removal of water"—water that the courts had, in fact, decreed to the lake people. Through H. Rex Lee, Myer replied reassuringly that "funds for this development are not included in the pending appropriations bill and we have, accordingly, instructed the field office [i.e., Fryer] to discontinue surveys for the canal and distribution system." Grateful, McCarran had this reassurance published in the Nevada press to show his white constituents what their senator, who was up for reelection, had done to protect them from his red constituents and their superintendent (see "No Appropriation for Development," *Reno Gazette*, September 22, 1950).

Next Myer notified Superintendent Fryer that he was to be moved on October 15 to the Colville Agency in Washington, where he would be safely out of harm's way. Hearing of the proposed transfer, Ruth Muskrat Bronson, a Cherokee who was executive director of the National Congress of American Indians (NCAI), and two associates went to see Myer and protested that it was at the behest of McCarran, that it weakened the Paiutes' will to stand up for their rights and made them feel let down by the Indian Service, and that Fryer had done a superb job in their behalf:

> Commissioner Myer indignantly denied that McCarran had anything to do with the transfer of Fryer, and gave us . . . the impression that Fryer himself had initiated the transfer. What he actually said was, when confronted with the charge (by me) that McCarran had ordered the move because Fryer had been too faithful in doing his duty to defend the Indians, that Supt. Fryer himself had suggested that in view of the political situation he should be moved. We thereupon wired Supt. Fryer and asked if he wanted to be transferred. He wired back that he had not wanted a transfer, that he considered the transfer a repudiation of his fight to defend the rights of the Pyramid Lake Indians, and of the Nevada program, that he would be glad to stay at Carson Agency but only on condition that Commissioner Myer allow him

to continue in the same vigorous way to protect the rights of these people he was employed to protect. . . . Upon his own request I went back to talk with Commissioner Myer about his reasons for making this transfer. I got nothing from him which changed my conviction that the move was being made to please Senator McCarran. He said to me the reasons for the transfer were: (1) that McCarran told him that ex-Commissioner [John Ralph] Nichols had promised he would move Supt. Fryer, and that Nichols denied it; (2) that he (Myer) had known Fryer a long time.

[to Oliver La Farge, September 30, 1950, AAIA]

It was true, as we have seen, that Myer had known Fryer a long time.

Perhaps with the earlier case of Superintendent Bowler on his conscience, Harold L. Ickes threw himself publicly into the fight against Fryer's transfer ("McCarran and the Paiute Indians," *Washington Post*, October 13, 1950). To a correspondent he characterized Myer's order as "one of the worst moves I have ever seen made by the Indian Office" and added that "I have been working for almost a week now, trying to have this order suspended" (to Glenn Coykendall, October 13, 1950, JCP). Backed by the NCAI and other Indian rights groups, Ickes took the issue directly to the White House and on the eve of Truman's departure for his historic conference with General Douglas MacArthur in the Pacific, the president intervened personally by staying the order for Fryer's removal (NCAI Press Release, October 15, 1950, AAIA).

A few days later Ickes reported to Collier that Myer had been to see him at his own request and had "admitted that he was pretty mad when word reached him" that his order had been countermanded:

> I did not mince any words with him on that subject. He insisted that, although McCarran had been in to see him to protest against Fryer and to ask for the transfer, he had not transferred Fryer for that reason but for others. Of course, this could be true and I do not think that Myer is a man who would deliberately tell a lie, least of all to me. So I told him that I accepted his word, although the circumstances in relationship in point of time were such that it would be difficult for any one not to believe that the two events were related. I then told him that, politically, it was naivete of high order. He admitted that perhaps it was.

[November 6, 1950, JCP]

No doubt remembering his earlier praise of Myer's "indestructible integrity" in his recommendation of the Medal for Merit, Ickes was plainly straining to believe the unbelievable. It was a doomed attempt: "I know of a certainty now," he later wrote Collier, "that the effort to transfer Fryer was to appease McCarran" (March 21, 1951, JCP). Collier himself had long been an unbeliever for reasons he summarized in a letter to Morton Grodzins: "Myer has categorically stated that his actions were not occasioned by McCarran's intervention. Nothing except McCarran's intervention occasioned them—nothing else is even specified as having done so" (November 17, 1950, JCP). Nothing else had been so specified, that is, except in Myer's statement to Ruth Bronson, Oliver La Farge, and others that Fryer himself had approved his transfer, and that lie had been shot down by Fryer's telegraphed denial.

The victory hardly did more than convince Ickes that Myer's integrity was destructible. In his telegram to the NCAI Fryer had made it clear that he wanted to remain at his post, but only if requested to do so by the commissioner and "GIVEN ASSURANCES THAT POLICY PLACE PYRAMID LAKE INDIANS IN POSSESSION AND ENJOYMENT OF THEIR PROPERTY BE VIGOROUSLY PURSUED" (September 29, 1950, AAIA). A few days later he wrote Collier that "I strongly object to being pushed out of Nevada by McCarran—if it is true" and yet "Pyramid Lake is McCarran's obsession, and any superintendent who works to place the Indians in physical possession of the repossessed lands and fights for their actual use, will commit career suicide unless given strong backing by the Office" (October 2, 1950, JCP). Lacking any such assurances and backing from the commissioner, Fryer resigned from the Indian Service two months later to take a much better paying job with the Point Four program (Technical Cooperation Administration) in the State Department. Through Myer's good offices, the people had lost another defender and McCarran had gained a supine superintendent. Under the circumstances Ickes did not blame the departing career official unduly, but still wished "that he had stuck to his Indian job because, to me, his resignation seems to serve notice on the Indian Service generally that all have to yield to McCarran or get out" (to Collier, December 22, 1950, JCP).

With Fryer out of Nevada, McCarran stepped up the war. Without water for their repossessed land, the Pyramid Lake Indians might be starved out. The only way they could regain their water rights, decreed to them by the U.S. District Court in 1926, was to urge the suit prepared by their attorneys. So McCarran rose up in the Senate to speak in behalf of his old friends the lake people and other Indians everywhere as their protector against precisely such "champertous," grasping attorneys:

> I want the Indians to get whatever is coming to them, for their own benefit; but I do not want them, somewhere along the road, to be mulcted of part of what is their due by way of or under the guise of attorney's fees. True, the Indian may need counsel in connection with some particular activities, but

the Bureau of Indian Affairs, I think, has all the counsel necessary for the Indian's advice, and there is nothing to prevent the Bureau of Indian Affairs from seeing to it that the Indian is taken care of, and that he gets his money.
[*Congressional Record*, August 6, 1951, p. 9703]

McCarran knew that for Indians to have no representation outside the Bureau of Indian Affairs, presided over by his protégé, meant that the lake people would have no representation of their own and therefore no water of their own. And he had already taught Myer much of his lore about desert nomads who were not "agrarian Indians." When the contract of their general counsel, James E. Curry, ran out in February 1951, the commissioner refused to allow them to renew it, except under his own terms, and forbade the band to pay Curry any fees out of their own money. With Curry immobilized, Judge E. P. Carville, who had been brought in to advise him on Nevada law, remained inactive and eventually dropped out of the case.

Said by A. J. Liebling to look "like a straight featured Japanese," Avery Winnemucca was chairman of the people's tribal council and for a living worked for the U.S. Forest Service. A lot had happened to their lake since the day of his great-grandfather, old Chief Winnemucca. A cycle of dry years and withdrawal of water from the Truckee River for the "beneficial use," as McCarran would have it, of white irrigators and power companies had dropped the surface of the lake about fifty feet, increased the salinity, brought in silt, and made it impossible for fish to swim upriver to spawn. The cutthroat trout that had so pleased Frémont and his men seemed to have disappeared. The unique fish had not, but were so scarce no one would have thought of calling the band the Cui-Ui Eaters—fishing was no longer an important source of food and cash income (Liebling, *New Yorker*, January 15, 1955, p. 33). For a living the people had their stock, which needed hay to get through the winters. To raise hay for their cows and horses, they had the 600 acres "under the ditch" and the 5,745 acres of bench land Superintendent Fryer had intended to irrigate, all of which was useless without water. Lacking that, reservation families tried to subsist on about ten acres each. Of the thirty or so young men who joined the armed forces in World War II, none had any land to come back to. Those who survived came back to the smaller war with McCarran and the white squatters. For them the Humboldt code was not ancient history.

Like his great-aunt Sarah, Avery Winnemucca had a keen sense of their people's wrongs and claims. Head of the militants in the band, he advocated direct action and accepted James E. Curry's counsel that they had a right, in the light of the court decisions, "to retake possession of

Pyramid Lake, n.d. "Set like a gem in the mountains," thought John C. Frémont, this remnant of prehistoric Lake Lahontan has shrunk rapidly in this century— the base of the five-story-high "pyramid" offers mute witness to the falling level of the gray-green water.
[Nevada Historical Society]

their own property, including the necessary ditches" (Liebling, *New Yorker*, January 1, 1955, p. 38; January 15, 1955, p. 36; January 22, 1955, p. 40). An admirer of Alida Bowler and Si Fryer, he deplored the fact that one had been driven out and the other "kicked upstairs." Coming on the heels of this latest setback, Myer's nullification of the contract with their attorneys made their situation desperate and moved him to seek a showdown. On September 20, 1951, the tribal council endorsed his strong letter of protest to Interior Secretary Oscar L. Chapman against the commissioner's assumption of "the power to hire and fire our attorneys so that he can control their actions. We believe that Mr. Myer is working in cooperation with Senator Pat McCarran and against the interests of the tribe" (*Nevada State Labor News*, September 28, 1951). The tribal council also voted to send a delegation to the capital for a direct face-to-face confrontation while Congress was still in session.

Addressed to the people back at the lake, Avery Winnemucca's "Re-

Nevada Indians Make Protest in Washington, November 2, 1951. The Paiute delegates "with the attorney they seek to hire. Left to right are Elizabeth R. Roe Cloud, field secretary of the National Congress of American Indians; Mrs. Ruth Muskrat Bronson, executive director of the Congress; Warren Tob[e]y, a member of the Pyramid Tribal Council; Avery Winnemucca, chairman of the Tribal Council; James E. Curry, attorney; and Albert Aleck, secretary-treasurer of the tribe."
[The New York Times]

port of Delegation to Washington to Obtain Approval of Attorney Contract and Restoration of Land Rights" was a classic account of how the Indian Service was still playing with men as though they were children (n.d., JCP). To protest and appeal the commissioner's paralyzing blow, delegates Albert Aleck, Warren Tobey, and Winnemucca had to get the commissioner's approval to spend their own tribal funds for their mission. On September 20 they asked for their money and six days later Myer replied by questioning whether the interests of tribal members were sufficiently involved to justify the expenditure and noted that he planned to visit Pyramid Lake in the near future and then they could all sit down for a good talk: "I sincerely believe that it would be preferable to deal with the problems in this way rather than having the tribe going to the expense of sending a delegation to Washington" (see also *Reno*

Evening Gazette, October 10, 1951). Their local father and new super-intendent, Burton A. Ladd, also tried to talk them out of their needless extravagance and admonished that if they would not be sensible, the BIA would "tie up" their funds for at least ten days in addition to the two weeks they had already waited. On October 12 Alexander Lesser of the AAIA wired the tribal council a loan of $540, friends in Reno took up a collection for the delegates, and finally they boarded a Grey-hound bus bound for the national capital, where they arrived at 3:00 A.M. on October 17.

Five days later and two days after Congress had adjourned, Myer, Ladd, and company untied tribal funds and airmailed them from Los Angeles. The unwelcome runaways thus received some of their own money a month and more after they had first requested it. As they con-cluded their report:

> Although we asked for our tribal money on September 20, we did not receive it until October 24. And then we received only part of what the Council had authorized us to use. The money we received on October 24 is owed to the Association on American Indian Affairs, since the money they gave us was not a gift but a loan. As you know, our friends in Reno collected some money for us. If it were not for these friends, this delegation could not have come to Washington at all. We have received some additional small contributions since we arrived and we hope to get some more outside help so that we can stay here until this fight is won.

To one of their friends in Reno, Winnemucca expressed their determi-nation "to avoid the mistake other Indian delegations have made—that is to get discouraged, or run out of money, and to go home before they get what they want. . . . We intend to 'squat' here in the Capital (just like the white people have been 'squatting' on our lands) until we get our rights. The first right we demand is to use our own money to hire our own lawyer to help us fight our legal battles" (to Alma Mayer, Oc-tober 18, 1951, JCP). It was to be a long and hard squat. Three weeks later in an appeal to John Collier for help, he reported that he still sat squat, but just barely: "I am living on borrowed money while two of our delegates have had to return home" (November 11, 1951, JCP).

For tribal delegates in the capital, nothing fundamental had changed in the seventy-one years since Sarah Winnemucca had first asked the Great White Father for their rights.

CHAPTER IX

"Wily" Indians

The wily, more competent Indians . . . [are] capable of making the Bureau of Indian Affairs appear as a group of paternalistic bureaucrats who will not allow them to handle their own affairs.

> —*Dillon S. Myer*
> *to Interior Secretary Douglas McKay,*
> *March 20, 1953*

"The Indians"—after fourteen months in office Dillon Myer questioned "most seriously" whether "the atmosphere of recrimination and suspicion and antagonism which has been developed in certain areas is in the best interests of the Indians." Speaking to "the Indians" and others at the annual convention of the National Congress of American Indians, Myer patiently complained that, "obviously, we are not going to make any really substantial progress in our work if large numbers of the Indians become convinced that the Bureau is some sort of monster against which they desperately need protection." That was a perversion of the truth, asserted their guardian, as was the charge "that the Bureau is engaged in a kind of subtle, Machiavellian attempt to enlarge and expand its control and supervision over Indian affairs, through a new type of paternalism." As for the "loose criticism" of his policy on attorney contracts, it had been based "either on misunderstanding or deliberate misrepresentation." Under his direction the BIA had "*not* been handpicking attorneys for the tribes. We have *not* been discriminating against attorneys because they were outspokenly critical of Bureau policies" ("Address . . . St. Paul, Minnesota, July 25, 1951," NRC). For those familiar with the commissioner's style, his emphatic negatives were giveaways that he *had* been handpicking and discriminating. With his own bitter memories of what happened when inmates at Tule Lake finally secured the services of Ernest Besig and Wayne M. Collins, he had hardly needed McCarran's urgings to take action against James E. Curry and other "champertous" attorneys.

Actually, on taking over the BIA in 1950 Myer had assigned his former WRA solicitors the task of finding a legal basis for denying tribal peoples attorneys of their choice. Nonspecialists Edwin E. Ferguson and Lewis A. Sigler had ransacked the volumes of the Indian Affairs Manual, and after weeks of search they unearthed a seemingly serviceable antique, the act of May 21, 1872 (17 Stat. 136) that prohibited noncitizen Indians and tribes from hiring counsel without BIA approval. So armed, Myer had issued a memorandum on November 9, 1950, that subjected tribes to novel, minute, and detailed controls over their contracts for legal services ("Contracts Between Attorneys and Indian Tribes," NRC). These controls had already become operative, as we have seen in the case of the Pyramid Lake Paiutes, when Interior Solicitor Mastin G. White pronounced their statutory underpinnings sound in an opinion rendered on June 22, 1951 ("Authority of the Secretary . . . ," NRC). Still called "proposed regulations," despite the fact they had been implemented, Myer had them published two weeks after the NCAI convention (Federal Register, August 11, 1951). Public outcry then became so shrill that Interior Secretary Oscar L. Chapman felt compelled to call public hearings on his commissioner's handiwork, hearings we shall return to presently.

Now, it was breathtakingly fitting for Myer to have discovered authority for his regulations in a presumably obsolete statute of 1872. With the directness of a homing pigeon, he had flown straight back to the era of unabashed domestic imperialism and racism from which his homegrown tenets sprang. "The 1872 statute was in turn based upon an act passed a year earlier, the Act of March 3, 1871 (16 Stat. 544, 570)," explained Felix S. Cohen (to Alexander Lesser, October 25, 1950, JCP). "This was the same act that forbad the making of treaties with Indian tribes. The motivation of these twin attacks on the power of Indian tribes is indicated by the policy of the Commissioner of Indian Affairs at that time," whose annual report I have already had occasion to quote: "There is no question of national dignity, be it remembered, involved in the treatment of savages by a civilized power" (p. 176).

Commissioner Francis Amasa Walker (1840–97) had also believed in "scientific" management and had also known nothing about the tribal peoples he was mismanaging. In his *Report for 1872* he started out with the critical question: "What shall be done with the Indian as

an obstacle to the progress of settlement and industry?"* Just letting
these hindrances be or bypassing them was unthinkable: "They must
yield or perish." Their communal land ownership, their heathenism, indeed everything about them left them in "a position altogether barba-
rous and incompatible with civilization and social progress." With wild
men as with wild beasts, therefore, the question of dealing with them
came down to what was easiest and safest. It was easiest to permit
"tractable and peaceful tribes to gather a bare subsistence by hard work,
or what to an Indian is hard work." It was safest to buy off "the hostility
of the savages" in the dangerous "roving tribes," such as the "insolent"
Sioux and the "treacherous and vindictive" Apaches. Through use of
"the Military Arm" hostiles should be restrained "in their Ishmaelitish
proclivities" and "should be made as comfortable on, and as uncomfortable off, their reservations as it was in the power of the Government
to make them; that such of them as went right should be protected and
fed, and such as went wrong should be harassed and scourged without
intermission"—this chastisement was currently being administered to
Kintpuash's band of Modocs, and would soon be to Dull Knife's band
of Northern Cheyennes and to all the other errant bands scourged in
the grand finale of this first century of dishonor. Walker heartily rejoiced
that he could already see the beginning of this end and the day when
"the last hostile tribe becomes reduced to the condition of suppliants
for charity," or, in another memorable phrase, to being "pensioners
upon the national bounty." Whether "wild" or "tractable," all the Indian remnants had to be placed under federal laws, "judiciously
framed," that would subject them to *strict reformatory control by the
agents of the Government*" (emphasis added).

Supported by Commissioner Walker, the judiciously framed 1872
statute kept the red man from taking up the white man's legal weapons,
through an attorney of his choice, to fight on another battlefield for his
rights and against being deprived of his land without due process of law.

*On Indians as animated obstacles, compare Commissioner Myer's attempt at histor-
ical analysis eight decades later: during the frontier period "the Indians were frequently a
real menace to the advancing tide of settlement" ("The Program of the Bureau of Indian
Affairs," *Journal of Negro Education* 20 [Summer 1951]: 349). Before this onrushing tide
of white settlement was empty or unsettled space, save for the menacing impediments that
had to be bowled over or removed to reserves. The tidal metaphor had also appealed to
Commissioner Walker: "It is not feebly and futilely to attempt to stay this tide, whose
depth and strength can hardly be measured, but to snatch the remnants of the Indian race
from destruction from before it, that the friends of humanity should exert themselves in
this juncture, and lose no time." Both commissioners grounded their policies in the geno-
cidal assumption that tribal cultures were dying cultures and Indians a dying race—except
for those unsaving "remnants."

The statute facilitated land-grabbing on a scale that dwarfed Senator McCarran's larcenous schemes in the next century. Unadvised, persuaded, coerced, and tricked by Indian agents and white entrepreneurs, tribespeoples soon ceded, often for pittances, additional tens of millions of acres. When the General Allotment, or Dawes, Act was passed in 1887 (24 Stat. 388), they still held 138 million acres; when the Indian Reorganization Act was passed in 1934 (48 Stat. 984) and ended the allotment system, they had only 48 million acres left. Recourse to lawyers and courts might have saved some of their millions. In protest of Commissioner Myer's policy, which resumed denial of that recourse, Josephine Kelly and other members of the Standing Rock Sioux Tribal Council observed poignantly: "We believe that we need an attorney to protect us; that if we had an attorney during the last century we would not have lost the Black Hills" (to Assistant Interior Secretary Dale E. Doty, September 28, 1951, NRC).

In the main, Commissioner John Collier and two of his successors had recognized the right of tribes to hire their own attorneys. But when he assumed office in 1933, the Standing Rock Sioux and other tribes had no such recognized right; nor the rights to select their own representatives; to freedom from arbitrary arrest, trial, and imprisonment by Indian Service personnel; to speak their own languages and follow their own customs; to practice their own religious beliefs. BIA monopoly of control over the tribes was so nearly perfect, travelers first had to secure a BIA passport before crossing the frontiers of Indian country. Collier repudiated the cultural monism behind this "epoch of forced atomization, cultural prescription, and administrative absolutism," as he called it, and embarked upon the novel experiment of using the national state to foster cultural pluralism. Under his direction, the BIA respected the right of Indians to their own languages and customs and crafts, repealed all administrative restrictions on freedom of speech and religion, and even increased Indian landholdings. Whatever his successes and failures in using a calcified bureaucratic structure to achieve libertarian ends, Collier reshaped policy, and to a surprising extent public opinion, with the revolutionary proposition that Indians were not obstacles, but peoples. To his mind, indeed, they were peoples with much to teach whites about their forgotten, but intimate and mutually dependent, relationships with nature. Instead of "unilateral policy-making" descending from the dominant to the subordinate societies, he made the key to his Indian New Deal "the bilateral contractual relationship between the government and the tribes." Accordingly, Commissioner Collier had to recognize the right of the latter to employ attorneys to uphold their rights and check capricious authority—even his own.

As alike as two peas in a pod in their presuppositions and prejudices, Commissioners Walker and Myer could never have tolerated such dilution of their administrative absolutism. No less certain than the former that he knew what was "in the best interests of the Indians," Myer reintroduced the traditional policy so forcefully enunciated by Walker: the destruction of tribal cultures and organizations and the individualization of their landholdings. The day foreseen by Walker had long since arrived: former hostiles had been reduced to "suppliants for charity."

Myer reversed his predecessor's policy in one essential particular: Indians should be made as *un*comfortable on, and as comfortable off, their reservations as it was in the power of the government to make them. Harassed without intermission *on* their reservations, these "pensioners upon the national bounty" could be driven off to vanish in welfare rolls and the slums where Myer had already scattered so many of the Japanese Americans. And for this final relocation to happen, Myer, no less than Walker, needed to subject Indians to *"strict reformatory control,"* free from interference by meddlesome lawyers. The old pre-Collier monopoly of control could only be restored by weeding out lawyers lacking in appreciation and sympathetic understanding of the need for "administrative stability." Lawyers who were more tractable could be brought within the chain of command through Myer's close regulation of form and execution of contracts (in sextuplicate), their duration and means of termination, kind and amount of fees and expenses allowable, how often detailed reports had to be submitted on legal services performed, and the like.

The trouble was that since Commissioner Walker's time Native Americans had been made citizens by an act of Congress (43 Stat. 253, 1924). Just as in the case of the Japanese Americans in the camps, therefore, they had presumptive legal and constitutional rights as citizens. But if they could no longer be treated as wild beasts, they could be treated as "wards" whose citizenship had somehow been effectively cancelled by that peculiar status. No doubt building on the dubious work of BIA counsel Ferguson and Sigler—the staffs were separate—Interior Solicitor Mastin G. White took precisely that route in the opinion he rendered for Chapman ("Authority of the Secretary . . . ," June 22, 1951, NRC). In that "surprising document," as a critic characterized it, Solicitor White obligingly started out by misquoting the 1872 statute Myer had invoked:

No agreement shall be made by any person with any tribe of Indians * * * for the payment or delivery of any money or other thing of value, in present or in prospective, or for the granting or procuring any privilege to him, or any other person in consideration of services for said Indians relative to their lands, or to any claims . . . [unless such contract be executed as stipulated and bear the approval of the secretary of the interior and the commissioner of Indian affairs].

The three seemingly innocent asterisks hid a surgical mutilation not to be explained away by considerations of space. Cut out of the octogenarian law were six vital, relatively short words: "not citizens of the United States."

Known for his prickly honesty, forthrightness, and fierce loyalty to his friends, former Interior Secretary Ickes was in Maine when he received a copy of Solicitor White's opinion. Reading it carefully, he noted the asterisks and wondered about them but, with no records or law books at hand, naturally "concluded that this was an honest opinion of an honest lawyer to his superior," as he wrote his successor Chapman in a long, angry, formal letter:

I did not like what had been going on in the Indian Bureau recently, any more than I cared for the methods employed by the Bureau, or the misguided policy toward the Indians that permeated the Bureau. Yet, it never occurred to me that any one there or elsewhere in Interior would perform a major operation on the 1872 statute without even a local anesthetic and cut from it a vital organ. My astonishment may be imagined when I received a communication from the Association on American Indian Affairs, Inc., over the signature of Professor [Charles L.] Black. It was he who had discovered, at least so far as I am aware, the omission from the Solicitor's opinion of the significant words "not citizens of the United States." It was he who, logically and conclusively, argued just what this apparently deliberate elision would do to the body of the Indian law, and therefore to the Indians themselves, if the trick and "reverse English" opinion of the Solicitor were to be accepted as an official and authentic interpretation of law. . . . In my opinion, this is the greatest scandal that has ever been discovered in the Department of the Interior. I say this without forgetting the shameful behavior of an earlier Secretary, one Albert B. Fall [of Teapot Dome infamy], who in his own way was also a "surprising document."

[November 5, 1951, JCP]

Labeling White's opinion "a fraud and a snare for unwary feet," Ickes insisted that the elision of the six simple words could not have been done by mistake. It was the work of "the legal craftsmen—or were they butchers?—who were anxious that the Commissioner be permitted to have his will of the Indians, 'by hook or by crook,' and regardless of their duty to the Secretary [i.e., Chapman]. So they prepared a brew calculated to please the palate of the Indian Commissioner." With the help of such fellow conspirators, Myer had headed back to the good old days of the "'Walkerized' code" on tribal attorney contracts, "to return to which it is apparent that the present Indian Commissioner is exerting all of his strength, Indians being 'wild beasts' should have no rights except such as might be vouchsafed to them by an oppressive and ungenerous 'superior' race."

This flagitiously racist policy, the lies, the appointment of officials whose acceptability was in direct ratio to their general ignorance, and the "repression imposed by a police-state mind," all these sorry reversals in Indian affairs drove Ickes himself back to a reexamination of the more recent past and of his own responsibility for Myer: "And yet those of us who, although in good faith, mistakenly, applauded the appointment of the new Commissioner and predicted a fine administration for the Indians were careless in not looking back." He and Myer's other supporters should have looked back at Justice William O. Douglas's opinion in *Ex parte Endo* (323 U.S. 283, 1944) that the WRA had no right to detain "these people wholly on account of their ancestry even though the Government conceded their loyalty to this country" and at Justice Frank Murphy's concurring opinion that WRA detention was but "another example of the unconstitutional resort to racism inherent in the entire evacuation program." Since this police-state agency had been in his department and since he had so extravagantly praised its director and recommended him for the Medal for Merit, Ickes had to be pained by the upshot of this reexamination. "I concur with the statement that the War Relocation Authority constituted 'Our Worst Wartime Mistake' and that 'What is now proposed for the Indians may well be characterized as "Our Worst Peacetime Mistake,"'" he told Chapman. And that made Ickes himself, as the relentless old man was fully aware, a participant in the first and a contributor to the second of these "worst mistakes."

"So far as our American Indians are concerned, Commissioner Dillon Myer of the Bureau of Indian Affairs is a Hitler and Mussolini rolled into one," wrote Ickes in one of his *New Republic* columns, and in another he called his former subordinate "a blundering and dictatorial tin-Hitler [who had] tossed a monkey wrench into a mechanism that he was not capable of understanding" (124 [May 21, 1951]: 17; 125 [September 24, 1951]: 16). But only with extreme reluctance had Ickes finally charged Chapman with having permitted this dictatorial wonder to run "hog wild." He had known and liked the former since 1933, when he asked Roosevelt to appoint him assistant secretary of the interior. Before he took this final step of making his charges public he wrote "Dear Oscar" a personal and confidential letter reminding him of his unbroken faith:

> I am much older than you and I have been through too many tough fights to look forward with any relish to a public controversy with a man whom I have wanted to help since he became a member of the Cabinet, and not to hurt. I have been urged to go to President Truman on this Indian issue and explain to him fully just what it involves. I have never approached the subject with him except to say one day, as I promptly reported to you, that his administration might run into real trouble on account of Dillon Myer's misbehavior toward the Indians.
>
> [September 14, 1951, JCP]

Fruitlessly, he warned Chapman that "calculated injustice" in dealing with Indians could not "hurt White or Myer. They are nobodies. But you are somebody and you cannot afford, either on your own account or that of President Truman, to finish your administration on the note that you have permitted others to sound on Indian affairs." Currently, and until he got back to solid ground, Chapman was in "the unfortunate position of relying upon an Indian Commissioner who is a reckless, bullheaded fool, and a Solicitor who does not scruple to cheat you when you ask for an opinion on Indian law."

Born in 1874, just two years after the enactment of Commissioner Walker's judiciously framed statute, Ickes could look back from his late seventies on over a half century of tough fights against "sinister interests" such as the Chicago magnates Charles Tyson Yerkes and Samuel Insull and despoilers such as Secretary Albert B. Fall and Senator Patrick A. McCarran. With justifiable pride he could look back on almost as many decades of fights in behalf of tribespeople. Through his wife Anna Wilmarth Ickes, he had first become actively involved in Indian rights in 1916, joined the American Indian Defense Association in the 1920s, and initially sought the BIA post from Roosevelt in 1933 before raising his sights to the cabinet. Working closely with his commissioner and learning from him, Ickes had sturdily supported the Indian New Deal even after Collier's forced resignation. Inclined nearly always to side with the underdog, his commitment to tribal peoples was unquestionably deep and abiding. It was this and Myer's scrapping of Native American rights that had forced him to restudy and regret his role in the wartime onslaught against Japanese American rights. Not out of rhetorical recklessness and personal pique, then, had come his denunciation of Myer for turning the clock back and acting as "accessory, before or after the fact, to the further despoliation of the Indians." His outrage and sense of betrayal in these last embittered days of his life had roots extending back to the turn of the century.

Obviously still vigorous intellectually and morally, Ickes was declining physically, could not participate in Chapman's public hearings on the attorney contracts, and died the following month. With his voice stilled, his former subordinate could all the more easily have his will of the first despoiled Americans, by hook or by crook.

2

Secretary Chapman's hearings were held on January 3 and 4, 1952, by which time Avery Winnemucca had been squatting in Washington for over eleven weeks. He was one of the forty-four witnesses who appeared and spoke as with one voice against Commissioner Myer's regulations. Among the organizations condemning them were the American Bar Association, the Association on American Indian Affairs, the Indian Rights Association, the National Association for the Advancement of Colored People, the Congress of Industrial Organizations, the Women's International League for Peace and Freedom, and numerous other unions and civic groups. Even Roger Baldwin appeared for the American Civil Liberties Union to oppose his old ally and support the moral right of Indians to employ their own counsel without outside interference. The American Bar Association was represented by a special committee that had investigated Myer's handiwork for seven months, found it lacking in statutory authority, and stigmatized it as "a reversion to the doctrine that the 'Indian has no rights except those extended as privileges through rules and regulations and through mere sufferance.' . . . Moreover, the Committee has been unable to find evidence of any necessity to turn the clock backward so as to subject the Indian tribes to the minute and detailed controls which are prescribed in the proposed regulations" ("Report of Special Committee on Contracts of Lawyers with Indian Tribes, Administrative Law Section, American Bar Association," November 8, 1951, JCP).

"INDIAN WAR WHOOP MARKS HEARINGS," read the *New York Times* headline (January 4, 1952). It had sprung from the throat of Popovi Da, the former governor of the San Ildefonso Pueblos, a fullblood Indian engineer who had worked on the Los Alamos atomic bomb and who now "repeated the whoop of exultation that escaped him on that memorable [test] day in 1945." His meaning was clear: If the United States government had trusted him with its greatest wartime secret, why would it not trust him now to hire a lawyer of his own choosing? And if his cry did not mark a declaration of war, it did signal that Indians were on the warpath against Myer's regulations. Popovi Da, Avery Winnemucca, and twenty-two other delegates from bands, tribes, and intertribal organizations whose members totaled 300,000 had traveled thousands of miles to express their salty condemnation and thereby underscore the "atmosphere of recrimination and suspicion and antagonism" the commissioner pretended existed only "in certain areas." Selections from their statements in the transcript of the proceedings allow us to meet a few of the "wily" Indians he distrusted and give us invaluable glimpses of his style in the field and of the havoc wrought by his mere sufferance of their basic civil rights (Transcript of "Hearing on Proposed Regulations to Govern Indian Tribal Attorney Contracts," JCP).

Wily Indian #1. Since "I am the one who has been sitting here in Washington for weeks waiting for a decision on my contract," Avery Winnemucca appeared early in the proceedings to recount some of the background that we have already considered and along the way pinpointed an official lie that had made his band's long and desperate struggle seem ridiculous. Winnemucca quoted a letter Myer had written Ramona Kaiser of Cincinnati on November 15, 1951: "Currently the controversy is centered on . . . the illegal use and occupancy by the squatters of two tracts of land totaling 46.5 acres." The people's delegate pointed out that these 46.5 acres contained the residences of the squatters—making them a "pretty important 46.5 acres"—that the immediate dispute was over some 800 or 900 acres of land that remained waterless because the squatters had cut off the ditches, and that it was also over some 5,745 acres of land Superintendent Fryer had intended to irrigate. To his people back at the lake these thousands of acres represented "a fortune" and made the need of lawyers "to vindicate our rights to these lands" all the more imperative: "By his reference to the 46.5 acres, the Commissioner of Indian Affairs . . . is trying to laugh off our problems," charged Winnemucca. "But they are extremely important to us who have to raise families on such small amounts of land. This is a flippant way for any official to talk."

Wily Indian #2. "We want someone as our attorney on whom we can depend, and not someone who is picked for us and about whom we do not know anything," declared Governor Manuel Holcomb of the Pueblo of Santa Clara. "Now, a long time ago we used to be considered savages. At that time we were not allowed to carry arms and ammunition," said the governor, who had returned from the recent war missing a leg. "At the same time we were also not allowed to pick our own attorneys." His message too was plain: "I can truthfully say that when we were in the service the Great White Father overlooked the law about carrying arms and ammunition and treated us like other citizens. . . . But today, when we are in great need of legal help, he can see again very plain that we are savages and unable to take care of ourselves." In point was their money: "Again we have no right to ask for the things that belong to us. I put in a requisition for our money on August 20. Up to this date I have not heard a word. I have not even heard where the money is. We have to almost get the money out of our people's mouths to make a trip like this so that we can be heard here, so that the Secretary can hear our problems from our mouths." It seemed to him that the commissioner "just wants to get us in a fighting mood, instead of helping us." Added Cleto Tafoya, a Santa Claran elder statesman who had accompanied the governor to Washington: "I just want to tell you that everything he said is true, and everything that he said about our people being pushed around is even more true of the older people."

Wily Indian #3. Speaking for the Pueblo of Laguna, William V. Creager asserted that their attorneys, one of whom was Felix S. Cohen, "are our hired men. They don't tell us what to do. When Commissioner Myer testified before Congress on March 9, 1951 he said that our budget recommendations were 'prepared by Mr. Cohen or under his direction.' That is not true. Our budget recommendations were prepared in 1948, and Mr. Cohen did not know about them until more than two years later. At that time he took the matter up with the Indian Bureau at our request, and asked the Indian Bureau to do something about these recommendations. That was on September 13, 1950. We are still waiting for an answer to that request. . . . We want you to treat us like American citizens and not like savages." Their attorney Cohen had argued the case (*Trujillo v. Garley*, unreported [1948]) that finally gave them the right to vote in New Mexico elections and the case that brought social security benefits "to our old people, our blind people, and our dependent children." Through their attorneys, legislation had been drafted and passed by Congress that had given them title to over 100,000 acres of submarginal land. Their attorneys had "helped us to draw up an oil and gas lease that brought in $5,000 as an initial payment, which was about 10 times as much as we got under a similar lease made by the Indian Bureau. I am sorry to say that." These were among the reasons they needed their own hired men, who had never told them what to do. Unhappily, he could not say the same of the BIA under Myer:

> Let me give you a simple little example of what I mean, Mr. Secretary. Under our attorney's contract we have the right to pay the travel expenses of our attorneys out of our own Pueblo funds. Well, one of our attorneys, Mr. Cóhen, spent 10 days this last year at Laguna and travelling to and from Laguna on our business, and his total charge for meals during this period came to $13.40. That is an average of $1.34 a day. But the Indian Bureau thinks that Mr. Cohen is too extravagant in his tastes, and three times when he bought dinner for himself on the Santa Fe Railroad and paid more than $2.00, the Commissioner of Indian Affairs says that that bill is too extravagant, and we cannot pay it. Apparently, the Commissioner of Indian Affairs still thinks that we're savages who don't understand money when it get[s] over $2.00 (laughter).
>
> Mr. Secretary, we are here to ask that you treat us as responsible American citizens and not as savages. . . .

SECRETARY
CHAPMAN: Thank you. I want to say I am afraid I disagree with
MR. DILLON S. MYER   my Commissioner of Indian Affairs, who thinks that
(Commissioner of $1.38 is extravagant. Was that figure correct?
Indian Affairs):   So does the Commissioner.

No laughter greeted this mysterious sally.

Wily Indian #4. With his straight black hair in braids and clad in a bright blanket, Severino Martinez spoke through interpreter Paul Bernal in behalf of the Pueblo of Taos. In 1947 his people had selected Henry J. Hughes of Santa Fe as their attorney, signed a contract with him, and submitted it to their Superintendent Eric Hagberg, who, as other delegates also testified, habitually "lost" such documents. Five years later they were still "waiting for the approval of the contract by the Commissioner. The years have increased so many that we just felt like we were tied up against a tree, could not move anywhere." The BIA had bound and effectively gagged them, their predicament heightened by the fact that the Indian Claims Commission Act of 1946 (60 Stat. 1049) provided that all claims had to be filed within five years and Com-

Severino Martinez and Paul Bernal, April 17, 1961. Taken in New York at the annual meeting of the Association on American Indian Affairs, this photograph of the governor and his interpreter shows them looking pretty much as they had a decade earlier denouncing Myer's regulations on tribal attorneys.
[Theodore Brinton Hetzel]

missioner Myer had opposed enactment of a bill to give Indians more than a few additional months to hire lawyers and file their claims.* This was the essential background for the Taos Pueblo's confrontation with Myer in New Mexico:

> When the new Commissioner took over the job, Mr. Dillon S. Myer came out to the west. He was in Albuquerque. We made an appointment with Mr. Myer, Commissioner of Indian Affairs, and he gave us only three minutes to exchange a word with him. We asked him the question what he had done with our contract. He would not give us any information regarding it. We asked him again. "Would you approve our attorney's contract?" He said, "I will not approve Henry Hughes' contract as long as I am Commissioner of Indian Affairs."
>
> When I asked him why, he just grinned at me. He gave me no answer. I tried to clarify myself by telling him that we were talking about serious business, and there was nothing comical. He stated himself again that he would not approve our selected attorney's contract. I was hoping at the time when I met him he would furnish me the reason why the Indian Bureau would not approve Henry Hughes' contract. I asked him the reason, if Henry Hughes was a thief or he had some other serious offense against him, and those things we were anxious to hear from him but he would not say anything. He would not give his reason at all. He would not accept Mr. Henry Hughes' contract at all. He said himself that there is a law that the Indian Bureau would appoint an attorney for us.

Martinez and his people felt blocked in, "just corral[l]ed in the back seat."

Wily Indian #5. "Commissioner Myer seems to think that we are savages and that we don't know our own minds," said Ben Chief for the 11,000 members of the Oglala Sioux Tribe on the Pine Ridge Reservation in South Dakota. "When we opposed the budget put up by the Indian Bureau, Commissioner Myer told a committee of Congress that our lawyer put the words in our mouths. I was present at a meeting between our attorney, Felix Cohen, and the members of the tribal council. At that time, our attorney told us that we were adult Indians and we had to make our own decisions. Commissioner Myer doesn't think we should have the right to decide such things, or that we are able to

---

*"During hearings before the House Subcommittee on Indian Affairs on H.R. 2896, H.R. 3203, and H.J. Res. 210 (all bills to extend the time for filing under the Indian Claims Commission Act) Associate Commissioner H. Rex Lee, on July 3, 1951, presented a variety of reasons indicating that the requested one-year extension was unnecessary and advocating a six-month extension limited to those tribes which secured contracts approved by the Commissioner of Indian Affairs within the last six months of the allowed period for filing claims" (Felix S. Cohen, "Erosion of Indian Rights," *Yale Law Journal* 62 [1953]: 371n).

decide such things. Last March, Commissioner Myer promised that this
credit fund [of $140,000, appropriated by Congress,] would be un-
frozen in the near future. This was ten months ago and the money is
still frozen." Ben Chief emphatically asserted their need for an attorney
immediately, one subject to their orders and not to Myer's: "To hire a
lawyer under these regulations is like hobbling a horse and trying to
make him run. We want the hobbles taken off so he can fight for our
rights."

Wily Indian #6.   In "$40 cowboy language," Thomas Main spoke
for his Gros Ventre Tribe, the Fort Belknap Community, and the Montana Intertribal Policy Board, of which he was chairman. For the eight
tribes with more than 20,000 members scattered across the state, he
expressed "our firm and undying opposition to these proposed attorney
regulations." He found it hard to believe that Secretary Chapman could
"be a party to such a rank denial of basic human right as these regulations propose" and resented that "during the last couple of years that
attitude of paternalism, treating us like prisoners in a concentration
camp, has become an attitude of the Indian Bureau." And he drew the
moral for the secretary and the commissioner through a little story:

> On my way down here I saw some D.P.'s in the Union Depot at Chicago, and
> I was just thinking: Here are some people from some foreign land finding
> refuge and sanctuary in the land of the free and the home of the brave, that
> perhaps in the short space of five years they may become full-fledged citizens
> of the country. And I was also thinking: I wonder if these foreigners would
> have to have somebody's approval or san[c]tion for an attorney in case they
> needed one?

Wily Indian #7.   "I feel that we are just as patriotic as the other
citizens in the United States and we deserve consideration," said Chairman Rufus Wallowing of the Northern Cheyenne Tribal Council, speaking for the 1,958 souls in what had been Dull Knife's people. The son
of Bull Wallowing, a Contrary who had fought Custer, he presented a
specific and compelling case of their immediate need for consideration.
Located in southeastern Montana, their reservation contained 400,736
acres, of which about half were allotted and half tribal, and that total
included 90,000 acres in a good stand of yellow pine, 20,000 acres of
farmland, many thousands of acres of good cattle country, and beneath
the surface of all this an "abundance of coal. A depth of 12 feet deep
all over the reservation." Now, they needed an attorney to help them
develop their resources, for their timber, for their Crazy Head Springs

Rufus Wallowing and Montana Representative Wesley d'Ewart, n.d. James D. King, Sr., of the Northern Cheyennes, through whose courtesy this photograph of his uncle is reprinted, thinks it may have been taken when Wallowing was in Washington attempting to move Myer to approve their attorney contract.

summer resort, and for a revision of their charter, established under the Indian Reorganization Act, so as to facilitate their self-government:

> So this attorney Mr. James E. Curry who lives in Washington here we want him as our attorney. We chose him because he has the Indian at heart. . . . We do not have any other attorney in view. We have met him and we have

talked to him and we know that he has our welfare at heart and we want our contract approved. We entered [into] a contract with him in the summer of 1951 and the contract went to the Area Director first and it was pigeon-holed, it was delayed there and they never told us what they did to it. Now we want the Secretary of the Interior, Oscar L. Chapman[,] in behalf of the Northern Cheyenne tribe to approve this contract. We can do so much good on the reservation and the Bureau has lost enough interest in our welfare. . . . We want our reservation resources developed . . . so that it will create work opportunities for our people to stay on the reservation. It does not make sense to us that we have all these resources on the reservation and have to go through so much hardships, they can stay on reservation and work and develop these resources.

Under their contract with Curry, the Northern Cheyennes had agreed to pay him fifty dollars a month and the contract could be cancelled on ninety days' notice. It had been in Myer's office since June 30, 1951. "Can't it be approved at this time," asked Wallowing, "so that I can go back to my people with some good news?"

Such were the highlights of a handful of the presentations that were heard and of the hundreds of others that might have been heard in Secretary Chapman's conference room. Each of the bands and tribes across the country had a history no less long and complicated, if less immediately dramatic, than that of the Pyramid Lake Paiutes—through the latter I have merely suggested the complications of one such history and tried thereby to put a recognizable face on just a bit of the deprivation and the sufferings within Myer's vast domestic empire. And since we followed their Avery Winnemucca into the hearings, let us change guides and follow Rufus Wallowing out into the sequel. A month later the Northern Cheyenne's "Report on Attorney Contract" brought no good news to his hard-up people back in Lame Deer, Montana (February 15, 1952, JCP).

                                    3

The "runaround," as Wallowing called it, began immediately after the hearings. When he and his attorney tried to see Secretary Chapman, they were shunted off to Assistant Secretary Dale E. Doty, who in turn sent them to Commissioner Myer, who told them on January 7 that he did not know when he would get around to deciding and that he was waiting for a decision on the regulations from the secretary and for a possible investigation by the Senate Subcommittee on Indian Affairs. When they returned to Doty, he said he would talk to Myer and get back to them that day, but failed to do so. On January 11 they again saw Myer, who told them "that he still did not intend to act" and in any event "that he did not want to deal with the Chairman [i.e., Wallowing] about this matter but wanted to deal directly with the Tribal Council. We went back to see Doty to report, but were unable to see him that day." Thereupon Wallowing telephoned his council back in Montana and spent the next few days awaiting renewed authorization. It arrived in the form of a telegram from Secretary Eugene Little Coyote:

WE THE UNDERSIGNED MEMBERS OF THE TRIBAL COUNCIL INSIST THAT THE QUESTION OF OUR ATTORNEY CONTRACT BE SETTLED IMMEDIATELY BY AND DURING YOUR PRESENT TRIP TO WASHINGTON AND WE OBJECT TO ANY MOVE BY THE COMMISSIONER TO BYPASS YOU AND REFER THE MATTER BACK TO THE TRIBAL COUNCIL BEFORE THE CONTRACT IS APPROVED. WE THINK THAT ANY SUCH MOVE WOULD JUST BE AN EFFORT ON THE PART OF THE COMMISSIONER TO CAUSE FURTHER DELAY ON A MATTER OF GREAT IMPORTANCE TO THE TRIBE THAT HAS BEEN HANGING FIRE FOR MORE THAN SIX MONTHS.

Luckily, one of the commissioner's unintentionally revealing memoranda for the files confirms Wallowing's report and presents the runaround from his side of the desk (January 11, 1952, NRC). On January 7 Myer, backed by H. Rex Lee, had indeed conferred with Wallowing and James E. Curry and acknowledged "that the contract has been in the office for quite some time and that we had not taken any action on it because of the need for clarification of our responsibility under the policies relating to attorney contracts." Wallowing wondered how long he would have to stay around, "implying that it would be necessary for him to stay until we approved the contract. I told him that I did not think it necessary for him to stay in Washington," with his own clear implication that he could see no necessity for Wallowing ever to have come to Washington. Four days later Myer, backed by Lewis A. Sigler this time, again conferred with Wallowing and Curry and impatiently repeated that they would "review the contract within a reasonable time, as soon as we could get around to it. . . . Mr. Wallowing then raised the question if soon meant six months. I said I was hesitant in view of the time required by the lawyers and myself to set a time, but told him I would give him an outside figure of two or three weeks" and invoked "all of the other responsibilities that were facing us at the moment." To Curry's remark that it would take less than a half hour to do the job, Myer retorted stiffly "that we were the ones to determine what priority our work schedule should be, and I refused to be badgered into immediate action simply because he felt we should take action under his pressure." With the dignity of his office so spiritedly reasserted, Myer smugly recorded that "Mr. Curry and Mr. Wallowing then left my office, seemingly in a rather unhappy mood."

And then the memorandum for the files took a surprising turn. Later that same day, at 3:40 P.M., Assistant Secretary Doty called on the telephone about the contract:

> I had a call from Mr. Doty, saying that Mr. Curry was in his office, the contract was a one-page contract, and he saw no problem in getting it approved, if we would do so. I explained to Mr. Doty what I had told Mr. Curry and that I felt the request was unreasonable; that I made it clear I did not intend to do it today but would try to get it done within a reasonable time, and in any case, unless it was a clear approval, it should go back to the Tribe for acceptance. Of course, if I had orders from Mr. Doty, I would approve the contract now and without further discussion, but I had not had such orders. And without such orders, I would stick to the position outlined to Mr. Curry. Mr. Doty's reply was okay, and that completes my comment on the discussions relating to the Northern Cheyenne proposed attorney contract as of 3:45 P.M., January 11.

Assistant Secretary Doty had called mildly suggesting they stop the runaround and Commissioner Myer had in effect told his nominal superior to go to hell. How did he dare? "I think that the Commissioner is very angry about all the criticism that was made at the hearings of January 3 and January 4," Rufus Wallowing reported to the Northern Cheyennes, "and he has taken a very stubborn attitude."

"Very angry" was accurate but a little weak. For Myer the hearings had been more intolerable than the "demonstration . . . staged at Tule Lake for the benefit of the National Director" in November 1943—then he had had no worry about outsiders and could quickly crush "troublemakers." But at the hearings, "wily" Indians had told him to his face—before television cameras, reporters, superiors, tribal attorneys, the world—that he had been acting the Great White Father by treating them as savages, ridiculing their just aspirations, lying about their wrongs and claims, denying their basic human rights, pushing them around. As John Ross of the Cherokees had said in an earlier time of troubles, "I knew that the perpetrator of a wrong never forgives his victims." Myer had left the hearings unforgiving, vindictive, and fighting mad, as his exchange with Doty suggested.

Five days later he confirmed this mood in an insolent letter that made clear for his superiors, in case they still had any doubts, how he proposed to get away with defying them (to Doty, January 16, 1952, NRC). Peremptorily, he wrote that he wanted Chapman to take no action before the Anderson subcommittee had completed its investigations and hearings and that if the secretary proposed to accept the recommendations of the American Bar Association and the tribal lawyers, then "I am greatly perturbed and shocked. The adoption of the Bar Association approach represents, in my judgment, an almost complete abnegation of the Secretary's statutory duty as it has hitherto been interpreted." That is, hitherto interpreted by Dillon S. Myer—but has there ever been a cabinet officer not appalled by the prospect of a powerfully positioned subordinate charging him with flagrant failure to carry out his statutory duty? And then Myer made the threat explicit by invoking his congressional network: Chapman would be subject "to serious criticism in Congress" if he reached his decision on the attorney regulations without first consulting the chairmen "of the Senate and the House Subcommittees involved."

Chapman did have a statutory duty to keep his commissioner from stomping on Indians. A liberal with a creditable record in Indian affairs during the New Deal years, he had his reputation at stake as well as control over his department. Notwithstanding these stakes and the entreaties of Ickes, Collier, and other friends, he had failed to take timely action to reassert his own waning authority. Perhaps he had still had enough authority to act two months earlier when he unburdened himself to Felix S. Cohen, who passed on the essentials of their long conference to Oliver La Farge: "Chapman is thoroughly unhappy about Myer and finds himself in rather a spot concerning him. It seems that Chapman is finding him, as we do, stubborn and unable to learn. He has built himself extraordinary strength on the Hill, and maintains his own relations with Congress independent of the Department" (La Farge to Alexander Lesser, November 23, 1951, AAIA). On January 24, 1952, Chapman ignored Myer's threats to the extent of rejecting his regulations, but then weakly appointed a committee to look into the problem. Disdainfully ignoring the secretary's decision and his inactive committee, Myer continued to deny Indians attorneys of their choice on the specious ground that he was merely carrying out his own "statutory duty as it has hitherto been interpreted" and that was that. By then Chapman did not dare to keep his commissioner from running "hog wild" and apparently neither did the president: "I know that Chapman, with Truman's agreement, did make a very serious effort to get Myer out, some two or three months ago," wrote Collier, who had been close to Chapman since 1933, "and the Congressmen descended on Truman and dissuaded him from acting. And Myer has so 'steered' the Senate group, that in the matter . . . [of] atty. contracts etc. he has got Chapman boxed in" (to Joe Jennings, August 11, 1952, JCP). No Ickes he, Chapman had allowed himself to be buffaloed by Myer and his powerful friends.

Through H. Rex Lee, the commissioner had in effect moved the BIA from the executive to the legislative branch by establishing his base of power among the most rapacious of the lawmakers. Those who had descended on Truman to keep Myer from being sacked, if Collier's information was sound, no doubt included those most actively hostile to Indian cultures and most avidly covetous of Indian land, water, minerals, and timber. Mostly Westerners, they dominated the Indian Affairs Subcommittees—and the Interior Appropriations Subcommittees—in the House and in the Senate. They became Myer's lifeline within the Interior Department and his natural allies in the campaign against "wily" Indians and their "champertous" attorneys. In the House they included Toby Morris of Oklahoma, who as chairman of the Indian Affairs Subcommittee defended Myer as "a man of unimpeachable integrity . . . a very able administrator, one of the most able in our government"; Norris Poulson of California, who as a subcommittee member praised Myer for his fight to keep Indians from "being stolen blind by these attorneys"; and Henry ("Scoop") Jackson of Washington, who had formerly chaired the subcommittee and who could not commend Myer too warmly "for going after some unscrupulous attorneys" and for "trying to emancipate the Indians that are ready for emancipation" (see, e.g., *Cong. Rec.*, April 25, 1951, pp. 4370–79). A rising star soon to be known derisively as "The Senator from Boeing," Jackson might then have been dubbed "The Representative from Weyerhauser," for he wanted to emancipate the Colville Indians from their valuable timber reserve.

In the Senate the group of Myer defenders included, of course, Patrick A. McCarran and his Republican sidekick from Nevada, George ("Molly") Malone, who shortly made good on his threat to introduce a bill to "make Indians people" by introducing one to free them of all their tribal assets within three years; from nearby Arizona, Carl Hayden and Ernest McFarland, who were annoyed with tribal attorneys for winning the case (*Harrison v. Laveen*, 67 Ariz. 337, 196 P.2d 456 [1948]) that gave Indians the right to vote in their state for the first time in 1950; from nearby Utah, Arthur V. Watkins, who was destined to become known in the Eisenhower era as "the Great Emancipator" of Indians from their pasts and their possessions; and from nearby New Mexico, Clinton P. Anderson, who chaired the Indian Affairs Subcommittee— technically, a subcommittee of the Committee on Interior and Insular Affairs—and who was, perhaps second only to McCarran, one of Myer's most powerful allies.

A former secretary of the Agriculture Department under Truman, Senator Anderson had thereafter continued to champion the Forest Service in its battles with Indians over their land; as a legislator he represented agribusiness, banking, mining, timber, and defense interests. Another ally of McCarran's in his war against the Pyramid Lake Paiutes, Anderson was in the early years of his own long war with the Taos Pueblo people over their sacred Blue Lake and the surrounding 50,000 acres. A skeptic when it came down to Indian religions, Anderson could see nothing sacred about their Blue Lake and later demanded that they reveal their sacred rites and show just how and where they performed them day in and day out over all this real estate. Of the same mind exactly, on October 17, 1951, Commissioner Myer overrode the objections of Indian landowners and insisted his BIA personnel would stay in one of the Rio Grande Pueblos during certain ceremonies, notwithstanding the ancient custom that prohibited outsiders from being present at such times (Felix S. Cohen, "Erosion . . . ," *Yale Law Journal* 62 [February 1953]: 359). Of course, Anderson and Myer also shared the agriculture connection and basic assumptions about the need to turn Indians "loose" and about how to convert their communal holdings into individual ownership by siphoning off tribespeople into the mainstream. Finally, the senator was no less annoyed than the commissioner by tribal attorneys who prated about Indian rights—like his Arizona counterparts, Anderson had not welcomed the case that gave Indians the right to vote in New Mexico's 1950 elections and become for the first time a factor in some contests (*New York Times*, January 4, 1952). Out of such mutual repugnance and such shared assumptions, then, Myer and "Dear Clint," as the former's salutations read, joined forces against their common enemies.

For an interviewer who was putting together his oral autobiography years later, Myer recounted one of their signal victories. When tribal attorneys became "a thorn in my flesh," he had gone to Anderson, and the senator had helpfully set up a series of hearings before his subcommittee: "He practically chased one of them out of business with our help which we were very happy about. The lawyer's name was Jim Curry"

(Auto, p. 303). These were also the hearings Myer was brandishing over Chapman's head and continued to brandish, for they started on January 21 and were held sporadically thereafter until September 29, 1952.

For seven days in late January and early February Rufus Wallowing attended the hearings and reported back to the Northern Cheyennes: "They consisted mostly of attempts by Commissioner Myer and Senator Watkins and others to find something wrong with the conduct of our attorney, but they did not succeed. On most of these days, our attorney talked about the Northern Cheyenne contract and insisted that it should be approved immediately." Myer charged Curry with having solicited contracts, but "we know that Mr. Curry did not come to us; we came to him." Myer's smear tactics did not shake his confidence in their attorney:

> It looks as if Mr. Myer is just trying to hurt Mr. Curry, and not really to help the Indians. He also made some other charges against Mr. Curry such as that he has too much business, and that he told some lies. But Mr. Myer did not try to prove any of these accusations. He just made the charges and said he would submit his evidence to the Committee secretly. Mr. Curry is insisting that he prove these charges or back down on them.

From Myer's tactics Wallowing drew a perceptive conclusion:

> I think it is very important that we insist on getting this contract approved. If we cannot even hire our own lawyer, then we will never be permitted to run our own affairs. If we let them stop us from hiring our own lawyer, then we might as well close up shop and quit trying. We must fight this thing through. And even if it takes a long time, we have to keep on fighting. The reason they fight so hard on this is because it is so important to those who want to keep the Indians under the yoke. And if it is important to our enemies to keep us from getting our own attorney, then it is important to us to get him.

Instructed by his council to stay "till we finished," Wallowing unhappily concluded that he had done all he could in Washington: "the odds are against me" ("Report on Attorney Contract," February 15, 1952, JCP). After a month and a half spending his people's money for his expenses, he had to go back to them empty-handed.

Another spectator at the hearings was Avery Winnemucca. On February 22 the Paiute delegate just missed becoming an involuntary participant. After a letter sent out over his signature had been put into the record, he conferred with his attorney and walked out. When Anderson finished reading the letter he looked up and asked if Winnemucca was not in the room. Told that he had just left, the senator directed an aide to try to catch him and added, "the wicked fleeth when no one pursueth." Curry objected to Anderson's insulting maxim, was recalled to the stand, and asked if he had any part in drafting the letter that included this sentence: "This senatorial inquisition is another attempt to break Curry, to ruin his reputation, and in that way to scare all Indian lawyers so that they will be timid about defending Indian rights." Curry answered that "he did have a part in drafting it and the expense of sending the letter to Indian leaders would be borne by his office" ("Subpoena Out as Spectator Quits Hearing," *Washington Post*, February 23, 1952). It was as though the senators had never themselves sent out letters their legal aides had a hand in drafting. In their partial report, this incident was filed under "Misrepresentations": "Mr. Curry in perpetuating his untruths has gone so far as to use Indians as 'fronts' to sign propaganda letters drafted by him. One such letter, dated February 16, 1952, bearing the signature of Mr. Avery Winnemucca . . . Chairman of the Pyramid Lake Tribal Council, is replete with distortions and falsehoods attacking the conduct of these hearings and members of this subcommittee" (*Attorney Contracts with Indian Tribes*, January 16, 1953, JCP). For sheer viciousness, Senator Anderson's hearings rivaled those conducted by McCarran's friend and ally on the Judiciary Committee, Senator Joseph McCarthy.

For tribal delegates in the capital, justice had proved to be dear and not speedy. Now called "wicked" and labeled a "front," Avery Winnemucca had reason to be discouraged. "Avery had to go home because he seemed to be doing no good here in Washington," Curry reported to Collier long months later. "The friends of the Indians all seemed tired of listening to their woes. And I had to try to catch up on some of the regular work of my paying clients" (June 29, 1952, JCP). After eight months of squatting and living on borrowed money "until we get our rights," Winnemucca had to go back to his lake people without their rights and without much hope of ever getting them.

In his appearance before Anderson's subcommittee, Commissioner Myer had assumed that he shared with Congress "a diligent concern for the welfare of the tribal groups." For their own good, these "groups" had to be kept from signing contracts with "disreputable or unscrupulous lawyers, ambulance-chasers, and fomenters of trouble" ("Statement . . . January 21, 1952," NRC). On the basis of an interim report of the subcommittee on June 24, 1952, Myer disapproved Curry's contracts with Winnemucca's people and with Wallowing's Northern Cheyennes: "In view of the recommendations in the report of the subcom-

mittee and information disclosed in the investigation by this Bureau,"
he informed Wallowing, "I disapprove the choice of James E. Curry as
counsel for your tribe. If in these circumstances the Council finds need
for general counsel services, it is recommended that it submit to me for
my approval a proposed contract with other counsel" (August 8, 1952,
NRC). As the *Washington Post* editorialized, the BIA had "acted under
cover" and was "threatening to destroy a lawyer's business without a
hearing" (August 29, 1952). As Myer later crowed, Curry had been
"practically chased . . . out of business with our help," a victory memorialized by another *Post* item headlined: "CURRY SAYS HE WON'T
ACCEPT INDIAN CLIENTS": "He said the reaffirmation by Secretary
Chapman of a decision to nullify his contract with the Pyramid Lake
Paiute Indians of Nevada forced his withdrawal as an Indian attorney"
(October 30, 1952).

A former assistant solicitor in the Interior Department, Curry was
sufficiently scrupulous for Ickes to have become his associate counsel in
appeals against Myer's decisions, and for Ickes to have reprimanded
Chapman for allowing Myer to play "pretty rotten cricket" with the
attorney's contracts (Ickes to Collier, January 13, March 21, 1951,
JCP). Curry was sufficiently active in their behalf to convince Winnemucca, Wallowing, and other tribespeople that he had "the Indian at
heart." Also general counsel of the National Congress of American Indians, he kept watch on land-grab legislation in Congress and earned
the enmity of Indian-haters such as McCarran and Anderson. Finally,
he was brash and sometimes needlessly assertive, as his NCAI associate
Ruth Muskrat Bronson admitted in a letter to the president of the Association on American Indian Affairs:

> I know that Curry has managed—almost as if he worked at it—to make
> himself disliked even by people who ordinarily would have been disposed to
> help him. I confess that I myself find Jim irksome and distressing at times,
> and wish that by some legerdemain he might be whisked out of the picture
> altogether. But he has become the center of the fight and the symbol. I think
> Curry is incorruptible, and that this is part of the grim determination to
> destroy him.

But the principle at stake went beyond Curry, she continued, to the
right of Indians to control their own affairs:

> I think Myer is embarked on a plan to destroy the opposition to his program
> and policies by smear, or by any other means he can find at hand. It is work-
> ing very well, his campaign of smear, and if we let him succeed with Curry
> he will move on next to Felix Cohen, and the Association on American In-

dian Affairs. . . . It will not take much to snuff out of existence, by smear and innuendo, the National Congress of American Indians, for it is a new and not yet solidly financed organization. But if Myer is allowed to succeed at this, it will be easier for him to take on more solid opposition, until all vocal support of the Indians is destroyed. That would be [a] catastrop[h]e.
[Bronson to Oliver La Farge, August 24, 1952, AAIA]

With the Pyramid Lake Paiutes denied any legal help not dominated by Senator McCarran, with the Northern Cheyennes denied any legal help of their choice, and with other tribes also denied free access to the courts—"their last battle ground"—the NCAI executive director wrote "in a kind of feeling of desperation." Her desperation had ample cause and her reading of coming events was prescient. She had no way of knowing that Myer had long since moved on to the AAIA general counsel with any means he could find at hand.

CHAPTER X

"Fomenter of Trouble": Felix S. Cohen

Felix S. Cohen has written and circulated among Indians and
non-Indians a shocking memorandum. It is shocking, first,
because it is filled from start to finish with outrageous perversions of the truth. It is shocking, secondly, because it is obviously intended to spread terror among the Indians and to
fill their minds with fear and hatred against an agency of
their government. It is shocking, thirdly, because Mr. Cohen
admittedly made no effort to check on the subject of his
memorandum with responsible officials before putting it into
circulation.

> —*Dillon S. Myer,*
> *"Statement . . . , " n.d. (March 1952)*

The Blackfoot Indians adopted Felix S. Cohen into their tribe, calling
him "Double Runner." Philosopher Ernest Nagel of Columbia University called him "an outstanding contributor to ethical and legal philosophy." Ralph S. Brown, Jr., of the Yale Law School called him "a great
and noble teacher." Senator Hubert H. Humphrey called him "one of
the country's outstanding experts in legislative drafting" (*New Leader*,
March 2, 1953, p. 3). Assistant BIA Commissioner William Zimmerman identified him for the FBI as the colleague who "gradually became
recognized in the department as the best-informed lawyer in the field of
Indian law." Assistant Interior Solicitor William Flanery advised the FBI
that he was a former superior who had "done much to further legislation in the Indians' behalf while he was in the department" and in the
process "undoubtedly acquired . . . a vast knowledge of the Indian race
both as to its historical background and its present day setting." This
FBI report also incorporated the denunciation of an anonymous critic
who was interested in Alaskan timber stands, for whom he was odiously
"Felix Cohen, dep't of interior radical" (December 6, 1949, FBI 46-
16318).

In an earlier investigation under Truman's loyalty program, FBI agents had extracted basic data from Cohen's departmental personnel file that started out with "his birth at New York City on July 3, 1907, the son of MORRIS RAPHAEL COHEN, who was born in Minsk, Russia" (June 7, 1948, FBI 121-6680). A son of the world-renowned philosopher, he had graduated from the City College of New York (CCNY) in 1926, earned his Ph.D. degree in philosophy from Harvard in 1929, and his law degree from Columbia in 1931. He was the author of numerous essays and articles and of two books: *Ethical Systems and Legal Ideals* (1933), his revised doctoral dissertation, which compellingly established the implicit presence of ethical issues throughout the legal system and every other institution; and the *Handbook of Federal Indian Law* (1941), his monumental compilation and analysis of treaties, statutes, and regulations, which soon became the authoritative work on tribal sovereignty and Indian legal rights. After serving as assistant solicitor from 1933 and associate solicitor from 1943, Cohen had resigned from the Interior Department on January 2, 1948, to go into private practice in Washington and to become a visiting lecturer at CCNY and at the Yale Law School.

As an undergraduate at CCNY Cohen had fought compulsory military training and been active in the League for Industrial Democracy. FBI agents learned that the Washington, D.C., Police Department had once "reported him as a member of the Socialist Party at an unspecified date." The agents also alleged that he was on the mailing list of the United American Spanish Aid Committee and that he had withdrawn from the National Lawyers Guild "in the early 1940's, after fighting the Communists in the Guild and realizing it was a losing fight, according to Judge Lawrence Koenigsberger of the Tax Appeals Court, Washington, D.C." Even in those perfervid days building up to the loyalty mania, these bits could not be pieced together into a damning political profile. It was rather that of a libertarian socialist who had opposed communists and who had genuine distinction as a gifted teacher, a brilliant lawyer and legal theorist, and a scholarly fighter in behalf of Afro-Americans, immigrants, migratory workers, Native Americans.

These reports draw the portrait of Myer's antithesis.* Cohen's aim, said Ernest Nagel of Columbia, "was to open our minds to alternative possibilities, and thereby to make our judgments less provincial and more responsible." Myer's aim, said his every act, was to close our

---

*Recall the omen that turned up back in 1942 when Cohen passed on to the WRA director the embarrassing reminder that not all the inmates in his camps were "Japanese" (discussed in chapter 3).

minds to alternative possibilities and thereby to make our judgments more provincial and less responsible. It followed that in Cohen he saw his quintessential "fomenter of trouble." As he had with "troublemakers" in his WRA camps, Myer turned quite naturally to the FBI for help in extracting this thorn from his flesh.

2

In the summer of 1950 the new commissioner had conferred with the Montana tribes in Billings and received a request from the Blackfeet that they be consulted before he appointed another superintendent for their reservation. In the ensuing discussion Myer treated them as suppliants for charity by telling them and the other tribal representatives that when they paid their superintendent's salary, they might have the privilege of selecting him. Writing for the Blackfoot tribe as their general counsel, Cohen repeated their request and courteously suggested that such consultation would be one constructive way to ease tensions on a reservation that had been for many years "a battleground between Indians who bitterly resent paternalism and Indian Bureau officials who have been accustomed to dealing with Indians as they would deal with young children." It was customary to consult with the heads of foreign states before making important diplomatic appointments, with unions before appointing a secretary of labor, and the like, so why should Indians not be consulted beforehand in comparable appointments? Tired of "being insulted and pushed around," his clients had instructed Cohen to call the commissioner's attention to the fact that their tribe was "the largest tax-payer in Glacier County, and that the members of this tribe pay in Federal taxes a sum very much larger than the Federal Government spends on the Blackfeet Reservation. They feel, therefore, that even on a narrow financial view they have earned the right to a voice in the selection of the next Blackfeet superintendent" (to Myer, September 13, 1950, NRC). None of these arguments interested Myer: "I believe that my position was made quite clear at Billings when I stated that we would always be glad to receive suggestions, and I see no reason for further discussion of the point at this time. . . . I enjoyed very much my meeting with the representatives of the Indian groups in Montana and Wyoming on my recent field trip" (to Cohen, September 19, 1950, NRC). In the commissioner's lexicon, Indian tribes were *groups*, as though they were chance collections of individuals at a bus stop, and in his appointments, tribes were treated as though they were aggregations of young children. By installing Guy Robertson as the new Blackfoot superintendent on November 22, 1950, Myer disregarded the wishes of members of the tribe and guaranteed they would be strenuously pushed around.

Prior to the war, Guy Robertson had worked at this and that, for a construction outfit, in the purchasing department of a magnesium company, as a dude rancher, and as manager of some tourist camps near Jackson, Wyoming (Butte Special Agent, "Memorandum for Inspector M. E. Gurnea," February 12, 1943, FBI 100-164195). Then in 1943 he had become director of the WRA camp at Heart Mountain, in which position we encountered him scheming with Myer to crush the draft resistance of inmates and in particular to upset "the apple cart" of Kiyoshi Okamoto (p. 301). After the war, and before opportunity knocked again, he managed the Noble Hotel in Wyoming. Neither as a dude rancher nor as a people keeper inside and outside concentration camps had he learned anything about Indians. Robertson did know, however, that his old boss liked to run a tight ship, and that suited him perfectly. Chairman Thomas Main of the Montana Intertribal Policy Board undoubtedly had him in mind, among others, when he indicted "that attitude of paternalism, treating us like prisoners in a concentration camp" (Transcript of "Hearing on Proposed Regulations to Govern Indian Tribal Attorney Contracts," JCP).

One of the identifying characteristics of concentration camps, Myer's included, as we have seen, was the determined denial of due process—the intercepted letters, monitored telephone conversations, eavesdropping, networks of informers. Under Myer, BIA officials did their level best to get back to the day of Commissioner Walker, when reservations had in fact had many of these earmarks of concentration camps, and that made Robertson feel right at home on the Blackfoot reservation. On April 3, 1951, his superior in Billings, Area Director Paul L. Fickinger, reported to Myer on the constant surveillance of their disobedient children:

> Incidentally Mr. Cohen will be at Fort Belknap this weekend and at Blackfeet next week. Tom Main in particular and the Council as a whole at Fort Belknap are in constant telephone contact with Mr. Cohen. Apparently Felix is working for the tribe for nothing. I am trying to get copies of the correspondence that the Tribe has back and forth with Cohen but have not been very successful as yet. The boys seem to keep things pretty close, probably on Cohen's advice. So many of the things from Fort Belknap go direct to Mr. Cohen and from there on into other channels that we find ourselves a little hard pressed to keep up with things.
>
> [NRC]

In reply Myer agreed with Fickinger on his handlings of things, but did not reprimand him for his systematic campaign to breach the confidential relationship between a lawyer and his clients (April 9, 1951, NRC). Just like Japanese Americans, Native Americans had a constitutional right, as citizens, to privileged communication with untrammeled counsel, and just like the camp inmates before them, they had been effectively denied that right. Also like "pressure boys" or "problem boys" in the camps, many Indians on the reservations were men and not "boys"— Thomas Main, for instance, was sixty years old.

Superintendent Robertson was caught off guard by a contretemps during Cohen's presence in his bailiwick at Browning, Montana. After reporting the outrage by telephone, the next day he detailed what had happened for Area Director Fickinger in an agitated letter. On Saturday, April 14, 1951, he had been working in his office when he received word that a number of people and cars were congregated in front of a vacant house on the personnel circle. Going there immediately, he tore down a NO TRESPASSING sign that had been posted on the front door. Just outside the back entrance he found Felix Cohen and Chairman George Pambrun of the Blackfoot Tribal Business Council and inside the house found a tribal policeman, whom he ordered out: "We found that a basement window had been forced and entrance evidently made through it into the house and the back door then unlocked and opened." When he asked Chairman Pambrun if he did not know that breaking and entering government property was a grave offense, he was told that Cohen had said that the building was tribal property, had participated in occupying it, and would accept full responsibility for the act:

> After some heated discussion in which I attempted to tell Mr. Cohen how contemptible I thought his actions were to which he continually invited me to bring suit for possession of the building, I told him that as custodian of Government property, I had possession of the building, that I intended to retain that possession until advised to the contrary by my superior officers and that I would also continue to administer this government property regardless of opposition or consequences [that included for one tribal employee the threat of death]. I told Mr. Pambrun that I had known other persons who had flaunted Government authority and that they had come to no good end [viz., Okamoto and members of the Fair Play Committee at Heart Mountain]. . . . Mr. Cohen told me he was leaving last night. I want very much to bring charges against him and hope Mr. [George] Brunskill [BIA Area Law Enforcement Officer] will prepare a case.
>
> [Robertson to Fickinger, April 15, 1951,
> FBI 70-17072]

The trouble was that Robertson was playing Horatio at the Bridge on property that "by all ordinary standards of law, equity, and morality,"

Blackfoot Lockout, April 14, 1951. "WARPATH—George Pambrun and Cora Irgens of the Blackfoot Indian Tribal Council watch a workman tack up a sign on the warehouse as part of a legal dispute" reads the caption and legend of this photograph. The onlooker at the left was the Blackfoot "Double Runner," their General Counsel Felix S. Cohen.
[AP/Wide World Photos]

as Cohen put it, belonged to the Blackfeet. They had paid for the construction of the "broken and entered" house and other buildings on their reservation through offsets charged against their recovery in a claims case (*The Blackfeet Nation* v. *United States*, 81 Ct. Cl. 101 [1935]).

In contrast to Robertson, the Blackfeet acted with civil restraint and presented their side of the controversy through a model of mature argumentation. On advice of counsel, they had chosen to occupy the house "as the most expeditious way to bring the merits of this issue before the courts." If Robertson had a better way to suggest, their council would consider it, pledged their spokesman:

> Meanwhile, I would suggest that you caution subordinates who are less even tempered than you are against acts of violence that would seriously set back the cooperative relations we have tried to build up together. We propose to assert our claims of ownership in a public, peaceable, and orderly way, and

we hope you will cooperate in seeing that no acts of violence mar our efforts
to bring an important question before the courts.

[Pambrun to Robertson, April 16, 1951,
FBI 70-17072]

But Robertson and his superiors were not keen to have this important
question adjudicated, for the courts might well identify *them* as the
trespassers.

In accordance with a telephone conversation with Myer, Area Director Fickinger sent Enforcement Officer Brunskill up to the Blackfoot
reservation to conduct an investigation and forwarded a copy of Robertson's report:

Things are quiet at Blackfeet at the moment and I am keeping in daily
contact with the situation there. We will follow your instructions and in the
event there is an attempt at forcible entry again of any of the vacant buildings, no force will be used to keep the individuals out.

It is incredible to me, however, that any attorney, and particularly an
attorney who is serving as legal counsel for a Tribe of Indians, will advise
his clients to take the law into their own hands, as Mr. Cohen appears to
have done with the Blackfeet Tribal Council. This one act alone, to my way
of thinking, should clearly demonstrate Mr. Cohen's unsuitability to serve as
a legal counsel and adviser to a group of Indian people.

I am not forwarding a copy of the placard that was posted by the Tribal
Council since Mr. Robertson will have a copy with him when he arrives in
Washington.

[Fickinger to Myer, April 19, 1951, FBI 70-17072]

Like his chief, the area director presumed to pass on the suitability of a
legal counsel for a "group" of citizens. In their minds, the Blackfeet were
not mature enough to assess the merits of the "Double Runner" between
their tribe and the dominant culture.

Out of the conferences of Myer and Robertson in Washington and
their consultations on the telephone with Fickinger and others in Montana came a plan worthy of the way they had made up WRA law as
they went along. If charges against Cohen for breaking and entering
were likely to backfire, then maybe he could be prosecuted under some
other statute. On April 21 BIA Attorney Harlow Pease appeared at the
FBI office in Butte "and requested that an investigation be conducted
by the FBI under Section 372, Title 18, USC, on the theory of conspiracy
to hinder or impede a Federal Officer to discharge his duties. Mr. Pease
said his chief interest in requesting this investigation was to get a true
and clear picture of the Blackfeet Indian Reservation with respect to the
claim of the Indians, but he was not interested in any arrests of any
persons *as yet*" (Butte SAC to FBI Director, April 21, 1951, FBI 70-

17072; emphasis added). Such were the origins of the abortive investigation J. Edgar Hoover labeled "FELIX COHEN/BREAKING AND ENTERING OF BUILDINGS OF BLACKFEET INDIAN RESERVATION ON APRIL 14, 1951/CRIME ON INDIAN RESERVATION/CONSPIRACY" and laid to rest in a memorandum indicating that the appropriate U.S. attorney had declined to press criminal charges and advised that the issue of ownership of the disputed buildings would be determined by civil action (for Assistant Attorney General James M. McInerney, August 27, 1951, FBI 70-17072).

"Myer has also been defeated on virtually every point involving the Blackfeet," exulted the executive director of the Association on American Indian Affairs. "The tribe is now in fully confirmed possession of the buildings which they padlocked on Cohen's advice" (Alexander Lesser to Oliver La Farge, May 23, 1951, AAIA). While Secretary Chapman still exercised a measure of restraint, he had overruled his commissioner, and the BIA had admitted that the tribe possessed a proper equity in such buildings. Nevertheless, Lesser's celebration was premature, as Cohen later made clear in the *Yale Law Journal*: "The Bureau is still collecting the rentals; and, notwithstanding Commissioner Myer's promises to the Blackfeet Tribe, no tribal building of any substantial value has yet been turned over to the Blackfeet (or, apparently, any other) tribe" (62 [1953]: 368). Like his predecessor Walker, Commissioner Myer did not feel bound by promises to Indians. With his blessing, Superintendent Robertson retained BIA custody of Blackfoot property "regardless of opposition or consequences."

Concurrently, Myer was behind another abortive FBI investigation that involved Cohen and James E. Curry as legal counsel for the Oglala Sioux on the Pine Ridge Reservation in South Dakota (FBI 100-378472). On March 15, 1951, a letter bearing Secretary Chapman's signature had formally requested an investigation of the attorney general, alleging "that virtually a complete breakdown of law and order had occurred at the reservation. . . . The Secretary's letter also alleges that one of the members of the tribal council is reportedly an active Communist and that Communist organizers from Denver have recently spent some time on the reservation." When agents interviewed Chapman, however, he informed them "that he was vaguely familiar with the situation" and referred them to his commissioner, who in turn related "that most of the knowledge he has concerning the instant matter was related to him by Warren Spaulding, Area Director . . . Aberdeen, South Dakota." Agents doggedly followed up leads given them by Myer and unearthed reports that communists had sent old clothing to the reservation; that communists may have sponsored meetings of the Native American Church at which "Indians taking part in the service became doped"; and, still more luridly, that communists may have been the "certain individuals in black sedan automobiles . . . meeting with the Indians on the prairie at Allen, South Dakota."

Area Director Spaulding advised agents that so far as he could determine all the dissatisfaction and dissension at Pine Ridge dated from the appointment of Cohen and Curry as legal advisers. One of the ways Cohen had stirred up strife and suspicion was to charge that many BIA "employees do not treat Indians like human beings." What was more, he had done the same thing on the Blackfoot reservation, said Spaulding and "related that MR. PAUL L. FICKINGER of the Bureau of Indian Affairs at Browning, Montana has full particulars on this episode." But in the instant matter, "it is SPAULDING's opinion that CURRY and COHEN are deliberately inciting the Indian people on the Pine Ridge Reservation against the Government of the United States."

That was Myer's view exactly, and just a week after his drubbing during Chapman's hearings on the attorney contracts, he made certain that the investigation was his idea by asking Agent O. J. Keep if he had any good news for him: "Mr. Dillon S. Myer, Commissioner of the Bureau of Indian Affairs, asked concerning the status of a case previously referred by him to the Bureau. He said that the matter involved Communism among the Indian leaders and others on the Pine Ridge Reservation. . . . He was interested in whether or not the investigation had been completed and the results of the Bureau's inquiry" (January 10, 1952, FBI 100-378472). A production of "Prairie Communists and Red Lawyers on the Reservation" would have nicely complemented Senator Joseph McCarthy's "Card-Carrying Communists in the State Department" had Hoover's agents not again let Myer down. Curry, the general counsel of the National Congress of American Indians, would shortly be practically chased out of business by Senator Anderson's hearings, but Cohen, the general counsel of the Association on American Indian Affairs, had once again slipped through the commissioner's fingers.

3

Stymied in his attempts to sic the FBI on Cohen, Myer tried to silence him through a systematic campaign of vilification. To Philleo Nash, a future BIA commissioner who was then White House liaison with the Interior Department, Myer remarked that "Cohen when last seen on the

Blackfeet reservation was crawling out of a cellar window, etc." (the forced basement window of the "broken and entered" house, which no one had seen Cohen crawling out of). From that and other aspersions against their general counsel, Alexander Lesser drew the conclusion for Oliver La Farge that Myer "is making and has made a calculated effort to cause a break between the Association and Cohen—not only in his talks with you, but in things he has told Philleo. Philleo was amazed to discover that Cohen had no claims contracts and no financial interest in any—and pleased, and stated specifically that his earlier views were largely by way of Myer" (May 23, 1951, AAIA). Later in a congressional hearing Cohen testified for the AAIA and, according to Lesser, "his remarks were courteous, dignified, and controlled. Yet Myer rose at once, almost pathologically, to attac[k] Cohen personally. I have an independent witness to this fact. My own reaction is that in such a situation, I am for Cohen. He doesn't have to take the kind of abuse Myer hands him, to carry on his practice or earn a living. He does because of principle, and for no other reason" (to La Farge, June 30, 1952, AAIA).

Myer had been telling Philleo Nash and others that Cohen had a major financial interest in tribal claims presented under the Indian Claims Commission Act. But in 1949 the FBI had conducted a thorough investigation based on complaints that Cohen had violated the Hatch Act (Sect. 284, Title 18, U.S.C.) by acting as an agent for tribes within two years of completing his government service; the investigators had then discovered no such violation and no such financial interest. Their inquiries revealed that about sixteen law firms scattered across the country, called the "joint-efforts group," had joined together to have the New York firm of Riegelman, Strasser, Schwartz & Spiegelberg conduct common research on the interrelated questions presented by claims cases. As a partner in the Riegelman firm and head of its Washington office, Cohen had an annual retainer of $15,000, but no interest whatsoever in the tribal claims themselves. As he informed FBI agents on November 25, 1949, his work had consisted of compiling "tribal histories" comparable to "the sort of research job that went into Chapters 20 to 23 of the Handbook of Federal Indian Law. . . . He stated during the last two months his work has consisted largely of studying and preparing selective summaries of the reports of the Commissioner of Indian Affairs prior to 1880. He states his work has included the training of a staff of four attorneys in the methods and sources of research in Indian law and history" (FBI 46-16318). In fine, law firms had joined together to draw on Cohen's vast knowledge of Indian law and on his luminous under-

standing of American history, for which technical assistance he had
been, and was being, paid a fixed fee.

In testimony before the House Subcommittee on Interior Appropriations Cohen had cleared up the facts of this relationship with the joint-
efforts group shortly before Myer appeared before that subcommittee
to reiterate his aspersions: "Then, I believe that he has a broad interest
in a group of claims contracts, 20 or more, which are being pressed as
claims before the Indian Claims Commission. . . . I believe that his major interest from the standpoint of income from Indian contracts would
likely be in the claims contracts handled by the so-called joint-efforts
group of lawyers." On May 16, 1951, Cohen quoted these misstate-
ments and remonstrated with Myer: "I want very much to believe that
these remarks were made as a result of honest error, and that you will
want to set the record straight without delay when the error has been
called to your attention. . . . The fact is that I do not now have, and
never have had, any interest in any Indian claims contract" (JCP). Myer
stiffly acknowledged the letter, enclosed copies of his own letters to the
appropriate subcommittees correcting the record, and closed with this
half apology: "I am sorry if I misinformed the Subcommittee, and I
assure you it was unintentional" (to Cohen, May 21, 1951, JCP). Only
for the moment had the record been set straight. Myer had tilted it with
misinformation that was not unintentional, and his deliberate untruth
would crop up again. Control of lawyers meant control of Indians.
Cohen stood in the way of that control.

Any doubt that Myer sought the "*strict reformatory control*" enjoyed
by his predecessor Walker disappeared on January 29, 1952, when at
the request of the Indian Bureau the chairman of the Senate Judiciary
Committee introduced S. 2543 and shortly thereafter a companion bill,
H.R. 6035, went before the House Judiciary Committee with the
graphic title, "A Bill to Authorize the Indian Bureau to Make Arrests
Without Warrant for Violation of Indian Bureau Regulations, etc." In
introducing his ally's bill, the Indian-hating Senator McCarran put its
enormity in perspective by saying that he was "not wholly in sympathy"
with it and thought that it went beyond precedent and might undermine
civil liberties (*Cong. Rec.*, January 29, 1952, p. 569). As the general
counsel of the Blackfeet of Montana, the Oglala Sioux of South Dakota,
the San Carlos Apache of Arizona, and the Laguna Pueblo of New Mexico, Felix Cohen quickly warned the 20,000 red citizens in these tribes
of "the shocking implications of S. 2543" in a preliminary analysis

headed, "Memorandum on Bill Authorizing the Indian Bureau to Seize, Search, Arrest and Shoot Indians" (February 1, 1952, NRC).

"This is one of the most vicious misrepresentations of fact that I have seen in over 35 years of public service," fumed Myer when a copy of Cohen's privileged communication fell into his hands. "When the text of the memorandum was read at an open hearing of a Congressional Subcommittee on February 29 and Mr. Cohen identified himself as the author, one of the committee members stated that Mr. Cohen was not a fit person to represent the Indians." Myer's self-revealing condemnation of the attorney raised to high relief his resentments against "troublemakers" accumulated over all those years of public service and in the instant moment his fury over Chapman's hearings and his frustrations over the abortive FBI investigations. No doubt with the help of the serviceable Messrs. Ferguson and Sigler, Myer undertook to demonstrate Cohen's unfitness in a four-page "Statement by Commissioner of Indian Affairs Dillon S. Myer Concerning Felix S. Cohen's Memorandum on S. 2543" (n.d., NRC). Among the especially nettling "outrageous perversions of the truth" was Cohen's charge "that the bill is obviously part of the Indian Bureau's new program to reduce Indians to the condition of prisoners of the Bureau. It would apply to American citizens of the Indian race the same coercive measures that were applied during war-time to American citizens of Japanese descent in the concentration camps operated by Dillon S. Myer." No, said the former jailer of the Japanese Americans, from the beginning the foremost objective of the WRA had been to restore them "as rapidly as possible to ordinary American communities." Just another example of Cohen's "false and malicious" criticism, his entire memorandum was shocking because it was "obviously intended to spread terror among the Indians and to fill their minds with fear and hatred against an agency of their government." Thereupon Myer circulated thousands of copies of his "Statement" at government expense throughout the Indian country and elsewhere. When a copy reached Cohen in an envelope without any return address, he responded to "this scurrilous personal attack" with a nine-page memorandum, "The Indian Bureau's Drive for Increased Police Powers" (April 3, 1952, JCP).

In this battle of the memoranda, Myer was better financed, but hopelessly outclassed. In parallel columns, *The Indian Bureau Says* versus *The Actual Facts*, Cohen charitably skipped over "the hysterical name calling" and used his knowledge of Indian law and the weapons of a scholar to hew and slash the commissioner's "Statement":

The Indian Bureau Says

"The primary purpose of the bill is to provide these officers with the types of powers held by policemen in an ordinary American community."

"The powers conferred upon the Bureau's law enforcement officers are virtually identical with those now held by U.S. Marshals."

"Mr. Cohen said that the Department's bill would authorize Bureau employees to shoot Indians."

"Under our American system of justice no person charged with committing a crime can be punished without first being properly arrested, arraigned, and given a fair and impartial trial before a court of law."

"It is a well settled principle of our legal system that no act of Congress can authorize the enforcement of an unconstitutional regulation."

The Actual Facts

There is *no ordinary community in the United States* where a policeman has a right to arrest without a warrant anybody who violates an administrative regulation, promulgated by an official in Washington.

United States Marshals, under Section 3053 of the Code of Criminal Procedure, may make arrests without warrant only for felonies—not for misdemeanors—and certainly not for mere violations of executive regulations.

The bill authorizes Bureau employees to carry guns and make arrests, even for violations of Bureau regulations; it follows that the guns may be used to effect such arrests.

Under H.R. 6035 the Commissioner or his employee would be law-maker, law enforcement officer, prosecuting attorney, judge, and prison warden combined. [Just as Myer had been at Moab, Leupp, and the Tule stockade, Cohen might have added.]

When Mr. Myer was in charge of Japanese detention camps, he kept thousands of loyal American citizens of Japanese ancestry behind barbed wire. The United States Supreme Court later said this was illegal. . . . Judge [William] Denman, speaking for the Circuit Court of Appeals in the 9th Circuit, in the case of *Acheson* v. *Murikami*, 176 Fed. (2d) 953, said that conditions in the Tule Lake Center under Mr. Myer's administration were "in major respects as degrading as those of a penitentiary, and in important respects, worse than in any Federal penitentiary."

["Indian Bureau's Drive," April 3, 1952, JCP]

And so the columns marched on. "Your watchdog has done his barking now," Cohen concluded, and the rest was up to the tribes and their friends: "If the proposed bill becomes law, the chances are that it will affect the lives of hundreds of thousands of Indians not yet born, and will stand on the statute books long after Dillon Myer and Felix Cohen have passed on. The last time that kind of legislation was passed was in 1858, and it took until May 18, 1934 to get that legislation repealed."

Just as Myer had made up WRA law as he went along, so now he wanted to make up BIA law at will. Already subject to 800 special statutes and 2,200 regulations "just because they are Indians," as Cohen said, nearly half a million red citizens—not to mention those not yet born—would be subject through his bill to whatever additional repression he deemed desirable. At one stroke reservations would become concentration camps comparable to the WRA camps in everything but the barbed wire and watchtowers, and they could be added later. Indeed, the armed military police had remained outside the WRA camps—except to put down those "riots"—whereas under the proposed bill any number of Myer's current 12,745 employees could become pistol-packing police *inside* the BIA camps, searching, seizing, arresting, imprisoning without warrant, and, yes, shooting those who resisted. Surely stockades would spring up like weeds. Leupp might even be reopened; it was, after all, on Navaho land. Myer was bent on applying "to American citizens of the Indian race the same coercive measures that were applied during war-time to American citizens of Japanese descent," Cohen observed. In both instances, ancestry ordained who the victims would be and thereby branded the coercive measures as unmistakable expressions of their author's racism. In the second instance, "is it that our Indians are more dangerous than counterfeiters, enemy spies or convicted criminals serving terms of hard labor?" Cohen rather more politely asked as spokesman for the AAIA. "Could it be that those who propose such legislation still think of Indians as savages without rights?" (*Great Falls* [Montana] *Tribune*, April 14, 1952).

As commissioner, Myer was handicapped by the absence of any para-administrative organization comparable to the Japanese American Citizens League. No organization of Native Americans ran interference for him by singing his praises and welcoming his repressions as beneficences bestowed upon them for their own good. Instead, the National Congress of American Indians, composed of the larger tribes, fought him with all the slim resources Ruth Muskrat Bronson and her associates could lay their hands on. Also confronted by watchdogs who really barked, such as the late Harold Ickes and John Collier, Myer could no longer boast of his very cordial "relations with the Civil Liberties group." Even Roger Baldwin spoke out against his attorney regulations, as we have seen, and a spokesman for the ACLU remonstrated that under his law-and-order bill, "the civil rights of American Indians would suffer" (Jay B. Nash to Myer, May 12, 1952, JCP). But it was Cohen who spearheaded the fight against S. 2543 and H.R. 6035, testified for the AAIA against the latter, and provoked widespread editorial condemnations of the bill:

> "Indian Bureau Asks Gestapo Power. . . . This is one bill Congress would do well to file and forget pronto."
> [*Houston Post*, April 22, 1952]

> "No One Is Safe. . . . This measure appears to be a bald-faced attempt by the Indian bureau to seize dictatorial powers. . . . If America's Indian citizens can be so flagrantly deprived of their rights, none of us is safe."
> [*Gallup* (New Mexico) *Independent*, April 16, 1952]

> "No 'Cold War' on Indians. . . . It is amazing that an agency of our Government, for any reason, would put forth proposals such as these. Such a grant to bureaucrats of vast authority over Indians or any one else in this country hasn't a shadow of justification. It should be rejected."
> [*Philadelphia Inquirer*, April 17, 1952]

When the long hearings turned into a wake, the House Judiciary Committee laid Myer's bill to rest.

The commissioner had been stung but not disabled. The dictatorial powers he had hoped to legitimate were tellingly demonstrated even while his law-and-order bill was still pending in Congress. On April 16, 1952, Superintendent Guy Robertson wrote Chairman Walter S. Wetzel of the Blackfoot Tribal Council that he had learned of a bad situation at Heart Butte:

> I am told that many people congregate on Saturday and Sunday and that children engage in blackjack and hand games [or stick games, as Cohen explained, "a sort of aboriginal canasta"] and do not return to school for several days, and I would appreciate it very much if you call the peace officers in for a meeting and advise them of the situation and direct them to break it up and see that the children attend school.
> [NRC]

"I think Mr. Robertson's letter fully explains the action taken by him," Myer wrote Senator Carl Hayden, "which action I thoroughly approve" (May 16, 1952, NRC). When the superintendent gained no immediate satisfaction from the Tribal Council, he called a BIA policeman in and ordered him to break it up and see that Indians stopped playing their games by six o'clock on Sundays so they could get up bright and early on Mondays. And that same month, Robertson's "armed Bureau employees closed down a polling place on the Blackfeet Reservation where the tribe had announced a referendum vote on a tribal budget ordinance under the charter of self-government that still carried the unfaded signature of former Secretary of the Interior Harold Ickes" ("Policing the Indians," *New Republic* 126 [June 23, 1952]: 8). Before and after Myer's bill had been laid away, in fine, BIA law enforcement officers carried guns to make Indians behave; before and after his bill, the BIA asserted its right to run their elections even if this interference violated tribal charters of self-government. Just as during the war the lack of enabling legislation had not stopped Myer from exercising dictatorial powers in the WRA camps, so now that lack demonstrably did not stop him and his recycled WRA cohorts on the reservations.

"Once grant that expert government is better than self-government and there is no stopping the expansion of the Indian Bureau, or any other bureau, until it fills the whole space of the individual's life," Cohen had prophetically observed in the *Progressive*. Unlike Myer, he brought a measure of humor to their conflict by rejecting the "devil theory" of commissioners wherein, "according to the adherents of this popular view, the only good Indian Commissioner is a dead Indian Commissioner." Life was not that simple, and what had to be understood was the process of *colonialism* "by which great empires 'aid' and 'protect' backward peoples out of their independence, and impose a dependent status and a dependent psychology upon people who once managed their own affairs in a self-reliant way." Any white outsider who interfered with the imposition of that dependency became a "paid agitator" who stood in the way of "the unshirkable duty of the Indian Bureau to carry on its shoulders the 'white man's burden' of telling the Indians what to do." Drawing on his intensive study of thirty-six commissioners, Cohen went beyond devil theories and personalities to interrelate colonialism and racism, and to place Myer squarely within the psychology and philosophy "of colonial administration in all parts of the world." His analysis anticipated my attempt to understand Myer's "carceral systems" as complex coercive networks that shared critical functions and inner dynamics:

> Every now and then a Commissioner reveals the large number of dishonest officials that held jobs under a prior administration. But the real corruption of the Indian Bureau is institutional, not personal. It is like the corruption of

prisons, insane asylums, concentration camps, fascist and communist states, and other societies in which men cannot "talk back" to officials. It is what Lord Acton had clearly in mind when he pointed out that power corrupts and absolute power corrupts absolutely.

["Colonialism: U.S. Style," *Progressive* 15
(February 1951): 16–18]

Carceral systems corrupt. It is a pity the thirty-seventh commissioner could never accept his adversary's invitation to engage in a dialogue.

At bottom Cohen's message was the simple one he delivered to Area Director Spaulding and others at Pine Ridge, South Dakota: many BIA "employees do not treat Indians like human beings." But this was just the message Myer would not or rather could not hear, for he was one of those employees. A largely unconscious agent of the colonial process—"he doesn't even know what he himself is like," as John Collier had observed—he could not see Indians as human beings, adult human beings, and could only see Cohen as a "fomenter of trouble," a paid agitator. Why otherwise would the latter aid and abet "wily" Indians who tried to slip out from under reformatory control? So in his conferences with Philleo Nash and others, Myer vilified Cohen—who was often out of pocket in his work for red clients—as an ambulance-chaser who was after hundreds of thousands, millions, maybe even billions of dollars of public funds through Indian claims contracts. Yet as commissioner, Myer was in a position to inform himself of the precise details of the claims interest of any attorney, and that meant that he could have determined the particulars of Cohen's relationship with the joint-efforts group of lawyers before he fed his aspersions into the record of the House Subcommittee on Interior Appropriations. That he did not first seek the facts before vilifying was shocking in itself, but not, as Cohen hoped, the "result of honest error."

Months later dramatic evidence that Myer's misinformation was intentional cropped up and was given national circulation. In "'Justice' for Indians Comes High," the syndicated columnist Drew Pearson began with an attack on James E. Curry that had to have been based on a handout from the commissioner or from his misinformation specialist, Morrill M. Tozier. Pearson then went on to explain further "the bitter attacks on Myer":

> In the forefront of the attack on the Indian Bureau has been the Association on American Indian Affairs, whose general counsel is Felix Cohen, a former high official of the Interior Department. Cohen is also a partner in a syndi-

Portrait of Felix S. Cohen by Joseph Margulies, 1954.
[Morris R. Cohen Library at City College of New York]

cate seeking more than 4 billion dollars in Indian claims against the Government which Cohen on[c]e represented.

[*Washington Post*, August 14, 1952]

Like Myer before him, the columnist had to retract the aspersion:

Correction: Last month this column reported that Felix Cohen . . . was a "partner" in a syndicate seeking Indian claims against the Government. Testimony to this effect was given before the Senate [Anderson] Committee probing Indian attorneys. However, I now learn that Mr. Cohen . . . has a partnership agreement specifically providing that he shall have no fees from these Indian claims. Delighted to set the record straight.

[*Washington Post*, September 11, 1952]

Drew Pearson had fallen for, or lent himself to, Myer's renewed attempt to set the much-abused record crooked. His column helped change the mind of Oliver La Farge, who had been thinking of making Myer a new offer of cooperation in behalf of the AAIA, for it showed conclusively that the commissioner was "circulating information that he knows to be untrue. The man is a liar on a number of provable counts, and it would be folly to make peace with him" (La Farge to Ruth Muskrat Bronson, September 5, 1952, AAIA).

In a desk folder labeled "Cohen, Felix S.—Misc. Problems" (NRC), Myer left behind a copy of this little memorandum he had written for Secretary Chapman on August 3, 1952:

I believe you will be interested in seeing what the Communist-line press is doing these days with "news" items handed out by the Association on American Indian Affairs and undoubtedly inspired by Felix Cohen.

THE COMPASS, of course, is well-known for its consistent plugging of the party line. My understanding is that the Federated Press, which used to be a respectable labor news service, has fallen in recent years into Communist Party hands.

Dillon

CHAPTER XI

Terminator

I think my record will bear out the fact that I believe very
strongly that time is past due when many Indians should be
released from all types of Federal supervision. While I have
pointed out that many Indians do not wish this, I strongly
feel that the trusteeship and other special forms of government services to the Indians are holding the Indians back politically, socially, and economically. . . . For the benefit of the
Indians a strong hand will have to be taken both by the Department and Congress.

> —*Dillon S. Myer*
> to *Interior Secretary Douglas McKay,*
> *March 20, 1953*

For two years Myer's outstanding triumphs had been his drafts on the
U.S. Treasury. For the fiscal year of 1949 the BIA budget had been
$44,000,000. As the incoming commissioner he got even more money
from Truman for 1950, as we have noted, and by 1952 he was straining
to treble the budget over what it had been when he took office: "We
had wonderful cooperation from the President and the Bureau of the
Budget," he bragged at the annual meeting of the AAIA, "in the largest
budget ever presented to Congress—a total of $122,350,000" ("Speech
. . . ," March 26, 1952, NRC). Despite the comparably wonderful cooperation of his congressional allies, whom he modestly did not mention, the BIA later had to settle for a budget of $85,000,000 for fiscal
year 1953, but that was still nearly twice what Myer's predecessor could
command. And this vast increase in public expenditure took place while
the BIA was professedly withering away, or getting "this thing wound
up fast," as H. Rex Lee had advocated during the hearings on the Bosone bill in August 1950 (see p. 171). At the 1952 AAIA meeting, Myer
explained that the increase was necessary so that the BIA could "step
up the tempo looking to the completion of some of the obligations
which I believe should be completed before we withdraw." While Indi-

ans suffered reduced services and were being "freed" to fend for themselves, that is, the Indian Service needed more staff and money for "withdrawal operations." Myer, Lee, and their army of subordinates were a classic illustration of Parkinson's law postulating the increase of bureaucracies even when what they regulate decreases.

Only temporarily slowed by the defeat of the Bosone bill in 1950, congressional pressures to "terminate" Indians had built up, with Myer's help, and on July 1, 1952, finally pushed through the House a resolution (H.R. 698) that directed the Committee on Interior and Insular Affairs to conduct an investigation of the Bureau of Indian Affairs. Pursuant to this resolution, Chairman Toby Morris, Reva Beck Bosone, and other members of the Indian Affairs Subcommittee formally requested a detailed report from the BIA on how it was carrying out its responsibilities: in particular, on how it had "performed its functions of studying the various tribes, bands, and groups of Indians to determine their qualifications for management of their own affairs without further supervision of the Federal Government"; and, still more particularly, on the preparations it had made for "legislative proposals designed to promote the earliest practicable termination of all Federal supervision and control over Indians." Whether or not Myer had helped his allies on the committee draft their request, he obviously welcomed their charges as declarative of congressional policy: "I think it may be fairly said that current Congressional actions with regard to the Bureau of Indian Affairs and Indian appropriations indicate that future appropriations will be limited largely to financing items which will facilitate withdrawal," he declared in an important memorandum that directed all BIA personnel to collect the data requested by the subcommittee and to step up the tempo of termination (August 5, 1952, NRC). Even prior to legislative authorization, then, the commissioner had directed his forces in the field and his headquarters Division of Program to make Indians vanish by administrative edict.

Titled "Withdrawal Programming," Myer's directive was in effect a covert declaration of administrative war against Indians. It was covert, if not secret, since he had characteristically not bothered to consult tribespeople beforehand and afterward had not deigned to share this basic statement of policy with them. Weeks after it had been distributed to officials in Indian country, Frank George, the Nez Percé who had taken over as executive director of the National Congress of American Indians, came by a copy and ran off others for all tribal council chairmen: "Because it vitally concerns you and the future of your children, we believe that such a document, advancing such a radical change in Indian policy, should not be kept secret from you" (September 26, 1952, JCP). Frank George had been informed that Myer had fifteen termination bills ready to introduce in the next (83rd) Congress, but could not learn which tribes they would affect: "THEY MAY BE YOURS!"

The directive was a declaration of administrative war, since therein Myer commanded the Indian Service to put aside programs for tribal betterment and concentrate instead on tribal dismemberment. BIA personnel had to submit promptly in writing what they had done toward removal of trusteeship over tribal property and lands and toward withdrawal of tribal services such as schools, hospitals, and social welfare. Under his directive, indeed, *tribes* became transient *groups*, clusters of individuals programmed for relocation. But what had happened to Indian rights under the 389 treaties, 5,000 statutes, numerous tribal constitutions and charters, multifarious court decisions and executive orders, and all the other solemn national commitments? They had been written on the wind, as far as Myer was concerned, for he mentioned treaties in just one line of his thirty-four-page directive: "Describe any treaty rights, with citations, pertinent to withdrawal" (p. 28).

In 1952 Myer had thus made his own the basic principle of Commissioner Walker's policy in 1872:

WALKER: There is no question of national dignity, be it remembered, involved in the treatment of savages by a civilized power. [See my discussion in chapter 9.]

MYER: Agreement with the affected Indian groups must be attained if possible. In the absence of such agreement, however, I want our differences to be clearly defined and understood by both the Indians and ourselves. *We must proceed even though Indian cooperation may be lacking in certain cases.* ["Withdrawal Programming," p. 2; emphasis added]

Demonstrably, Myer saw no question of national dignity involved in his scrapping the promises and contractual obligations of the United States to those he called Indian groups.

For a century and more before the Hoover and Roosevelt administrations, commissioners had promised to save taxpayers a lot of money by working themselves out of a job, cutting BIA controls, and setting their charges free. All that while commissioners had made increased demands on taxpayers, strengthened BIA controls, and set their charges free of their lands. With infectious enthusiasm, they had heralded their secondhand policies as brand-new and glorified them with names such as "civilization," "assimilation," and "liquidation"—over this period Felix S. Cohen counted "more than 500 programs for liquidating Bureau activities" (*Progressive* 15 [February 1951]: 17). With this pattern in mind, John Collier stigmatized Myer's directive as a "hoax" in which "he announced and pursues as *a new policy* those social genocides of the earlier generations of dishonor toward Indians" ("The Hoax and Betrayal of Orderly Withdrawal," n.d., JCP). And the red thread tying his "new" policy of withdrawal to this dishonorable past was the collective animosity Herman Melville had called "Indian-hating." As a modern Indian-hater, Myer was simply the carrier and instrument of the traditional hostility of white America to the very idea of the survival of Indians as *peoples*.

2

While pushing his "Programming for Indian Independence" in the field and in articles, speeches, and interviews, the commissioner took for granted absolute Indian *dependence* and unmindfully revealed his own root assumption of Indian *inferiority*:

> I believe that we should move as fast as possible toward assisting the Indians in the country to become integrated into the general pattern rather than being maintained in segregated groups.
>
> [*Journal of Religious Thought* 7 (Spring/Summer 1950): 99]

> Many fail to distinguish between those Indians who have progressed a long way toward assimilation and those who have as yet had little opportunity to associate with non-Indians and to acquire the tools and habits of living in a highly complex industrial civilization, whose final goals and values have not been finally fixed.
>
> ["Statement . . . ," August 29, 1950, NRC]

> [Those who advocate what the Meriam Report calls the "glass case policy"] would make a deliberate effort to keep the Indians separated from the main currents of American life and would preserve them, in the words of the Report, "as museum specimens for future generations to study and enjoy." This approach, in my judgment, is fundamentally unrealistic.
>
> [*Journal of Negro Education* 20 (Summer 1951): 351]

> Over the years governmental programs for the Indians have nearly always been framed in terms of these basic land resources, and have had the effect of tying the Indians to the land perhaps more closely than any other segment of our population.
>
> ["Address . . . ," December 12, 1951, NRC]

The expansion and settlement of lands in the West led to the period of Indian wars which lasted approximately forty years. Some of the treaties and settlements that grew out of these wars resulted in the establishment of additional reservations. Many of these reservations were something akin to large detention camps for a period of years when the United States government found that it was cheaper to provide rations to Indians than it was to fight them. During this period we had practically destroyed the basis for their economy, which, of course, consisted largely of hunting, fishing, gathering of wild fruits, nuts, and berries; and limited farming operations.
["Address . . . ," December 9, 1952, NRC]

Unintegrated or unassimilated and therefore unprogressed; tied to the land; and, of course, former nomads who had hunted, fished, and gathered, while doing a little farming, and who for economy's sake had been penned up in near prisons—all these "segregated groups" were plainly not up to snuff. Irremediably inferior as they were where they were, their only possible chance to come up to white standards was for their keepers to cut their ties to kin and hearth, pull up their stakes, and move them as fast as possible away from their Indianness.

With his vision clouded by these ancestral presuppositions and prejudices, Myer could not *see* an Indian as an individual citizen. Confronted in Albuquerque by delegates from the Taos Pueblo, he could not see Severino Martinez as a man with a serious problem worthy of his consideration, but perceived in him merely an instance of "the Indian problem," a holdover from the primitive past, an amusing "museum specimen": the commissioner "just grinned at me" (Transcript of "Hearing on Proposed Regulations . . . ," JCP). Similarly, he could not see Avery Winnemucca, Rufus Wallowing, and the other Indian critics of his attorney policy as tribal patriots, but perceived in them merely "wily" redskins who threatened the administrative stability of his programming with their misbehavior and refusal to shed their Indianness.

Myer could not *see* Indian tribes as deeply rooted communities of people, but merely as "segregated groups." A nomadic bureaucrat himself, he blamed "governmental programs" for tying Indians to the land and could not see that tribes such as the Pyramid Lake Paiutes had their own ties reaching down into ground they had reverenced for thousands of years. The kind of rootedness to which he was oblivious had been celebrated a century earlier when one old Crow warrior said to another: "You are sunk in this ground up to your armpits."

> The land has given us our life,
> and we must give life back to it,

John Wooden Legs, n.d. Said this spokesman for his people: "You would have to be a Cheyenne to know what it meant when the Government in Washington kept its word."
[Theodore Brinton Hetzel]

agreed Simon J. Ortiz, the modern poet from the Acoma Pueblo, in showing how the land and the people "are in a family with each other." Said John Wooden Legs, from the same tribe as Wallowing, about this intimate relationship: "To us, to be Cheyenne means being one tribe— living on our own land—in America, where we are citizens. Our land is everything to us. . . . It is the only place where Cheyennes remember same things together. I will tell you one of the things we remember on our land. We remember our grandfathers paid for it—with their life." Avery Winnemucca, too, remembered, remembered that his great-grandfather the old gift-giver had fought for the lake people's land, that his great-great-uncle Truckee John had been killed farming it, and that his great-aunt Sarah had "promised my people that I would work for them while there was life in my body" (*Life Among the Piutes*, p. 241). Made up of their remaining lands, reservations were peoples' homes and last refuges, the sources of their lives, the grounds of their spiritual existence, places where peoples remembered "same things" together. But Myer saw them as enclaves of backwardness, rural slums, so many millions of acres that in white hands could be put to more beneficial uses. Like the WRA camps, reservations had to go when they had served their purpose. Now that it was no longer cheaper to have them than to fight Indians, as in Walker's day, they were embarrassing reminders of past wrongs and claims better forgotten and expensive anachronisms better abolished.*

Still not quite able to utter the words *concentration camps*, Myer saw and administered reservations as "something akin to large detention camps" and treated the inmates as though they were savages. Through staff members such as Paul L. Fickinger and Guy Robertson, he told Indians when to go to bed and when to get up; how to behave or be summarily searched and seized; who not to hire as a lawyer; for whom to vote in tribal elections; what to do with their money and when they might have it; if they could come to Washington to protest; whom they might not exclude from their sacred ceremonies; how to become normal by integrating "into the general pattern" or be programmed willy-nilly into the mainstream.

Later Earl Old Person, chairman of the NCAI and of the tribe that had adopted Felix S. Cohen, summarized the meaning of deracination and dispersion for the Blackfeet:

---

*Even prior to the passage of any of the termination bills, Myer had been whittling away at the Indian land base. From 1933 to 1949 it had grown by almost 4 million acres and from then to 1957 decreased by well over 2 million acres. Of course, the period of shrinkage covered years before and after Myer took office, but the figures available for his tenure show major increase in alienation of Indian land from trust status—see William A. Brophy and Sophie D. Aberle, *The Indian: America's Unfinished Business* (Norman, Okla.: University of Oklahoma Press, 1966), pp. 72–73, 219. Not surprisingly, the BIA offices reporting the largest losses were those presided over by two of Myer's favorites, Area Directors Warren Spaulding in Aberdeen, South Dakota, and Paul L. Fickinger in Billings, Montana.

It is important to note that in our Indian language the only translation
for termination is "to 'wipe out' or 'kill off.' " We have no Indian words for
termination. . . .
   You have caused us to jump every time we hear this word. We made
treaties with the U.S. Government which guaranteed our rights to develop
our reservations and to develop as a people free from interference. . . .
   But how can we plan our future when the Indian Bureau constantly
threatens to wipe us out as a race? It is like trying to cook a meal in your
tipi when someone is standing outside trying to burn the tipi down. . . .
   Why is it so important that Indians be brought into the "mainstream of
American life"? What is the "mainstream of American life"? . . . The closest
I would be able to come to "mainstream" would be to say, in Indian, "a big,
wide river." Am I then to tell my people that they will be "thrown into the
Big, Wide River of the United States"?
                                          [*Integrated Education* 5 (April–May 1967): 18–21]

Myer had undertaken to do just that.

Termination in Myer's Anglo-American language had a precise
meaning. It meant to bring "the Indian problem" to an end by cutting
the ties of tribal peoples to both the land and to one another. Envision-
ing relocation on a scale that would treble or quadruple that out of the
WRA camps, Myer had instituted a voluntary policy in the fall of 1950
and for his 1953 budget sought nearly $8 million "for training, place-
ment and relocation" ("Speech . . . ," March 26, 1952, NRC). Though
this was one of the items cut from his request, he moved ahead with a
program that was to be the model for those that followed during the
Eisenhower years, designed to entice "these people" off the reservations
and into "ordinary American communities." He drew on his WRA experience and on such experts as H. Rex Lee for a public relations campaign in which BIA field personnel put up posters and photographs
showing former reservation Indians living the easy life in cities such as
Los Angeles and Chicago—posing beside their new television sets and
gleaming refrigerators; making airplanes; and making it big in the
"highly complex industrial civilization" Myer held up as infinitely desirable for everyone.

   Less cajolery and more force were behind Myer's use of boarding
schools to effect the same end. "In connection with the Navaho education program," observed the former BIA official William Zimmerman,
"perhaps for the first time there appeared a flat statement by a Commissioner of Indian Affairs that 'the Federal off-reservation education of
Navahos is directed entirely toward the preparation of these children for
permanent off-reservation employment.' " Actually, this was only the

"Indian City" in Chicago, n.d. This street scene on Broadway south of Wilson
Avenue shows one of the "ordinary American communities" Myer and his staff
of ghetto-izers thought far preferable to the homelands of Native Americans.
[Virgil and Louise Vogel]

first flat statement of this objective in the recent past, for Thomas L.
McKenney, the first head of the BIA, had used the mission schools in
the 1820s to separate children from their families, batter their tribal
relationships, and strip away their native languages. Thirteen decades
later Myer was merely openly reinstituting this timeworn means of
breaking up "the tribal mass." As he put it with engaging frankness in
his autobiography, he had arranged to have "Navaho youngsters go to
school in other areas in order to get them out of the reservation complex
and milieu" (Auto, p. 261).

Indian families have always been the spiritual and cultural links between the generations of the past and of the future. One way to cut those
links, as Myer recognized, was to force their children to attend boarding
schools where they were explicitly or implicitly forbidden to speak their
own languages. Another way with even hoarier sanction was to remove
Indian children from their families completely and permanently. Following the slaughter of Pequots at Mystic and at Fairfield Swamp in 1637,
for instance, the Puritans divided up the spoils, including the few sur-

viving women and children. Roger Williams asked for the "keeping and bringing up of one of the Children. I haue mine eye on this little one with the red about his neck." Williams was merely an early seeker of a war orphan on the assumption that he knew and could foster the boy's "good and the common [good], in him," as he put it in his letter of thanks to John Winthrop (July 31, 1637). Over the three centuries separating the missionaries of Williams's day from the social pathologists of Myer's, countless tribal children had been forcibly placed in white homes and made hostages to their benefactors' bland assumption they knew the common good for everybody.

In an address to the National Council of the Churches of Christ, Myer appealed for help in solving "the problem represented by the Indian orphans and children from broken families." By BIA estimate, "there may be as many as 8,000 Indian youngsters of this type throughout the country," most of whom were in boarding schools:

> I believe very deeply that this is a fundamentally unhealthy situation and that these children should have the advantages of a normal home and family environment which should be the birthright of every American youngster. So I want to urge most strongly that you put your facilities to work, in cooperation with our Indian Service welfare people and with the appropriate local agencies, to find families in all parts of the country who will be willing to provide foster homes for these institutionalized Indian children.
>
> ["The Needs of the American Indian,"
> December 12, 1951, NRC]

Could no tribal families qualify as foster or adoptive parents? Should not members of an orphan's extended family be given preference, or at least a chance to apply for custody? Should the parents from a broken family be denied any say in the fate of their child? Were not child-custody proceedings of vital importance to the tribes? Did not bypassing their courts flagrantly deny their right to self-government and undercut their most basic right, the right to survival? Had someone raised these questions, Myer would surely have been surprised, since from his point of view they were "fundamentally unrealistic." And he could count on his audience sharing his assumption that "a normal home" was a home away from the reservation. All he was proposing, after all, was that these Indian youngsters be made the fortunate recipients of a chance to live like white youngsters.

John Collier rightly traced these various strands of Myer's "*new policy*" straight back to the old policies "of the earlier generations of dishonor," and he took his repugnance a step farther, as we have seen, by identifying them all as "social genocides" ("The Hoax and Betrayal of Orderly Withdrawal," JCP). Had he exaggerated? Or might a careful student of Myer's assault on Indian tribes properly say that he was committing *genocide*?

When Collier used the word, it was of very recent origin. Raphael Lemkin had coined it in his *Axis Rule in Occupied Europe* (1944) from the Greek *genos* (race or, most interestingly, tribe) and the Latin *cide* (killing) and used it to refer to the deliberate destruction "of a nation or of an ethnic group." On December 11, 1946, the General Assembly of the United Nations unanimously adopted a resolution recognizing genocide as "a crime under international law" and on December 9, 1948, unanimously passed a "Genocide Convention" to prevent and punish the crime of denying peoples the right of existence. In the convention genocide meant "any of the following acts committed with intent to destroy, in whole or in part, a national, ethnical, racial or religious group, as such," and of the five specified acts that began with "(*a*) Killing members of the group," the last had direct application to Myer's policy: "(*e*) Forcibly transferring children of the group to another group." On January 12, 1951, the convention became effective upon the ratification of the necessary twenty member nations, although the United States had not ratified it and for the next three decades would leave it bottled up in the Senate Foreign Relations Committee. But Collier was a close student of such matters, knew that the convention had become international law in 1951, and plainly had grounds for charging that Myer was engaged in "social genocide."

Under the hopeful heading "Are The Indians A Dying Race?" Myer himself later confirmed this conclusion in his autobiography (Auto, p. 292). Yes, "The Indians" were "on the way out as a separate or isolated people, but it may take hundreds of years. I feel quite strongly that integration is already in process." With the old rites—"puberty" and such—on the way out, probably in 500 years we white Americans "will not have an Indian problem" (Auto, p. 294). Only slightly chastened by his experience with Indians who had stubbornly refused to vanish on demand, he still felt "quite strongly" they should be hurried to their graves as a race. Every strand of his policy had been designed to hasten the end forbidden by the Genocide Convention—namely, to destroy them as a "racial . . . group, as such."

Using his inroads on "the Indian problem" for ammunition in Congress and elsewhere, the terminator launched his campaign for reappointment well in advance of the 1952 elections. With some small

The Adopted Chippewa, 1952. Posing for this photograph in a war bonnet was perhaps Myer's most friendly gesture toward the "Dying Race."
[The Bancroft Library]

comfort, John Collier reported to the superintendent of the Eastern Cherokees that he had "pretty good confidence that [Adlai E.] Stevenson if elected would not reappoint Myer. This, however, is as *of now*. But since Myer is concentrated on the sole object of holding his job, and is without scruple (I mean, without the mental make-up within which scruple can even be born), one must not underestimate his power. And he is just what a lot of Congressmen want" (to Joe Jennings, August 11, 1952, JCP). Not one to underestimate his adversary's power, Collier sent lengthy memoranda "On Why Dillon S. Myer Should Not Be Reappointed as Commissioner of Indian Affairs" to both candidates. To Dwight D. Eisenhower he pointed out that the incumbent's "implacable commitment, subordinating all else, to a program of 'relocation and withdrawal'" had many parallels with "the authoritarian, racist, and stereotyped administration which he directed for the Japanese-Americans in World War II." In his cover letter to the candidate's brother, Collier explained that he had touched "on the WRA record because, in terms not greatly changed, it has become the Indian record under Myer" (to Milton Eisenhower, October 29, 1952, JCP).

Also convinced that Myer had to go, Oliver La Farge of the AAIA suggested to Ruth Muskrat Bronson of the NCAI "that we must work to ensure a change of commissioners regardless of who is elected President" and accordingly drafted "Considerations on 'a Bill of Particulars'" on the incumbent's misdeeds (September 5, 23, 1952, AAIA). After Eisenhower's victory, "The Situation" remained desperate, according to a memorandum Alexander Lesser prepared for a meeting of the AAIA executive committee: "No procedure to secure a change of Commissioner should be left untried." Given Myer's ties to Republicans in Congress, "securing his removal is not to be taken as an easy or settled matter. Myer has built bridges in Congress and with the Eisenhower camp, and hedged during the election. It should be assumed that he wants to carry over" (November 14, 1952, AAIA). Beyond doubt Myer did, but his resignation was requested and accepted by the new president (*New York Times*, March 20, 1953).

Why?

Probably Milton Eisenhower had passed on Collier's memorandum to his brother, as he had said he would (to Collier, October 31, 1952, JCP); and this may have played a part in the new president's decision. Perhaps the opposition of La Farge and Bronson and their respective organizations had helped to prevail against the power of Myer's congressional allies. Perhaps Milton Eisenhower himself had given up on the former protégé to whom he had handed the WRA in 1942—he had to have been pained by Collier's reference to "the authoritarian, racist, and stereotyped administration" of what had been his agency in the first place. Quite possibly Collier assumed such a falling-out, for Felix S. Cohen had earlier reported hearing "that Dillon Myer has a very low opinion of Milton Eisenhower and considers him a man totally devoid of imagination and therefore incapable of appreciating the true merits of characters like Dillon Myer. I hope this feeling is reciprocated, and that the danger of Dillon Myer's reappointment in the event of an Eisenhower victory is not very great" (to Collier, July 23, 1952, JCP). By then that feeling may well have been reciprocated, in which case Milton Eisenhower may have intervened on his own behalf to block

Myer's reappointment. And maybe Cohen himself reached influential members of the incoming administration with his "Erosion of Indian Rights, 1950–1953: A Case Study in Bureaucracy," a timely and devastating essay that laid out in meticulous detail Myer's assault on tribal peoples (*Yale Law Journal* 62 [February 1953]: 348–90). For whatever combination of reasons, possibly these and no doubt others, the terminator had to look for another job.

3

In the swan-song memorandum for incoming Secretary Douglas McKay quoted in the epigraph to this chapter, Myer sounded all his refrains of the preceding three years. The "general supervision of lawyers who mislead Indians" had been a vexing problem and especially so in the cases of those who used certain organizations as their "fronts," such as James E. Curry of the National Congress of American Indians and Felix S. Cohen of the Association on American Indian Affairs. With Curry practically driven from his Indian law practice, Myer now centered his fire on Cohen and reiterated all the essentials of his scurrilous personal attack:

> In my judgment he has used this [AAIA] organization as his front. He has either directly or indirectly put out falsehoods, distorted information and misrepresentation of the worst type while posing as an idealistic lawyer whose main interest lies in helping the Indian people. Actually Mr. Cohen has a very substantial personal financial stake in the Indian law business, both in terms of direct representation of the Indian tribes for a fee and through his consultant fees from the joint efforts groups.
>
> [March 20, 1953, NRC]

Cohen had succeeded "in aiding and abetting a group of alleged tribal leaders with a modicum of Indian blood, some of whom have exploited other tribal members who are less competent than they are, through shady real estate deals or utilization of tribal funds to maintain themselves in power," Myer declared. He formally proposed that Cohen be targeted for "further investigation."

With such lawyers out of the way, his successor would find it easier to "*bring under control those people who want to maintain their trust status*" (emphasis added), his poorly concealed goal all along. In fact, Myer confessed to McKay, he left office without having solved the problem of those "wily, more competent Indians":

These same people refuse to accept trust free patents to all of their property when such an offer is made to them. The problem as to *how to eliminate the trust* in such cases is one which we have been exploring for some months and on which we still have not found the answer. Part of the answer probably lies in the review of treaties and in the length of the trust period. . . . . It may require new legislation to help solve the problem.

[ibid.; emphasis added]

Like Commissioner Walker eighty years earlier, Myer left office calling for "judiciously framed" legislation that would solve, unilaterally, the problem of those nuisances called treaties.

Secretary McKay, a car dealer from Salem, Oregon, could not have agreed more with Myer on the need "*to eliminate the trust.*" McKay and the next terminator, Commissioner Glenn L. Emmons, a banker from Gallup, New Mexico, took over intact Myer's congressional outfit and his ramrod on the Hill, H. Rex Lee, who stayed on as assistant commissioner. With the support of this network, and especially of Senator Arthur V. Watkins of Utah, McKay and Emmons took up the termination bills Myer had left behind ready for enactment, added more of their own, and pushed the lot through Congress. Before the spate of termination bills subsided (1954–62), fourteen such acts became the means by which the United States unilaterally withdrew its recognition of nearly a hundred tribes, bands, and rancherias (in California), cut off services to them, and sold off their reservations. Taking their cue from Myer, McKay and Emmons did not bother about first obtaining the *consent* of Indians before selling off their land and forcing them off their reservations. Instead they engaged in *consultation*, and that meant confronting the tribes with their extinction, requesting their assent, and then, if necessary, proceeding without it. In expanded form, Myer's "Operation Relocation" became a key part of their detribalization program—just as in the WRA, individuals received one-way tickets to the ghettos.

The first to be destroyed as racial groups were four bands of Paiutes in Utah, cousins of the people at Pyramid Lake, and they were followed by the Klamaths, the Menominees, and all the others who became lost peoples, separated from one another and from their places of collective remembrance. Those who escaped outright destruction for the moment lived in fear that it might come in the next mail or government car. In the meantime, they had to try to survive with their hospitals transferred to local authority or shut down. With health services reduced, infant mortality rose, along with the incidence of tuberculosis. Reservation roads deteriorated. Surviving tribes became increasingly subject to hostile state systems of law and order (Public Law 280, August 15, 1953). Most demoralizing of all was the impossibility of thinking with any confidence that the chain of generations would continue.

Of such suffering there is no measure. The prototypal terminator can fairly be claimed to have laid the programmatic and administrative groundwork for it all. Those who followed in Dillon S. Myer's footsteps inherited the betrayal and the destruction already under way. Already waiting just over the horizon was what D'Arcy McNickle, a Flathead Indian and former BIA official, named in careful words, "a holocaust in the making."

Epilogue

As you might expect, I did not and do not like the idea of the
term concentration camps instead of relocation centers for
the reasons set forth in my book, *Uprooted Americans*. I especially do not like the adopted term, because I do not want
to go down in history as a director of concentration camps.
> —*Dillon S. Myer,*
> *"Written Testimony," CWRIC, July 12, 1981*

Forced out of the Bureau of Indian Affairs in March 1953, the slightly
scarred elder statesman left unrepentantly and reluctantly. Next he became executive director of the Group Health Association, a comedown
position he occupied until November 1958.

In March 1959 Dillon S. Myer returned to the field of hemispheric
benevolence as the senior expert in public administration for the United
Nations in Caracas, Venezuela. His job was to coordinate the work of
UN experts with three contracting agencies in what he described as an
all-out effort to revamp the "old traditional patterns" and bring Venezuela's administrative procedures "into the twentieth century." He felt
"very fortunate" to have a UN car, a good apartment, and all the other
fringe benefits accruing to nation builders. But when it came to mod-
ernizing, the Venezuelans proved balky. In particular, he had problems
with a certain "Dr. Lopez Gallagos who was not happy in the presence
of 'gringos'" (Auto, p. 365). These problems mounted so that by June
1960 he was glad to get out of Caracas and leave the UN mission
behind.

On an unexplained mission of his own to Saigon, Vietnam, meanwhile, Myer had met Professor Milton Esman and had then agreed to
teach a course for him sometime (Auto, p. 372). Accordingly, on his
return from Caracas he lectured for a term in the Graduate School of
Public and International Affairs at the University of Pittsburgh.

In the aftermath of the Cuban revolution, and while the new Kennedy administration vigorously pushed forward secret plans for the Bay of Pigs invasion, Myer temporarily became a people keeper again. In February and March 1961 he directed the Cuban Refugee Program. Before handing the Cubans over to a more permanent director, he and Jenness Wirt Myer spent a pleasant month or so in Miami.

Later in 1961 he chaired a personnel panel for the newly formed Agency for International Development and spent several months in Seoul, Korea, helping organize an AID public works program "financed largely by U.S. products" (Auto, p. 380).

In February 1962 the omni-administrator received a one-year appointment as a personnel consultant for the Organization of American States, a position in which he drew on his experience as the former president of the Institute of Inter-American Affairs. Unfortunately, Myer soon found himself again at odds with restive Latin Americans, entered into an acrimonious dispute with a certain Señor Magana, and resigned from the OAS before the year was out.

Finally, in 1964 Myer retired at the age of seventy-three. He lived on in the Washington area near the scene of his many administrative triumphs.

Washington, Tule Lake, Pine Ridge, Caracas, Seoul, Saigon—it was entirely fitting that Myer should have shown up, however briefly, at the last-named outpost of the American empire, the setting for Graham Greene's haunting novel *The Quiet American* (1955). Alden Pyle, the title character, was a young man based on another outrider of empire, a U.S. secret agent in Saigon, but otherwise shared with Myer all the fundamental features and trappings of American "innocence." Pyle, too, was "impregnably armoured by his good intentions and his ignorance" and determined "to do good, not to any individual person but to a country, a continent, a world. Well, he was in his element now with the whole universe to improve" (p. 18). Well, that read like an outline of Myer's career, for he, too, had been in his element doing good to the Japanese immigrants, the Japanese Americans, the Native Americans, the Latin Americans, the Asians—the ever-widening circles of his most recent peregrinations suggested that, had he not retired, he might have moved on out into the universe to do good to it too. And like his fictional counterpart, he had generated much misery in his wanderings. As Greene put it with piercing insight into this national style, such "innocence is like a dumb leper who has lost his bell, wandering the world, meaning no harm" (p. 37).

Of course, Myer did not look back on his career that way at all. As he summed it up in an interview for his oral autobiography, "All in all, I have had a wonderful life with many opportunities for learning and development in my many jobs" (Auto, p. 396). Despite all the fomenters of trouble, his life had been so rewarding precisely because of those timeless values he had internalized as a farm boy:

> It was my good fortune to have been born of wonderful parents, and to have been reared on a farm at a time when thrift and hard work were virtues. The farm tasks and responsibilities, which were hard at times, were accepted as a major part of a farm boy's life. The work habits that were formed in early life were important assets in later years.
>
> [Auto, p. 395]

Secure in this sense that behind him stretched a homespun lifetime of solid achievement, he and Jenness Wirt Myer enjoyed his retirement in their home above Rock Creek Park in the northwest part of the District of Columbia, with two of their three daughters located in nearby Chevy Chase and with all of their eleven grandchildren close enough for visits over the holidays and on other special occasions.

Yet unexpected happenings soon stripped the gilt off Myer's golden years. Out of the generous expectations and the social upheavals of the sixties emerged the phenomenon of "Sansei activists," third-generation Japanese Americans angered by the way Mike Masaoka and the JACL had collaborated with their jailers two decades earlier, sharply critical of the quietism of the Nisei, and unable to understand why they had not resisted through any means available, legal and illegal. These veterans of the civil rights and antiwar movements and of the campus revolts helped establish Asian American studies programs that reopened old questions and old wounds—as JACLer Bill Hosokawa complained, they "would keep alive the memory of that sorry national experience" (*Pacific Citizen*, April 25, 1980). In fact, increasingly conscious historically of that sorrowful event, they conducted pilgrimages into the desert to view the places where their parents had been confined. And joined by a few exceptional Nisei, such as Sue Kunitomi Embrey of the Manzanar Committee, they became the driving force behind the committees that succeeded, after intense struggle against those who resented this return of the repressed, in putting up historical markers at Manzanar (1973), Topaz (1976), and Tule Lake (1979) that called a spade a spade by naming them the sites of *concentration camps*. Concurrently, the historian Roger Daniels and the victim Michi Weglyn wrote widely read books (1971, 1976) with the tabooed words in their title or subtitle. "As early as August 29, 1973," Myer later testified, "I heard about the use of this offensive terminology and thought it was popular just among some of the younger Japanese Americans. . . . I found it useless to protest at the time and believed that any public protest from me would only set the argument more deeply."

Like the rustle of autumn leaves outside Myer's alcove, foreboding sounds that the argument would not go away filtered in even from his former para-administrative allies. Knowing all too well that Sansei activists looked on the JACL as irrelevant at best on the issues of racism and poverty, its Nisei leaders tried to find some timely means of luring this younger generation into the organization so that it would have a future. The Nisei search for relevance and the Sansei demand that it be found finally moved the JACL—prodded by Edison Uno, members of the Seattle chapter's Redress Committee, William Hohri, and others—to take up the long-simmering issue of redress. In the early seventies it passed several resolutions to that end, and in 1978 it formally adopted a redress proposal. Subsequently it backed off from trying to push redress legislation through Congress and instead launched a campaign for what became Public Law 96-317 when President James Earl Carter signed it on July 31, 1980. Heralded by the JACL as a step toward redress, the bill established the Commission on the Wartime Relocation and Internment of Civilians, which was charged with gathering "facts to determine whether any wrong was committed against those American citizens and permanent resident aliens affected by Executive Order Numbered 9066." Suddenly the can of falsehoods the keepers thought closed forever had been opened, and wrongs spilled out in the survivors' testimony at the CWRIC hearings that followed. Naturally as one of the responsible officials still alive, Myer felt threatened and took the "Internment" in the commission's title almost as a personal affront, since he had always insisted that the only camps meriting that name were those run by the Justice Department for "disloyal" Issei. And galling beyond words was the fact that JACL lobbyist Mike Masaoka had piloted this loathsome act though Congress.

In that forsaken time Myer "with whole-hearted consent and appreciation" formed an alliance with Lillian Baker, a part-time journalist for the *Gardena Valley News* in California, author of the comprehensive *Collector's Encyclopedia of Hatpins and Hatpin Holders* (1976) and speaker on a variety of topics, including "Feminism vs. Femininity," "Hatpins as Weapons," and "Relocation Center versus Concentration Camp." A World War II widow who had lost her first husband in a Japanese prison camp in the Philippines, she maintained that while the

Japanese and Germans had had such places, the Americans had never had anything but humane relocation centers, in which the necessarily evacuated people had had good medical care, three square meals a day, and freedom to leave at will—freedom, that is, for all save those who had, as she later testified, "not only lent 'aid and comfort' to the enemy, but committed acts of treason." She fiercely opposed the wording on the markers at Manzanar and Tule Lake, the JACL's redress movement, and the objectives and title of the national "Internment" commission. A redoubtable propagandist, she appeared on radio and television talk shows, and in these and in her speeches and writings expressed what can only be described as an intemperate contempt for those with whom she disagreed, as in her characterization of Senator Daniel K. Inouye of Hawaii as "a blackguard who dares blaspheme a Country he has taken an oath to defend." In Myer, Baker believed that she had found unanswerable authority that the United States had never had concentration camps. In Baker, Myer found a tireless champion and his most voluble defender.

Too infirm to appear before the CWRIC in the summer of 1981, Myer helped sponsor Baker's trip to Washington, her representation of his feelings, and her emotional appeal to the commissioners: "Listen to this man, for dear honor's sake!"* At subsequent hearings in Los Angeles on August 4 she again appeared as his representative and informed them that she had "written testimony that Mr. Dillon S. Myer has authorized me to read into the record. These are his words, not the words of Lillian Baker."

The words had a genuine Myer ring. He did not like the term *concentration camps*, as the epigraph to this epilogue shows. They had been "wayside shelters," "self-governing" communities from which his WRA had attempted to relocate *all* the uprooted Americans. True, there had been armed guards, but "these guards, in addition to other problems, helped protect the people in the centers from misguided attacks from local citizens." Had anyone inside been shot, he would have known of it. "I have no memory, nor is there such a record of anyone being shot while trying to escape," he avouched in the face of his full knowledge, at the time it took place, of the lethal shooting of James Hatsuaki Wakasa at Topaz on April 11, 1943 (see my discussion in chapter 3). The 1940s web of intentional falsehoods had become the 1980s automatic

---

*Myer's former aide Leland Barrows appeared before the commissioners in his stead to discuss WRA administration and operations and testify "about this extraordinary, and I hope unique, American experience."

falsifications of memory. By then he probably had "no memory" of the Wakasa and other shootings, the penal colonies and stockade, the slave labor, the beatings, the mass denial of elementary rights, and the rest.

Myer did have a fresh and lasting recollection, however, of the many testimonials showered upon him by the JACL:

> Leading these tributes was Washington representative of the Japanese American Citizens League, Mr. Mike M. Masaoka, who today has joined with those who have demeaned me and my staff of dedicated individuals, most of whom are no longer here to defend themselves and their honorable war-time actions.
>
> When I learned the names of those who are now using the term concentration camp and are asking for redress and reparations, I was moved to tears and could not help recalling that it was these very men who had kissed my hand in gratitude. . . .
>
> Why has this man and those who paid tribute now forsake[n] me and my country[?] Why do they dishonor both?

Autres temps, autres moeurs—other days other ways of responding to Myer's "courageous and inspired leadership."

To this written testimony Lillian Baker added a postscript in her own words:

> I want that man—and I think every American of Japanese ancestry owes that man a happy ending. He said to Mrs. Myer that he wished he had not lived long enough to see this happen, and I promised Mrs. Myer that this man was going to die a happy man, knowing that our history books would not reflect Dillon S. Myer as a director of concentration camps.

As it turned out, she could not keep her promise. Dillon S. Myer died of cardiac arrest on October 21, 1982, at the age of ninety-one.

2

In *The Far Eastern Policy of the United States*, published in 1938, A. Whitney Griswold carefully traced the anti-Oriental clamor on the West Coast down through the decades to the blatantly anti-Japanese immigration act of 1924 (43 Stat. 153) and to a perplexing conclusion: "Yet every one of the Presidents and Secretaries of State who tried to restrain the exclusionists was to a greater or lesser degree converted by them. All were compelled to recognize the fact that orientals were, if not impossible of assimilation, at least more difficult than any other immigrants" (p. 376). Yet both coasts shared the racism that made capture of Washington each time by "unbridled sectionalism" less perplexing than predictable. And, thus amended, Griswold's conclusion directly anticipated Franklin Delano Roosevelt's Executive Order 9066 a few years later.

Surely no West Coast exclusionists had to convert Roosevelt to racism. Thanks to Christopher Thorne's extraordinary research for *Allies of a Kind: The United States, Britain, and the War Against Japan, 1941– 45* (1978), we now know that the president considered it fit to joke to White House aides that Puerto Rico's "excessive" birthrate could be solved by "the methods which Hitler used effectively": "It is all very simple and painless—you have people pass through a narrow passage and then there is a brrrrr of an electrical apparatus. They stay there for twenty seconds and from then on they are sterile." At Yalta he weightily informed Joseph Stalin that the Vietnamese were little pacifists, or, in his own words, "people of small stature . . . and not warlike." And to Winston Churchill, whose arrogance toward nonwhites matched his own, he confided that he had "never liked the Burmese and you people must have had a terrible time with them for the last fifty years. Thank the Lord you have He-Saw, We-Saw, You-Saw [i.e., Prime Minister U. Saw] under lock and key. I wish you could put the whole bunch of them into a frying pan with a wall around it and let them stew in their own juice" (*Allies*, pp. 6, 159).

For the commander in chief the war in the Pacific was at bottom a racial war that had originated in the first place from the inborn nature of the Japanese to be aggressors and as such to be a separate species from the peace-loving white Americans. In the summer of 1942 FDR informed the British Minister Sir Ronald Campbell that he believed crossbreeding with Europeans might improve certain Asian peoples such as the Chinese, but definitely not "the Japanese-European mixture, which was, he agreed, thoroughly bad." "The President had asked the Professor [Ales Hrdlicka of the Division of Physical Anthropology at the Smithsonian Institution] why the Japanese were as bad as they were, and had followed up by asking about the Hairy Ainus. The Professor had said the skulls of these people were some 2,000 years less developed than ours. . . . The President asked whether this might account for the nefariousness of the Japanese, and had been told that it might, as they might well be the basic stock of the Japanese" (*Allies*, pp. 158–59, 167– 68). The president put the professor to work on this proposition, but the latter died in 1943 before all of the evidence was in.

When the secretary of war took up "the west coast matter" with FDR on February 11, 1942, therefore, Henry L. Stimson "fortunately found that he was very vigorous about it and told me to go ahead on the line that I had myself thought the best" (cf. p. 35). True enough, but fortune had nothing to do with the vigor of the response from the White House. The president viewed the Japanese and their descendants as innately bad, wherever they were, and as such fit for the great roundup just weeks away. No doubt their cunning and treachery stemmed from the less developed skulls of their basic stock.

No West Coast exclusionists had to convert Stimson to his chief's racial attitudes. In an effort to dissuade Archibald MacLeish from delivering a speech decrying the army's discrimination against Afro-Americans, Stimson informed him of their incompetency "except under white officers." As he recorded in his diary on January 24, 1942, he had pointed out to the poet "that what these foolish leaders of the colored race are seeking is at the bottom social equality, and I pointed out the basic impossibility of social equality because of the impossibility of race mixture by marriage." And as members of another "colored race," the Japanese Americans were innately treacherous: "Their racial characteristics are such that we cannot understand or trust even the citizen Japanese," he noted in his diary the day before he learned that FDR also vigorously distrusted them. "This latter is the fact but I am afraid that it will make a tremendous hole in our constitutional system to apply it" (p. 35).

And no West Coast exclusionists had to convert Stimson's right-hand man. Indeed, when John J. McCloy implemented his hero's feckless "fact," it created a constitutional chasm bigger and dirtier than any we have hitherto surmised. Through documents recently released under the Freedom of Information Act, Peter Irons has demonstrated in *Justice at War* (1983) "a legal scandal without precedent in the history of American law" (see especially pp. viii, 206–18, 278–302). The Roosevelt administration stacked the deck against the handful of Japanese American test cases by suppressing, altering, and destroying evidence critical to their defense, and thereby presented the courts with a fundamentally tainted record.

The master tainter was McCloy. On April 19, 1943, he received via air express two printed and bound copies of the Western Defense Command's *Final Report: Japanese Evacuation from the West Coast, 1942*. Hot off the press, it arrived over the signature of General John L. DeWitt, but was primarily the handiwork of that lawyer in uniform, Colonel Karl R. Bendetsen (discussed in chapter 3). Opening the document, McCloy found especially objectionable the general's frank admission that it had been "impossible" to determine the loyalty of the "Japanese," no matter how much time he had had for the task: "It was not that there was insufficient time in which to make such a determination; it was simply a matter of facing the realities that a positive determination could not be made, that an exact separation of the 'sheep from the goats' was unfeasible." In a word, both oriental sheep and oriental goats were ultimately inscrutable.

Unwilling to release this dangerously straightforward "racial characteristics" justification of the roundup, McCloy dressed Bendetsen down for not letting him see the galleys "before you printed it up," ordered him back to Washington, and put him to work with his staff on a compromise that removed the offensive words and replaced them with an offhanded reference to the absence of "ready means . . . for determining the loyal and the disloyal with any degree of safety." McCloy then instructed DeWitt to send a second transmittal letter, as though it were his first, with the final version of his *Final Report*. Captain John M. Hall, McCloy's legal deputy, reported on June 7 that "War Department records have been adjusted accordingly." And after his return to the Presidio in San Francisco, Bendetsen went beyond adjustment when he ordered Warrant Officer Theodore E. Smith to oversee the destruction of all the relevant background materials in the files of the Western Defense Command: "I certify that this date," Smith reported on June 29, "I witnessed the destruction by burning of the galley proofs, galley pages, drafts and memorandums of the original report of the Japanese Evacuation." Necessarily imperfect at both ends, this memory-hole operation could not have removed "every trace of the initial submission," as Peter Irons has contended (p. 211), since the very process of recalling it generated transcripts of telephone calls, telegrams, and memoranda. But it was close enough to perfect to cover up the truth for decades.

"The War Department's shell game," as Irons has aptly called it (p. 212), kept DeWitt's report out of the hands of Justice Department lawyers who needed it to prepare their briefs for the 1943 test cases. Attorney General Francis Biddle and Edward J. Ennis of the Alien Enemy Control Unit pressed their request for a copy in person, but were put off and assured by McCloy "that it was not intended to print this report" (Irons, *Justice*, p. 212). Not given access to the original report (or its successors), the drafters of one of the briefs (*Hirabayashi* v. *United*

States, 320 U.S. 81) made the lack of sufficient time a significant factor in the army's decision to go ahead with mass exclusion and not attempt loyalty hearings: "Many months, or perhaps years, would be required for such investigations." DeWitt's original formulation of the "racial characteristics" justifications mocked that claim and in fact would have blown it out of the water, had the Supreme Court justices only known of the suppressed version of his *Final Report*.

And then the plot thickened. According to even the revised DeWitt, "the Japanese race is an enemy race." It followed that the path from "racial characteristics" had led directly to the "military necessity" of the roundup, since Japanese Americans were innately more liable than any other class of West Coast residents to commit acts of sabotage and espionage. This free-floating prejudice found moorage of sorts in his flat assertion that "there were many evidences of the successful communication of information to the enemy" from the mainland. All this was as his rank prejudice had postulated, but the trouble was that there were no such "evidences" and in truth, as he had ample reason to know, not a single authenticated case of shore-to-ship signaling or of illicit radio transmission.

After a copy of the final *Final Report* finally arrived at the Justice Department in January 1944, Ennis and John L. Burling, his assistant who was working on the upcoming *Korematsu* v. *United States* (323 U.S. 214), sought confirmation of DeWitt's charges from the FBI and the Federal Communications Commission, and in the reports from these agencies confronted incontrovertible proof that there had been *no* confirmed Japanese American espionage. Faced with the problem of presenting to the Supreme Court a key military report based on what they themselves called "suppression of evidence" and riddled with "lies" and "intentional falsehoods," Ennis and Burling inserted a crucial footnote in the Korematsu brief that flagged for the justices the "contrariety" of evidence on the espionage allegations and their own disavowal of War Department veracity.

Of course, McCloy objected to the footnote, intervened personally with Solicitor General Charles Fahy, and, as Irons's documents make warrantedly assertable (pp. 287–92), prevailed on Ennis's superior to excise the government's oblique confession that there had been no "military necessity" for the enormity. The master scene shifter had once again kept the justices from glimpsing the truth.

Overruled by Solicitor Fahy, Edward J. Ennis and John L. Burling brought themselves around to sign the Korematsu brief, which contained no repudiation of "these lies," as they called them, in DeWitt's report (Irons, *Justice*, p. 292). Therewith the Justice Department became a player in the "shell game" that amounted to a fraud on the courts.

With the exception of Harlan Fiske Stone and Owen J. Roberts, all of the justices were liberal New Dealers. Yet perhaps even the Roosevelt Court might have balked at "this legalization of racism," as Justice Frank Murphy stigmatized it in his Korematsu dissent, had they known of the intentional falsehoods they were leaning on for their majority opinions. And perhaps not, for Chief Justice Stone accepted outright the "racial characteristics" argument in his opinion for the Court in the Hirabayashi case: "We cannot reject as unfounded the judgment of the military authorities and of Congress that there were disloyal members of that population, whose number and strength could not be precisely and quickly ascertained." And Justice Hugo L. Black, who wrote the Court's opinion in the Korematsu case, also believed in the innate untrustworthiness of the "Japanese." Decades later he was still vigorously defending the opinion, and in 1967 he spelled out for an interviewer how he had arrived at it:

> I would do precisely the same thing today, in any part of the country. I would probably issue the same order were I President. We had a situation where we were at war. People were rightly fearful of the Japanese in Los Angeles, many loyal to the United States, many undoubtedly not, having dual citizenship—lots of them.
>
> They all look alike to a person not a Jap. Had they [i.e., the Japanese forces] attacked our shores you'd have a large number fighting with the Japanese troops.
>
> [*New York Times*, September 26, 1971]

Plainly, a justice capable of convincing himself that "they all look alike" demonstrated a certain disdain for the truth and needed only the barest of excuses for believing the lies the War Department and the Justice Department had put before him.*

---

*As I write this, in San Francisco U.S. District Judge Marilyn Patel has just ruled—in response to a petition for a writ of error coram nobis—that the internment was illegal and unjustified and has reversed the conviction of Fred Toyosaburo Korematsu forty years ago for violating orders that gained him a sentence of five years on probation for remaining in his hometown. In this extraordinary ruling, Judge Patel has told the Supreme Court that it was wrong, rejected the pleas of the Justice Department attorney to let bygones be bygones, and specified unsubstantiated assertions, distortions, and racism as instances of official misconduct (*San Francisco Examiner* and *Oakland Tribune*, November 11, 1983). And in Seattle, as this is being readied for the printer, District Judge Donald S. Voorhees has just overturned the conviction of Gordon K. Hirabayashi for defying the exclusion

All three branches of the government shared this inability to differentiate between foreign foes and Americans who happened to look like
them. Mis-seen as indistinguishable from flesh-and-blood enemies, the
Issei and the Nisei became targets of the righteous wrath officials directed against "Japs" everywhere. The urge to punish American citizens
for Japan's sins extended up through the echelons of the Roosevelt
administration to the White House itself.

After the so-called riot at Tule Lake, Assistant Attorney General Tom
Clark called FBI official D. M. Ladd and "stated that the Attorney General seemed to think that we should do something about the matter;
that he thinks it is 'kind of warm.' . . . [Later that evening Clark called
again, after speaking to Assistant Secretary of War McCloy, and] then
expressed the desire to see some of the Japs who incited the riot incarcerated. I told him we would also look into this angle, but reiterated
that we would make no investigation" (memorandum for E. A. Tamm,
November 8, 1943, FBI 62-70564). Shortly the FBI disinclination to
cooperate with the WRA was overruled dramatically and revealingly:
"At 7:15 P.M. on November 10th I telephonically contacted ASAC
[H. C.] Van Pelt of the San Francisco Office," D. M. Ladd reported to J.
Edgar Hoover, "at which time I read to him the note from the President
to the Attorney General, instructing that an investigation be made of
the Tule Lake Relocation riots" (November 11, 1943, FBI 62-70564).
Roosevelt himself was the source of the heat, though perhaps Francis
Biddle and surely Tom Clark themselves wanted to see "some of the
Japs" chastised. Handling the matter for his superiors, Clark persisted
in urging the FBI to bring some sort of charges against the "rioters": "I
advised [Clark] that most of the ringleaders were citizens and cannot
be interned. He stated in this case . . . maybe there is some statute that
they can be prosecuted under" (D. M. Ladd, memoranda for E. A.
Tamm, November 9, December 7, 1943, FBI 62-70564). Again the inmates' presumptive rights as citizens proved a hindrance to the Roosevelt administration's desire to punish them still more severely.

One of the documents that turned up during the FBI investigation of

---

orders. In an opinion similar to Judge Patel's, Voorhees found that the government had
improperly concealed from the defense and from the Supreme Court evidence challenging
the military necessity for the internment (see "Settling a Debt from World War II," *New
York Times*, February 16, 1986). The "legal cloud" that has hung over Japanese Americans for decades seems to be lifting, as Hirabayashi has jubilantly suggested, and the
opinions of Judges Patel and Voorhees may well bolster the multibillion-dollar class action
lawsuit in which the victims seek redress, now pending in the Federal District Court in
Washington, D.C. (discussed in the notes and bibliographic essay to the epilogue).

Tule Lake was the report of B. J. Glasgow of the Military Intelligence Service. As we have observed, Hoover passed on a copy of that explosive report to Attorney General Biddle and then reminded him a week later of this unimpeachable evidence of duress and beatings in the Tule administration building on the night of November 4, 1943 (see p. 138). And since the White House had made the matter "kind of warm" and initiated the investigation, Biddle or Clark may well have reported the beatings to FDR; later Hoover may well have incorporated passages from Glasgow's report in his summary memorandum for FDR, though I have been unable to unearth that document.* At all events, the liberal attorney general knew of the night of terror and Clark knew and may well have felt that it went some way toward meeting his desire for vengeance.

Stimson and McCloy had to know of the terror and sufferings at Tule Lake, for MIS Agent Glasgow was their man on the scene. When Cordell Hull expressed the State Department's concern that events there might close off prisoner exchanges with Japan, however, the secretary of war preemptorily denied any official wrongdoing with international implications: "No internee in the stockade or elsewhere has been brutally beaten by any representative of the United States Government," restraint made all the more admirable in the light of a fact he cited earlier—"this element is vicious" (memorandum for Hull, January 18, 1944, NA, RG 210). That vicious nature of the hundreds in the stockade no doubt made Stimson less unwilling to pile another lie on the pyramid.

Probably the drafter of Stimson's denial, McCloy had a toughminded readiness to treat inmates as guinea pigs, as we have seen, and could easily accommodate himself to rough-and-ready questioning techniques designed to "find out what they are thinking about" or, better yet, to "influence their thinking in the right direction" (McCloy to Alexander Meiklejohn, September 30, 1942, JERS, 67/14, E1.020). Pearl Harbor had been a central event in his life, and four decades later his thirst for vengeance had still not been entirely slaked.

In his memorable appearance before the CWRIC on November 3, 1981, the eighty-seven-year-old McCloy appeared still vigorous, quick

---

*On a memorandum of D. M. Ladd for the director, November 15, 1943, FBI 62-70564, Edward A. Tamm typed that he did not "think we should submit progress reports to the White House on this matter. I think it would be better to wait until we have completed our investigation and then submit the material in one summary memorandum" and Hoover initialed his agreement. In the absence of that summary, precisely what the FBI told the White House about the night of terror must remain conjectural.

of mind, and with total recall of the mystifications of the forties. The roundup of "our then Japanese population was reasonably undertaken and thoughtfully and humanely conducted." He had visited the camps and observed that the residents were "not distressed." In fact, out of their benign treatment had come a positive consequence: "On the whole the deconcentration of the Japanese population and its redistribution throughout the country resulted in their finding a healthier and more advantageous environment than they would have had on the West Coast following the Pearl Harbor attack and the reports of Japanese atrocities in the Philippines and the Southwest Pacific." Furthermore, the commissioners should not advocate policies that would prevent another forcible relocation because of ancestry—suppose that Cuba, "within 90 miles of our shores," invaded Florida in a decade or two or three hence, "wouldn't you be apt to think of moving them [i.e., the Cuban Americans] if there was a raid there? You can't tell."

All in all, McCloy maintained, conditions in the camps had been "very pleasant," "our Japanese population" had not been adversely affected, and besides, everybody had to make sacrifices in wartime. In a caustic tone, Commissioner William M. Marutani, a former camp inmate, asked just the right question: "What other Americans, Mr. McCloy, fought for their country while their parents, brothers and sisters were incarcerated?" McCloy did not like the word *incarcerated*. "Well, all right," shot back Marutani, "behind barbed wire fences." It was as if McCloy had finally heard a distressed voice speaking to him from behind his barbed wire. Visibly shaken, he let down his guard on "racial characteristics" for a second. Lots of Americans had made comparable sacrifices, he declared: "I don't think the Japanese population was unduly subjected, considering all the exigencies to which—the amount it did share in the way of retribution for the attack that was made on Pearl Harbor." After a heavy moment of silence, Marutani asked the stenographer to read that inadvertence back. This time McCloy did not like his own word *retribution*. It was out of the bag, however, an ugly cat that equated "our Japanese" with enemy Japanese and made both look-alike targets for richly deserved punishment.

Such was the bedrock of punitive racism on which the keepers had erected their "relocation centers." In them Roosevelt had succeeded in doing to the Nikkei what he could only fantasize Churchill doing to the Burmese, namely, "put[ting] the whole bunch of them into a frying pan with a wall around it and let[ting] them stew in their own juice."

This unpalatable truth brings Dillon S. Myer's role as tender of the flames into sharper focus. At the war's end, as we have seen, he was still stewing his charges in their own juice, still trying to Americanize Americans, still trying to bring their "Oriental inscrutability" bubbling to the surface, still trying to skim off his "unknown and unrecognizable minority." His unremitting efforts were absurd, but instructive. "The trouble is not with the Japanese mind," foresaw the sociologist Robert E. Park in 1914, "but with the Japanese skin. The Jap is not the right color." Decades later the real trouble was with the mind of Roosevelt, Stimson, McCloy, and their cohorts, who filled the "Jap camps" with their own specters and then made Myer their keeper. In their appointment of this "good sleeper" as their head jailer they emphasized white America's historic contempt for nonwhites by putting them in the hands of a man who literally knew nothing about them and their cultural heritage. And even after the Endo case, Truman rubbed this contempt in by awarding Myer the nation's Medal for Merit for illegally detaining American citizens.

Very recently dubbed "the most influential private citizen in America," McCloy made manifest in his testimony that such contempt is still on the loose, combustible, ready to be touched off by a foreign policy flare-up. Tomorrow it may blaze away at Cubans, Iranians, Arabs, Central Americans, or other imaginary enemies in our midst. And right now there is a Myer-like bureaucrat out there in some agency, no less certain that it is the destiny of the wise white man to rule the dark fool, just biding his time, more than willing to seize an opportunity to become another director of concentration camps.

3

"Like the miner's canary," observed Felix S. Cohen in the *Yale Law Journal*, "the Indian marks the shifts from fresh air to poison gas in our political atmosphere; and our treatment of Indians, even more than our treatment of other minorities, reflects the rise and fall of our democratic faith" (62 [February 1953]: 390). Truman's appointment of Myer as commissioner of Indian affairs—that "shitty ass job," as the president revealingly thought of it—was a dramatic illustration of that truth. To put half a million souls in the hands of a man who had not the slightest acquaintance with them as peoples and who cared even less about their cultures marked a fall back into an atmosphere poisoned by earlier generations of Indian-hating.

Early warning of poison gas came from the band we followed down through the years since their "discovery." The drooping Pyramid Lake Paiutes never did perk up after Myer's onslaught. Decades after he stepped down as commissioner they were still despondently fighting to have an attorney of their own, still fighting to hold on to their lands, still fighting to save their lake: "We're just like ants down here," said a spokeswoman ("Nevada Indians Fight for a Lake," *New York Times*, February 25, 1969). No longer tribal chairman, Avery Winnemucca was living quietly with the old gift-giver's people, all of whom were so "desperately poor" only *two* of the 500 did not qualify for the federal surplus food program. The *Times* reporter apparently did not interview Winnemucca, but did encounter another veteran delegate, Warren Tobey, seated in an old station wagon on the shore of the lake, selling fishing permits and looking back in anger: "When I first saw the lake in 1918 the water was up to those rocks, 300 yards from where it is now." And then on June 24, 1983, the Supreme Court handed down another crushing setback for the people by denying their rights to water for the purpose of maintaining their Lahontan Cut Throat Trout Fishery (*Nevada v. United States*, 77L. Ed. 2d 509). Yet after all this, the Numa still try to keep their lake from being turned into a chemical swamp.

On July 8, 1970, President Richard M. Nixon publicly repudiated the policy of termination in a special message to Congress, but for all bands and tribes the threat of Myer-like programmed extinction remains as timely as yesterday's newspapers. In January 1983 Secretary of the Interior James Watt echoed Myer's contention that reservations "nowadays lead . . . to a welfare type of state" (Auto, p. 290) by calling them socialist failures: "If you want an example of the failures of socialism, don't go to Russia. Come to America, and see the American Indian reservations. . . . If Indians were allowed to be liberated, they'd go and get a job and that guy [the tribal leader] wouldn't have his handout as a paid government official" (*Washington Post*, January 20, 1983). Sharp protests from Indian country moved Watt to say that he did not say what he had said, as it were, and his boss outlined a policy that would pursue "self-government for Indian tribes without threatening termination" (*New York Times*, January 25, 1983). But this new crop of liberators had tipped their hand, and many tribal peoples remained shrewd unbelievers: "The Reagan Policy Is Termination," editorialized *Wassaja*, the national Indian newspaper (July/August 1983).

Also just the other day the farm boy's old outfit—now grown to a powerful 3.2-million-member organization—called for the liquidation of treaties and reservations. At the national convention of the American

Farm Bureau Federation in January 1983, delegates passed a termination resolution that read as though it had been drafted by Myer: "We
favor abolition of the Bureau of Indian Affairs and termination of special treaty rights by purchase or negotiation for fair compensation."
Now, as decades ago, the nation's affluent white farmers shrug off the
solemn commitments embodied in treaties and prefer not to be reminded of the historical verities recently outlined by the National Indian
Youth Council:

> Indian reservations are not concentration camps but, rather, homelands. In-
> dians in the past gave up millions of acres of land in order that they be
> allowed to keep a little for themselves and to get certain services from the
> government. This is our covenant with the American People. Of all groups
> in this country, Indians are the only ones that have paid in advance for the
> services that they have.
>
> [*Americans Before Columbus* 11, no. 1 (1983)]

But right now out there in the BIA's vast domestic empire, or in some
other agency, there is a Myer-like colonizer more than willing to step in
as another liberator of Indians, treat their reservations as concentration
camps, burn down their tipis while they are trying to cook a meal inside,
cut their ties to past and future generations, and let them sink or swim
by dropping them individually into the "mainstream of American life."

An accident of chronology has masked the underlying meaning of
Myer's termination policy. Had he been commissioner of the BIA *before*
he became director of the WRA, then the continuities stretching from
the reservations to the camps could hardly have been missed and the
fundamental sameness of his treatment of Native Americans and Japanese Americans would have elicited close analysis long ago. Just as his
termination of Native Americans meant their *relocation* in ghettos, so
his *relocation* of Japanese Americans across the country meant the *termination* of their communities (Little Tokyos) on the West Coast and
the breakup or attempted breakup of their subculture. In both instances
he and his staffs energetically grubbed up the roots of their charges and
gave them one-way tickets away from their places of shared recollections. Of course, the Japanese Americans were not tribal, but they had
been made targets of the same destruction: "To a people for whom community was the essence of life," said Joy Kogawa of the comparable
Canadian dispersal, "destruction of community was the destruction of
life" (*Obasan* [1982], p. 311).

Like Cohen and John Collier, Harold L. Ickes came to see parallels
between Myer's records as head of the WRA and of the BIA and even

approached an understanding of their inner identities: "I concur with
the statement that the War Relocation Authority constituted 'Our Worst
Wartime Mistake' and that 'What is now proposed for the Indians may
well be characterized as "Our Worst Peacetime Mistake"'" (to Oscar
L. Chapman, November 5, 1951, JCP). That was a generous admission
for Myer's former superior, but sufficiently wide of the mark to be a
near miss. The WRA under Myer was not a "mistake," but what Roger
Daniels has correctly characterized as "the logical outgrowth of over
three centuries of American experience, an experience which taught
Americans to regard the United States as a white man's country in which
nonwhites 'had no rights which the white man was bound to respect.'
These infamous words, from Chief Justice Roger B. Taney's 1857 decision in Dred Scott v. Sanford, were merely echoed by the United States
Supreme Court during World War II" (CC, p. xiv). And the BIA under
Myer was not a "mistake," but an explicit reversion to these ingrained
racist themes Ickes abhorred and had fought in behalf of Native
Americans.

   Then why had he been so uncaring or rather so enthusiastic about
what his subordinate was doing to the Japanese Americans?

   Because Myer was doing what liberals almost to a man extolled. The
ethnic goal of the Roosevelt administration, with the partial exception
of the indigenous peoples, was to make everyone alike through "Americanization," "assimilation," "integration," the great end that McCloy
the Republican was still celebrating forty years later when he lauded
"the deconcentration of the Japanese population and its redistribution
throughout the country." His rhapsody merely echoed Roosevelt's
strong advocacy of "dissemination and distribution" as final solutions
for the "Japanese problem" (quoted and discussed in chapter 4). Dispersion was "one of the best means of promoting assimilation," agreed
the liberal sociologist Robert W. O'Brien ("Selective Dispersion as a
Factor in the Solution of the Nisei Problem," Social Forces 23 [Decem-
ber 1944]: 140–47). "Many nisei realize that it was a mistaken policy
to develop 'Little Tokyo's,'" applauded the liberal Quakers Clarence E.
Pickett and Homer L. Morris ("From Barbed Wire to Communities,"
Survey Midmonthly 79 [August 1943]: 210–13). "Goodbye Mr.
Moto," cheerily waved the liberal publicist Carey McWilliams after the
gardener and all the others had been torn out of "these in-grown Japanese communities" and sent packing off across the mountains: henceforth "Beverly Hills matrons will have to get someone to replace Mr.
Moto, the indefatiguable and highly reliable gardener" (ms., n.d., Hoo-

ver Institution Archives, Stanford, California). By breaking up the "virtual ghettos on the Pacific Coast," chorused John Haynes Holmes, Arthur Garfield Hays, and Roger Baldwin, the trio of ACLU liberals, Myer had shown "far-sighted statesmanship" (to Myer, October 8, 1942, CHS 3580). Hence, Ickes did no more than express this liberal consensus in his high praise of Myer for converting one of the "most locality-bound" minorities into a "widely distributed one" (Ickes to President Harry S. Truman, May 8, 1946, NA, RG 48).

"All bunched up in groups as they were along the Coast," as Myer put it, the Japanese immigrants and their children were to blame for the racism of their white neighbors. Had they not followed the "mistaken policy" of huddling together in their Little Tokyos and instead flung themselves across the continent, then in a generation or two they might have been blanched and engulfed by white America. They were themselves guilty of not being like everybody else by assimilating, and by "assimilation" white liberals of course meant to "our" standards—this traditional tendency to "blame the victim" was as routine as cops beating up inoffensive citizens and then charging them with assault and battery or "riot," as at Tule Lake. Pretty much outside the liberal consensus in the case of the Native Americans, Ickes still swallowed this egregious nonsense about Japanese Americans not by "mistake" but because of his decades of conditioning as a Progressive.

If "the men who ran America's concentration camps were liberals of the genus New Deal," as I have ventured in chapter 1, their superiors such as FDR, Stimson, and Ickes all had their moral and intellectual roots in the era of Theodore Roosevelt and Woodrow Wilson.* All shared with that earlier generation of reformers a zeal to cleanse, purify, and perfect industrial America by imposing an orderly existence on backward farmers and inefficient workers; on "new" immigrants just off the boat; on tramps and paupers; on criminals, lunatics, and idiots; on loose women and prostitutes; on Native Americans, Afro Americans, and Chicanos; later on Puerto Ricans and Asian Americans—on everybody. At bottom the protean term *Progressivism* meant reform from the top down through repression—the subjection of individuals, families, and kinship societies to the organized discipline of centralized power. Militaristic abroad and therapeutic at home, Progressives marched onward and upward to control everything through a vastly expanded state.

---

*And of course Wilson's Secretary of State William Jennings Bryan—recall the Great Commoner's trail-blazing proposal to scatter the Japanese Americans all around the country (CC, pp. 1, 155n).

They were driven forward and sustained by their limitless faith in the benevolence of this Leviathan and in its power to "Do Good" when in the hands of "scientific" experts such as themselves.

A "helping professional" from the time he became a county agent, Myer was a white-cane expression of this blind faith. Progressivism bred the affective dissociation that enabled him to see not peoples but "problems," backward farmers, inscrutable inmates, holdover redskins. Always the disinterested expert and the friendly helper, he maintained great psychic distance from his victims, especially when they were of a different complexion. In Myer we have seen the disastrous consequences of coupling three centuries of racism to the positivistic scientism of the Progressives.

Yet this coupling of racism and scientism went back far beyond the Progressive era. Commissioner Francis Amasa Walker (1871–73), with whom I have repeatedly compared Myer, also wanted to whiten the countryside by removing those unsightly red blotches through a "scientific" Indian policy. Also enamored of the "social sciences," and another candidate for the "scientific" elite, Walker, too, looked on Indians as animated obstacles and ridiculous—albeit then still dangerous—holdovers from the primitive past. And the unquestioned assumption underlying his and Myer's policy had been enunciated decades earlier by Commissioner Thomas Hartley Crawford (1838–45) in a succinct formulation: "Common property and civilization cannot coexist." Ultimately this White Anglo-Saxon Protestant (WASP) axiom went back at least as far as the Puritan drive to banish mystery from the world, strip it of its human idiosyncracies, and subject it to regimented reason. It had existed a very long time before Myer and survived him down to the instant moment, as the new crop of terminationists makes all too clear. And throughout it has represented what Louis Hartz identified in *The Liberal Tradition in America* (1955) as "the mood of America's absolutism: the sober faith that its norms are self-evident" (p. 58). Applied to Indians, it has led to the "understandable but just fatal defect" that former Commissioner Philleo Nash (1961–66) has pointed out: WASPs "assume that the value system of the Anglo-Saxon is universal, and that the individual ownership of property is the only natural way for people to live."

Finally Myer has settled into his proper historical context. His long career raises issues as close as the pronouncements of a member of Ronald Reagan's cabinet and as remote as the European invasion of this continent. A professional remover and relocator, Myer imposed *compulsory* assimilation on both Native Americans and Japanese Americans in the service of the same set of prejudices. As jailer and as terminator, he was no more and no less than a carrier of America's absolutism, which meant WASP values—those "tenets which I had grown up with." His scattering of Japanese Americans from the camps had precedents that were already timeworn when the first Japanese immigrants arrived in the United States. And over a century after the Reverend Jacob Little had remarked that "snakes, wolves and Indians abounded" in Licking County, Myer was energetically trying to flush the last of this linkage group out of their remaining refuges in the deserts and plains and mountains. Thoroughly up to date about the latest dicta of the administrative theorists, Myer still showed that his "scientific" programming rested on those bedrock tenets of the distant past—in deed and in word he projected a vision that resembled a Norman Rockwell cover of the *Saturday Evening Post* or a Currier & Ives print of a small, nineteenth-century town much like Hebron, Ohio.

Have nonwhites no rights which the white man is bound to respect? At the time Myer's most acute critic saw that this was the perennial American question that he emphatically posed as a domestic colonizer, "U.S. Style." And in "Americanizing the White Man" (*American Scholar* 21 [Spring 1952]: 177–91), Felix S. Cohen might have been addressing his simple answer directly to the then commissioner: "None of us knows enough about the other fellow's way of life to have a right to wipe it out." The real American way of life, Cohen thought, is the Indian way in which "each man has respect for his brother's vision": "The real epic of America is the yet unfinished story of the Americanization of the White Man, the transformation of the hungry, fear-ridden, intolerant men that came to these shores with Columbus and John Smith" (pp. 180, 191). Read rightly, Dillon S. Myer's life stands as a monument to that sadly unfinished story, and could serve as a summons to all of us to give it, at long last, a happy ending.

Notes and
Bibliographic Essay

PROLOGUE

I quote from the paperback edition of Jeanne Wakatsuki Houston's *Farewell to Manzanar* (1973; reprint, New York: Bantam Books, 1974), p. 137.

More by title than contents, Eugene V. Rostow's "Our Worst Wartime Mistake," *Harper's* 191 (September 1945): 193–201, made the great internment seem a careless miscalculation, inadvertence, or aberration. It was by no means, I shall argue, that sort of bumbling stupidity.

Useful on the Navaho's Long Walk and their captivity at Fort Sumner is Clifford E. Trafzer, *The Kit Carson Campaign: The Last Great Navaho War* (Norman, Okla.: University of Oklahoma Press, 1982).

I am indebted to Simon J. Ortiz for permission to quote excerpts from "West: Grants to Gallup, New Mexico" and "Relocation." The complete poems appear in *The Way: An Anthology of American Indian Literature*, ed. Shirley Hill Witt and Stan Steiner (New York: Random House, Vintage Books, 1972), pp. 84–85, 88–89.

Indian Agent D.N. Cooley's indictment of "the California Digger" was quoted by Sherburne F. Cook, "The Destruction of the California Indian," *California Monthly* 79 (December 1968): 15. For a full-scale treatment of this grim topic, see Cook's *The Conflict Between the California Indian and White Civilization* (1940–43; reprint, Berkeley and Los Angeles: University of California Press, 1976).

For the background, characterization, and outcome of the Modoc War, see Robert H. Ruby and John A. Brown, *Indians of the Pacific Northwest* (Norman, Okla.: University of Oklahoma Press, 1981), pp. 211–22. On p. 53 Ruby and Brown quote Peter Skene Ogden on the happiness of the Klamaths.

See "Termination bill: Don't underestimate AFBF [American Farm Bureau

Federation]," *Americans Before Columbus* 11, no. 3 (1983): 2, for the former Klamath official's verdict on termination as genocide.

Our Worst Peacetime Mistake: In a letter to Interior Secretary Oscar L. Chapman, Harold L. Ickes concurred with the contention that termination or "what is now proposed for the Indians may well be characterized as 'Our Worst Peacetime Mistake'" (November 5, 1951, JCP).

Ruth Gruber's description of Myer appeared in her *Haven: The Untold Story of 1,000 World War II Refugees* (New York: Coward-McCann, 1983), p. 20.

"The gray president" who exulted over the bombing of Hiroshima was, of course, Harry S. Truman. In *A World Destroyed: The Atomic Bomb and the Grand Alliance* (New York: Alfred A. Knopf, 1975), p. 221, Martin J. Sherwin quoted HST's "vile remark."

For Hannah Arendt's insight, see her indispensable *Eichmann in Jerusalem: A Report on the Banality of Evil* (New York: Viking Press, 1963). For the controversy it provoked, see *Hannah Arendt: The Jew as Pariah*, ed. Ron H. Feldman (New York: Grove Press, 1978), pp. 240–79.

CHAPTER I. THE WRA STORY OF HUMAN CONSERVATION

Established early in 1942 with generous university and foundation support, the Japanese American Evacuation and Resettlement Study tried to cover the roundup and great imprisonment from beginning to end. A rural sociologist, Dorothy Swaine Thomas had a staff of some fifteen younger social scientists, twelve of them Japanese Americans, who studied the camps from the inside. In return for government cooperation, the Thomas group pledged not to publish or discuss the camps publicly during the war; still, as we shall see, relations between the JERS and the WRA were not always harmonious. Afterward the JERS brought out three books: Dorothy Swaine Thomas and Richard S. Nishimoto, *The Spoilage: Japanese-American Evacuation and Resettlement During World War II* (Berkeley: University of California Press, 1946), a study of the sizable number of inmates who renounced their citizenship; Dorothy Swaine Thomas, *The Salvage: Japanese-American Evacuation and Resettlement* (Berkeley and Los Angeles: University of California Press, 1952), a collection of case histories of those who were "dispersed" to the Middle West and East; and, most impressive of the three, Jacobus tenBroek et al., *Prejudice, War and the Constitution: Causes and Consequences of the Evacuation of the Japanese Americans in World War II* (Berkeley and Los Angeles: University of California Press, 1954), an analysis of the legal aspects of removal and imprisonment. A fourth book by a former staff member was published over JERS protest: Morton Grodzins, *Americans Betrayed: Politics and the Japanese Evacuation* (Chicago: University of Chicago Press, 1949), a reworked dissertation that contained much useful data, but exaggerated the responsibility of economic pressure groups. Finally, yet another book with JERS origins was published decades later: Tamotsu Shibutani's empathetic *The Derelicts of Company K: A Sociological Study of Demoralization* (Berkeley and Los Angeles: University of California Press, 1978).

For the first WRA director's revealing account, see Milton S. Eisenhower,

The President Is Calling (New York: Doubleday, 1974), pp. 93–127. There, to piece "together the story that I did not know on March 18, 1942," he drew primarily on Stetson Conn, "Japanese Evacuation from the West Coast," in Stetson Conn et al., *United States Army in World War II: The Western Hemisphere: Guarding the United States and Its Outposts* (Washington: Government Printing Office, 1964), pp. 115–49; see p. 140 for Stimson's notes on the cabinet meeting of February 27, 1942. Eisenhower supplemented the army's official history with other sources, including the memoirs of two cabinet members: Francis Biddle, *In Brief Authority* (Garden City, N.Y.: Doubleday, 1962); and Henry L. Stimson and McGeorge Bundy, *On Active Service in Peace and War* (New York: Harper & Brothers, 1948).

My own summary of the reasons behind the exclusion also draws on Stetson Conn's detailed documentation, on the Henry Louis Stimson Diaries, Manuscripts, and Archives at the Yale University Library, and on three books by Roger Daniels: *The Politics of Prejudice* (Berkeley and Los Angeles: University of California Press, 1962); *Concentration Camps USA: Japanese Americans and World War II* (New York: Holt, Rinehart and Winston, 1971); and *The Decision to Relocate the Japanese Americans* (Philadelphia: J. B. Lippincott, 1975). Building on Conn's analysis, Daniels has argued, to my mind rightly, "that political decisions by civilians, in and out of uniform, were more significant than a largely fictitious 'military necessity,' and that a racist ideology was much more important than economics," as he put it in his bibliographical essay, "American Historians and East Asian Immigrants," *Pacific Historical Review* 43 (November 1974): 449–72. And for general bibliographies of a background that is largely outside the perimeters of the present study, see Edward H. Spicer et al., *Impounded People: Japanese Americans in the Relocation Centers* (Tucson: University of Arizona Press, 1969), and Audrie Girdner and Anne Loftis, *The Great Betrayal: The Evacuation of the Japanese-Americans During World War II* (New York: Macmillan, 1969).

For Hannah Arendt's typology of concentration camps, see *The Origins of Totalitarianism*, 2nd ed. (New York: Meridian Books, 1958), p. 445. Like Eisenhower and Myer at the time and since, Americans have commonly rejected parallels between their camps and those elsewhere.

James Hatsuaki Wakasa was only one of those who endangered their lives by movement. For an incomplete list of inmates wounded or killed by sentries, see Girdner and Loftis, *Great Betrayal*, p. 243.

Myer discussed how he became director in *Uprooted Americans: The Japanese Americans and the War Relocation Authority During World War II* (Tucson: University of Arizona Press, 1971), p. 3. For this "inside story," as the publisher would have it, Myer had the editorial assistance of Morrill M. Tozier, and indeed his book hardly amounts to more than a gloss on the latter's *WRA: A Story of Human Conservation* (Washington: Government Printing Office, 1946), the principal source of data in the text on the camps.

All the other major publications of the agency also came out of the Government Printing Office in Washington: *Administrative Highlights of the WRA Program* (1946); *Community Government in War Relocation Centers* (1946); *The Evacuated People: A Quantitative Description* (1946); *Impounded People:*

Japanese Americans in the Relocation Centers (1946; the 1969 University of Arizona Press edition by Edward H. Spicer et al. contains a new preface and the useful bibliography already mentioned); *Legal and Constitutional Phases of the WRA Program* (1946); *The Relocation Program* (1946); *Wartime Exile: The Exclusion of the Japanese Americans from the West Coast* (1946); and *The Wartime Handling of Evacuee Property* (1946).

After the war the WRA supposedly deposited a complete set of its files in the Bancroft Library to round out those of the JERS. But the Bancroft holdings must be supplemented by WRA records in the National Archives, Social and Economic Records Division, Record Group 210 (cited as NA, RG 210).

Among the few historians who have refused to pass on the WRA story of human conservation uncritically is Roger Daniels. In the bibliographical essay already cited he called for "a thorough study of this agency of benign incarceration." Arthur A. Hansen has also been skeptical: see his and David A. Hacker's "The Manzanar Riot: An Ethnic Perspective," *Amerasia Journal* 2 (Fall 1974): 112–57, and the collection of essays and interviews he and Betty E. Mitson edited, *Voices Long Silent: An Oral Inquiry into the Japanese American Evacuation* (Fullerton, Calif.: California State University at Fullerton Oral History Program, 1974). Some younger Japanese American scholars are also far from accepting WRA propaganda at face value: see especially Gary Y. Okihiro, "Japanese Resistance in America's Concentration Camps: A Re-evaluation," *Amerasia Journal* 2 (Fall 1973): 20–34. Finally, one of the victims has written a critical account that is outstanding: Michi Weglyn, *Years of Infamy: The Untold Story of America's Concentration Camps* (New York: William Morrow, 1976).

CHAPTER II.   FARM BOY

Published in three volumes the year of Dillon Myer's birth, Henry Howe's *Historical Collections of Ohio*, Centennial edition (Columbus: Henry Howe & Son, 1889, 1891), is invaluable for understanding past and contemporary attitudes and circumstances of the residents of Licking County. Parenthetical citations to "Howe" by volume and page numbers refer to this source.

Some Myer biographical data come from headstones in the Hebron cemetery and from interviews with local residents, but most come from Dillon Myer's oral autobiography. In the latter Myer conjectured that his paternal ancestors migrated to America from Germany in the middle or late eighteenth century (Auto, introduction).

Edward Eggleston of course meant that neither Puritanism nor Methodism *was* "very agreeable to live with, maybe"—*The Circuit Rider* (New York: Charles Scribner's Sons, 1897), p. 159.

For William Holmes McGuffey's parallelism of the dark man and the fool, see his *Eclectic First Reader for Young Readers* (Cincinnati: Truman and Smith, 1837), p. 29. On the readers generally, see Richard D. Mosier, *Making the American Mind: Social and Moral Ideas in the McGuffey Readers* (New York: Columbia University Press, 1947).

Hebron's present population is only about 2,000, even as an automobile suburb. Still useful for understanding such nineteenth-century villages is Ed Howe's

Story of a Country Town (New York: Harper & Brothers, 1883). See also Lewis F. Atherton, *Main Street on the Middle Border* (Bloomington: Indiana University Press, 1954); David Graham Hutton, *Midwest at Noon* (Chicago: University of Chicago Press, 1946); and Solon T. Kimball and James E. McCellan, Jr., *Education and the New America* (New York: Vintage Books, 1962). Kimball, incidentally, was on Myer's WRA staff.

Theodore Roosevelt's definition of *national efficiency* was quoted by Samuel P. Hays in *Conservation and the Gospel of Efficiency* (New York: Atheneum, 1969), p. 125. For the rise of middle-class specialists and technicians generally, see Burton J. Bledstein, *The Culture of Professionalism* (New York: W. W. Norton, 1976).

Lawrence Goodwyn's *Democratic Promise: The Populist Moment in America* (New York: Oxford University Press, 1976) sympathetically portrays the movement twentieth-century business leaders hoped to leave behind through their promotion of commercialized agriculture. See also Richard Hofstadter, *The Age of Reform* (New York: Alfred A. Knopf, 1956). Still useful on the key figure in the transition is *The County Agent* by Gladys Baker (Chicago: University of Chicago Press, 1939).

Outstanding on the Byzantine politics of agriculture during the first half of the twentieth century is Grant McConnell's *Decline of Agrarian Democracy* (Berkeley and Los Angeles: University of California Press, 1953). I have also drawn on A. Whitney Griswold, *Farming and Democracy* (New York: Harcourt, Brace, 1948). For the Mount Weather Agreement and the rivalry of AAA and SCS, see Murray Reid Benedict, *Farm Policies of the United States, 1790– 1950* (New York: Twentieth Century Fund, 1953), pp. 394–96. For a provocative discussion of agriculture as "neither public nor private enterprise," see Theodore J. Lowi, *The End of Liberalism*, 2nd ed. (New York: W. W. Norton, 1979), pp. 67–77.

Myer exaggerated his "major victory for the SCS" a little. A few years after he left to become director of the WRA, the American Farm Bureau Federation and the Extension Service vigorously renewed their attack on the SCS—see McConnell, *Decline*, pp. 128–34. McConnell's remarks quoted in the text are from ibid., p. 72.

For the more imaginative Ohioans, see Louis Bromfield, *The Farm* (New York: Harper & Brothers, 1933), and Sherwood Anderson, *Winesburg, Ohio* (New York: B. W. Huebsch, 1919). Anderson's words on his endless search for a lost dream were quoted by Maxwell Geismar, *The Last of the Provincials* (New York: Hill and Wang, 1959), p. 283.

Russell Lord is quoted in McConnell, *Decline*, p. 165.

For Alexis de Tocqueville's observation on Americans and nature, see *Democracy in America*, ed. Henry Steele Commager (New York: Oxford University Press, 1947), p. 292.

In 1929 H. J. Spinden estimated that "about four-sevenths of the agricultural production of the United States (farm values) are in economic plants domesticated by the American Indian and taken over by the white man" ("Population of Ancient America," Smithsonian Institution, *Annual Report* [Washington, D.C., 1929], p. 465n). For Lyman Carrier's earlier estimate of at least a third, see *The Beginnings of Agriculture in America* (New York: McGraw-Hill, 1923), p. 41. The first white explorers and settlers encountered extensive farming operations along the Atlantic. Various sources attest that near Narragansett Bay farmers had cleared the land of timber for a distance of eight to ten miles from the coast. To the south on Chesapeake Bay were three thousand acres of cleared land near present-day Hampton, according to the calculations of Philip A. Bruce, *Economic History of Virginia* (New York: P. Smith, 1896). For an able modern account of the farming skills of Indians, see Carl Ortwin Sauer, *Sixteenth-Century North America* (Berkeley and Los Angeles: University of California Press, 1971), especially pp. 286–95.

Archaeologist Cyrus Thomas effectively attacked the fanciful lost-race theory in "Report on the Mound Explorations of the Bureau of Ethnology," Smithsonian Institution, *Annual Report* (Washington, D.C., 1894). Gerard Fowke drew extensively on it for *Archaeological History of Ohio: The Mound Builders and Later Indians* (Columbus: Ohio State Archaeological and Historical Society, 1902). Geographer John Wells Foster's racist *Pre-historic Races of the United States of America* (Chicago: S. C. Griggs, 1873) went through five editions by 1881. For a modern summary of this revealing controversy, see Robert Silverberg, *Mound Builders of America: The Archaeology of a Myth* (Greenwich, Conn.: New York Graphic Society, 1968).

CHAPTER III.   DIRECTOR

The chapter epigraph is from U.S. Senate Subcommittee of the Committee on Military Affairs, *War Relocation Centers*, 78th Cong., 1st sess. (Washington, D.C.: Government Printing Office, 1943), p. 53.

The Problem of Nomenclature: In the case of John J. McCloy, his perplexity over what to call Japanese Americans has lasted a lifetime. On November 3, 1981, he appeared before the Commission on Wartime Relocation and Internment of Civilians (CWRIC), established by Congress (Public Law 96–317, July 31, 1980) to determine whether citizens and aliens had suffered any wrong under Executive Order 9066. Even at this late date McCloy fell back into invoking the thoughtful and humane official action "in regard to our then Japanese population" (*Personal Justice Denied: Report of the Commission on Wartime Relocation and Internment of Civilians* [Washington, D.C.: Government Printing Office, 1982], p. 383).

Though General DeWitt was formally responsible for the army's *Final Report: Japanese Evacuation from the West Coast* (Washington, D.C.: Government Printing Office, 1943), Colonel Karl R. Bendetsen wrote most of the document. Bendetsen rarely called the Nisei "Japanese Americans" and was no doubt responsible for the explanation in the *Final Report*, p. 34: "The word 'Japanese' includes alien Japanese and American citizens of Japanese ancestry."

The navy had comparable problems. In an ONI document on the camp at Heart Mountain, Wyoming, dated December 13, 1944, the writer refers to the Issei and then has to explain they are "Japan born Japanese" (FBI 62-69030). By implication, then, the Nisei were "American-born Japanese."

Myer and his staff eschewed the epithet "Japs," but at one conference Jerome

Project Director Paul A. Taylor spoke of "having some Japs come to the project from Dallas," and Myer did not reprimand him for breaking the taboo—see Little Rock Project Directors Conference, February 1–3, 1943, JERS, 67/14, E2.11B.

Inscrutable Orientals: California Governor Culbert L. Olson was quoted by Togo W. Tanaka, "How to Survive Racism in America's Free Society," in *Voices Long Silent*, ed. Arthur A. Hansen and Betty E. Mitson (Fullerton, Calif.: California State University, 1974), pp. 94–95. For Earl Warren's testimony before the Tolan Committee, see Leo Katcher, *Earl Warren: A Political Biography* (New York: McGraw-Hill, 1967), p. 144. After Warren became governor, Katcher noted, the limit of his "tolerance was still determined by pigmentation" (p. 148). In June 1943 Warren warned his fellow governors that continued release of Japanese Americans would make it so "no one will be able to tell a saboteur from any other Jap" (quoted by Daniels, *CC*, p. 149).

Carey McWilliams's "Goodbye Mr. Moto," a draft of "Evacuation—A Military Necessity," and other MSS furthering and defending the roundup and penning of Japanese Americans are in the Hoover Institution Archives, Stanford, California. An expanded, revised, and retitled version of "Goodbye Mr. Moto" appeared as "Moving the West Coast Japanese," *Harper's* 185 (September 1942): 359–69. McWilliams later changed his mind about the necessity for exclusion but still rejected the term *concentration camps* for the detention phase—see his *Prejudice: Japanese Americans: Symbols of Racial Intolerance* (Boston: Little, Brown, 1945). Throughout, McWilliams served as an influential apologist for WRA policies.

For the long history of white supremacist groups agitating against the "yellow peril," see especially Jacobus tenBroek, Edward N. Barnhart, and Floyd W. Matson, *Prejudice, War, and the Constitution: Causes and Consequences of the Evacuation of Japanese Americans in World War II* (Berkeley and Los Angeles: University of California Press, 1954); Roger Daniels, *The Politics of Prejudice: The Anti-Japanese Movement in California and the Struggle for Japanese Exclusion* (New York: Atheneum, 1968); and Stuart C. Miller, *The Unwelcome Immigrant: The American Image of the Chinese, 1785–1882* (Berkeley and Los Angeles: University of California Press, 1969). See also Morton Grodzins, *Americans Betrayed: Politics and the Japanese Evacuation* (Chicago: University of Chicago Press, 1949), and Myer's chapter on "The Continuing Battle of the Racists," *UA*, pp. 91–107. Daniels traced the origin of the term to "Kaiser Wilhelm II's vaporings about a *gelbe gefahr* [sic] threatening Europe and all Christendom (he meant a Chinese invasion à la Genghis Khan)" (*Politics of Prejudice*, p. 68). Miller found faint stirrings of yellow perilism in the United States during the Opium War and posited a much longer time span for the notion: "No doubt the yellow peril concept goes back at least to the thirteenth-century European reaction to Genghiz Kahn" (*Unwelcome Immigrant*, p. 110). No doubt Europe's inner demons arrived on this continent with the first European invaders. At all events, as the works of Miller, Daniels, et al. demonstrate, *racism* in its anti-Oriental form was by no means limited to the West Coast.

For C. Wright Mills's discussion of "the inner core," see *The Power Elite* (New York: Oxford University Press, 1956), pp. 288–90. In a letter to the executive director of the CWRIC, dated July 24, 1981, John J. McCloy of One Chase Manhattan Plaza in New York recalled that he "had much to do with the early aspects of the relocation program while I was The [*sic*] Assistant Secretary of War following the Pearl Harbor attack." In his oral testimony before the CWRIC on November 3, 1981, McCloy again referred to himself as "The" assistant of Stimson. Surely he was that as he was "The" key figure in the chain of command from the White House to the Western Defense Command—see Stetson Conn, "Japanese Evacuation from the West Coast," in Stetson Conn et al., *Guarding the United States and Its Outposts* (Washington, D.C.: Government Printing Office, 1964), pp. 115–49. On June 4, 1943, McCloy wrote William S. Merchant of the San Francisco Down Town Association: "The War Department is aware that many of the evacuees, both citizens and aliens, are disloyal and in some instances even potentially dangerous" (FBI 62-69030). In truth, he knew nothing of the sort, but thought he did and was in a position to implement his prejudices.

In 1949, as U.S. high commissioner in Germany, McCloy assumed responsibility for, and control over, convicted war criminals. He freed all the convicted industrialists, as I have noted, perhaps partly in response to those "automatic sympathies" mentioned by the German periodical *Die Gegenwart* (September 1, 1949) as then accruing to the defendants (quoted in Raul Hilberg, *The Destruction of the European Jews* [Chicago: Quadrangle Books, 1961], p. 697n). The chief champion of "the single-bullet theory" and the sole champion of the "killer-instinct theory" to explain Lee Harvey Oswald's motives, McCloy served on the Warren Commission not so much to discover the truth as to dispel rumors and advance the national interest: it was of paramount importance, he informed Edward Jay Epstein in 1965, to "show the world that America is not a banana republic, where a government can be changed by conspiracy" (*Inquest: The Warren Commission and the Establishment of Truth* [New York: Bantam Books, 1966], p. 30). McCloy also knew something about changing governments in "banana republics"—in addition to the positions I have listed, he served as director of a number of companies, including the United Fruit Company (Thomas P. McCann, *An American Company* [New York: Crown, 1976], p. 56).

Most unrewarding for any attempt to understand the role of the secretary of war is Henry L. Stimson and McGeorge Bundy, *On Active Service in Peace and War* (New York: Harper & Brothers, 1948). Elting E. Morison's *Turmoil and Tradition: A Study of the Life and Times of Henry L. Stimson* (New York: Atheneum, 1964) is not much more helpful. See instead Stimson's diaries and other papers in the Yale University Library and Richard Nelson Current, *Secretary Stimson: A Study in Statecraft* (New Brunswick, N.J.: Rutgers University Press, 1954), the source for Stimson's and Hoover's conversation about the white man's burden (p. 120). In *The Valor of Ignorance* (New York: Harper & Brothers, 1909) Homer Lea prophesied a Japanese American war, with Japan seizing the Philippines and the Pacific states. See also Lea's *Day of the Saxon* (New York: Harper & Brothers, 1912) and discussions of him by Roger Daniels, *Politics of Prejudice*, pp. 72–74, and Richard Hofstadter, *Social Darwinism in American Thought* (Boston: Beacon Press, 1955), pp. 190–91.

For an account of World War II exclusion in Canada, see Ken Adachi, *The Enemy That Never Was* (Toronto: McClelland and Stewart, 1976). The Canadians rounded up and placed in detention and labor camps nearly 21,000 persons, three-fourths of whom were Canadian citizens, confiscated and sold their property, threatened to deport them if they did not scatter themselves across the interior provinces, and refused to allow them to return to British Columbia for almost four years after the end of the war. The Canadian counterpart of the WRA was the British Columbia Security Commission (BCSC), and like Myer's outfit it had language rules or euphemisms for its pens—they were not concentration camps but "interior housing centres," "relocation centres," or "interior settlements." The Japanese Canadians who did relocate discovered, Adachi wrote, "that racial prejudice was spread uniformly over the whole of Canada" (p. 286). Like FDR, Prime Minister Mackenzie King had the goal of settling "the Japanese more or less evenly" throughout the country (p. 335). Adachi's conclusion applies equally to U.S. events: "The dominant element in the development of the evacuation programme was racial prejudice, not a military estimate of a military problem" (p. 224). The underlying racism in both countries produced similar phenomena, a truth that can be highlighted by careful comparisons and contrasts. For a step in that direction, see Roger Daniels, "The Decisions to Relocate the North American Japanese: Another Look," *Pacific Historical Review* 51 (February 1982): 71–77. In addition to Adachi, see David R. Hughes and Evelyn Kallen, *The Anatomy of Racism: Canadian Dimensions* (Montreal: Harvest House, 1974); and Ted Ferguson, *A White Man's Country: An Exercise in Canadian Prejudice* (Toronto: Doubleday, 1975).

Our understanding of the Japanese Canadian experience has been enriched by two books published since this chapter was written. Ann Gomer Sunahara has supplemented and extended Ken Adachi's findings through the use of government files for her *Politics of Racism* (Toronto: James Lorimer, 1981). And in *Obasan* (Boston: David R. Godine, 1982), Joy Kogawa gave voice to her raped generation through a superbly written novel that is the best fictional treatment of the uprooting and penning to have appeared on either side of the border.

A copy of McCloy's important letter to Alexander Meiklejohn (September 30, 1942) was typed by former Tule inmate Frank Shotaro Miyamoto, a sociologist member of the JERS team who had access to WRA records when he was in Washington with Morton Grodzins in the fall of 1943. The copy is undoubtedly authentic. On October 5, 1942, General DeWitt wrote McCloy: "I am told by Colonel Bendetsen that you are sympathetic toward the development of a plan to determine whether an opportunity is now within reach for learning more about the Japanese as a people than is known at the present time" (quoted in *YoI*, p. 101). And in his appearance before the CWRIC on November 3, 1981, McCloy was questioned about treating "these people as 'guinea pigs' "— as quoted by Richard Drinnon in " 'Jap Camps,' " *Inquiry* 4 (April 27, 1981): 29—and in response obligingly acknowledged that such thoughts "may have crossed my mind" (Drinnon, personal notes).

In his continuing espousal of "selective evacuation," Myer may have meant what the FBI had already carried out in the days following Pearl Harbor, namely the apprehension and internment of about 2,000 Issei suspects (*YoI*, p. 46).

Whether even this "may have been justified" is highly questionable. As Director Edward J. Ennis of the Alien Enemy Control Unit in the Department of Justice explained to Milton Eisenhower on June 18, 1942: "I might say for your information that a large number of Japanese were apprehended, not because there was any indication that the individual himself was suspected of subversive activity but because the occupation group or association to which he made a contribution was suspect, for example, fishermen and Heimusha Kai [Military Service Men's League]" (JERS, 67/14, C1.05). Myer later found fault with the army's rationale for mass evacuation, stating that General DeWitt's reasons "make out a case of racial bias" (UA, p. 285). But in 1943 he advanced those selfsame reasons as his own; in 1971 he was attempting to distance himself from the racism he belatedly acknowledged in DeWitt.

In 1969 Edward H. Spicer drew parallels between the policies of forced compliance not only characteristic of the camps "but also of Indian reservations in the United States, the colonial countries before independence, and a host of modern national government programs for the improvement of life at the local level in various parts of the world" (Introduction, Impounded People [Tucson: University of Arizona Press, 1969]). Later—after Poston—Spicer became head of all the WRA community analysts, as they were called, and after the war properly placed Myer's program in its larger colonial context. His critique of WRA paternalism, though written long after the fact, is noteworthy.

In The Governing of Men: General Principles and Recommendations Based on Experience at a Japanese Relocation Camp (Princeton, N.J.: Princeton University Press, 1945), Alexander H. Leighton introduced the useful typology of "people-minded" versus "stereotype-minded" keepers (p. 84) and established passim tangible connections between prior experience administering Native Americans and current problems in administering Japanese Americans.

For Collier's desire to head up the WRA, see Kenneth R. Philp, John Collier's Crusade for Indian Reform (Tucson: University of Arizona Press, 1977), pp. 208–10. Collier's discussion of his conflict with Myer over Poston appeared in From Every Zenith (Denver: Sage Books, 1963), pp. 300–301. After their quarrel Collier drafted a "Statement of Policy for the Residents of Poston," undated, to represent "the joint views of Mr. Dillon Myer and Myself" (JERS, 67/14, J1.11). It encouraged permanent employment outside the camp, but recognized the fact that Poston would be home for many until the end of the war, and for them, "it is our intention to develop as full a community life as possible." Needless to note, Myer did not sign the document. On August 11, 1943, Poston Project Director Wade Head wrote Collier recommending that the BIA sever the connection: "We are held responsible . . . without any real influence or control of the policies governing our administration. We are forced to put into effect policies which we are convinced are contrary to the best interests of the evacuees, and in conflict with your own policies and principles" (NA, RG 48). On December 31, 1943, the BIA officially turned the camp over to the WRA.

For the shooting at Topaz, see Russell A. Bankson, "The Wakasa Incident," May 10, 1943, NA, RG 210. The army acquitted the sentry Gerald B. Philpott of violating any military law in shooting Wakasa and acquitted the sentry Bernard W. Goe "upon the specification and charge" of feloniously shooting to death Shoichi Okamoto at Tule Lake camp. Of course Myer knew of the shoot-ings—see, e.g., the Tule information specialist Allen L. Markley to Myer, May 25, 1944, NA, RG 210. In response to a letter from Myer dated July 14, 1944, Topaz's project director, Louis T. Hoffman, answered his query as to whether Wakasa and the other inmates had been warned not to go near the fences: "The Topaz Times [camp newspaper] frequently carried notices urging residents to use the gates and not to crawl over or under the fences. The WRA could hardly have been in a position to specify the action the military would take in case persons approached the fence or attempted to go through or over it" (July 25, 1944, NA, RG 210). According to a State Department memorandum quoted by Michi Weglyn, "examination of the Army's reports on the shootings gives the impression that the Army's shooting rule comes close to making death, rather than up to 30 days arrest as provided in Article 54 of the Geneva Con-vention, the penalty for attempted escape" (*YoI*, p. 312n). In these instances the army's shooting rule anticipated its Mere Gook Rule (MGR) in Indochina de-cades later—see Richard Drinnon, *Facing West: The Metaphysics of Indian-Hating and Empire-Building* (New York: New American Library, 1980), pp. 454–55.

In *Japanese Americans: The Evolution of a Subculture* (Englewood Cliffs, N.J.: Prentice-Hall, 1969), pp. 34–39, Harry H. L. Kitano discussed some of the "positive" aspects of camp life and pointed out that inmates could break out of their minority-group roles to become captains of athletic teams, cheer-leaders, and the like.

"Community" Government: In "Collective Protest in Relocation Centers," *American Journal of Sociology* 63 (November 1957): 264–72, an article based on his Ph.D. dissertation of the same title (University of California, 1955), Nor-man R. Jackman reported finding little or no self-government in the camps: "The center was, at best, a benevolent authoritarianism." From WRA social scientists the word *community* had much the Orwellian ring of the word *truth* from the lips of a minister of misinformation. For an egregious example, see John H. Provinse and Solon T. Kimball, "Building New Communities During War Time," *American Sociological Review* 11 (August 1946): 396–409. In his comment on their essay in the same issue, Leonard Bloom remarked incisively that "a very good case could be made that the camps were hardly communities or, at best, only in the sense that prisons are communities" (p. 409).

Institutionalized Racism in the WRA Camps: Especially insightful on the "self-hate" this fostered among the inmates was Daisuke Kitagawa, *Issei and Nisei: The Internment Years* (New York: Seabury Press, 1967).

Servants: "Please tell me who or how I can arrange to get a Jap couple as maid and yard man for my home," M. A. Parker of Knoxville, Tennessee, asked Harold Ickes. "I have contacted the F.B.I. here and they know nothing about it" (May 3, 1943, NA, RG 75). The businessman may have written to the secretary of the interior in part because Ickes had just received a good deal of notoriety for having placed seven former Poston inmates on his estate, Headwaters Farm, at Olney, Maryland (*Washington Times-Herald*, April 15, 1943). Four were poultrymen, three of whom were accompanied by their wives: "Neither would the War Relocation Authority spokesman disclose whether the wives will be

employed as maids by Mrs. Ickes, or how much the seven parolees will be paid."
In wartime, the reporter pointed out, "because they are so scarce, good maids
and good poultrymen have no price ceilings in the Washington area." Secretary
of Agriculture Claude Wickard also attempted to hire former inmates for his
farm, according to the *Los Angeles Times* (June 20, 1943), and letters streamed
into the WRA and the FBI asking how to go about getting maids and cooks,
houseboys and gardeners. A friend of J. Edgar Hoover's even asked for his personal help in getting some "American-Japanese" to work in her New York
flower shop (October 12, 1945, FBI 62-69030).

A headline in the *Philadelphia Bulletin*, April 17, 1944, said it all: "HOUSE-
WIVES HERE NOT PREJUDICED AGAINST HIRING JAP AMERICANS; 129 now on
Waiting List to get them for Work as Domestic Servants; WRA Places Some."
The article revealed that the WRA had already placed about fifty Issei and Nisei
"in servants positions here. That's about 25 per cent of the total relocated Japanese given jobs through the Philadelphia office, but it doesn't even come close
to meeting all the domestic demand for them." Obviously, the WRA was imple-
menting Myer's "relocation" program in part by serving as an employment
agency for domestics. The Tule Lake WRA personnel involved in what Ernest
Besig called "a slave labor racket" had understandably yielded to the temptation
to get their hands on these splendid servants while they were still in their custody. The melancholy fact, inside and outside the camps, was that many Anglo-
Americans evinced much greater eagerness to have the impounded people as
servants than as free equals.

Obviously making inmates into servants provided psychological as well as
physical satisfactions for the Prospero-like administrators of the WRA. On the
origins of the former gratifications, see K. M. Abenheimer, "Shakespeare's 'Tempest': A Psychological Analysis," *Psychoanalytic Review* 33 (October 1946):
399–415; Otare Mannoni, *Prospero and Caliban* (New York: Frederick A.
Praeger, 1964); and Philip Mason, *Prospero's Magic* (London: Oxford University Press, 1962).

Robert L. Brown was Ralph P. Merritt's reports officer. For his characteri-
zation of Merritt as "a big man," see his interview in *Camp and Community:
Manzanar and the Owens Valley*, ed. Jessie A. Garrett and Ronald C. Larson
(Fullerton, Calif.: California State University, 1977), p. 37.

To protect the confidentiality of his sources and his own physical safety, Richard Nishimoto tried to keep his work for Dorothy Swaine Thomas under
wraps—the full citation of the work they later coauthored is *The Spoilage: Japanese-American Evacuation and Resettlement During World War II* (Berkeley:
University of California Press, 1946). There is good reason to believe that if
Thomas had not secured permission to carry on her study from Milton Eisenhower in the first months of the WRA—"with no strings attached," as she put
it—the JERS team would never have received Myer's approval. As it was,
Thomas wrote Nishimoto on April 27, 1944, John H. Provinse (chief, WRA
Community Management Division) "came over to my office and demanded that
I give him carbon copies of everything that our staff was sending in from the
projects" (JERS, 67/14, W1.25). To her credit she managed to fend him off, and
to my knowledge she never betrayed the trust of her vulnerable staff and their

sources. This was no small achievement, for JERS members were harassed in the camps. For instance, Thomas wrote Nishimoto on August 11, 1944: "I had lunch with Mr. [Regional Director Robert] Cozzens yesterday, and he told me that [Project Director Leroy] Bennett and others at Gila [River] had been complaining bitterly about . . . [JERS member Rosalie Hankey]. They claim that she is 'against all government and has been inciting the evacuees to anarchy'" (JERS, 67/14, W1.25B). Like other administrators of total institutions, the project directors disliked "outsiders" in the camps, and their distaste was shared by their national director. For the former JERS staff member's views, see Rosalie Hankey Wax, *Doing Field Work* (Chicago: University of Chicago Press, 1971).

CHAPTER IV.   SCATTERER

The chapter epigraph is from Dillon S. Myer, Press Conference, May 14, 1943, JERS, 67/14, E2.04.

In an interview with Hiroshi Suzuki on February 21, 1978, Myer said that he had first consulted with John J. McCloy about his leave regulations and found him "very sympathetic" (Suzuki, "Dillon S. Myer and Federal Relations with American Japanese and Indians," M.A. thesis, George Washington University, 1978, p. 22).

Apparently the WRA invoked its assumed power to recall inmates from leave only once. Recalled for aiding some escaped German prisoners, a family group obediently returned to their camp. "The WRA asked the assistance of the Justice Department to enforce a recall, should this be necessary, but Francis Biddle refused, saying he knew of no legal authority to do this" (Audrie Girdner and Anne Loftis, *The Great Betrayal* [London: Macmillan, 1969], p. 344).

"Caucasian" References: In the WRA regulations "Issuance of Leave for Departure from a Relocation Area," Administrative Instruction No. 22 (Revised), November 6, 1942, item no. 8 of the application instructed the inmate: "Give the names and addresses of references not to exceed five in number. These need not be Caucasians, but good Caucasian references may be particularly helpful." This was the preference Myer mentioned to J. Edgar Hoover and my reason for observing that overt racism was built into the application process itself.

In the WRA leave regulations issued on September 26, 1942, Myer listed the requirements for eligibility: offer of a job, community acceptance, and so on. But the first requirement disclosed the basic purpose of the process: "There must be no evidence of disloyalty to the United States."

Michi Weglyn has conveniently reproduced "Leave Clearance Interview Questions—25 August 1943" (*YoI*, pp. 196–99). As she observed, that document comes from the files of the assistant secretary of war (ASW 014.311 WDC Segregation-Japs, NA, RG 107) and that meant that McCloy and his staff may have had a hand in formulating Myer's questions.

"An Evacuee's an Evacuee": This conviction was implicit in a letter Myer wrote Stimson on March 11, 1943. One of his operating assumptions, he explained to the secretary of war, "is that all American citizens and law-abiding alien residents of the United States should be treated by the government, *insofar*

as possible under wartime conditions, without racial discrimination" (*UA*, p. 161; emphasis added).

William Byrd's famous advocacy of miscegenation appeared in his *History of the Dividing Line*—see Louis B. Wright, ed., *The Prose Works of William Byrd of Westover* (Cambridge, Mass.: Harvard University Press, 1966), pp. 160–61. For a discussion of its context and meaning, see Richard Drinnon, *Facing West* (New York: New American Library, 1980), pp. 85, 479–80.

For the Sioux Red Dog's suggestion about putting Indians on wheels, see Peter Nabokov, ed., *Native American Testimony* (New York: Harper & Row, 1978), p. 184. For the Great Commoner's proposal to scatter the Japanese Americans all around the country, see Roger Daniels, "William Jennings Bryan and the Japanese," *Southern California Quarterly* 48 (September 1966): 227–40.

For the WRA propaganda barrage designed to blow Nisei and Issei eastward, see also "THE NISEI PROBLEM—EVACUEES SELL WEST COAST PROPERTY IN TREND TOWARD EASTERN SETTLEMENT," *San Francisco Chronicle*, February 28, 1944. After such WRA-inspired articles were published, Philip J. Webster of the San Francisco regional office sent copies to reports officers in all the camps for immediate use to persuade the inmates to forsake their former homes (March 9, 1944, JERS, 67/14, E1.020).

Census figures measure precisely the relative failure of Myer's "dispersal" program: Of all the persons of Japanese ancestry in the continental United States in 1940, 88.5 percent (112,353) lived in Pacific Coast states; in 1950, 58.2 percent (98,310); and in 1970, 64.6 percent (239,678). By contrast, white Canadians were much more successful, in part because their restrictions on movements of Japanese Canadians lasted until 1949—see Roger Daniels, "The Japanese Experience in North America: An Essay in Comparative Racism," *Canadian Ethnic Studies* 9 (1977): 91–100.

For Nanette Dembitz's discussion of "the theme of benefaction," see her "Racial Discrimination and the Military Judgment," *Columbia Law Review* 45 (March 1945): 202–3; the origin of that theme, I have ventured, takes us all the way back to Shakespeare's Prospero.

CHAPTER V. SEGREGATOR

Decades after Myer's admission that the WRA penal colony at Moab, Utah, was "nothing more than a concentration camp," he still sought to hide that fact behind his "definitions." In a letter to Judy Tachibana dated September 24, 1978, he denied that inmates of the penal colony were "prisoners in the normal sense": "We never considered the isolation centers to be jails in the normal sense other than for isolation in order to keep peace among the remaining populace" (quoted by Rita Takahashi Cates in her informative "Comparative Administration and Management of Five War Relocation Authority Camps: America's Incarceration of Persons of Japanese Descent During World War II," Ph.D. diss., University of Pittsburgh, 1980, pp. 457–58). Thanks to this word-magic, if "we never considered" jails jails, then they were never jails, "in the normal sense."

Publicly WRA officials insisted that the American camps had no parallels with other camps anywhere, but privately they were not above drawing on the experience of their European counterparts. On December 7, 1944, for instance, John H. Provinse, chief of the Community Management Division, wrote a memorandum for Myer proposing the "safety valve" of allowing determined Issei who sought repatriation status as war internees:

> In advocating the extension of the safety valve principle which we are considering for Tule Lake to the other centers, I am recalling the fairly well substantiated reports of the Russian success in bringing even German army prisoners around to anti-Nazi points of view while still in Russian prison camps. This has been done as nearly as I can find out by eliminating the principal die-hard Nazi leaders (by segregation and otherwise) and by working hard to educate the next group of leaders that comes to the top. In another memorandum, I am elaborating some of this same experience so far as what I feel are our responsibilities in utilizing our loyal Issei and Nisei in preparing for our post-war adjustment with Japan. [JERS, 67/14, U1.22]

In their inner councils WRA leaders thus recognized full well that their camps were comparable to prison camps elsewhere. Their totalitarian aspiration to emulate Stalinist successes in behavior modification—in "brainwashing," as that coercive conversion came to be called in the 1950s—made explicit their assumption that the WRA camps were indoctrination centers and that "our" imprisoned Issei and Nisei were the subject guinea pigs.

All the major congressional hearings and reports came out of the 78th Cong., 1st sess., and were published in Washington, D.C., by the Government Printing Office in 1943. See U.S. Senate (Chandler) Subcommittee of the Committee on Military Affairs, *War Relocation Centers: Hearings on S. 444, A Bill Providing for the Transfer of Certain Functions of the War Relocation Authority to the War Department*, and *Report on Japanese War Relocation Centers*. Also see U.S. House (Costello) Subcommittee of the Committee on Un-American Activities, *Hearings on Japanese War Relocation Centers, Report on the Tule Lake Riot*, and, finally, *Majority and Minority Report*.

The Los Angeles newspapers especially gave extensive coverage to the Costello subcommittee's seizure of Masaoka's JACL files—see the issues of the *Los Angeles Times* and the *Los Angeles Examiner*, June 15–20, 1943.

JACL: The biographical data on Mike Masaru Masaoka come mostly from Bill Hosokawa's admiring portrait in *Nisei: The Quiet Americans* (New York: William Morrow, 1969), pp. 202–5. The FBI agent's conclusion that Masaoka was "not altogether scrupulous" found some confirmation in Hosokawa's description of him as a "brash, outspoken, sometimes delightfully devious *Nisei*" (p. 202). No doubt he was delightful to his admirers and less so to those on the receiving end of his deviousness. In his appearance before the Costello Subcommittee, Agent Ranstad reported, Masaoka testified "that he had advised the FBI" of the denunciation of Roosevelt by a Manzanar inmate (memorandum of D. M. Ladd, July 7, 1943, FBI 62-69030). Indeed, FBI documents indicate that Masaoka and his associates at JACL national headquarters in Salt Lake City "advised" the agency on a wholesale basis—see, for example, the sixty-page report on "Subversive Activities at War Relocation Centers" from the SAC in Salt Lake City (March 13, 1943, FBI 100-140363).

In *The Colonizer and the Colonized* (New York: Orion Press, 1965), Albert Memmi pointed out that "rejection of self and love of another are common to all candidates for assimilation. Moreover, the two components of this attempt at liberation are closely tied. Love of the colonizer is subtended by a complex of feelings ranging from shame to self-hate" (p. 121). (For Daisuke Kitagawa's analysis of the selfsame self-hate, see *Issei and Nisei* [New York: Seabury Press, 1967], pp. 26–36.) As prime candidates for assimilation, Masaoka and other JACLers were prime cases in point.

Among the early test cases opposed by the JACL were those of Gordon Kiyoshi Hirabayashi, a Nisei college student whose conviction of curfew violation was ultimately sustained by the Supreme Court (320 U.S. 81 [1943]), and Minoru Yasui, a Nisei lawyer in Portland, Oregon, and a lieutenant in the army reserve, who deliberately violated the curfew by walking into a police station late at night. Judge James Alger Fee found the curfew "void as respects citizens"—later reversed by the Supreme Court in the Hirabayashi decision—but found Yasui guilty on the ground that he had lost his citizenship by working before the war for the Consulate General of Japan. For his appeal Yasui sought help from the national JACL and from friends in the camp at Minidoka, Idaho. The latter formed a "Civil Liberties League" and vowed "to see the Yasui case to a finish." On January 23 and 24, 1943, Masaoka spelled out what he meant by his warning that the JACL was *"unalterably opposed to test cases."* According to a confidential ONI report, he appeared at Minidoka, denounced the organization of the Civil Liberties League as a "stab in the back," and pressured its members into disbanding. Masaoka's logic was impeccable: If uncomplaining submission to the government's "humane and democratic resettlement of us unfortunate people" was the acid test of their loyalty, then legal challenges to the program—not to mention "troublemaking"—were sure proofs of disloyalty. Stabs in the back. For the JACL view, see Bill Hosokawa, *JACL in Quest of Justice* (New York: William Morrow, 1982).

The most extensive discussion of the general strike at Poston I appears in Alexander H. Leighton, *The Governing of Men* (Princeton, N.J.: Princeton University Press, 1945), pp. 162–244. But see also Edward H. Spicer et al., *Impounded People* (Tucson: University of Arizona Press, 1969), pp. 129–35. JACLer Togo Tanaka's firsthand account of the Manzanar revolt in Dorothy Swaine Thomas and Richard S. Nishimoto, *The Spoilage: Japanese-American Evacuation and Resettlement During World War II* (Berkeley: University of California Press, 1946), pp. 49–52, remains useful. For an outstanding recent analysis, see Arthur A. Hansen and David A. Hacker, "The Manzanar Riot: An Ethnic Perspective," *Amerasia Journal* 2 (Fall 1974): 112–57—the authors concluded "that there is strong reason to believe that the overwhelming majority of internees fully endorsed" the beating of JACLer Fred Tayama (p. 139). And for a valuable comparison of the events at Poston and at Manzanar, see Gary Y. Okihiro, "Japanese Resistance in America's Concentration Camps: A Re-evaluation," *Amerasia Journal* 2 (Fall 1973): 20–34.

Over the decades no one has done more than Bill Hosokawa to fulfill Masaoka's offer to have "Japanese Americans laud the work of the War Relocation Authority." A native of Seattle and a graduate of the University of Washington (1937), Hosokawa worked on English language newspapers in the Far East until just before Pearl Harbor, when he returned to join other members of the Seattle chapter of the JACL in pledging to inform on Issei and if necessary take them into protective custody. Interned in the Wyoming camp, he became editor of the *Heart Mountain Sentinel,* from which rostrum he enjoined compliance with WRA regulations, denounced "troublemakers," and lambasted "Tokyo's militarism" in words that caught the attention of outside newspapers: "Others would do well to remember that race is the only thing that a Tokyo Jap has in common with the Japanese American and his parents who repudiated their native land 30 or 40 years ago to make their future with the United States" (*Rocky Mountain News,* April 28, 1943).

Illustrating the symbiotic relationship of the WRA and JACL, Dillon Myer wrote a long letter on August 26, 1943, recommending this "young man in whom many of us are very much interested" to the publisher of the *Des Moines Register:* "His editorials, in the eyes of the WRA, have been extremely well written. . . . He has demonstrated beyond all possible doubt an intense loyalty to the United States and has been responsible for an unceasing program of Americanization in the Heart Mountain Center." After Myer helped him get a job with the *Des Moines Register,* Hosokawa moved on to the *Denver Post,* where he became editor of the editorial page before retiring. Along the way he has tirelessly advanced the WRA-JACL line in books and articles, including *Nisei: The Quiet Americans* and his "From the Frying Pan" column for the *Pacific Citizen:* "There was no intent to keep the evacuees penned up indefinitely. That's the reason the camps were called relocation centers," he wrote in his column for April 25, 1980. "And this is the reason Dillon Myer is saddened to hear the WRA centers referred to as concentration camps in the rhetoric of those who would keep alive the memory of that sorry national experience." Hosokawa's most recent effort to bury that memory and explain away "the undeserved hostility JACL had experienced from Nisei during the war years" was the 1982 organizational scrapbook he called *JACL in Quest of Justice,* which includes a photograph with the legend "An American concentration camp for United States citizens—Heart Mountain, Wyoming, Winter 1942–43." Can a suppressed "troublemaker" be hiding behind Hosokawa's affable exterior?

Myer had to know that "the attempts of the J.A.C.L. to claim leadership of the evacuees has been almost universally repudiated," for Solon T. Kimball of the WRA Community Government Section had so reported in 1942—see *Community Government in War Relocation Centers* (Washington, D.C.: Government Printing Office, 1946), p. 16. Yet he continued to ask the national secretary for his "judgments"—and for those of his successors after Masaoka went into the army—for he needed the JACL as a para-administrative arm. In return he bypassed the Issei and the critical Nisei to deal with the JACL as the only viable organization of all those of Japanese ancestry (the Nikkei). I am indebted to Frank Chin for the insights in his unpublished "Statement to the Commission on Wartime Relocation and Internment of Civilians," September 9, 1981.

In "Comparative Administration of Five War Relocation Authority Camps," Ph.D. diss., University of Pittsburgh, 1980, Rita Takahashi Cates dealt critically with the punitive attitude of JACL "American flag-waving zealots" (see esp. pp. 16–20, 79–94, 365). In November 1942, for instance, Ken Tashiro, editor of the camp newspaper *Gila News Courier,* demanded "stern and immediate punishment" for agitators and troublemakers: "Project Directors should revise their 'lenient attitudes'; temporizing, appeasing methods should be discarded. . . ." In his recommendations to Myer on segregation, Masaoka thus faithfully reported the taste for punishment of his "key people," who confronted challenges to their WRA-bestowed "leadership" with vindictiveness that outcolonized the colonizers'.

In "Our Worst Wartime Mistake," *Harper's* 191 (September 1945): 194, Eugene V. Rostow pointed out that "sympathy with the enemy is no crime in the United States (for white people at least) so long as it is not translated into deeds or the visible threat of deeds." Under Myer, the WRA made alleged sympathy a de facto if not de jure crime for the nonwhite Nikkei. In "The Japanese American Cases—A Disaster," *Yale Law Journal* 54 (June 1945): 490, Rostow cited *Keegan* v. *United States*, in which the Supreme Court reversed the conviction of members of the German-American Bund for conspiracy to obstruct the draft, and other cases involving persons who actively propagandized for the Axis cause.

Segregation: At a staff meeting in Washington on November 12, 1942, Myer noted that John J. McCloy was "very strongly sold now on the segregation policy . . . thinks we should move toward a segregation policy, in which I agree with him, but I told him we had all those other considerations" (JERS, 67/14, E2.11A). On December 14, 1942, Myer assured McCloy that "we are formulating a program of segregation of disloyal people and agitators, but I must say this phase of it is not so simple in view of the fact that the real agitators are not easy to locate" (JERS, 67/14, E6.00). Myer appointed a "segregation committee" composed of Solicitor Philip M. Glick, Chief of Community Management John H. Provinse, and Head Community Analyst John Embree. For the differing views of key staff members, see Glick's memorandum to Myer of March 5, 1943, JERS, 67/14, E6.00. Along with means, space continued to be a problem—on December 15, 1942, for instance, Myer asked McCloy to have men from the War Department inspect a location in Alexandria, Louisiana, where the Department of Justice had an internment center (JERS, 67/14, E2.05). Long before May 31, 1943, in fine, Myer had come out for mass segregation, had been trying to work out a program to implement it, and had no need to "capitulate" to the importunities of his project directors. In the meantime piecemeal segregation had proceeded on the basis of Myer's "unnumbered instruction relating to the removal of aggravated and incorrigible troublemakers" (John H. Provinse to Myron E. Gurnea, March 17, 1943, FBI 62-69030).

Even for aliens the legality of the friendly arrangement between Myer's WRA and Edward J. Ennis's Alien Enemy Control Unit was doubtful. As FBI Inspector Myron E. Gurnea observed in his comprehensive report: "It is also problematical whether Hearing Boards will intern alien Japanese who are only known troublemakers and have not engaged in any subversive activities jeopardizing the security of this country" (transmitted by Hoover to Myer, March 22, 1943, FBI 62-69030). The pity was that the immigrants, aged about sixty, had no rights any official bothered to treat with respect. Even had their arbitrary internment been legal, it was unconscionable. After the war, incidentally, Ennis became a member and later chairperson (1969–77) of the board of directors of the American Civil Liberties Union. In Washington, D.C., on November 2, 1981, he represented the ACLU at the hearings of the Commission on Wartime Relocation and Internment of Civilians. In his testimony he said nothing about his disregard for Issei civil rights decades earlier, though he did marvel as he looked back upon that era: "I don't know why I didn't resign."

At the conference with project directors in Denver on January 30, 1943, an amusing exchange took place during Myer's discussion of the "problem boys" he wanted to segregate. The WRA could "go all out on a mass segregation program again just like another evacuation" but that did not yet seem to him a "sound" plan. Commented Solicitor Glick quickly: "It's unconstitutional" (JERS, 67/14, E2.11B). That interjection was exquisite in view of the fact that Glick headed up a staff of eleven attorneys charged with seeing that the camps operated "within constitutional and statutory limits" (YoI, p. 143). It became even more exquisite once the defective data from the mass oath came in and Myer adopted precisely the plan Glick had himself tagged "unconstitutional."

Even Myer later admitted that "a bad mistake was made in the loyalty question" and tried to distance his agency from the chaos produced by the questionnaire: "The handling of the registration and the loyalty questionnaires was planned by the adjutant general's office, and the plans were completed and put into execution before WRA was consulted" (UA, pp. 72, 243). But the WRA had in fact been consulted, as Glick "altogether unofficially" told an interviewer on October 12, 1943, when he blamed "the whole mess" on Myer subordinate Thomas Holland, who had reviewed the forms and expressed no objection to questions 27 and 28 (Morton Grodzins, "Second Glick Interview," JERS, 67/ 14, E2.12). And at the time the WRA was "very glad" to have the War Department "conduct loyalty investigations of Japanese-American citizens," as Elmer M. Rowalt, Myer's deputy director, confirmed in a letter to McCloy on February 2, 1943 (JERS, 67/14, E2.06). The evidence confirms the charge of Francis S. Frederick: the effort of the WRA "to make it appear that the registration was an army order WHICH IT NEVER WAS shows WRA in its true light—playing the role of benefactor and attempting to hide behind the skirts of [an] ARMY ORDER" (to Robert F. Spencer, December 9, 1943, JERS, 67/14, S1.10).

In his presidential address "Anthropology and the Coming Crisis," *American Anthropologist* 79 (June 1977): 293–308, Walter Goldschmidt characterized the incarceration as "a case of rape," but then went on to note that "the anthropologists who went into the War Relocation Authority felt that they could serve to ameliorate this situation even if they could not stop it, and this they did" (p. 298). This a significant number of the twenty anthropologists (and seven sociologists) did not, as has been compellingly demonstrated by Peter T. Suzuki, a former inmate at Minidoka and a professor of urban studies at the University of Nebraska—see his "Anthropologists in the Wartime Camps for Japanese Americans," *Dialectical Anthropology* 6 (August 1981): 23–60. (Summaries of his findings and attempted rebuttals by former community analysts appeared in the *Omaha World-Herald*, October 4, 1981, and the *New York Times*, October 5, 1981.) Suzuki's painstaking research demonstrated that not a few social scientists—one of whom, as it happened, taught me sociology when I was an undergraduate—became informers and helped the keepers indoctrinate and control and punish their charges. Concentration camps corrupt.

CHAPTER VI.   "TROUBLEMAKERS"

The chapter epigraph is from Dillon S. Myer, Press Conference, May 14, 1943, JERS, 67/14, E2.04.

The invaluable "case histories" of Masao I. and other resisters (in JERS, 67/14, S1.20A) bothered Myer and his staff more than a little, as we shall see, when they were compiled by Leupp Internal Security Officer Francis S. Frederick.

A minor irony of the "real mess" at Tule Lake was the presence of Major S. L. A. ("Slam") Marshall as head of the army recruiting team. Given his assignment by McCloy's office in the War Department, Marshall had assisted in preparing the questionnaires, after his arrival assisted Coverley in bringing pressure on inmates to fill them out, and even after learning that doing so was optional, never revealed that fact while he was in the camp. Whether the historian was justified in making his veracity also optional remains a delicate question—afterward Marshall went on to become the chief historian of the European theater of operations in World War II and the much-honored author of more than thirty books about tactics and the American soldier in combat.

Forced Labor: Other resisters at the old CCC camp also testified to the army's role in the forced labor. Wherever he went, one Kibei later wrote at Leupp, "I was followed by [a] sentry with [a] bayonet. I have been put to work as [a] compulsory worker and if I refused the Lieutenant said a punishment of a 6x6x10 feet deep hole was waiting for me" ("Statement of Seio K . . . ," August 1943, JERS, 67/14, S1.20A). As a result of Attorney Bernhardt's warnings, the keepers eased up after a couple of weeks, as an intercepted letter of Yoshio Y. (#4) to his wife on March 16 showed: "Until last Saturday we were forced to work—dig ditches and cement works—like slaves. Then from Monday just the volunteers are asked to work with the threatenings that no work—not eat & put in jail pits. But officials are hesitating to enforce the threatenings. At present time I'm not working." Later at their "trials" whether or not an individual had worked "frequently made a difference of five or ten days in the length of sentence meted out," according to Frank Shotaro Miyamoto ("Crisis").

"WRA Law": From his end, Myer urged the FBI to bring charges against resisters under the Espionage Act "or some other way," a desperate catholicity that excluded no possibility, including that of bringing inmates before the bar of justice for loitering in their concentration camp—in fact, as we shall see, some were later sent to jail for "unlawful assembly" in their penal colony. From his end, Coverley explained to an FBI agent "that the policy was for the project officials to place into isolation or jails any and all Japanese who were causing any sort of trouble or disturbance, notify the USA[ttorney] with said facts and background, who in turn would secure a warrant and have the U.S. Marshal pick them up and return them to San Francisco for their hearings. . . . Upon returning to San Francisco the writer contacted Assistant U.S. Attorney A. J. ZIRPOLI for the details of the aforementioned arrangement between COVERLEY

and the U.S. Attorney's Office. Mr. ZIRPOLI admitted the above was the practice but stated that it was not too satisfactory" (Pieper to Hoover, April 29, 1943, FBI 62-70564). (Thus were troublesome Issei arbitrarily interned under the friendly arrangement worked out by Myer's WRA with Edward J. Ennis's Alien Enemy Control Unit in the Department of Justice.) Not celebrated for their devotion to civil liberties, FBI agents were nonetheless surprised—or awed—by the rough-and-ready way WRA officials made their own laws.

The WRA and the FBI: The interagency dispute at Tule Lake led to an exchange of letters between Myer and Hoover, with the latter laying out in emphatic detail why the FBI had exclusive jurisdiction, under executive orders, over violations of the draft law and sedition statutes (March 24 and 31, 1943, FBI 62-69030). Matters went from bad to worse a few weeks later when "Mr. Dillon Myer telephonically advised Assistant Director D. M. Ladd that he was quite disturbed over the fact that he had been advised that this Bureau was conducting investigations concerning three American-born Japanese who had been brought to Washington to work as stenographers for the War Relocation Authority," as Hoover reported to Attorney General Biddle. "Mr. Myer was advised that the investigations were being conducted on the request of the Office for Emergency Management and that the rooms of these individuals were not searched by Special Agents of this Bureau. He was also informed that in view of the feelings which he had expressed . . . the investigations were being discontinued, as well as all other investigations of employees or applicants for employment with the War Relocation Authority" (June 3, 1943, FBI 62-69030).

Alarmed, Myer tried to see Hoover to recreate their "harmonious relationship," but in the event had to settle for an audience with Assistant to the Director Edward A. Tamm: "Mr. Myer stated that he had made a mistake when he called Mr. Ladd recently . . . that he was all steamed up at the time he made the call, and that he did not realize that the investigation was in the nature of an applicant inquiry but thought the Bureau was checking up on 'suspicious Japanese.' . . . Myer talked at some length and ultimately stated that the War Relocation Authority would be 'sunk' if the Dies Committee learned that the Bureau had refused to conduct any further investigations for that agency" (memorandum for Hoover, June 22, 1943, FBI 62-69030). Despite this self-abasement, Myer was advised that in view of all the bickering and altercations the FBI preferred "not to be mixed up in their matters in any way." And that remained Hoover's attitude, as his numerous scrawls on documents attested: "such an outfit"; "shameful mess"; "that outfit can't be depended upon" (FBI 62-69030 and FBI 62-70564).

While inmates were effectively cut off from informed legal counsel, WRA Attorneys Edgar Bernhardt and Kent Silverthorne and of course Project Attorney Anthony O'Brien interviewed prisoners in jail and in the subcamp and energetically attempted to build sedition cases against them. O'Brien in particular was not fond of Japanese Americans, as his expressed wish to have a machine gun for five minutes hinted. His detailed letter of March 17 revealed how he went about accumulating evidence of sorts from "our latest informer," talking to Solicitor Glick in Washington "via the Tactical Line," joining "a flying squadron of we Caucasians" in a raid to capture inmates, and then grilling "them all the rest of the night" (O'Brien to Glick, JERS, 67/14, R6.20). He suspected that Yoshio Y. (#4) was the author of an antiregistration pamphlet: "He will not admit it but he was one of the principal speakers at the Block 23 meeting and we hope that the additional evidence which we expect to obtain tomorrow will pin this act on him." It never did, but that suspicion and Yoshio Y.'s temerity in exercising his First Amendment rights were sufficient to have him sent off to the penal colony before he had his day in "court." And as Masao K. (#5) recorded, for the defenseless prisoners who did have their "trials," O'Brien acted as "defense attorney for the W.R.A.," or as he himself might have put it, for "we Caucasians."

"If the U.S. government [had] wanted to run death ovens," the former Topaz inmate Harry H. L. Kitano has remarked, then "we would have marched quietly to our doom with only slight hesitation." In *Japanese Americans: The Evolution of a Subculture* (Englewood Cliffs, N.J.: Prentice-Hall, 1969), pp. 103–5, Kitano attributed this ominous readiness mainly to "the *Enryo* Syndrome," with the Japanese word *enryo* meaning restraint, shyness, submissiveness. Undoubtedly this cultural norm emphasizing conformity and obedience played directly into the hands of the WRA jailers. But, as Gary Y. Okihiro and other young Japanese American scholars have argued, the docility of their impounded forebears has often been exaggerated. In point were the Block 42 petitioners and those who followed in their footsteps notwithstanding the WRA's terroristic campaign against "agitators." And as a block resident admitted to an FBI agent, "the Block, almost to the man, was sympathetic to the cause of the petitioners" (Pieper to Hoover, March 10, 1943, FBI 62-70564). Under the circumstances such resistance and such sympathetic support were intractable assertions of self-respect and little short of heroic.

The "case histories" of the five resisters discussed in the text were, then, but the very tip of the iceberg. Had enlarging their number to ten or fifteen furthered our inquiry, I might easily have added that many more. Of the five, individual attitudes ranged from Masao K. (#5), who stated simply, "I have more sympathy for Japan," to Yoshio Y. (#4), who thought of himself "as being 100% American and wants to rear his children as true citizens of this country." With a brother in the U.S. Army and the rest of his immediate family in Japan, Kentaro T. (#2) had mixed feelings, a bit like the Kibei who was asked through an interpreter if he was loyal to the United States:

> "Well," he hesitated, "I don't know. I'm all mixed up. I'm half loyal to America and half loyal to Japan."
> Cozzens repeated the statement to Sgt. Tsukahara to be sure he heard right. "He says he's half loyal to the United States and half loyal to Japan?"
> The Kibei answered in broken English, nodding his head up and down contemplatively. "Yes, half loyal American, half loyal Japan. . . ."
> "You can't be loyal to both countries." ["Crisis"]

But he was and his loyalty, I have ventured, undivided or Janus-faced, was none of the business of Robert B. Cozzens or any other WRA official.

The Kibei interview just quoted comes from Frank Shotaro Miyamoto's "The Registration Crisis at Tule Lake," written while he was still on Thomas's JERS team. A member of the Seattle chapter of the JACL before Pearl Harbor, Miyamoto equated resistance to registration with "an anti-American stand" and vigorously searched for such "proof" of pro-Japan sympathies among the resisters. For all that, he was a conscientious, honest field observer and his running account of what Coverley called the "registration bedlam," based on his extensive notes and documents collected at the time, is indispensable for understanding events from the beginning of resistance through the "trials." "Project officials were convinced," Miyamoto observed, "that the resistance could be traced to 'pro-Japanese agitators' (Japanese nationalists) whose removal would break the back of the resistance, and the failure of evacuees to divulge information about members of their own group was interpreted, in the light of their resistance to registration, as indicative of their lack of 'loyalty' for this country." He assembled evidence that demolished this line of Coverley and company and, though he obviously wished otherwise, found the foundation of resistance instead "in the general mass of the population." After the war he reworked his materials in "The Career of Intergroup Tensions: A Study on the Collective Adjustments of Evacuees to Crisis at the Tule Lake Relocation Center," Ph.D. diss., University of Chicago, 1950. Subsequently, he became a professor of sociology at the University of Washington.

For a definition of *total institutions* and their need for secrecy, see Erving Goffman, *Asylums* (Garden City, N.Y.: Anchor Books, 1961), pp. xiii, 9, 105–6. The essential point is that "carceral systems," as Michel Foucault calls them, are complex coercive networks that share critical functions and inner dynamics—see his *Discipline and Punish*, trans. Alan Sheridan (New York: Pantheon, 1977); see also Gresham M. Sykes, *The Society of Captives* (New York: Atheneum, 1966). In their internal security appointments Myer and his aides recognized this close connection of their agency with other policing and penal organizations. One obvious example was the penologist they put in charge of security at Moab/Leupp. Another was National Chief of Internal Security Willard E. ("Huck") Schmidt, who came to the WRA from long service in the Berkeley, California, Police Department. Later (1944) Schmidt became chief of security at Tule Lake and was replaced by a still more explicit example: National Chief of Internal Security Arthur W. James, who advised the FBI "that he was formerly with the Federal Bureau of Prisons and had been released to the WRA Internal Security Division for the emergency" (SAC, Los Angeles, to Hoover, June 11, 1945, FBI 62-69030; see also N. J. L. Pieper to J. C. Strickland, January 25, 1944, FBI 62-70564). Like captors everywhere, furthermore, WRA leaders responded angrily to any challenge to their authority and quickly concluded, as did Myer and Coverley in response to the resistance at Tule, that "troublemakers" were behind it. This conspiratorial view of uprisings has a long and continuing history in prisons across the country—in 1971, for instance, officials in the Attica Correctional Facility pinned the explosion there on "leftwing radicals and 'troublemakers'" (New York State Special Commission on Attica, *Attica* [New York: Bantam Books, 1972], p. 104). And like captors at Attica and elsewhere, Myer and his aides established the practice of transferring "troublemakers" from one prison to another.

Troublesome guards were also shifted from prison to prison. Gila Director Leroy H. Bennett tried to have Francis S. Frederick transferred to Tule Lake and wrote Coverley on February 9, 1943, that "we are very anxious to complete this transfer and would appreciate your acceptance by teletype." The following day Coverley was advised by his assistant Joseph O. Hayes that this proposed transfer was "somewhat of a mystery. We are dubious of it in that it may be Mr. Frederick has had trouble at Gila and they are anxious in view of this to dispose of him to another project" (JERS, 67/14, R1.40). The Tule officials guessed correctly and were right to be wary—they might have found the obstreperous Frederick hard to handle. In "Cultural Politics in the Gila River Relocation Center, 1942–1943," *Arizona and the West* 27 (Winter 1985): 327–62, Arthur A. Hansen put the troubles in that camp in an illuminating context and briefly noted Frederick's role therein and his conflict with his superior, W. E. Williamson.

A graduate student in anthropology, Robert Spencer worked for Dorothy Swaine Thomas at Gila and elsewhere while studying the extent to which Japanese social customs had been carried over into the daily lives of the Nikkei. After the war he completed "Japanese Buddhism in the United States, 1940–1946," Ph.D. diss., University of California, Berkeley, 1946.

For Frederick's version of how he dispensed summary justice in the penal colony, see his memorandum to Raymond R. Best, "Facts Leading to the Arrest and Disposition of Twenty-One Residents of Moab Isolation Center for Unlawful Assembly," April 19, 1943, JERS, 67/14, S1.10).

A glimpse into what it meant for Moab Director Best to have the four Manzanar men "in a separate barracks under constant guard" came out in a letter from another member of the group: "The four were moved out and now they are living in a different building. They are watched by soldiers equipped with fixed bayonets at meal time, in the shower room and at the lavatory" (Tamotsu K. to Manzanar Block Leader 17, February 14, 1943, JERS, 67/14, S1.20A).

Airy authority for the WRA punitive system came from the following: the unnumbered administrative instruction, "Removal . . . of Aggravated and Incorrigible Troublemakers," February 16, 1943; it was superseded by Administrative Instruction No. 95, June 5, 1943 (see p. 105); that in turn was superseded by Manual Sections 30.1.100 to 30.1.113, sections that appeared in Manual Releases No. 6 and No. 39, both of which were finally cancelled by Manual Release No. 84 (NA, RG 210). In addition there were Administrative Instructions No. 84 on "arrests" and No. 85 on "trial and punishment," both issued on February 26, 1943. I list all of these instructions merely as bureaucratic curiosities, for WRA officials habitually broke their own rules. The administrative instruction on arrests (No. 84), for instance, provided that an arrested person be promptly informed of the charges against him and that "his case shall be docketed for trial before the Project Director or before the evacuee Judicial Commission within 48 hours [*sic*], and that the cases on the trial dockets shall be heard as promptly as possible," as Myer stiffly instructed Ernest Besig of the NCACLU on March 26, 1943 (CHS 3580).

Writing Robert Spencer on August 20, 1943, Frederick noted that his case histories were "hurriedly done but there is a lot of meat in them"—if the JERS team would guard them with their lives, he would send them for copying. Of course Spencer wanted them and on September 25 acknowledged their receipt with thanks, adding that he and "the boss . . . agree that there is some tremendously valuable information" therein (JERS, 67/14, S1.10). There surely was, and why Dorothy Swaine Thomas made so little use of the case histories in *The Spoilage* (1946) is curious—it was as if they were too hot for her to handle immediately after the war.

Half acknowledging and half bragging that his case histories had aroused the hostility of top WRA officials, Frederick told Spencer he honestly believed that "they are afraid of me—the sissies!" A few weeks later he reported that he had discovered "to my satisfaction that the WRA engineered my being drafted. It solved their problem in getting rid of me." Later he still thought so "but am not sure as yet" (December 7, 1943, JERS, 67/14, S1.10). One thing he could have been sure of—had Myer wanted to keep him out of the draft, he could have done so.

Hisato K.: The enormity and complexity of Myer's lockups—the eleven camps, counting the penal colony, the different conditions and "incidents" in each, the thousands shifted back and forth during segregation, and the hundreds placed in tight inner or remote prisons called "Isolation Centers"—all this has left individual victims faceless and unidentified, save for a few exceptional resisters such as Joseph Kurihara at Manzanar and George Kuratomi at Tule Lake. "The experiences of individual human beings, of the *people* who suffered because of the evacuation," Judy Tachibana has rightly observed, "should not be lost in the overall history of the event" (see her "Indefinite Isolation: The World War II Ordeal of Harry Yoshio Ueno," *Rafu Shimpo Supplement*, December 20, 1980, a sensitive tracing of the experiences of one sufferer). Compared with Kurihara and Ueno, with whom he did time at Moab/Leupp and then accompanied to Tule Lake, Hisato K. was a nobody, unknown then and unknown today right down to his surname. But his very anonymity gives his experiences special meaning—like the unknown soldier's story, if it could be unearthed, that of this unknown victim speaks for the many that must remain untold.

For data on the grim conditions at Tule Lake when Hisato K. and the other Leupp men arrived, see John P. Frank to Interior Undersecretary Abe Fortas, March 9, 1944, NA, RG 48. Ostensibly the army returned control of the main camp—not the stockade—to the WRA on January 15, 1944. But Lieutenant Colonel Verne Austin, the commanding officer at Tule, explained to the FBI that this was merely a public relations move originating in a demand of the Department of State

> that the Center be returned to the WRA as an aid in State Department negotiations with the Japanese Government relative to repatriation of nationals. AUSTIN said that in reality there will be no change in the functions being carried on by the Army at the Center inasmuch as the WRA is in no position to handle the camp and provide order at this time. He characterized the above procedure as "white wash" and "window dressing" by the State Department. He pointed out that this procedure makes his position, as well as that of the WRA, more difficult in view of the fact that any publicity which will reveal the true state of affairs will be regrettable. [N. J. L. Pieper to J. C. Strickland, January 25, 1944, FBI 62-70564]

Behind the window dressing was the ugly reality of the stockade, the key component of the terroristic operation. After a dispute with the army over how it should be run, the WRA took full charge of the stockade on May 24 and that finally meant resumption of control of the entire camp.

Problem Boys, Hardboiled Boys, Pressure Boys: One of the five men in Carl Mydans's photograph (p. 115) was obviously middle-aged and all were obviously adult, but they were still "boys" in the eyes of their captors. In his testimony before the Chandler subcommittee on November 24, 1943, Myer discussed the troubles at Tule Lake and mentioned some "boys" who had assaulted a white doctor:

> Senator [Chapman] Revercomb: You said "some boys." What age boys?
>
> Mr. Myer: When we speak about boys, they are usually between 18 and 25. Most of the people who serve in the capacity of strongarm boys are people who have been in Japan most of their lives and come back; they are the ones who normally cause real trouble. . . . They are generally the front boys. [U.S. Senate Subcommittee of the Committee on Military Affairs, *War Relocation Centers*, 78th Cong., 1st sess. (Washington, D.C.: Government Printing Office, 1943), part 4, 235]

More than another illustration of Myer's paternalism, the term of contempt had roots in the timeworn racist assumption that adult nonwhites are perennially childish. In his use of the epithet he unwittingly echoed the vocative "Boy!" when a century earlier a Southern planter or a British colonial summoned a gray-headed slave or an elderly manservant.

Circulated by the Student Relocation Council, excerpts from Thomas R. Bodine's report came to the attention of Tule Director Raymond R. Best, who complained about them to Community Management Chief John H. Provinse, who in turn wrote a stiff letter of reproach to Homer L. Morris of the American Friends Service Committee—Bodine attached copies of the report and of Provinse's reproach to his letter to Ernest Besig, September 28, 1944, CHS 3580. Provinse assured Best that he would take the matter up with the field secretary and noted that, "prior to receiving your letter I had seen excerpts from Bodine's letter and I was quite disturbed about them myself. His emotionalism is entirely unnecessary" (JERS, 67/14, R1.40). In the margin next to Bodine's remark about Hisato K.'s photograph in *Life*, one WRA official, possibly Best, had penciled "Don't like this!" and another, possibly Provinse, had agreed: "No!" Plainly the keepers did not like criticism and were disturbed by "emotional" reports and not by the haunting faces of men in their lockup.

One last particular in Hisato K.'s case suggests that he was probably let out of the stockade later that spring in time for him to be reapprehended in the main camp. On the night of July 2, 1944, Yaozo Hitomi, general manager of Tule Lake Coöperative Enterprises, Inc., and widely regarded as the camp's number one *Inu*, or informer, was stabbed to death by a person or persons whose identities were never established. But the keepers suspected former and present stockade prisoners of having incited the murder, and among those they picked up for questioning was Hisato K. Both angry and apprehensive, WRA employee Anne Lefkowitz surreptitiously informed Alice Adams, Ernest Besig's secretary in San Francisco, that the camp police were using methods "hardly short of murder":

> One of the Leuppe [*sic*] boys, Hisato K . . . was arrested and questioned all night. His questioning included what one might call third degree methods.

> This boy had been in the stockade before—in fact you might have seen his picture in *Life*, he was the one playing the guitar. . . .
> If you write to K . . . do so in a way that will suggest you are answering a query from him. You see all the mail to the stockade is censored and they might not let him see the letter if they thought it was the first one. He may not be in the stockade now but I am sure his mail will now be watched. [July 14, 1944, CHS 3580]

A confidential letter from Tule Community Analyst Marvin K. Opler to his superior Edward H. Spicer confirms this additional abuse of "the kid whose picture was in the March issue of *Life* strumming a guitar" (July 15, 1944, MKO). In or out of the stockade, Hisato K. was still doing hard time.

In his interview with Morton Grodzins, Myer concluded his ruminations on Leupp by observing that he "had hoped to send Glick and Provinse out to regularize the whole thing and perhaps even work out a scheme for liquidating the camp—but you know what has happened since it was set up. But I still hope to get rid of the thing. Don't ask me when" (JERS, 67/14, E2.10). On Grodzin's copy of the interview appears this handwritten notation: "At staff meeting 10/6/43—Myer announced conferences being held looking forward to closing up of Leupp." Francis S. Frederick's case histories were obviously helping Myer make up his mind.

CHAPTER VII. JAILER

The chapter epigraph is from "Address by Dillon S. Myer, Director of the War Relocation Authority, at Eagle Rock, California, June 19, 1945," NA, RG 48.

In the fall of 1943 Morton Grodzins and Frank Shotaro Miyamoto were in Washington working with WRA materials (Miyamoto to Dorothy Swaine Thomas, September 20, October 18, 1943, JERS, 67/14, W1.25C). Apparently Grodzins typed out his notes immediately after his interview with Myer on September 29.

For Roger Nash Baldwin, see Dwight Macdonald's profile, "The Defense of Everybody," *New Yorker*, July 11, 1953, pp. 31–55, and July 18, 1953, pp. 29–59, which Baldwin did not like very much. To understand the conflict between Baldwin and Ernest Besig and their respective offices, one needs to know that in those days "affiliates" such as the NCACLU in San Francisco and the SCACLU in Los Angeles—A. L. Wirin's bailiwick—were only tenuously related to the New York ACLU. The NCACLU had its own officers, budgets, and some members who did not belong to any other civil liberties group. Called "the Union," the New York group was very much its founder's creation. Asked once how important he was to that organization, General Counsel Arthur Garfield Hays said simply: "The American Civil Liberties Union *is* Roger Baldwin," and by that he had to mean the New York office thereof. (After Baldwin retired from the directorship in 1950, Macdonald pointed out, the structure became more democratic and the national organization is now separate from the New York City branch, which has its own officers and headquarters.) In effect, Baldwin's office was merely another city branch, but one that presumed to be the national trunk. This was the structural context of his demand that the San Francisco office abide by "national" decisions or get out: "Of course your committee is entirely free to withdraw from the Union and take another name, and it may be that your committee will regard that as the best solution" (to Besig, March 10, 1943, CHS 3580). To the end Besig neither withdrew nor allowed the NCACLU to be reduced to the status of Baldwin's agency: "If you want to proceed against us, I suppose you can always kick us out of the Union" (to Baldwin, September 21, 1945, CHS 3580).

The Seymour Resolution: After the war Baldwin told Dwight Macdonald, "I hated to write that one, and I'm ashamed of it now" (*New Yorker*, July 18, 1953, p. 52). Lucille Milner, Baldwin's secretary in the New York office for twenty-five years, supported the resolution, however, and discussed its background and the ensuing infighting in her *Education of an American Liberal* (New York: Horizon Press, 1954), pp. 295–308. In *Justice at War* (New York: Oxford University Press, 1983), pp. 108–9, Peter Irons maintained that the ACLU board of directors was split into factions led by Arthur Garfield Hays and by Morris Ernst, lawyers who shared the title of ACLU general counsel. Whether Hays or Norman Thomas led one faction and Ernst or Whitney North Seymour the other is of no consequence for our understanding of the controversy over what was, after all, called the Seymour resolution.

"Totalitarian Liberals": In addition to Norman Thomas's article in the *Christian Century* (59 [July 29, 1942]: 929–31), see his *Democracy and Japanese Americans* (New York: Post War World Council, 1943). Among other candidates for Thomas's bitter tag "totalitarian liberals," along with Baldwin, Ernst, John Haynes Holmes, and Arthur Garfield Hays, were Carey McWilliams, whom we have already encountered cheering on the exclusion, and Clarence Pickett of the American Friends Service Committee, who with Myer's help sent the telegram of misadvice to the Tuleans.

The cozy collaboration of reputed defenders of freedom of expression in the New York ACLU and official underminers of that freedom in the Roosevelt administration has yet to receive the attention it merits. When Baldwin became in effect an agent of the WRA, his General Counsel Morris Ernst had already become in effect an agent of the FBI by naming names for his "Dear Edgar," by sharing ACLU internal reports, memoranda, minutes of meetings, copies of letters, and the like, and by serving as Hoover's voice in ACLU councils—see Harrison E. Salisbury, "The Strange Correspondence of Morris Ernst and John Edgar Hoover, 1939–1964," *Nation* 239 (December 1, 1984): 575–89; and Frank J. Donner, *The Age of Surveillance* (New York: Alfred A. Knopf, 1980), pp. 146–47.

Except for A. J. Muste of the Fellowship of Reconciliation, Besig, and a few others, Thomas was almost the only nationally known figure on the Left who consistently denounced the uprooting and impounding of Japanese Americans. The World War II superpatriotism of the American Communist Party has been established too often to need restatement here. In New York the handful of Nisei Marxists in the Japanese-American Committee for Democracy championed the exclusion as an exercise in democracy and a contribution to the Allied cause (*Pacific Citizen*, June 25, 1942). Pointing out that Carey McWilliams served on the Japanese-American Committee's advisory board and citing other evidence of communist-liberal collaboration, William Petersen has argued that this approbation of the camps was the "consummation" of the Popular Front of the 1930s and has charged liberals with being frequently linked to the support, wittingly or unwittingly, of totalitarianism. I think he has exaggerated the extent of communist influence on organizations such as the ACLU—his thesis fits McWilliams better than it does Baldwin and Meiklejohn and it fits Besig and Wayne M. Collins not at all. Yet for all their overtones of red-baiting/liberal hating, Petersen's analyses merit close consideration—see his *Japanese Americans* (New York: Random House, 1971), pp. 72–79, and his "Incarceration of the Japanese Americans," *National Review* 24 (December 8, 1972): 1349–50, 1367–69.

The Korematsu case continued to be a bone of contention between the San Francisco and New York offices on into 1944 and all the way up to the Supreme Court. On June 5, 1944, Besig wrote Baldwin that Wayne M. Collins, Korematsu's counsel, had no objection to the New York office filing a further amicus curiae brief, but was opposed to sharing time for argument, and that no purpose would be served by appealing to him personally: "He feels very strongly that the National Office has been a hindrance and not a help in testing the exclusion and the detention of the Japanese" (CHS 3580).

ACLU-JACL-WRA: Evidence abounds that close working relationships kept the national line taut. Myer rode in tandem with Masaoka, as we have seen, and also shared information and documents with Baldwin. On August 31, 1943, for instance, he sent Baldwin the "confidential" case history of Roku M. (NA, RG 210), the former chief of the warehouse at the Heart Mountain Hospital and currently an inmate of Leupp. In turn Baldwin shared data and views with Myer and the JACL secretary—see, for example, his memorandum "for— Ernest Besig, A. L. Wirin, Mike Masaoka," April 19, 1943, CHS 3580. After talking on the telephone with Edward J. Ennis about Tule Lake and then "speaking today with Dillon Myer," Baldwin's aide Clifford Forster sent Besig a "confidential memorandum" on August 21, 1945, with carbon copies for "A. L. Wirin, [JACL President] S. Kido, RNB" (CHS 3580). On August 24, 1945, Besig responded sardonically: "I am very much impressed with receiving a 'confidential memorandum.' Is this top drawer stuff? Or may I show it to a few people in the Civil Liberties Union? The influence of Washington upon the Civil Liberties Union certainly shows itself at every turn. What you tell me is no more definite than that which I have already learned from other sources" (CHS 3580). He might have added that the influence of the JACL on the union, and vice versa, showed itself at every turn.

Solicitor Glick did his best to pull Besig into the fine understanding the keepers enjoyed with civil libertarians. On August 4, 1942, for instance, he wrote that he had "had a very pleasant discussion of our common interests with Dr. Alexander Meiklejohn yesterday afternoon" (CHS 3580). But Besig fortunately never accepted the WRA definition of "our common interests" and also refused to share Baldwin's enthusiasm for the JACL: "I think Mike Masaoka is as much a politician as the rest of them. The League won't contest any action that the government takes. It is prepared to play along and get the best deal possible" (to Baldwin, March 21, 1942, CHS 3580).

For Baldwin's account of Roosevelt as the ACLU's man and his recollections of that golden era, see Peggy Lamson, *Roger Baldwin: Founder of the American Civil Liberties Union* (Boston: Houghton Mifflin, 1976), pp. 254, 255–56. When Lamson reminded her subject that Dwight Macdonald had called his reaction to the evacuation "feeble and confused," she was surprised to hear him defend it in Nixonian terms: "Terrible, yes, sure. But, well—perhaps in wartime very difficult to say that national security shouldn't be the first consideration. After all, you have to win a war. You can't lose it" (see pp. 237–41, esp. 239).

> Here in the exiles'
> Monotonous life
> Only the seasons change.
> [Quoted in Patricia Ward Biederman,
> "Non-White Americans and Our 'Kid-Glove
> Concentration Camps,'" *Colleague* (SUNY, Buffalo)
> 6 (Fall 1969): 4]

The poignant protest in such *senryu* poems, along with *Kabuki* theater, *utai* singing, *kendo* fencing, and *sumo* wrestling, produced a flowering of Japanese fine arts and sports that Tule Community Analyst Marvin K. Opler called "culture revivalism" (for his discussion of Japanese wrestling in the camp, see "A 'Sumo' Tournament at Tule Lake Center," *American Anthropologist* 47 [January–March 1945]: 134–39). Forever blind to the truth that this cultural efflorescence represented the desperate effort of Tuleans to reassert their dignity and social identity, Myer and Best could see in it only the subversive cunning of their projected "pro-Fascist trouble-making minority." It was more than or other than that, of course, and Opler's insight merits more systematic study than it has received, for it invites comparative study of this "pent-up, hopeless people" with Native Americans and their Ghost Dance religion and with other colonized peoples elsewhere. For the underlying theoretical assumptions, see Anthony F. C. Wallace's seminal "Revitalization Movements," *American Anthropologist* 58 (April 1956): 264–81. In "Japanese Resistance in America's Concentration Camps," *Amerasia Journal* 2 (Fall 1973): 20–34, Gary Y. Okihiro contributed to the kind of analysis we need, recognizing the colonization of his people and citing "Japanese parental resistance to administrative efforts to win over the minds of their children. WRA intentions included the 'Americanization' of the Japanese to make them 'assimilable' into white America. Thus, anything which emphasized traditional Japanese roots was to be discouraged" (31).

Kiyoshi Okamoto: While still at Heart Mountain, this plucky inmate had written to the national ACLU asking for help in testing the constitutionality of drafting citizens from behind barbed wire. Roger Baldwin then responded with a letter he released to the press (*Heart Mountain Sentinel*, April 15, 1944). In it he laid down the law for Okamoto and the resisters: although the latter had "a strong moral case," they had "no legal case at all. . . . Men who counsel others to resist military service are not within their rights and must expect severe treatment." Neither Okamoto at Heart Mountain nor Kentaro T. (#2) and Yoshio Y. (#4) at Tule Lake, nor any other camp inmate, could expect support from Baldwin, who had himself gone to jail at the end of World War I for his opposition to the draft. But why did Baldwin make his letter public and help break the back of the Fair Play Committee? In "Heart Mountain: The History of an

American Concentration Camp," M.A. thesis, University of Wyoming, 1970, pp. 153–54, Douglas W. Nelson discussed evidence that "implies that Baldwin's action was initially requested by the Japanese American Citizens League's Salt Lake headquarters." Had he known of the national ACLU-JACL-WRA axis, he might have found his evidence more compelling and less surprising. (Nelson's able study was published in 1976 under the same title at Madison by the Wisconsin State Historical Society.)

Okamoto's case provides another vivid illustration of how Myer and his aides dealt with their critics. Born in Hawaii, intelligent and well-educated, Okamoto had turned over the name of his Fair Play Committee to draft-age inmates in February 1944 and thereafter gave them guidance "but not as a participant," he told Besig. "I had no reason, I was beyond the age limit" (interview, July 10, 1944, CHS 3580). Notwithstanding his inactive role, the Heart Mountain Director, Guy Robertson, expressed alarm over Okamoto and assured his boss that he was watching him closely and "would be able to upset his apple cart pretty soon" (to Myer, February 12, 1944, NA, RG 210). When FBI agents came up empty-handed, Myer nonetheless asked Hoover for "the considerable amount of information" they had supposedly collected, assuring him "that the privilege of using the report . . . would assist us materially in maintaining order in the Center and protecting the national interest" (April 28, 1944, FBI 100-164195). Hoover had practically no evidence, as Solicitor Glick disappointedly informed Myer (May 25, 1944, NA, RG 210), but evidence was beside the point in the hearing Okamoto was granted "looking toward transfer to Tule Lake," as Glick put it.

A few days after his interview with Besig at Tule Lake, Okamoto was the government's principal target in an indictment that included Frank Seichi Emi and the other five men I have named in the text. It also included James Matsumoto Omura, Mike Masaoka's antithesis in his testimony before the Tolan Committee in 1942 (see book epigraph), and subsequently the English language editor of the Denver *Rocky Shimpo*, in which position he had provided a public platform for the Fair Play Committee. In November 1944 a Cheyenne jury acquitted Omura of conspiracy against the draft, but found Okamoto and the other six men guilty; only after a year in prison were they released when the Tenth Circuit Court of Appeals found that the judge's instructions to the jury had been improper. In sum, Okamoto's experience confirmed his earlier charge that, like "Hitler and Stalin," WRA officials punished any inmate who dared protest their absolutism.

In the meantime sixty-three Heart Mountaineers had accepted the logic and moral thrust of the Constitution and the Bill of Rights, as they read them, had refused induction, and had then been indicted at WRA behest, found guilty, and sentenced to three years' imprisonment (*CC*, p. 127). But in California U.S. District Judge Louis E. Goodman dismissed indictments against twenty-seven Tuleans charged with Selective Service violations: "It is shocking to the conscience," said the judge in words Okamoto might have used, "that an American citizen be confined on the ground of disloyalty and then, while so under duress and restraint, be compelled to serve in the armed forces or be prosecuted for not yielding to such compulsion" (*Newell Star*, July 27, 1944). In a confidential communication to "All Project Directors," Dillon Myer warned that this setback would play into the hands of draft evaders and add to the flood of requests for expatriation and changes in answer to the loyalty question: "There is reason to believe that many of these actions were prompted by a desire to facilitate draft evasion. The recent decision of Judge Goodman dismissing the prosecutions against Tule Lake evacuees who refused to obey Selective Service calls will provide an additional incentive for evacuees at other centers to take action which they believe will result in denial of leave clearance and transfer to Tule Lake [and thereby escape from the draft]" (August 10, 1944, NA, RG 210). Myer's vengeful hounding of draft evaders and draft resisters and their supporters like Okamoto and Omura stood in ironic contrast to his own "embarrassing" and evasive exemption that had made him feel "a bit of a slacker" during World War I (Auto, p. 147). His total inability to identify with his charges and to look at anything from their point of view meant that his conscience would never be shocked by what seemed so plain to them—and to Judge Goodman.

Shortly after his return from Tule Lake, Ernest Besig wrote WRA employee Katherine Hobbie: "Goodness knows that I should have visited the Center long before this, because I can see now that the present administration takes the attitude that the end justifies the means, even if civil liberties are abridged" (July 13, 1944, CHS 3580). It was unfortunate, if understandable, that he did not get up to Tule Lake during the loyalty oath/registration crisis of February–March 1943. But once he did make the trip and found out what was happening, he kept his promise "to see that the WRA was put in its place."

WRA personnel were thorough in their denial of due process. In addition to eavesdropping on Besig's interviews, they also monitored telephone conversations and intercepted written communications between the stockade prisoners and their counsel. For instance, San Francisco SAC N. J. L. Pieper reported that one man had written "a letter to Besig dated July 21, 1944, in which he instructed Besig to proceed with the cases on their behalf" (August 17, 1944, FBI 62-70564).

Later Wayne M. Collins wrote to a "renunciant" in Tokyo: "For your information I have absolutely no use whatever for the JACL, the American Civil Liberties Union of New York, a corporation of which Roger Baldwin is a director, Al Wirin of Los Angeles, or of any of the officers, directors or agents. . . . This is because I know said entities to be more interested in the betrayal of civil liberties issues than in their preservation and because they have for some three years steadily endeavored to interfere with the legal rights of these unfortunate people" (to Frank Akira K., July 7, 1948, CHS 3580). When a copy of the letter was forwarded to John Haynes Holmes, the chairman of the national board of the ACLU, Holmes complained to Bishop Edward L. Parsons that Collins's charges were not only "unwarranted, but are indecent and scandalous." Parsons in turn forwarded the correspondence to Besig with a chuckle: "They are naturally stirred up to think that a member of the local board affiliated with them thinks that they are betraying civil liberties" (October 19 and 28, 1948, CHS 3580).

Patently, Collins could be painfully direct. Bill Hosokawa reported that he told him he had nothing but "utter detestation for the JACL; they're nothing but a bunch of jackals." When JACLer Hosokawa pressed him for details, he reportedly said: "The JACL pretended to be the spokesman for all Japanese Americans but they wouldn't stand up for their people. They didn't speak up for the *Issei*. They led their people like a bunch of goddam doves to the concentration camps" (*Nisei* [New York: William Morrow, 1969], p. 423). But he complained that even this denunciation had been bowdlerized and fell short of the immeasurable contempt for "jackals" he never disguised. To Donald Collins of Athens, Georgia, he wrote explaining that "Bill Hosokawa wrote the 'nisei.' It is trash. It quotes me, but the quote is a misquote because what I said to him the one time he talked to me by phone was a damned sight harsher than the quotes he credits to me" (July 14, 1971, WCP, 78/177).

WRA employee Anne Lefkowitz was another of Besig's sources on the beatings in November 1943. After he spoke with her on his visit to Tule the following July, she was called into an assistant director's office, grilled about her connection with the NCACLU director, whether she had asked him to come, had given him names, and the like. Gloria Waldron reported this harassment to Besig with an apt comment: "The concentration camp atmosphere isn't all on the colony side of the fence" (July 19, 1944, CHS 3580).

Old boys from the Soil Conservation Service stuck by one another. The network included Myer, Best, and Clarence E. Zimmer and branched out in all directions. For instance, Tule Chief of Agriculture Clifford Kallam identified Regional Director Robert B. Cozzens "as a good friend of his" who had helped him get the job. FBI agents reported this as the return of an earlier favor: "He advised that he has known COZZENS for the past twenty years and met him at Watsonville, California when COZZENS was engaged in the construction business. According to KALLAM, COZZENS lost money on two jobs and found it necessary to obtain other employment. KALLAM advised that through his efforts, he procured a job for COZZENS with the Soil Conservation Corps, United States Department of Agriculture." And so on and on.

The "Riot": In his affidavit in Wayne M. Collins's *Abo v. Clark* case [77 F. Suppl. 806 (1948)], former Tule Legal Aid Counsel Tetsujiro Nakamura stated flatly: "On November 4, 1943, the troops were called into the inner camp to suppress a riot which never occurred and which was never even threatened." Apart from such major exceptions as Michi Weglyn, writers have simply perpetuated the WRA's suspect claims without subjecting them to close scrutiny and without investigating counterclaims such as Nakamura's. The most recent instance in point is to be found in the report of the Commission on the Wartime Relocation and Internment of Civilians, *Personal Justice Denied* (Washington, D.C.: Government Printing Office, December 1982), p. 210: "When the rioters moved toward the project director's house, the military guard was called in" and the commissioners' endnote refers the reader to Dorothy Swaine Thomas and Richard S. Nishimoto, *The Spoilage: Japanese-American Evacuation and Resettlement During World War II* (Berkeley: University of California Press, 1946), pp. 142–46. But Thomas and Nishimoto too trustingly relied exclusively on the WRA's *Semi-Annual Report*, July 1 to December 31, 1943, pp. 21–23, and quoted extensively from that document for their "bare facts" without independently investigating what were more probably bald untruths. Alas, the commissioners have compounded the sloppy scholarship of 1946 by putting their 1982 imprimatur on the WRA's cover-up.

While the mass demonstration was being "staged" on November 1, a separate group of inmates clashed with Tule Chief Medical Officer Reese M. Pedicord in the hospital and beat him. Director Best advised FBI agents that the beating "was provoked by the fact that Peddicord [sic] was disliked by the Japanese, as he runs the hospital in his own way, takes no dictation from Japanese, and refers to the Japanese as 'yellow bellies,' without respect for their feelings." Later interviewed, Doctor Pedicord said "he has never met any really good Japanese doctors" and advised the FBI agents

> that if he were left to his own methods he could identify all of his assailants. He said that he would do this by "beating the living tar out of them" until they would admit their participation or inform of [or on] those who did participate. . . . Dr. Pedicord said that he served two years in the army and that he believes in firm disciplinary action. He indicated by several remarks made in the course of the interview that he favored the use of third degree methods in obtaining confessions from the Japanese. He indicated this by favorable comment on the activities of some of the WRA police regarding the Japanese after the riot occurred. [Gurnea, FBI 62-70564]

Sharing the widespread urge to punish "yellow bellies," Doctor Pedicord was plainly one of those staff members who believed that inmates "were at last getting 'exactly what they deserved,'" as Emily Light recorded.

Stories of Emily Light's scandalous behavior were rife among staff members. One "Caucasian" (C) told FBI agents she was one of the schoolteachers of "an 'overly sentimental missionary type' who made a special point of inviting Japanese to their homes in order to show that they had no prejudice so far as race or color is concerned. [C] said that she was sure that no immorality was involved in these visits and that it was a case of 'pure silliness' on the part of the persons who did this. . . . According to [C] most of the stories concerning Miss LIGHT were spread by the former project attorney ANTHONY O'BRIEN, who evidenced a great dislike for the Japanese." A worthy successor, Project Attorney Kent Silverthorne advised agents that "one Emily Light and other members of the Fellowship of Reconciliation were commonly seen with their arms around Japanese women." Worse yet, Colonel Austin had personally seen her embracing a "Japanese" man: "He further advised that she had been observed on various occasions hugging Japanese upon their departure from the Center and that her latest demonstration of affection in this regard took place on November 10 when the Colonel personally saw her with her arm around a Japanese just as the Japanese was ready to board the train." Inspector Myron E. Gurnea carefully sifted these "wild rumors," concluded that in fact "at least one employee was seen on numerous occasions with her arms around evacuees," and formally recommended "that any relationship beyond necessary administrative contacts with the evacuees be absolutely forbidden except with the express authority of the Project Director" (FBI Investigation, "Tule Lake Relocation Center," November 12 to December 15, 1943, FBI 62-70564).

In her own interview, Emily Light practically condemned herself by frankly explaining to agents "her views concerning the intermarriage of persons of different races. She stated that she felt that if two persons such as a white person and a Negro or a white person and a Japanese were really in love, she could see no objection to their marriage." Moreover, "she advised that in her opinion, the Japanese who were taken from their homes and brought to the camp have been very unjustly treated, particularly the Nisei group and she believes that individual investigation should have been conducted and only those who were determined disloyal segregated" (Gurnea, FBI 62-70564).

"*Belligerent*" *Pacifists*: In their total institution WRA officials had long found worrisome, if not intolerable, the presence of clerical employees such as Gloria Waldron and Anne Lefkowitz—who discovered after Besig's visit that she was "not considered reliable"—and schoolteachers such as Light and Jean McKay of the Northern California Fellowship of Reconciliation (NCFOR). An analytical study of their presence in the camp and of the reactions to them by the rest of the WRA staff is badly needed. During the loyalty oath/registration crisis, Dillon Myer sent the then Director Harvey M. Coverley a confidential list of names that included those of McKay, Light, Goldie Nicholson, and fourteen other suspect teachers, calling his particular attention to the fact that

> two of the women mentioned (Miss Nicholson and Miss Light) are described as dangerous to administration and as leaders in the anti-war propaganda organizations which is [sic] reported as active at Tule Lake. Why the Tule Lake schools are so disproportionately staffed with pacifists of such belligerent type is not understood here, but if such is the case early corrective measures must be taken. . . . Since most of the appointees concerned have been on WRA rolls less than a year, no formal charges need precede their dismissal. Records should be developed, however, and specific reasons for dismissal should be assigned, if resignations are not secured. . . . The people concerned are probably well-meaning and sincere, though it would not be surprising to find on closer analysis a heavy trace of frustration and martyrdom. In any event, their presence on the project in such numbers and with such zeal for their beliefs is extremely undesirable at the present time. [March 31, 1943, JERS, 67/14, E2.04]

In the event, Myer's "belligerent" teachers were not dismissed en masse, as he demonstrably wanted, though Jean McKay and others were induced to resign. Like Emily Light, most stayed on and were on hand the next winter to be depicted by the press as "plants"—namely, white pacifists "who had incited the Japanese to riot," as McKay (by then NCFOR field secretary) complained to FBI agents and the *San Francisco Examiner* (see the issues of December 7, 8, 1943). Hence, not only did "the concentration camp atmosphere" mentioned by Gloria Waldron make a casualty of truth, at the same instant it made another of the First Amendment for both inmates and dissident staff members.

"*Renunciants*": On April 29, 1948, U.S. District Judge Louis E. Goodman entered a surprising interlocutory judgment in favor of Collins's many desperate clients. Judge Goodman again came up with just the right words of sharp reprimand: "It is shocking to the conscience that an American citizen be confined without authority and then while so under duress and restraint for his Government to accept from him a surrender of his constitutional heritage" (*Abo v. Clark*, 77 F. Suppl. 806). A concise statement of the background of this case appeared in the June 1948 issue of Besig's *ACLU-News*:

> It had no backing from any organized group except the ACLU of Northern California. Indeed, even the national office of the ACLU opposed any intervention because the renunciants had been labeled "disloyal." It forbade the filing of a mass suit by the local

Executive Committee, but then supported "administrative relief" in well-screened cases. Finally, it agreed to the filing of a few test suits, which the local branch opposed in the absence of an agreement with the Justice Department that the remaining renunciants would not be shipped to Japan while suits were pending. The renunciants finally engaged Attorney Wayne M. Collins, a member of the local committee, to file a mass suit, and the local committee voted to support the suit. After many months, the Union's national office endorsed the mass suit "in principle." The suit charged duress by the W.R.A., the Justice Department, and the Army, while the Union's national office wanted to absolve these Governmental agencies of responsibility and merely charge duress by pro-Japanese individuals and groups as well as parents. Judge Goodman's decision found, however, that there was Governmental duress.

On March 23, 1949, Judge Goodman entered a final judgment declaring all renunciations unconstitutional. The government appealed and a year later the Ninth Circuit Court of Appeals found that Goodman had erred in "lumping the cases." Collins then faced truly Augean labors: henceforth, the cases of his clients, who had come to number 5,000, had to be handled individually, a task that consumed his next eighteen years (*YoI*, pp. 262–63).

In early 1946 Collins's mass suits had been grievously weakened and the government's subsequent appeal of Judge Goodman's decision commensurately strengthened by *Murakami* v. *United States* (176 F. 2d 953), a prior case filed in the same court in behalf of three renunciants represented by Abraham Lincoln Wirin and J. B. Tietz, both attorneys from Los Angeles, acting on behalf of the New York ACLU. This intrusion into the San Francisco committee's bailiwick and the conspicuous failure of Wirin and Tietz to charge official duress triggered the NCACLU's denunciation of the New York ACLU for "playing the government's game": unwilling or unable to try Collins's nearly 1,500 clients (at that point), the government naturally welcomed trying only three and the bargaining factor of the mass action was lost in the process (Besig to board of directors, March 11, 1946, CHS 3580). Collins was also convinced there had been "connivance on the part of the ACLU of New York and Southern California with Justice Department and WRA officials. . . . The entering of judgment in the *Murakami* case first—by by-passing mine—set up conditions which enabled the same court to order the mass suits re-opened to allow the Justice Department to introduce additional evidence" (*YoI*, p. 323n).

Left with the disastrous consequences of this setback on his hands, Collins warned all his clients not to "be alarmed by any newspaper or magazine article you have read or may read about these cases. . . . Spokesmen for the JACL, the ACLU of New York and other persons who know nothing about the cases and are ignorant of your rights have made false statements concerning the cases. They long have been unfriendly to renunciants. Do not trust or rely upon any publications or statements of spokesmen for the JACL and the ACLU of N.Y. about the cases. Those people are not friendly to you" (December 29, 1951, WCP2).

In view of this conviction, which he carried with him to his grave, the eulogy that appeared in the *Pacific Citizen* on August 9, 1974, was more than ironic: "Seldom in history," said JACL Executive Director David Ushio, "does there appear a person possessing the moral courage and finely-honed sense of justice comparable to Wayne Collins." Collins might have snorted that those he called "jackals" were still hunting in packs and feeding on the defenseless. In contrast, I think he would have been moved by Michi Weglyn's words of sorrow and dedication: "Wayne Collins passed away suddenly on July 16, 1974, yet he lives on in the memory of thousands who were the beneficiaries of his fierce dedication to justice" (*YoI*, p. 322n).

On November 29, 1864, White Antelope sang his death song in front of his lodge at Sand Creek, Colorado, until U.S. soldiers cut him down—see Angie Debo, *A History of the Indians of the United States* (Norman, Okla.: University of Oklahoma Press, 1985), pp. 194–95.

For the fight over the wording on California Registered Historical Landmark No. 850, see "Manzanar—the Continuing Struggle: An Interview with Sue Kunitomi Embrey," in *Voices Long Silent: An Oral Inquiry into the Japanese American Evacuation*, ed. Arthur A. Hansen and Betty E. Mitson (Fullerton, Calif.: California State University, 1974), pp. 161–89, esp. 175. An unquiet Nisei, Sue Kunitomi Embrey had been managing editor of the *Manzanar Free Press*; in the late 1960s she became one of the founders of the Manzanar Committee.

For Bruno Bettelheim's analysis of the psychological impact of the "extreme situation" inmates experienced in the Nazi camps, see his essay on schizophrenia in the *American Journal of Orthopsychiatry* 26 (1956): 507–18, and *The Informed Heart* (Glencoe, Ill.: Free Press, 1960).

When Technical Sergeant Zentaro A. was killed in action in Italy the WRA publicized his death as a newsworthy first: "The WRA said this was believed to be the first death of a Japanese-American soldier whose parents are living at the Tule Lake center. Sergeant A . . . leaves five brothers and two sisters, also at the segregation center" (*Sacramento Bee*, July 22, 1944). (As noted in the text, two months later Myer could add another forty-four bodies to the count.) When the dead sergeant's mother wrote Besig a year later, Mrs. Tane A. probably had assistance in composing her letter—perhaps she was helped by Tule Legal Aid Counsel Tetsujiro Nakamura. At all events, "the utter desolation" of her heart was all hers. A week later one of her daughters, Yukuye Dorothy, also wrote Besig confirming the family's despair and wondering, with all the others, "is there any hope for me?" (September 13, 1945, WCP, 78/177).

And then there was a letter to Besig from Mr. and Mrs. Kentaro N., two citizens who had become "renunciants" because of their "intention of visiting parents who were residing in Hiroshima City, Japan, but having learned of the complete destruction that desire of visiting them is all gone" (September 2, 1945, WCP, 78/177). Was there any hope for them?

CHAPTER VIII.   COMMISSIONER

In addition to his speeches (all in the NRC), Myer's major statements of policy appeared in the following: "The Program of the Bureau of Indian Affairs," *Journal of Negro Education* 20 (Summer 1951): 346–53; and "Indian Administration: Problems and Goals," *Social Service Review* 27 (June 1953): 193–200, a paper originally presented at the Western Governors' Conference in Phoenix the preceding December. See also Dean Frank T. Wilson, "Interview with Dillon S. Myer," *Journal of Religious Thought* 7 (Spring/Summer 1950): 93–100.

Myer's BIA "demolition enterprise": Collier compiled "A Partial List of Personnel Changes," October 1, 1952, JCP, that went on for three pages and began with his note: "The following are but a partial list. . . . There have been a total of approximately 24 key personnel changes in addition to those listed below." See also Harold L. Ickes, "The Indian Loses Again," *New Republic* 125 (September 24, 1951): 16; and the *Nation* editorial, "The New Commissioner of Indian Affairs" 170 (June 10, 1950): 560. In "The Erosion of Indian Rights, 1950–1953: A Case Study in Bureaucracy," *Yale Law Journal* 62 (February 1953): 348–90, Felix S. Cohen discussed some of the personnel changes in Washington and noted that "on the reservation level, some of the best of the older Indian superintendents have been pushed out of the service; increasingly their places have been taken by former detectives and prison wardens" (pp. 383–84). Cohen cited two cases: "Thus a superintendent suspected of being too 'soft' (*i.e.*, sympathetic) to the Indians and Eskimos of Alaska was replaced by a former F.B.I. agent, and a superintendent suspected of being too 'soft' towards the Blackfeet Indians of Montana was replaced by a former warden of a W.R.A. detention camp" (p. 384n). In Alaska the shift was from Don C. Foster, who had antagonized whites by standing up for native rights, to Hugh J. Wade, a former cop with no Indian experience; in Montana it was from Rex D. Kildow to Guy Robertson, whom we have previously encountered as director of the WRA camp at Heart Mountain, Wyoming, and whom we shall meet again, after we consider the still more dramatic case of the superintendent of the Carson Indian Agency in Nevada.

After her resolution was defeated in 1950, Reva Beck Bosone (D., Utah) reintroduced it in the second session of the 82nd Congress. It then became H.J. Res. 8, the bill that carried the "final termination" language. Concurrently (April 10, 1952) in the Senate two staunch Myer supporters, Clinton P. Anderson (D., New Mexico) and Arthur V. Watkins (R., Utah), introduced S. 3005, a bill "to facilitate the termination of Federal supervision over Indian affairs in California." Spearheaded by Western congressmen, "the final termination" of "the Indian problem" was thus a bipartisan campaign that gained momentum under Truman and culminated with the dismembering legislation finally passed during the Eisenhower years.

A. J. Liebling's four-part Pyramid Lake series "The Lake of the Cui-Ui Eaters" appeared in the *New Yorker*, January 1, 8, 15, and 22, 1955. I am indebted to Liebling for his perceptive profile of Senator Patrick A. McCarran and his war against the Paiutes, for the quotation of Lieutenant J. M. Lee on the murderer of Truckee John, and, of course, for his interview of Superintendent Alida Bowler. Sarah Winnemucca Hopkins was married to her last husband, Lewis H. Hopkins, when she wrote *Life Among the Piutes: Their Wrongs and Claims*. Edited by Mrs. Horace Mann, the book was privately printed in Boston and New York in 1883. In 1969 it was reprinted by the Chalfant Press in Bishop, California. Gae Whitney Canfield's *Sarah Winnemucca of the Northern Paiutes* (Norman, Okla.: University of Oklahoma Press, 1983) contains careful research on which I have drawn freely for biographical details, including Indian Agent

W. V. Rinehart's affidavits against the "Harlot and drunkard" (p. 173), the Humboldt code (p. 49), and William Tecumseh Sherman's telegram on Kintpuash and the other Modoc prisoners of war (p. 83).

For Indian Commissioner Francis Amasa Walker's *Report for 1872*, see Wilcomb E. Washburn, ed., *The American Indian and the United States* (New York: Random House, 1973), I, 176–84, esp. 179.

In addition to A. J. Liebling's shrewd analyses of the hearings on McCarran's perennial Pyramid Lake bill, see the columnist Marquis Childs's assessment of one version, "McCarran Strikes Again," *Washington Post*, October 13, 1950.

The National Congress of American Indians (NCAI) had been founded in 1944 by the larger tribes and its legal counsel was not incidentally James E. Curry. The NCAI coordinated the fight against the transfer of Superintendent E. Reeseman Fryer—see the NCAI press release of October 15, 1950, AAIA. NCAI Executive Director Ruth Muskrat Bronson wrote Dillon Myer on October 31, 1950, enclosed a copy of her letter to Oliver La Farge, and noted that "La Farge must have had my letter at hand when he talked with you in Albuquerque. We have no indication that you did not tell him much the same thing you told us about the situation" (NRC). A writer and the president of the Association on American Indian Affairs, La Farge did talk with Myer in New Mexico and later included this first in a list of charges he pulled together against the commissioner: "The removal of E. R. Fryer and the Commissioner's statement to various people, including the President of this Association, that his transfer from Carson City was ordered with his agreement and approval. The point should be made that this transfer was arbitrary and contrary to the wishes of both Fryer and the Indians." As a result of this experience and others, he wrote in another context, "I am convinced that the man's a liar and I hope we can get the point across" ("Considerations on 'a Bill of Particulars,'" September 23, 1952, AAIA). On this occasion in particular Myer did not follow through on the old army motto, "Cover your ass," though he tried, belatedly, to set the record "straight." In a "Memorandum Relating to the Testimony by James E. Curry before the Senate Committee on Interior and Insular Affairs on Attorney Contracts with Indians, January 28, 1952," Myer recorded:

> On page 341, Mr. Curry made the statement, "The result was that the superintendent who tried to help the Indians was fired." This statement is not true. It just so happened that the superintendent was asked to transfer to another reservation at the same grade. The proposal to transfer has no relationship whatsoever, as far as the Indian Bureau is concerned, to the land and water problems of the Pyramid Lake Paiute Indians. [February 6, 1952, NRC]

In "Go East, Young Indian!" *New Republic* 125 (September 3, 1951): 17, Harold L. Ickes cut through Myer's lame denials:

> When questioned about the incident, Commissioner Myer admitted that McCarran had asked for the transfer of Fryer, while denying that the removal was the result of McCarran's request; it was merely coincidental—or so Myer would have people believe—that his "quickie" order of transfer followed McCarran's demand. He did not explain why a subordinate [certainly H. Rex Lee] promptly called McCarran's office to apologize and to explain that the removal order had been stopped, regrettably, by the White House.

These niceties of detail, gathered from Ickes's former subordinates in the Interior Department, left Myer's just-so story dangling.

During the fight over his proposed transfer, Fryer wrote Collier asking if some national magazine might not assign a reporter to do an article on Mc-Carran and his land-steal legislation: "Alida Bowler believes, and she is here, that an inquisitive reporter might find facts which might possibly tie him up with both the gambling and dope interests in Nevada" (October 5, 1950, JCP). This was the kind of thorough investigation A. J. Liebling published in the *New Yorker* five years later, but by then McCarran was dead and Myer was no longer commissioner. Collier added a postscript on Fryer in *From Every Zenith* (Denver: Sage Books, 1963), p. 373: Fryer "is now back in Indian Service, as Director of Indian Resources, through appointment by present Indian Commissioner Philleo Nash."

In the hearings on McCarran's first bill (1937), Collier outlined the process whereby the squatters took possession of the people's land and cited the murder of Truckee John, whereupon Senator Elmer Thomas interrupted with this comment: "As far as I am personally concerned, I have very little interest in that ancient history." A dozen years later the Humboldt code on which the murderer acted was still not ancient history to the lake people, as Avery Winnemucca's testimony in the 1949 hearings made plain: "There at . . . what is known as the Hill Ranch, in 1867, July 4—this date stands out vividly among the Indians. . . . some white men who wanted that field, because it was all irrigated, they killed Truckee John, shot him in the back, killed him outright because they wanted his field." No so outright and so bloody in the twentieth century, the Humboldt code survived in the lack of interest of Senator Thomas and his brethren, in the tenacious encroachments of whites on Indian land, and in assorted individual abuses. Delegate Albert Aleck, Winnemucca's brother-in-law who drove the schoolbus on the reservation, told A. J. Liebling of one case in point: "When we go to Washington, we see plenty of buck. Buck they pass. But back when my father had a little farm down by Wadsworth and a white man wanted it, they got him off fast enough. The agent came down to the house one night and said, 'Here's twenty dollars. Get out.' My old man got out" (*New Yorker*, January 15, 1955, pp. 49, 56). And after all, McCarran's war against the Paiutes was simply the Humboldt code in modern dress.

For additional details on Myer's paternal solicitude for the funds of the Pyramid Lake Tribal Council, see the letters to the editor of Avery Winnemucca et al.—and the editor's note thereto—and of Alexander Lesser in the *Washington Post*, October 27, November 2, 1951.

CHAPTER IX. "WILY" INDIANS

The chapter epigraph is from Dillon S. Myer, memorandum for Interior Secretary Douglas McKay, March 20, 1953, NRC.

Francis Amasa Walker's *Report for 1872*, an abridged version of which was cited in chapter 8, was also published in the April 1873 issue of the *North American Review* and as *The Indian Question* (Boston: James R. Osgood, 1874), wherein will be found his advocacy of "*strict reformatory control*." In

Iron Cages: Race and Culture in Nineteenth-Century America (New York: Alfred A. Knopf, 1979), pp. 181–88, Ronald T. Takaki discussed the commissioner's ignorance of his charges and advocacy of "scientific management." See also James P. Munroe, *A Life of Francis Amasa Walker* (New York: Henry Holt, 1923). The Native Americans were "a recognized evil," Walker noted in his report, and he gloated openly over their destruction: "Never was an evil so gigantic environed, invaded, devoured by forces so tremendous, so appalling in the celerity and the certainty of their advance."

To read the reports of successive Indian commissioners is to encounter variations on this theme of smashing the tribes, breaking up their landholdings, and making the surviving red individual over into what John Collier rightly called "an imitation white man." In his *Report for 1906*, for instance, Francis E. Leupp—after whom the school where Myer later had his penal colony was named—declaimed that "the legislation of recent years shows conclusively that the country is demanding an end of the Indian question and it is right" (Wilcomb E. Washburn, ed., *The American Indian and the United States* [New York: Random House, 1973], II, 747–66). Collier's particular bête noire was Charles Henry Burke, commissioner from 1921 to 1929. Accompanied by Interior Secretary Hubert Work, Burke invaded the Taos Pueblo's council "to tell them that they were 'half-animals' by virtue of their 'pagan worship' " (*From Every Zenith* [Denver: Sage Books, 1963], p. 136). In this and in his rabid assimilationist policies, Commissioner Burke was the precursor of Commissioner Myer. Said the former: "I believe in making the Indian take his chance, just the same as white folks do" (quoted in Herbert Corey, "He Carries the White Man's Burden," *Colliers*, May 12, 1923, p. 13).

In addition to Collier's autobiography, just cited, see his *Indians of the Americas* (New York: W. W. Norton, 1947). On his policy, I have been quoting in the text from his "Genesis and Philosophy of the Indian Reorganization Act," in *Indian Affairs and the Indian Reorganization Act: The Twenty Year Record*, ed. William H. Kelly (Tucson: University of Arizona Press, 1954), p. 5. For differing assessments of his Indian New Deal, see Kenneth R. Philp, *John Collier's Crusade for Indian Reform, 1920–1954* (Tucson: University of Arizona Press, 1977); Graham D. Taylor, *The New Deal and American Indian Tribalism* (Lincoln: University of Nebraska Press, 1980); and Lawrence C. Kelly, *The Assault on Assimilation: John Collier and the Origins of Indian Policy Reform* (Albuquerque: University of New Mexico Press, 1983). In *The Nations Within: The Past and Future of American Indian Sovereignty* (New York: Pantheon Books, 1984), Vine Deloria, Jr., and Clifford Lytle scrupulously weighed the strengths and weaknesses of Collier's innovations.

The groundwork for a new Indian policy had been laid when Collier assumed office in 1933. Some of the changes recommended by Lewis Meriam et al., *The Problem of Indian Administration* (Baltimore: Johns Hopkins University Press, 1928)—called the Meriam Report—had been initiated by Commissioner Charles James Rhoads, who nevertheless continued the traditional policy of individualization and assimilation. The Indian New Deal reversed the direction and emphases of this policy and nowhere more than in the matter of Indian rights. Indispensable for understanding how sharp the change was between the pre- and post-Collier years is Felix S. Cohen's "Erosion of Indian Rights," *Yale Law Journal* 62 (February 1953): 348–90. Useful overviews that also include the Myer years are Theodore H. Haas, "The Legal Aspects of Indian Affairs from 1887 to 1957," and William Zimmerman, Jr., "The Role of the Bureau of Indian Affairs since 1933," in the symposium "American Indians and American Life," *Annals of the American Academy of Political and Social Science* 311 (May 1957): 12–22 and 31–40. "White Americans seem continually to be rediscovering the Indians," observed symposium editors J. Milton Yinger and George Eaton Simpson, and twenty years later, they repeated their observation in another *Annals* symposium on "American Indians Today": though there had been changes, reprinting their original foreword might "suggest the distance we have yet to go before the country has truly redefined its racial and ethnic practices." In like fashion and like Columbus, Commissioner Myer had made his own misdiscovery of *Los Indios*, "the Indians," and delayed significantly that fine day of redefinition. In this symposium, see Raymond V. Butler, "The Bureau of Indian Affairs: Activities since 1945," and James E. Officer, "The Bureau of Indian Affairs since 1945: An Assessment," *Annals* 436 (March 1978): 50–60 and 61–72.

On Harold L. Ickes, see his *Autobiography of a Curmudgeon* (New York: Reynal and Hitchcock, 1943) and his *The Secret Diary of Harold L. Ickes*, 2 vols. (New York: Simon and Schuster, 1953). For his early years I have found useful Linda J. Lear's *Harold L. Ickes: The Aggressive Progressive, 1874–1933* (New York: Garland, 1981). During Secretary Chapman's hearings on attorney contracts, Ickes wrote that he had wanted to appear to present his views on the proposed "deceits and injustices": "Unfortunately, I am laid up, with a very painful and enervating disease, at Georgetown University Hospital and it is quite impossible for me even to attempt to attend this hearing" (Ickes to Chapman, January 4, 1952, JCP). He hoped it would be kept open until he could present his views in person, but that too proved impossible. The game old man died a few weeks later—see Walter Lippmann's obituary, "Harold Ickes: American Fundamentalist," *New York Herald Tribune*, February 7, 1952.

Editorial opposition to Myer's attorney regulations appeared in the *New York Times*, October 15, 1951; the *Washington Star*, January 6, 1952; and the *Washington Post*, August 29, 1952. A useful series by Anthony Leviero on the "Antagonisms Rife over Indian Policy" appeared in the *New York Times*, November 1, 2, and 3, 1951.

Especially after Chapman's hearings, Myer seethed with animus against the "wily, more competent Indians." Not lacking his own wiles, the commissioner sent out other letters misrepresenting the Pyramid Lake controversy. Elizabeth H. Baker of State College, Pennsylvania, for example, showed that she had been taken in by one: "It is easy to see from your letter that this case has been misrepresented. You state that 46.5 acres are involved: the enclosed clipping sent to me by a friend gives the figure as 2000 acres" (Baker to Myer, November 26, 1951, NRC).

Compare the account of how Myer "just grinned" at the delegation from the Pueblo of Taos with that of Elizabeth C. Bumgarner, the president of the Ute Indian Affairs Organization, who with her husband was granted an hour of the commissioner's time when he visited their reservation in Utah:

He allowed us 1 hour of his time in which he sat and toyed with his keys and watched his watch as though he was so disgusted with what we were saying. I presented to him things that I stated that I could prove about Tribal Business and my husband presented things concerning happenings of the government work here. The Commissioner did not even note down one thing that I or my husband said. . . . In fact he told us we were too emotional and that we had chips on our shoulders. . . . Now the thing I don't seem to be able to grasp is how the Commissioner intends finding out the Indian problems if he doesn't let someone tell him what they are. [Bumgarner to Senator George W. Malone, December 3, 1951, NRC]

Instances abound of Myer's laughing off or impatiently dismissing the grievances of his charges. See especially the official "Transcript of Meeting of August 21, 1952, at the Fort Peck Indian Agency Between the Tribal Executive Board and The [sic] Commissioner of Indian Affairs," NRC.

The runaround suffered by Rufus Wallowing was standard operating procedure in Myer's BIA. In the spring of 1951 he issued regulations that required tribal governing bodies to obtain special permission from him to send delegates to Washington. As Collier commented to Ickes, "It amounts to telling the tribes: 'No use seeing or communicating with the Commissioner. . . . "Runaround" is my, Myer's, formula for all of you'" (April 5, 1951, JCP). When he could not head off some delegations, such as that from Pyramid Lake, he refused to see them or saw them briefly and impatiently, as in Wallowing's case. For the runaround given the Standing Rock Sioux, see Ickes's "'Justice' in a Deep Freeze," *New Republic* 124 (May 21, 1951): 17. Or as Paiute delegate Albert Aleck put it, "when we go to Washington, we see plenty of buck. Buck they pass."

Amusingly, BIA officials outside the charmed circle also experienced the runaround, as former Assistant Commissioner Willard W. Beatty reported after his resignation: "Dillon also accepted the present dictum of the administrative theorists that no man should have more than six people 'reporting to him' most seriously and made himself inaccessible to all but Rex Lee, his Chief Counsel [Edwin E. Ferguson], Bart Greenwood [Lee's aide], and [the inevitable Morrill M.] Tozier (the head of Information). In theory, Pop Utz and John Provinse had access to the royal ear—but in practice, John was soon left in outer darkness and relegated to Rex Lee as a Court of Last Resort" (to Collier, August 10, 1954, JCP). Of course, tribal delegates such as Wallowing sought their rights from Myer and officials such as Provinse merely sought his royal ear, so the runaround had a different meaning to the keepers and the kept.

For John Ross's observation on unforgiving victimizers, see Michael Paul Rogin, *Fathers and Children: Andrew Jackson and the Subjugation of the American Indian* (New York: Alfred A. Knopf, 1975), p. 231.

Collier's contention that both Chapman and Truman wanted to get rid of Myer found confirmation in a report of Alexander Lesser, executive director of the Association on American Indian Affairs. With access to Philleo Nash, the White House liaison with the Interior Department, William Zimmerman, and others, Lesser learned shortly after the hearings "that Chapman is now utterly convinced that Myer must go. . . . Chapman discussed this with the President and the Pres agrees. In fact Chapman tried to suggest a place to which Myer could be kicked upward, but the President refused to consider Myer for 'a promotion' but wanted him out. The fact that Chapman is definitely set on getting

Myer out is now known to Myer, therefore in all probabiloty [*sic*] to [Senator] Anderson. As I suggested earlier, it seems . . . that Myer's present lifeline is a combination of his new Budget, and the defense of it, and the continuation of the Anderson hearings" (to Oliver La Farge, February 16, 1952, AAIA). But then those congressmen had descended on the White House to save Myer from being an example of Truman's celebrated motto: "The buck stops here." If this was in fact what happened, as seems likely, then Myer had boxed in both the interior secretary and the president, no small achievement for a farm-reared lad from Ohio.

Myer's lifeline had already brandished his hearings over Chapman's head: "Senator Anderson urged Secretary Chapman to hold up approval of pending lawyer contracts until after the subcommittee inquiry. He said he hoped to open it in December or early January" (*New York Times*, November 9, 1951). Only Anderson's illness kept him from anticipating Chapman's hearings; it delayed his own until January 21, 1952, but then he and Myer quickly made up for lost time. On June 24, 1952, Anderson's subcommittee issued a two-page interim report charging Chapman to be vigorous and vigilant in protecting "the rights of Indians against unscrupulous activities," a charge that underscored and reaffirmed the threat Myer had already sent to the secretary. That warning was renewed once again in the Anderson subcommittee's partial report, issued on January 16, 1953, by which time it simply rubbed in Myer's victory over Chapman (see U.S. Senate Committee on Interior and Insular Affairs, *Attorney Contracts with Indian Tribes*, report No. 8, 83rd Cong., 1st sess. [Washington, D.C.: Government Printing Office, 1953], pp. 1–25). For Anderson's war against the Pueblo of Taos and his Indian-hating generally, see the concise discussion in Edgar S. Cahn, ed., *Our Brother's Keeper: The Indian in White America* (Cleveland: World Publishing, 1969), pp. 108–10, 165–68. In 1963 Anderson turned over his chairmanship of the Interior and Insular Affairs Committee to Senator Henry Jackson, who continued his advocacy of the interests of white Americans and the abolition of the special status of red Americans.

"Chapman is still holding our arms while Myer, Anderson and McCarran slit our throats," James E. Curry wrote Collier on June 29, 1952. "If you think this is an overstatement, read the enclosed resolution that Avery [Winnemucca] and I drafted before he went home. It tells how the Pyramid Lake Indians were hoodwinked. This happened only because Chapman has refused to permit these people to have legal help. . . . McCarran now thinks he has me on the run and has come out [in the Senate, June 25, 1952,] with a direct personal attack on me. I am sending you also a copy of his attack and a copy of my reply" (all of which are in the JCP). In "Speaking for Indians," an eloquent counterattack and defense of his record that appeared in the *Washington Post* of August 30, 1952, Curry outlined how he was being investigated to death and concluded with a realistic prediction: "I expect that I, a single 'mouthpiece' of the Indian, can and will be destroyed. But the voice of the national conscience will not thereby be permanently stilled." When Curry had charged Myer to his face with trying to put him out of business, the latter dictated another interesting memorandum for the files: "I made it quite clear to Mr. Curry that he was the one who had assumed that we were trying to put him out of business, that I had never made such a statement. . . . He further stated that this action would bankrupt him. I told him I had no knowledge that this would be the case, excepting his statement" (February 13, 1951, NRC). The commissioner had cunningly not made the lawyer privy to the truth: "we were very happy about" his being chased out of business (Auto, p. 303).

CHAPTER X. "FOMENTER OF TROUBLE":
FELIX S. COHEN

The chapter epigraph comes from "Statement by Commissioner of Indian Affairs Dillon S. Myer Concerning Felix S. Cohen's Memorandum on S. 2543," n.d., NRC.

The biographical data on Felix S. Cohen come from the FBI reports cited in the text and from *Felix S. Cohen: A Fighter for Justice*, ed. Theodore H. Haas (Washington, D.C., Chapter of the Alumni of the City College of New York, 1956), the source for the quotations of Ernest Nagel (p. 13) and Ralph S. Brown (p. 16).

Area Director Paul L. Fickinger was one of those who "lost" tribal attorney contracts: "Take the Ft. Belknap group[,] for example[,] which has been trying for about 16 months to get a Cohen contract approved, and can get no action of any kind. The neighboring Blackfeet have Cohen, and his staunch action for them and against Fickinger and his ilk have cost him the stubborn enmity of that man and those who support him from higher up" (Alexander Lesser to Oliver La Farge, October 9, 1950, AAIA).

Area Director G. Warren Spaulding, with Myer's approval, was indeed using federal credit funds to beat down criticisms of waste and corruption, as Oglala delegate Ben Chief charged (Transcript of "Hearings on Proposed Regulations . . . ," JCP) and as documents the agents collected during their investigation fully confirmed (see FBI 100-378472).

On Blackfoot Superintendent Guy Robertson treating Indians as children— whether young or old in years—by telling them when to go to bed, see also George Dixon, "Washington Scene," *Washington Times-Herald*, May 15, 1952. For Myer's justification of Robertson's calling out armed BIA employees to close down a tribal polling place and otherwise deny the tribe its charter-mandated rights, see his letter to Secretary Chapman, May 28, 1952, NRC.

Were character assassination ever funny, Myer's unceasing efforts to develop the maximum possible distrust of Cohen would have been ludicrous. As we have seen, he worked for the Blackfeet and other tribal clients as their general counsel, and that work had no connection with any claims they may have been pressing before the Indian Claims Commission. And had he accepted claims cases after January 2, 1950, by which time the necessary or statutory two years after leaving government service had elapsed, he would have been doing nothing illegal. That even after that date he had separated himself completely from claims work represented higher ethical standards than the Hatch Act required. Thus, "Commissioner Myer's false charge of Cohen's interest in claims would have no validity for discrediting him even if true," Oliver La Farge explained to a member of the AAIA Board of Directors, "except that when one says, 'millions of dollars,' everyone pricks up his ears and begins looking for skulduggery." The plain truth was that the AAIA general counsel was not after the big money:

> I happen to know that he has never received any compensation of any kind, including expenses, for his work for the All-Pueblo Council. As that work involves travel among other things, he is heavily out of pocket. I have good reason to believe that in several other instances the token payments he receives do not even begin to cover his costs. In personal communication to me he has shown somewhat my own feeling about my involvement with Indian affairs—it is an unconscionable drain of time and strength that one can ill afford. [La Farge to Charles de Y. Elkus, September 30, 1952, AAIA]

Within his family and among his friends, Cohen's selflessness was legendary. Lucy Kramer Cohen had to exert prodigious effort to get him to buy an extra suit or topcoat, and they did not own a car until 1951, when he bought a relic for $100.00.

CHAPTER XI. TERMINATOR

The chapter epigraph is from Dillon S. Myer, memorandum for Interior Secretary Douglas McKay, March 20, 1953, NRC.

On December 3, 1952, Myer submitted to the Indian Affairs Subcommittee the detailed information it had requested—see U.S. House Committee on Interior and Insular Affairs, *Report with Respect to the House Resolution Authorizing the Committee on Interior and Insular Affairs to Conduct an Investigation of the Bureau of Indian Affairs* [pursuant to H.R. 698], House Report No. 2503, 82nd Cong., 2nd sess. (Washington, D.C.: Government Printing Office, 1953). Two former WRA applied anthropologists played key roles in laying out the theoretical justifications for Myer's termination policy. See the *Report* just cited for John H. Provinse's "Withdrawal of Federal Supervision of the American Indian," a paper presented at the National Conference of Social Work, San Francisco, April 15, 1947 (*Report*, pp. 179–88). In "The Indian Bureau and Self-Government," *Human Organization* 8 (Spring 1949): 11–14, John F. Embree held up the WRA as a model for phasing out the BIA: "The basic problems of liquidating wardship and a bureau which encouraged it were much the same, if on a smaller scale, as are found today in Indian reservations and the Indian Bureau" (p. 12n). Embree's piece was in effect a call for Myer to come in and repeat his marvelous feat of assimilation and dismantling. It appeared, not incidentally, in the journal of the Society for Applied Anthropology, whose president was Assistant Commissioner John H. Provinse.

In response to Frank George's letter to all the tribal council chairmen, Myer circulated a memorandum in which he did not apologize for withholding his plans for "withdrawal programming" but did make explicit the threat he was holding over every tribe in the country: "Should all reasonable efforts fail to develop a joint program, then it would be incumbent upon me to present the facts to Congress and make suitable legislative recommendations" ("General Position of the Bureau with Respect to Withdrawal," October 10, 1952, NRC).

For Herman Melville's overview of the terrain of racial hatred, see his chapter "The Metaphysics of Indian-Hating" in *The Confidence-Man: His Masquerade*, ed. Elizabeth S. Foster (New York: Hendricks House, 1954). I follow Indian-haters across the span of Anglo-American history in *Facing West: The Metaphysics of Indian-Hating and Empire-Building* (New York: New American Library, 1980).

On the meaning of Northern Cheyenne land to the tribe, see John Wooden Legs's statement in Angie Debo's *History of the Indians of the United States* (Norman, Okla.: University of Oklahoma Press, 1970), pp. 314–15. Incapable ever of seeing anything from the tribal point of view, Myer lamented in his autobiography that "the matter of holding onto lands just because they are Indian lands is one that has developed into a real problem" (Auto, p. 298).

On Myer's use of boarding schools to get "Navaho youngsters" off their reservation, see William Zimmerman, *Annals of the American Academy of Political and Social Science* 311 (May 1957): 35. Unlike Felix S. Cohen, Zimmerman did not have a firm grasp on the history of the Indian Service or he would have known that the charter of the first Navaho boarding school, established at the turn of the century, stated that its fundamental purpose was "to remove the child from the influence of his savage parents," and that was precisely Myer's purpose a half-century later. I discuss Thomas L. McKenney's similar use of the mission schools in *Facing West*, pp. 187–88.

Roger Williams's correspondence about the Pequot war "orphan" appears in the *Winthrop Papers* (Boston: Massachusetts Historical Society, 1943), III, 436–37, 458–59.

Abusive Indian-child–welfare practices had a long history leading up to Myer and continued apace after he left office. In the mid-1970s the AAIA estimated that one third, or nearly 100,000, of the tribal children were living apart from their families in foster homes, group homes, institutions, or boarding schools. Not until November 8, 1978, did Congress pass the Indian Child Welfare Act (Public Law 95-608) in an attempt to protect the integrity of tribal families and their governments and to curb child placement against the will of the family and other abuses Myer had systematically programmed.

Genocide: In *Axis Rule in Occupied Europe* (Washington, D.C.: Carnegie Endowment for International Peace, 1944), p. 79, Raphael Lemkin applied the term to actions aiming "at the destruction of essential foundations of the life of national groups, with the aim of annihilating the groups themselves," an application cut to fit Myer's termination policy like a glove. For the background and text of the Genocide Convention, see the *Yearbook of the United Nations, 1948–49* (New York: Columbia University Press, 1950), pp. 953–60. In the debate over earlier drafts, a UN committee had at first included an article forbidding "cultural genocide," but "at its 83rd meeting, the committee decided by twenty-five votes to sixteen, with four abstentions, not to include provisions relating to cultural genocide" (p. 954). Nevertheless, the fifth act forbidding the forcible transfer of children was a holdover from the secretariat's consideration of cultural genocide and that had direct application to what Myer was doing. Hence, Collier could justifiably charge the commissioner with committing "social genocide." For wide-ranging and thoughtful analyses of this topic generally, see Leo Kuper, *Genocide* (New Haven: Yale University Press, 1982) and *The Prevention of Genocide* (New Haven: Yale University Press, 1985).

Knowledgeable about Native Americans, Oliver La Farge of the AAIA revealed his utter ignorance of Japanese Americans during the desperate pre-election search for an alternative to Myer: "I heartily agree with you about picking some candidates for the commissionership. Have you any suggestions? A friend of mine here [in Santa Fe] suggested Bendetsen, now Assistant Secretary of the Army, as a desirable Republican. The suggestion, I think, came mostly from his personal admiration for the man, and I have no reason to believe that he would be interested in accepting the job" (to Charles de Y. Elkus, September 5, 1952, AAIA). Karl R. Bendetsen, the reader will recall, had been John J. McCloy's man in the Western Defense Command during World War II, and as such a prime mover in the uprooting and penning of the Japanese Americans. Even fleetingly to think of replacing Myer with Bendetsen was to think of compounding infamies.

In his autobiography, Myer made his pages on Native Americans a compendium of the racist clichés accumulated over the Indian-hating centuries since the European invasion of the continent (see Auto, pp. 284–92). Myer made his contempt for their pasts and their treaties explicit by his ridicule of one tribe that had a treaty

> which provided that they should get a certain number of yards of calico each year under the treaty and in spite of the fact that their population had increased and that each one would only get a quarter of a yard of calico apiece they insisted upon having the calico doled out each year to each member of the tribe! I presume this was important to them as a[n] indication that the treaty was still in effect. . . . So they weren't willing to abandon even this one. There were many other items that were holdovers, I am sure, from the early days and from early treaties. [Auto, p. 257]

The high symbolism of treaties for tribal peoples was lost on their programmer, who did not see in these documents the embodiments of historic commitments of the United States. As with the museum pieces fetishistically clutching their bits of calico, so such parchment "holdovers" had to be abandoned to the childish early days.

Termination: For the disastrous consequences of the termination program and acts, see William A. Brophy and Sophie D. Aberle, *The Indian: America's Unfinished Business* (Norman, Okla.: University of Oklahoma Press, 1966); Gary Orfield, *A Study of Termination Policy* (Chicago: University of Chicago Press, 1966); and Kirke Kickingbird and Karen Ducheneaux, *One Hundred Million Acres* (New York: Macmillan, 1973). Useful for both analysis and bibliography is Frederick J. Stefon's "The Irony of Termination: 1943–1958," *Indian Historian* 11 (Summer 1978): 3–14.

Myer and his staff had vainly attempted to rebut Cohen's essay in the *Yale Law Journal* (62: 348–90) with some rambling "Indian Bureau Comments on an Article by Felix S. Cohen, 'Erosion of Indian Rights, 1950–1953: A Case Study in Bureaucracy,'" n.d., NRC. In his memorandum for Secretary McKay, Myer cited that essay as an instance of his nemesis's ability "to capitalize on any weak points" in laws, regulations, and procedures (March 20, 1953, NRC).

In addition to the article and the essay already cited, see Cohen's "Alaska's Nuremberg Laws: Congress Sanctions Racial Discrimination," *Commentary* 6 (August 1948): 136–43; "Americanizing the White Man," *American Scholar* 21 (Spring 1952): 177–91; "First Americans First," *New Leader* 36 (January

26, 1953): 15–18; and "Indian Wardship: The Twilight of a Myth," *American Indian* 6 (Summer 1953): 8–14. The last article cited was reprinted, along with other relevant pieces, in *The Legal Conscience: Selected Papers of Felix S. Cohen*, ed. Lucy Kramer Cohen (New Haven: Yale University Press, 1960), pp. 328–34.

Had Secretary McKay and Commissioner Emmons requested the "further investigation" Myer called for, it would never have had a chance to get underway. On October 19, 1953, Cohen died of lung cancer at the untimely age of forty-six. The Blackfeet lost their brother and we lost a man capable of writing the kind of great work on the first Americans that Henry David Thoreau had underway before his still more untimely death a century earlier. To his final breath Cohen was an honest and brilliant "Double Runner" between the tribes and white Americans. Perhaps John Collier said all that needed saying in his letter of condolence:

> Felix's death has shattered me as no death since my Mother's and my Father's, in boyhood, has done. Indeed, I do not know the whole of the reason myself. The agony is on account of all the Indians—and of you and your children—but it is yet more. . . . I daren't come to the funeral tomorrow—No more. Felix is my highest experience of power of thought united with disinterested power of action. [Collier to Lucy Kramer Cohen, October 20, 1953, JCP]

D'Arcy McNickle's reference to "a holocaust in the making" appeared in his biography of Oliver La Farge, *Indian Man* (Bloomington, Ind.: Indiana University Press, 1971), p. 161.

EPILOGUE

My data on Myer's career after he left the Indian Service come from his oral autobiography (Auto); see also Robert M. Kvasnicka and Herman J. Viola, eds., *The Commissioners of Indian Affairs* (Lincoln, Nebr.: University of Nebraska Press, 1979), p. 298.

Graham Greene based his title character in *The Quiet American* (1955; reprint, New York: Penguin Books, 1977) on Edward Geary Lansdale, the Central Intelligence Agency official who led the first team of American fighting men into Indochina in 1954. I once thought of discussing Myer as Lansdale's mainland counterpart in *Facing West: The Metaphysics of Indian-Hating and Empire-Building* (New York: New American Library, 1980); for Lansdale, see pp. 374–442. Both gained their reputations handling natives, with Myer the domestic side and Lansdale the overseas side of the same coin. In Alden Pyle, Greene captured their likenesses.

"*Sansei Activists*": For a makeshift, ambivalent account of the background and early stages of the "search for redress," see Bill Hosokawa, *JACL* (New York: William Morrow, 1982), pp. 321–59. Unfortunately still not in print is the unapologetic "Repairing America: An Account of the Movement for Japanese-American Redress" (1984) by William Minoru Hohri of the National Council for Japanese American Redress. On March 16, 1983, the NCJAR sued the government for 27.5 billion dollars on behalf of 125,000 victims (*William Hohri et al. v. United States*, U.S. District Court for the District of Columbia,

Civil No. 83-750). On May 17, 1984, Judge Louis Oberdorfer dismissed the suit because the statutes of limitations had run out. Hohri et al. appealed and on January 21, 1986, a three-judge panel of the U.S. Court of Appeals for the District of Columbia Circuit, in a two-to-one decision (no. 84-5460), overturned Oberdorfer's dismissal and remanded the suit back to the lower court. Judges James Skelly Wright and Ruth Bader Ginsburg ruled that the statutes of limitations did not bar the plaintiffs' claims for unjust takings of property under the Fifth Amendment. Normally these statutes would apply, they held, but the founding fathers had "also most certainly assumed that the leaders of this Republic would act truthfully. In the main, history has proved the Founders correct. We have also learned, however, that extraordinary injustice can provoke extraordinary acts of concealment. Where such concealment is alleged, it ill behooves the government of a free people to evade an honest accounting." As this is being readied for the printer, the class action lawsuit is very much alive, in fine, and Judges Wright and Ginsburg have just handed down their opinion that "today, now that the truth can be known, the government says that the time for justice has passed. We cannot agree."

In the legislative branch a number of redress bills have been introduced over the past few years. Currently the House Judiciary Subcommittee on Law and Governmental Relations has scheduled hearings for April 28, 1986, on H.R. 442. The companion redress bill in the Senate is S. 1053.

Myer's "Written Testimony" appears in the CWRIC hearings in Los Angeles, August 4, 1981, pp. 288–99. It contains a plug for his ally: "I am not very happy with my efforts with writing the introductory remarks for Lillian Baker's book 'Watergate West, the Concentration Camp Conspiracy,' but I hope her book will be published and widely purchased" (p. 298).

In the event, Baker changed the title to *The Concentration Camp Conspiracy: A Second Pearl Harbor* (Lawndale, Calif.: AFHA [Americans For Historical Accuracy] Publications, 1981) and advertised this anthology of inaccuracies with other plaudits from Ronald Reagan, Karl R. Bendetsen, and Milton S. Eisenhower. From the cover come most of the data "About the Author" and from the text her characterization of Senator Inouye as "a blackguard" (pp. 288–89) and her testimony before the CWRIC in Washington on July 16, 1981 (pp. 22–27). For her allegation that Japanese Americans "committed acts of treason" during the war, see her testimony before the Subcommittee on Administrative Practice and Procedure, U.S. Senate Committee for the Judiciary, Hearing on S. 1520, the World War II Civil Liberties Violations Redress Act, and Reports of the Commission on Wartime Relocation and Internment of Civilians, July 27, 1983.

In her *Concentration Camp Conspiracy*, Lillian Baker observed that "Americans are becoming aware of this redress and reparations movement and have been reacting negatively. Many have begun to associate the American dissidents with our former enemy, Japan, and some are unfortunately including all Asians into a grouping of anti-America and anti-American factions" (p. 245). By her text and subtitle, *A Second Pearl Harbor*, she did her best to fuel this historic misassociation. The inability of white officials to differentiate between Japanese enemies and American citizens who happened to look like them sparked the enormity in the first place. And for Myer to write his approving "Introductory

Remarks" (dated December 3, 1979) and otherwise embrace this exercise in the paranoid style meant that with his last public act he endorsed and defended what Justice Frank Murphy had rightly stigmatized as the "racism inherent in the entire evacuation program" (*Ex parte Endo*, 323 U.S. 309 [December 18, 1944]).

Published a couple of months after Myer's death, the CWRIC report, *Personal Justice Denied* (Washington, D.C.: Government Printing Office, December 1982), suggested the commissioners had heeded Lillian Baker's exhortation, "Listen to this man, for dear honor's sake!" They eschewed the term *concentration camps*, since the WRA facilities "were not extermination camps, nor did the American government embrace a policy of torture or liquidation of the ethnic Japanese" (p. 27n). But who had ever charged that the WRA camps were *extermination* camps? Had Myer lived to witness the commissioners' vanquishing of imaginary controversialists and their adoption of his red herring *relocation centers*, he would have died a happier man. (For a rigorous analysis of this and other weaknesses in the commissioners' handiwork, see Raymond Okamura's review in *Hokubei Mainichi*, May 28, 1983; see also my criticism of their naive use of suspect WRA sources in the notes for chapter 7.)

After emendations, A. Whitney Griswold's *The Far Eastern Policy of the United States* (New Haven: Yale University Press, 1938) is still valuable on anti-Orientalism from coast to coast. Vital on the subject of FDR's racism is Christopher Thorne's *Allies of a Kind: The United States, Britain, and the War Against Japan, 1941–45* (New York: Oxford University Press, 1978).

For an analysis of the lethal consequences of Roosevelt's division of humankind "into two species: an 'aggressor' species and a 'peace-loving' species," see Louis J. Halle's "Our War Aims Were Wrong," *New York Times Magazine*, August 22, 1965. Applied to the Germans and Italians, FDR's division produced what Halle, a former member of the State Department's Policy Planning Staff, rightly labeled "nonsense"; applied to the Japanese abroad and the Nikkei at home, it produced a full-blown racism.

In 1942 Roosevelt was explaining to friends that the Japanese were militaristic and generally nefarious because of their less developed skull pattern and almost to the day of his death was still rattling on about the skulls of nonwhites. On his return from Yalta in 1945 he told reporters that Queen Wilhelmina of the Netherlands "was planning to give Java and Sumatra independence soon, New Guinea and Borneo only after a century or two. The skulls of the New Guineans, the Queen had explained, were the least developed in the world" (as paraphrased by James MacGregor Burns, *Roosevelt: The Soldier of Freedom* [New York: Harcourt Brace Jovanovich, 1970], p. 592). The war against the racist Third Reich had its ironies.

Supreme Court: For the "legal scandal," see Peter Irons, *Justice at War* (New York: Oxford University Press, 1983). For the revised General DeWitt, see U.S. Army, *Final Report: Japanese Evacuation from the West Coast* (Washington, D.C.: Government Printing Office, 1943).

"They all look alike . . . " or so Justice Hugo L. Black adamantly insisted in the 1967 interview he granted on condition that it not be published until his death. For this uncompromising defense of his reasoning in *Korematsu*, see the

New York Times obituary, September 26, 1971; see also Gerald T. Dunne, *Hugo Black and the Judicial Revolution* (New York: Simon and Schuster, 1977), pp. 211–15. As late as 1974 Justice William O. Douglas was also reaffirming his position on *Korematsu*, but shortly before his death recanted and acknowledged that the alleged inability to differentiate between Japanese enemies and Japanese Americans "was not much of an argument, but it swayed a majority of the Court, including myself" (*The Court Years, 1939–1975* [New York: Random House, 1980], p. 279).

I have drawn on my notes at the time for McCloy's CWRIC testimony in Washington on November 3, 1981. For his exchange with Commissioner William M. Marutani, who is a Court of Common Pleas judge in Pennsylvania, see the CWRIC files for that date, pp. 34–37; see also the *New York Times*, November 4, 1981. Beyond doubt McCloy's word *retribution* was a slip that revealed deep-set feelings. Later in a television talk show he avoided the word, but not the substance: "I accept the notion of relocation. I said it was—I say it's a just result and a just and natural consequence of the sneak attack on Pearl Harbor, and that in itself justifies [relocation] fully, without going into whether or not the Japanese [*sic*] were thought to be loyal or whether they were thought not to be loyal. There was a great deal of evidence which was never brought out here which would indicate that large segments of the population were disloyal. We didn't know who they were" ("MacNeil-Lehrer Report," June 16, 1983, Transcript #2014, pp. 5–6). Recently another historian, Alan Brinkley, dubbed McCloy "the most influential private citizen in America" in his awestruck "Minister Without Portfolio," *Harper's* 266 (February 1983): 31–46: "He is one of the last of a line, one of the last representatives of the establishment tradition in the days of its greatest glory."

McCloy's timely caution to the CWRIC "not to advocate policies that might someday prevent the forcible relocation of other American citizens because of ethnic background" (*New York Times*, November 4, 1981) obviously did not raise the specter of herding WASP citizens into camps. He had particularly in mind the Cubans, "roughly a hundred thousand people, thoroughly trained, thoroughly equipped, well trained in modern warfare, that are being set up to serve as proxies for the Soviet Union in the various strategic parts of the world." Should that David launch a raid on this Goliath, he imagined U.S. officials again faced with the impossible task of separating the sheep from the goats, Cuban Americans from Cuban enemies.

The 1980 boatlift from Mariel had brought 125,000 Cubans into the country and nearly 1,000 into federal prisons, where they were held indefinitely. In Topeka, Kansas, on December 31, 1980, U.S. District Judge Richard Rogers ruled that this indefinite detention violated international law and treaties, the United Nations Charter, and a basic human right to a rapid resolution of their status. "You just cannot hold people without giving them a definite time for their release," said Judge Rogers, who might have been speaking of the Japanese Americans four decades earlier. "There was expert testimony that people held without a time limit are under more mental strain than an ordinary prisoner" (*San Francisco Chronicle*, January 2, 1981). In response to this ruling, the Justice Department proposed to move the Cubans out of federal prisons to "refugee camps" where they could be held "temporarily" indefinitely ("NBC News," January 13, 1981). *Plus ça change* . . . Had the proposed name been "relocation centers," and had they been for citizens as well as aliens to meet the need McCloy foresaw, then surely a Myer-like bureaucrat would have stepped in to run them.

"Japanese Skin": For Robert E. Park's pinning the "trouble" to its color, see "Racial Assimilation in Secondary Groups. . . ," *American Journal of Sociology* 19 (March 1914): 611.

A Postscript on Tribal Attorneys: In the sixties Robert Leland, an attorney in Carson City, Nevada, came by evidence that a land developer and a BIA official had acted in cahoots to steal more of the people's land along Pyramid Lake. For his pains Leland was suspended by the BIA without pay for fourteen months, even though, according to him, his charges against the land developer were later sustained. Only after additional official obstacles had been overcome was he able to go back to work for the Pyramid Lake Paiutes—see Edgar S. Cahn, ed., *Our Brother's Keeper: The Indian in White America* (Cleveland: World Publishing, 1969), p. 131. Earlier in Montana the Northern Cheyennes of Rufus Wallowing and John Wooden Legs had also been steam-rollered by the BIA. In 1957 their keepers put up for sale 1,340 acres of their prime grazing land. Anxious to hold on to this key area, they sold off $40,000 worth of cattle to buy it. Let Angie Debo summarize their sad tale:

> The Bureau, claiming the right of supervision, got control of the money and held it. As the date of the sale approached, the tribe frantically petitioned for its postponement, and members of Congress from Montana added their protest. The land was sold to a white bidder for $22,485; a year later he offered it to the Indians for $47,736, but by that time they had to use their money to bid on other allotments as they were offered. [*A History of the Indians of the United States* (Norman, Okla.: University of Oklahoma Press, 1970), p. 314]

Had Myer not practically chased the obstreperous James E. Curry out of business, the tribe's former attorney might have prevented or at least impeded this administrative absolutism.

For a discussion of the American Farm Bureau Federation's termination resolution from a Native American point of view, see "Termination Bill: Don't Underestimate AFBF," *Americans Before Columbus* 11, no. 3 (1983): 2–3.

Native Americans/Japanese Americans: The basic identity of Myer's response to his nonwhite wards in both the BIA and the WRA illustrated what the anthropologist Stanley Diamond calls the ongoing kin-civil conflict, "the basic struggle in human history" (*In Search of the Primitive: A Critique of Civilization* [New Brunswick, N.J.: Transaction Books, 1974], p. 9). Seen in this light, Myer was the state's bureaucratic weapon against families. He first attacked the families of inmates, of course, but Native American families had been the first victims of comparable assaults and that was the tradition he picked up and pushed forward later. And general historians of the family, I have suggested elsewhere, would do well to remember that its present plight was prefigured by such battering of Native American kinship and family structures—see Richard Drinnon, "The Red Man's Burden," *Inquiry* 1 (June 26, 1978): 22.

For the inner meaning of the Canadian dispersal, see Joy Kogawa's novel

Obasan (Boston: David R. Godine, 1982). For a useful discussion of Canadian liberals who also "blamed the victim," see Ann Gomer Sunahara, *The Politics of Racism* (Toronto: James Lorimer, 1981), pp. 131–32. Before the advent of multiculturalism and cultural pluralism on both sides of the 49th parallel, liberals demanded that the victims keep away from one another and jettison their cultural heritage.

Shaped by the Progressive era in his early years, Myer was working his way up through the Extension Service and the Soil Conservation Service at the same time that dissent was being institutionalized and homogenized by other liberals. Clifford Forster, who was special counsel for the New York ACLU from 1941 to 1950, approvingly outlined Roger Baldwin's trajectory for Dwight Macdonald: "The Union began outside the legal system and in opposition to the government. But in recent years it has gradually become assimilated into both" ("The Defense of Everybody," pt. 2, *New Yorker*, July 18, 1953, pp. 57–58; see also Forster's update in Peter Irons's *Justice at War*, p. 361). This benign "assimilation," this refusal to take "an unfriendly, adversary position," played right into Myer's hands, as we have seen, and left unchallenged his attempts to force social "assimilation" on the Nikkei. In fairness to Roger Baldwin, who in times past generously encouraged my own work on Emma Goldman, I should note that he began as a maverick outside the legal system and as an adversary of the government made a lasting contribution to civil liberties in the United States. Of the final, less courageous and more contradictory chapter in his career, his old teacher might well have said what she said about other individuals who fell away from their earlier principles: "We've had the best of him."

In *The Inner Civil War* (New York: Harper & Row, 1965), pp. 201–5, George M. Fredrickson portrayed Commissioner Walker as a representative postbellum "new intellectual as social scientist and scientific reformer." My source for Commissioner Crawford's dictum about "common property and civilization" is Harold E. Fey and D'Arcy McNickle, *Indians and Other Americans* (New York: Harper & Row, 1970), p. 72. Former Commissioner Nash was quoted by Edgar S. Cahn, ed., *Our Brother's Keeper*, p. 171.

"America's Absolutism": See Louis Hartz, *The Liberal Tradition in America* (New York: Harcourt, Brace & World, 1955), p. 58 et passim.

To the end Myer remained unaware of the absurdities of his attempts to Americanize Americans, whether of Japanese or indigenous ancestry. "What is distinctive about America is Indian," contended Felix S. Cohen: "The American way of life has stood for 400 years and more as a deadly challenge to European ideals of authority and submissive obedience in family life, in love, in school, in work, and in government. For four and a half centuries Government officials have been trying to stop Indians from behaving in un-European ways" ("Americanizing the White Man," *American Scholar* 21 [Spring 1952]: 178).

Index

Compositor: Wilsted & Taylor
Text: 10/13 Sabon
Display: Sabon
Printer: Murray Printing Co.
Binder: Murray Printing Co.